Iran under the Mongols

The Ehsan Yarshater Center for Iranian Studies and The Persian Heritage Foundation

Persian Studies Series Number 22

Iran under the Mongols

Ilkhanid Administrators and Persian Notables in Fars

Denise Aigle

Supported by the Persian Heritage Foundation

I.B.TAURIS

LONDON • NEW YORK • OXFORD • NEW DELHI • SYDNEY

I.B. TAURIS
Bloomsbury Publishing Plc, 50 Bedford Square, London, WC1B 3DP, UK
Bloomsbury Publishing Inc, 1359 Broadway, 12th Floor, New York, NY 10018, USA
Bloomsbury Publishing Ireland, 29 Earlsfort Terrace, Dublin 2, D02 AY28, Ireland

BLOOMSBURY, I.B. TAURIS and the I.B. Tauris logo are trademarks of Bloomsbury Publishing Plc

First published in Great Britain 2024
Paperback edition published 2026

Cover design: Holly Capper
Cover image: Execution of Bûqâ Amîr (© BnF - National Library of France, Department of Manuscripts, Persian Supplement 1443 f.238v)

Buqa's execution at Arghun's behest, Shams al-Dīn Kāshānī, Shāhnāma-i Chingīzī, Bibliothèque nationale de France, Supplément persan 1443, fol. 238v.

A catalogue record for this book is available from the British Library.

Library of Congress Cataloging-in-Publication Data
Names: Aigle, Denise, author.
Title: Iran under the Mongols : Ikhanid administrators and Persian notables in Fars / Denise Aigle. Other titles: Ikhanid administrators and Persian notables in Fars
Description: London ; New York : I.B. Tauris, [2024] | Includes bibliographical references and index. | Summary: "What were the effects of Mongol rule in Iran? Using a wide variety of sources including official and semi-official historiography; non-official historiography; local sources and geographical and biographical works, this book examines Ilkhanid rule in Fars from a local perspective. Charting the fortunes of successive rulers, her research shows that the failings of individual rulers, as well as intriguing by Persian notables, were the principal reasons for Shiraz and Fars's economic decline under the Mongols in comparison with the more successful neighbouring province of Kerman. Including a glossary, chronology and genealogical tables for the major Ilkhanid dynasties, as well as analysis of the latest manuscript sources, Iran under the Mongols is a vital contribution to our understanding of the effects of Mongol rule in Iran"– Provided by publisher.
Identifiers: LCCN 2024005749 (print) | LCCN 2024005750 (ebook) | ISBN 9780755645732 (hardback) | ISBN 9780755645770 (paperback) | ISBN 9780755645756 (epub) | ISBN 9780755645749 (ebook)
Subjects: LCSH: Ilkhanid dynasty–Iran–Fārs. | Mongols–Iran–History–To 1500. | Kings and rulers–Iran–Fārs–Biography. | Fārs (Iran)–History. | Iran–History–1256–1500.
Classification: LCC DS289 .A34 2024 (print) | LCC DS289 (ebook) | DDC 955/.026–dc23/eng/20240206
LC record available at https://lccn.loc.gov/2024005749
LC ebook record available at https://lccn.loc.gov/2024005750

ISBN: HB: 978-0-7556-4573-2
PB: 978-0-7556-4577-0
ePDF: 978-0-7556-4574-9
eBook: 978-0-7556-4575-6

Typeset by Newgen KnowledgeWorks Pvt. Ltd., Chennai, India

For product safety related questions contact productsafety@bloomsbury.com.

To find out more about our authors and books visit www.bloomsbury.com and sign up for our newsletters.

In memory of Jean Aubin

Contents

List of Maps x
Preface xi
Author's Note xiv
List of Abbreviations xv

Introduction 1

1 Notes on the Sources 9
Official Historiography 10
Non-official Historiography 14
Local Historiography 16
Historical Geography and Biographical Dictionaries 21
Hagiographic Sources 22

2 Establishing and Governing an Empire 25
Legal and Administrative Foundations of the Great Mongol State (1220–58) 26
Administrative Breakdown under the Ilkhans (1258–1336) 30
Destructive Impact of the *Ordu* 33
Land Status and Insecurity of Property Titles 34

3 Competent Governance under Abū Bakr Salghur 39
Establishment of the Salghurids in Shiraz 39
Abū Bakr's Territorial Expansion in the Persian Gulf 41
Autonomy in Exchange for Allegiance to the Great Qa'an 43
Establishment of a New Fiscal Policy 45
Abū Bakr, a Ruler Concerned about His Power 47

4 Progressive Administrative Control of the Ilkhans over Fārs 51
Ineptitude of Abū Bakr's Successors 51
Two Capable Turko-Mongol Administrators 57

Inkianu: A Competent Turkish Administrator and Victim of *Ordu* Intrigues 58
Rigorous Administration of the Mongol Sughunchaq Noyan 59
Consequences in Shiraz of Political Instability at the *Ordu* 63
The Mongol Bulughan Resists Aḥmad Tegüder 64
Abish Khātūn and the *Injūs* in Fārs 66
Return to Matters of Sayyid ʿImād al-Dīn Abū Yuʿlā 67
Boldness of the Mongolian Princess 68

5 Ilkhanid Policy in Fārs 73
Arghun and the Crown Lands 73
Arghun's New *Dīvān* Team: Repercussions in Fārs 76
Persistent Difficulties in Tax Collection in the Gaikhatu Era 78
Mongols and Trade 79
Ghazan's Administration in Fārs 84
Setbacks of Malik al-Islām at the *Ordu* 85
Division of Fārs into Tax Districts 86
The *Dīvān* in Search of Financial Resources 88
The Return of the Ṭībī Merchants to the Tax Farm 89
A Yazdī Sayyid in Charge of Tax Collection 90
Injuids Governors of Shiraz 92

6 Fārs amid the Rivalries of Chupanids, Injuids, and Muzaffarids 97
Five Military Campaigns: Alliances and Counter-Alliances 99
First Campaign: Chupanid–Injuid Alliance 99
Second Campaign: Chupanid–Muzaffarid Alliance 99
Third Campaign: New Chupanid–Injuid Alliance 100
Fourth Campaign: New Chupanid–Injuid Alliance 101
Fifth Campaign: New Chupanid–Muzaffarid Alliance 103
Uncertain Political Line of Shaykh Abū Isḥāq Īnjū 106
Capture of Shiraz 108
Role of Tribal Members in the Injuid and Muzaffarid Armies 112
Muzaffarids and *Pahlavāns* 114
Paradox of Muzaffarid Ideology 117
Amīrs' Campaigns in Fārs 120
First Campaign: Chupanid–Injuid Alliance 120
Second Campaign: Chupanid–Muzaffarid Alliance 120
Third Campaign: New Chupanid–Injuid Alliance 120

Fourth Campaign: New Chupanid–Injuid Alliance 120
Fifth Campaign: New Chupanid–Muzaffarid Alliance 121

7 Persian *ḥukkām*: "Games of the Swords" or Corrupt Officials? 123
Previous Instances of Economic Decline 123
Reasons for Recurring Administrative Dysfunctions 124
Venality of Local Officials 126
Great Traders Caught in the Turmoil 127
Consequences of Corrupt Local Agents 130
Chaotic Return to Traditional Sharing Zones 131

8 Epilogue: Other Principalities in Southern Iran 135
Principalities on the Eve of the Mongol Invasion 135
Confirmation of Power in Exchange for Submission 139
Supplying the Ilkhans with Troops in Exchange for Peace 143
Consequences of Insubordination to the Ilkhans 144

Notes 151
Bibliography 203
Index 221

Maps

Preface

Iran is often viewed as a completely independent political entity, mostly because of the significance of the periods when it was politically united under a single prince and dynasty. However, on the eve of the Mongol invasion, the concept of Iran as a separate entity did not exist.[1] Writing between 1224 and 1229, Yāqūt does not include an "Iran" entry in his geographical dictionary, the *Muʿjam al-buldān*; Iranian cities and provinces are instead mentioned individually. Without ignoring the intellectual community that formed the bedrock of Iranian and Islamic culture, there are many other features that urge us to study pre-Safavid Iran and closely examine its specificities, as Western historians have done with regard to their own history. Indeed, there were many "Iran-s" in the plural, just as there were many "Spain-s" or "Germany-s." In fact, "Iranity" may be experienced through the sense of belonging to "regional homelands."[2] With regard to Iran's regional diversity, Jean Aubin pointed out in 1971 that local history is the natural framework for all research and that "only an analysis at the level of cantons and cities, which are the cells of the Iranian body, makes it possible to determine … the remarkable continuity of Iranity throughout crises and invasions, a continuity that is due … to a cohesion and interplay of social forces."[3]

The division of the country into several large historical areas represents one of the most marked characteristics of medieval Iran. In the northeast, Khurasan and Transoxiana are the mountainous regions that were hit hard by nomadic invasions. In the south, Fārs, Kirmān, and ʿIrāq-i ʿajam are more diverse from a geographical and climatic viewpoint, making them less subject to influences from exogenous populations. Azerbaijan in the northwest is marked by a strong Turkic tribal settlement. Finally, the regions bordering the Caspian Sea (Māzandarān, Gīlān, and Ṭabaristān) form the fourth area of Iranian particularism. They form "a world apart,"[4] where resistance to Islam was manifested through their inhabitants' tendency to embrace alternative religious currents, particularly Shiʿism.

This diversity is clearly evident in the Mongol period. The largely destroyed Khurasan was rapidly annexed to the Mongol Empire. Azerbaijan later became the seat of the Ilkhanid state, where the Ilkhan's court, the *Ordu*, was established and where the densest concentration of Turko-Mongol settlements was found. In the south, Fārs was better preserved from an ethnic and cultural perspective, thus retaining its Islamic cohesion through its capital Shiraz. The incorporation of these different areas into Hülegü's *ulus* made them subject to a common administrative and fiscal regime, even though distinctive rules were applied to each area.

Nevertheless, in this Mongol Iran, as soon as the authority of the Ilkhans crumbled after Abū Saʿīd's death in 736/1335, new political groups surfaced with different aspirations according to their geographical location in the northwest, east, and south. Diverse Iranian societies began to be revived, as they gradually emerged from the upheavals of Mongol rule. In the northwest and Upper Mesopotamia—regions subject to tribal struggles—a Mongol dynasty, that of the Jalayirids, maintained its authority with its double capital inherited from the Ilkhanid tradition, with Tabriz as the summer capital and Baghdad as the winter capital. In the east, the tribal formations quickly ceded some of their power to local rulers such as the Sarbedars of the Bayhaq. In Fārs, despite the presence of Turkmen nomads, the Mongol tribes did not penetrate into this area. Since the end of the thirteenth century, this province wielded an ever-growing cultural influence over the Mongol Empire that was in the process of Islamization. For a while, Fārs along with the Injuids was even the guardian of Iranian identity.

In this monograph, the study of these "Iran-s" during the Mongol period will thus be conducted from a double perspective. On the one hand, it is necessary to take into account the unity of the Mongol Empire, which, to varying degrees and at different times, expanded its administrative system, its regulations, and often its abuses over the whole territory of Iran. On the other hand, the course of events occurring in the different areas of the Empire must be studied jointly with the policies pursued in the *Ordu*, while taking into account the social and economic conditions specific to each region. This is what I endeavored to do in this study of the rich region of southern Iran known as Fārs.

An earlier version of this work was published in the Cahiers series. Studia Iranica n° 31, *Le Fārs sous la domination mongole. Politique et fiscalité*

(XIIIe-XIVe s.), Paris, 2005. I would like to thank Rika Gyselen for giving me permission to publish a revised English version. I am most grateful to the Persian Heritage Foundation for their generous donation in support of the publication of this volume.

Author's Note

For the spelling of Mongol and Turkic proper names, I follow the system adopted in J. A. Boyle, *The History of the World Conqueror*, London; New York, 1958.

The Arabic names conform to the standards set in *Mamluk Studies Review*; these are also applied to Persian, except for *wa*, transliterated as *va*.

For the Mongol terminology, I use the system found in *The Secret History of the Mongols. A Mongolian Epic Chronicle of the Thirteenth Century*, translated by Igor de Rachewiltz, 2 vols., Leiden, 2004.

Dynasties are written without diacritical marks: Ilkhanids, Injuids, Salghurids, etc.

Quotations from the Qur'ān are taken from the translation of A. J. Arberry, *The Kuran Interpreted*, New York, 1950.

Some specific terms are not always translated:

- *bitikchi*, "secretary." The term can apply to literate Mongol *amīrs* as well as to Turko-Mongol or Persian members of the administration.
- *Dīvān* designates the department of the central administration, although *dīvān* written with a lower case refers to a regional or princely administration. The neologism "divanian" is used to designate members of these services.
- *ḥākim* (pl. *ḥukkām*) is usually translated as "governor." Nevertheless, I prefer "administrator," because there may be two or even several co-*ḥākim* in the same constituency (e.g., the *ḥukkām* of Shiraz).
- *malik*, title of variable meaning, sometimes: "king," "prince," "lord," or applied to different kinds of elite persons, or granted as a distinction to a military leader or distinguished individual.
- *nā'ib* (pl. *nuvvāb*), "assistant," "deputy."
- *nöker*, "companion," but subordinate.
- *noyan* refers to a Mongol leader, while *amīr* refers to a non-Mongol leader.
- *Ordu* is the royal camp of the Mongol sovereign.

Abbreviations

Primary Sources

Aharī	Abū Bakr Quṭbī Aharī, *Tārīkh-i Shaykh Ūvais*, ed. J. B. Loon, 's-Gravenhague, 1954.
Bar Hebraeus, *Chronicon Syriacum*	Bar Hebraeus, *Chronicon Syriacum*, ed. Paul Bedjan, Paris, 1890.
Bayḍāvī	Nāṣir al-Dīn Abū 'Abd Allāh Bayḍāvī, *Niẓām al-tawārīkh*, ed. Mīr Hāshim Muḥaddith, Tihrān, 2003.
Budge	Bar Hebraeus, *The Chronography of Gregory Abû'l-Faraj (1225–1286)*. English translation by Ernest Wallis Budge, London, 1932.
Dhayl-i Tārīkh-i guzīda	Zayn al-Dīn Qazvīnī, *Dhayl-i Tārīkh-i guzīda*, ed. Īraj Afshār, Tihrān, 1993.
Ḥāfiẓ-i Abrū, *Jughrāfiyā*	Ḥāfiẓ-i Abrū, *Jughrāfiyā-i Ḥāfiẓ-i Abrū*, ed. Ṣādiq Sajjādī, 3 vols., Tihrān, 1997–9.
Ḥāfiẓ-i Abrū, *Zubdat al-tawārīkh*	Ḥāfiẓ-i Abrū, *Zubdat al-tawārīkh*, ed. Sayyid Kamāl al-Dīn Javādī, 2 vols., Tihrān, 1993.
Hazār mazār	'Isā Ibn Junayd Shīrāzī, *Hazār mazār*, ed. Nūrānī Viṣāl, Shīrāz, 1975–6.
Ibn Balkhī	Ibn Balkhī, *Fārs-nāma*, ed. Guy Le Strange and Reynold A. Nicholson, London, 1921.
Ibn Baṭṭūṭa	Ibn Baṭṭūṭa, *The Travels of Ibn Baṭṭūṭa, A.D. 1325–1354*. English translation by Hamilton Alexander Gibb, 4 vols., Cambridge, 1958–94.
Ibn al-Fuwaṭī, *Talkhīṣ*	Ibn al-Fuwaṭī, *Talkhīṣ majma' al-adāb fi mu'jam al-alqāb*, ed. Muṣṭafā Jawād, 4 vols., Damascus, 1962–7.

Ibn Ḥajar ʿAsqalānī, *Durar al-kāmina*	Ibn Ḥajar ʿAsqalānī, *al-Durar al-kāmina fī aʿyān al-miʾa al-thāmina*, 4 vols., Hyderabad, 1929–32.
Ibn al-ʿImād, *Shadharāt al-dhahab*	Ibn al-ʿImād, *Shadharāt al-dhahab fī akhbār man dhahab*, ed. ʿAbd al-Qādir Arnaʾūṭ and Maḥmūd Arnaʾūṭ, 11 vols., Beirut, 1986–95.
Ibn Khallikān	Ibn Khallikān, *Wafayāt al-aʿyān*, ed. Iḥsān ʿAbbās, 8 vols., Beirut, 1968–72.
Juvaynī/Boyle	*The History of the World Conqueror*. Translation by J. Andrew Boyle, 2 vols., Manchester, 1958.
Juvaynī/Qazvīnī	ʿAlāʾ al-Dīn ʿAṭāʾ Malik Juvaynī, *Tārīkh-i jahāngushā*, ed. Muḥammad Qazvīnī, 3 vols., Leiden; London, 1912–37.
Khwāndmīr, *Dastūr al-vuzarāʾ*	Ghiyāth al-Dīn Khwāndmīr, *Dastūr al-vuzarāʾ*, ed. Saʿīd Nafisī, Tihrān, 1938–9.
Khwāndmīr, *Ḥabīb al-siyar*	Ghiyāth al-Dīn Khwāndmīr, *Ḥabīb al-siyar fī akhbār afrād bashar*, ed. M. Dabīr Siyāqī, 4 vols., Tihrān, 1955–6.
Khwāndmīr/ Thackston	*Habibu's-Siyar. Classical Writings of the Medieval Islamic World. Persian Histories of the Mongol Dynasties* (vol. II). Translated and annotated by Wheeler M. Thackston, London, 2012.
Kutubī	Maḥmūd Kutubī, *Tārīkh-i Āl-i Muẓaffar*, ed. ʿAlī Navāʾī, Tihrān, 1955–6.
Majmaʿ al-ansāb	Muḥammad b. ʿAlī Shabānkāraʾī, *Majmaʿ al-ansāb*, ed. Mīr Hāshim Muḥaddith, Tihrān, 1984.
Mīrkhwānd, *Rawḍat al-ṣafāʾ*	Mīrkhwānd, *Rawḍat al-ṣafāʾ*, ed. ʿAbbās Parvīz, Tihrān, 1960.
Mujmal	Aḥmad b. Jalāl al-Dīn Faṣīḥ Khwāfī, *Mujmal-i Faṣīḥī*, ed. Muḥammad Farrukhī, 3 vols., Mashhad, 1960–1.
Naṭanzī	Muʿīn al-Dīn Naṭanzī, *Muntakhab al-tawārīkh-i Muʿīnī*, ed. Jean Aubin, Tihrān, 1957.
Nuzhat al-qulūb	Ḥamd Allāh Mustawfī Qazvīnī, *Nuzhat al-qulūb*, ed. and trans. Guy Le Strange, 2 vols., Leiden, 1915, 1919.
Qashānī	Abū l-Qāsim Muḥammad Qashānī, *Tārīkh-i Ūljaytū*, ed. M. Hambly, Tihrān, 1969.
Rashīd al-Dīn, *Mukātibat*	Rashīd al-Dīn Faḍl Allāh Hamadānī, *Mukātibat-i Rashīdī*, ed. Muḥammad Shafīʿ, Lahore, 1974.

Rashīd al-Dīn/ Alizade	Rashīd al-Dīn Faḍl Allāh Hamadānī, *Jāmiʿ al-tawārīkh*, III, ed. A. A. Alizade, A. A. Romaskevich, and A. A. Khetagurov, Baku, 1957.
Rashīd al-Dīn/ Karīmī	Rashīd al-Dīn, *Jāmiʿ al-tawārīkh*, ed. Bahman Karīmī, Tihrān, 1959–60.
Rashīd al-Dīn/ Rawshan and Mūsavī	Rashīd al-Dīn, *Jāmiʿ al-tawārīkh*, ed. Muḥammad Rawshan and Muṣṭafā Mūsavī, 4 vols., Tihrān, 1994.
Rashīd al-Dīn/ Thackson	*Jamiʿu't-Tawarikh. Classical Writings of the Medieval Islamic World. Persian Histories of the Mongol Dynasties* (vol. III). Translated and annotated by Wheeler M. Thackston, London; New York, 2012.
Rashīd al-Dīn, *Tārīkh-i mubārak-i Ghāzānī*	Rashīd al-Dīn Faḍl Allāh Hamadānī, *Tārīkh-i mubārak-i Ghāzānī*, ed. Karl Jahn, s'-Gravenhague, 1957.
Sakhāwī, *Ḍawʾ al-lāmiʿ*	Shams al-Dīn Abū l-Khayr Muḥammad Sakhāwī, *Ḍawʾ al-lāmiʿ fī aʿyān al-qarn al-tāsiʿ*, 12 vols., Cairo, 1934–6.
Samarqandī, *Maṭlaʿ-i saʿdayn*	ʿAbd al-Razzāq Samarqandī, *Maṭlaʿ-i saʿdayn*, ed. ʿAbd al-Ḥusayn Navāʾī, Tihrān, 1975.
Secret History	*The Secret History of the Mongols. A Mongolian Epic Chronicle of the Thirteenth Century.* Translated by Igor de Rachewiltz, 2 vols., Leiden, 2004.
Shadd al-izār	Muʿīn al-Dīn Abū l-Qāsim Junayd Shīrāzī, *Shadd al-izār*, ed. Muḥammad Qazvīnī, Tihrān, 1948–9.
Shīrāz-nāma	Ibn Zarkūb, *Shīrāz-nāma*, ed. Ismāʿīl Vāʿiẓ Javādī, Tihrān, 1971–2.
Subkī	ʿAbd al-Wahhāb Subkī, *Ṭabaqāt al-shāfiʿiyya*, ed. Nūr al-Dīn Sharība, 10 vols., Cairo, 1906.
Tārīkh-i guzīda	Ḥamd Allāh Mustawfī Qazvīnī, *Tārīkh-i guzīda*, ed. Ḥusayn Navāʾī, Tihrān, 1983.
Tārīkh-i Shāhī	*Tārīkh-i Shāhī Qarākhitāyān*, ed. Muḥammad Ibrāhīm Bāstānī Pārīzī, Tihrān, 1976.
Vaṣṣāf	Vaṣṣāf, *Tajziyat al-amṣār va tazjiyat al-aʿṣār*, Lithograph, Bombay, 1852.
Yāqūt	Yāqūt, *Muʿjam al-buldān*, 5 vols., Beirut, 1986.

Secondary Literature

BSOAS	*Bulletin of the School of Oriental and African Studies*
Doerfer	Gerhard Doerfer, *Türkische und mongolische Elemente in Neupersischen*, 4 vols., Wiesbaden, 1963–75.
EI²	*Encyclopédie de l'Islam* (second edition)
EIr	*Encyclopædia Iranica*
IrSt	*Iranian Studies*
JESHO	*Journal of the Economic and Social History of the Orient*
JRAS	*Journal of the Royal Asiatic Society*
Lughat-nāma	Dihkhudā, *Lughat-nāma*, 16 vols., Tihrān, 1999.
REMMM	*Revue des Mondes Musulmans et de la Méditerranée*
StIr	*Studia Iranica*
StIsl	*Studia Islamica*

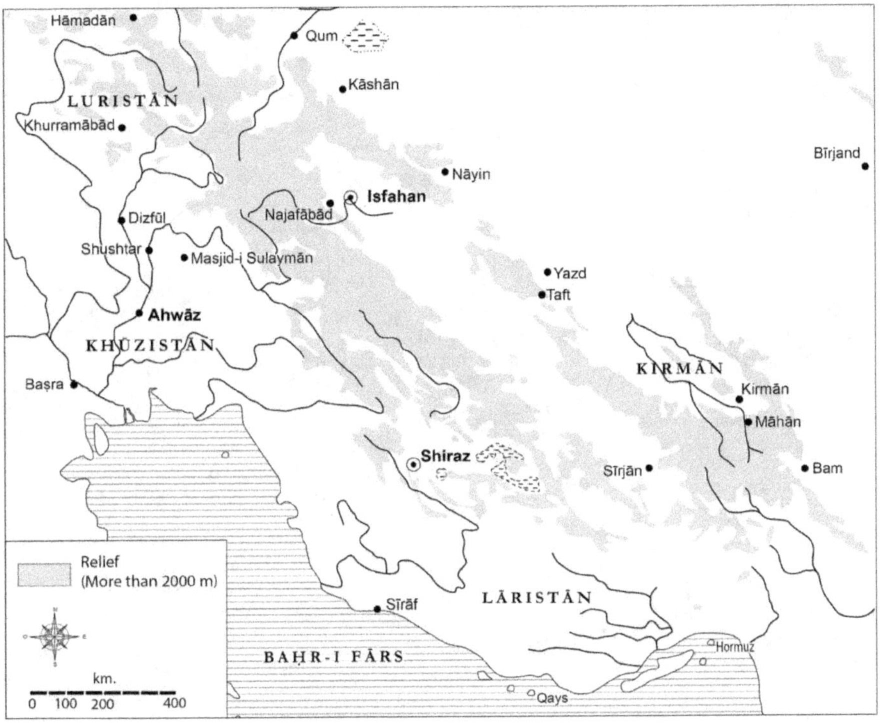

Map 1 Meridional Irān

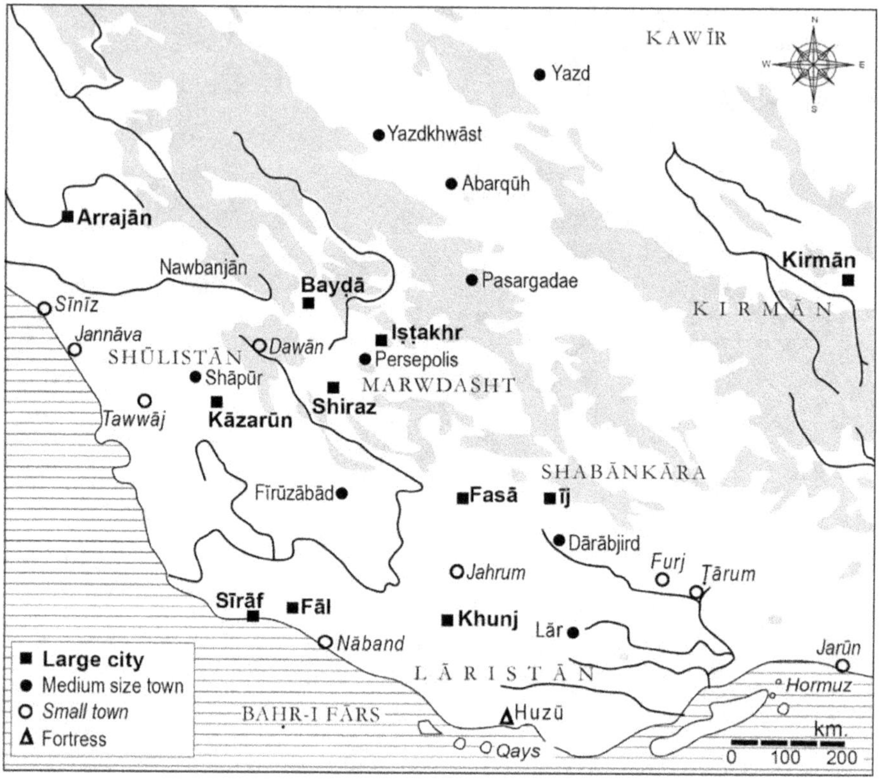
KAWĪR
Yazd
Yazdkhwāst
Abarqūh
Arrajān
Nawbanjān
Bayḍā
Pasargadae
Kirmān
KIRMĀN
Sīnīz
Jannāva
SHŪLISTĀN
Dawān
Iṣṭakhr
Persepolis
Shāpūr
MARWDASHT
Tawwāj
Kāzarūn
Shiraz
SHABĀNKĀRA
Fīrūzābād
Fasā
Īj
Dārābjird
Furj
Ṭārum
Jahrum
Sīrāf
Fāl
Khunj
Lār
Nāband
Jarūn
LĀRISTĀN
Hormuz
BAHR-I FĀRS
Huzū
Qays
Large city
Medium size town
Small town
Fortress
km.
0 100 200

Map 2 Fārs

Introduction

> God has spoken with me and has said:
> "I have given all the face of
> the earth to Temüjin
> and his children and
> named him Chingiz Khan.
> Bid him administer justice
> in such and such fashion."[1]

Originally a tribal people of Manchuria, the Kitans founded the Liao dynasty (907–1125) that ruled over Manchuria, Mongolia, and parts of northern China.[2] When this empire was created in the tenth century, it was the most complex of the nomadic confederations of the early Middle Ages.[3] The state model developed by the Liao was later adopted by the Jürchens of the Tungus ethnic group as well as the Manchus and the Mongols, who created the largest contiguous empire in human history following their successful mobilization of the human and material resources of their newly conquered lands. All the subjects of the empire, whether nomadic or sedentary, townspeople, artisans, or farmers, were required to support the imperial cause of the Mongols. Thomas Allsen points out that Hülegü's siege of Baghdad was not merely a confrontation between the Mongols and the Abbasid Caliph; it was rather a clash of the human, financial, material, and technological resources of northern China, Central Asia, Russia, the Caucasus, and Iran with those of the caliphate.[4] Nevertheless, the Mongol Empire would have quickly fallen if the conquerors had not been able to efficiently and successfully use the acquired resources.[5] The key factor in their long-term success was the competence of the Mongol administrative system comprised of an amalgamation of Chinese, Turkic, and

Muslim elements. During the first Mongol campaigns in China (1211–27), many local officials, mostly Kitans, Chinese, and some Jürchens,[6] had entered the service of the Mongols, bringing their administrative knowledge with them. Appointed to important positions, these administrative officials were responsible for organizing tax collection among others. They were imperial agents referred to as *darugha* or *darughachi*, meaning "one who affixes a seal."[7]

The death of Chinggis Khan in 1227 temporarily halted the expansion of the empire. During the reign of Ögödei Qa'an, the Armenians and the Georgians voluntarily rallied behind the Mongols in 1236, and following the victory of the Mongol commander Baiju over Kaykhusraw II at Köse Dagh in 1243, the Saljuqs of Anatolia were also subjected to Mongol power. As a result, they became a tributary state of the Great Qa'an and, as such, they were to provide troops (*cherig*)[8] to reinforce the Mongol armies during their campaigns. Following the conquest of eastern Iran under Chinggis Khan, the entire country fell definitively under the rule of Möngke Qa'an, the son of Tolui, who, after fratricidal struggles between the princes of the blood, was enthroned for a second time along the Kerülen river in the summer of 1251.[9] Möngke Qa'an commissioned his younger brother Hülegü to conquer Muslim countries and subject them to Mongol rule.[10] Beginning his campaign in 1253, Hülegü and his generals destroyed the main Ismā'īlī strongholds of the Qūhistān and southern Caspian during the early months of 1256. This campaign ended with the capture of Alamūt on November 19, 1256. Hülegü then continued to Azerbaijan, which became the center of Mongol power in Iran. Soon after, in late 1257, Hülegü started moving toward Baghdad. The siege of the city began in early 1258, and on February 13, it fell to the Mongols who thus seized Mesopotamia. Hülegü retreated again to Azerbaijan from where he launched his invasion of Bilād al-Shām, although his advance was halted at 'Ayn Jālūt in 1260 by the troops of the Mamluk Sultan Quṭuz.

Möngke Qa'an sent Hülegü to Iran because of the tensions arising between the princes of the blood after the death of Chinggis Khan, which stemmed from their desire to control the conquered territories. The power struggles were particularly fierce in Khurasan and Transcaucasia, which were under the direct authority of the Great Qa'an.[11] Iran was thus transformed into a khanate, along with the Jochid and Chaghatayid, as supported by numismatic data.[12] However, the title of *īlkhān*, which was conferred on Hülegü by Möngke, indicates that the former was the subordinate to the Great Qa'an of Mongolia.[13] The term *il* (Persian *īl*) of Turkic origin signifies "tribe, people," although in the Mongol period, it denoted "submissive, subordinate."[14] In the orders of submission sent to all the rulers of the earth, this term is found in opposition to the word *bulgha* meaning "rebel."[15]

Medieval chronicles and even contemporary historiography often describe the Mongol domination of the Iranian principalities as one of the darkest periods in Iranian history, which marked an important rupture. The death of the last Abbasid Caliph al-Musta'ṣim bi-llāh has been the subject of contradictory historical accounts by medieval historians in both the East and the West.[16] These accounts represent how historians wanted the Caliph to be remembered and what his death meant for the various social groups at the time. The Persian philosopher and Imāmī-Shī'ī scholar Naṣīr al-Dīn Ṭūsī (d. 672/1274), for example, who joined the Mongols when they captured the castle of Alamūt in 1256, is said to have advised them about killing the Caliph.[17] The unpredictable catastrophe of the Mongol conquest placed Muslim Iran in an unprecedented situation. Iranian society, hitherto established according to the precepts and customs of Islam, came under the domination of a people of Shamanist, Buddhist, and Christian beliefs, whose conception of the world and conduct were completely different.[18] Through the eyes of those who lived through the events and strived to understand their causes, they were interpreted as God's punishment for a sinful society based on the Qur'ānic verse: "He is the [One] Able to send upon you affliction from above you or from beneath your feet."[19] 'Aṭā' Malik Juvaynī, who served the new rulers of Iran, compared the Mongol invasion with the punishments inflicted on people who disobeyed God in ancient times.[20] But can the Mongol invasion of Iran be viewed as a more radical break than the seventh-century Arab conquest, whose ideology was not only to conquer new territory but also to expand the frontiers of Islam? The response is certainly not. Although the arrival of the Mongol hordes wreaked havoc in Iran, the cultural and religious foundations of Iranian society were not profoundly affected. Iran still remained a Muslim country even after decades of non-Muslim rule, since the Mongols did not impose a new religion.

The Ilkhanate was subject to a dual judicial system. On the one hand, Qur'ānic law, namely the *sharī'a*, was freely exercised as a private right of Muslims, being articulated by their *fuqahā'* and enforced by their *quḍḍāt*. On the other hand, Mongolian law, the *yasa* (Persian *yāsā*), was a public law applicable to all religious communities in political terms.[21] Judgments were pronounced by a Mongolian judge, the *yarghuchi*, before a special court, the *yarghu*.[22] The incompatibility between the *yasa* of Chinggis Khan and the precepts of the Qur'ān was mainly evident in matters of taxation and land status. However, the various religious communities under non-Muslim regimes embraced these novelties (*bid'āt*) from which they profited, even though they were in violation of Islamic law. Although fervent Muslims sought to understand the theological meaning of the catastrophe, those who collaborated with the new regime, including members of the clergy, enjoyed its benefits. 'Alā' al-Dawla Simnānī, a harsh censor of the moral depravity of his age, believed that a pagan ruler's justice was preferable to injustice and chaos.[23] The reign of Abaqa was indeed a long period of *pax mongolica* during which Persian culture once again flourished, as evidenced by the Juvaynīs.

Ruptures never occur on the precise date of the historical events that trigger the changes. Indeed, it takes at least one generation, often several, for the changes to come into effect. This was the case with the alleged decline of Iran, which is said to have been the direct consequence of the devastation triggered by the shock of the Mongol conquest, although its roots go back much further. The decline began in Fārs in the late tenth and early eleventh centuries and spanned several centuries. The weakening of the Buyids contributed to the unrest of the Shabānkāra tribe who stirred up trouble in the region, which was further accentuated by the decline of the Saljuqs.

The establishment of Mongol rule in Iran mostly outraged the population because of its brutality: the destruction of the large cities of Transoxiana and Khurasan, the flight of the population, the ruin of the irrigation system during the first Mongol hordes between 1218 and 1222, and, finally, the capture of Baghdad and the abolition of the Abbasid caliphate in 1258. The conquest of Baghdad, which brought with it a culture completely foreign to Islam, was experienced as a trauma by the Muslim population. However, in the eleventh century, the Turkic Saljuq invaders had no particular ideology, and they were rapidly accepted by Islamic society. And yet the consequences of the Turkic conquest continued to be felt in the long term, particularly with the growth of nomadism and the subsequent destruction of Khurasan, Azerbaijan, and Kirmān with the frequent ravages of the Ghuzz.

The massive influx of these tribes led to the creation of small local Turkic dynasties in Iran. Qāvurd, the nephew of the Saljuq Sultan Tughril, established a local dynasty in Kirmān that continued for 150 years until the Ghuzz tribes seized Khurasan in 1186. The subsequent decline of the Saljuqs favored the independence of the local atabeks or Turkish slaves who were military leaders and were originally appointed as guardians of the Saljuq princes in the provinces. The atabeks eventually amassed real power, as was the case with the Eldegüzids in Azerbaijan and the Salghurids in Fārs.

During the first decades of their rule, the Mongols marked a break in the history of Iran. In addition to the destruction of cities and the influx of tribes, the Mongols brought new political practices. However, their domination did not apply in equal measure to the whole territory. For practical reasons, the Mongol tribes largely settled in areas with sufficient pastures for their cattle, mainly in Khurasan and Azerbaijan where the Ilkhans established their royal court, the *Ordu*. By contrast, they allowed small states in the provinces of Māzandarān and Gīlān around the Caspian Sea to continue their rule. They also preserved the dynastic tradition in the region of Herat, thus keeping the Karts, a family of Afghan origin, in power. In Kirmān, they treated the Qutlughkhanids, recent converts to Islam, in the same way, and in Fārs, the power was shared between two rival states, the Salghurid Turkish atabeks of Shiraz and the old local kings of Shabānkāra. These dynasties retained their throne and territory but became subjects of the Great Qa'an. As their submission avoided military confrontations, these local rulers, well aware that they were unable to resist the Mongol forces, thus preserved their power and relative autonomy. Moreover, given their lack of administrative experience, the Mongols preferred to maintain the existing administrative structure through these vassal states. Indeed, maintaining these local powers under their control was the most convenient way for the Mongols to exploit the resources of these regions.

Before the establishment of the Ilkhanate, the conquered lands were ruled in the name of the Qa'an of Mongolia, based in Qaraqorum. The local dynasties that had sworn allegiance to him inscribed his name on their coins as a sign of their loyalty.[24] The Qa'an retained the prerogative of appointing Mongol officials in the provincial courts of the vassal states, while the local rulers received an official recognition of their authority directly from Qaraqorum.

Ibn Yaʿqūb Sayfī, author of *The History of Herat*, described the enthronement ceremony of the new ruler of the Kart dynasty, Shams al-Dīn Muḥammad (r. 643–76/1245–78), who came to the throne thanks to the Mongols.[25] His investiture took place in a large tent in which the emperor bestowed on him a robe of honor as well as a letter of investiture and three tablets (*paiza*), which gave him safe passage throughout the empire.[26] Similar procedures are attested for the ruler of Kirmān Quṭb al-Dīn Muḥammad (r. 650–5/1252–7) as well as the sultans of Anatolia.[27]

Loyalty to the Qa'an accorded special advantages to these local rulers. The ruling house of Shabānkāra received six thousand gold dinars annually for its administrative services to the Mongols. The sultans of Anatolia received four hundred gold bars (*bālīsh*) during a difficult period. Shams al-Dīn Muḥammad Kart received a sum of sixty thousand dinars when he was at the imperial camp of Möngke in 1251. According to Thomas Allsen, the generosity of the Qa'an toward the members of the Kart dynasty may be explained by the fact that a few years before the enthronement of Möngke, they had made a trip to Mongolia to pay tribute. In an effort to establish their dynasty at the Mongol royal court, the Karts had also sent large sums of money to Qaraqorum.[28]

There is currently a lack of research on the regions that survived the direct shock of the Mongol conquest and retained a certain autonomy in the empire. These semi-autonomous regions have been investigated in the framework of more general works on the Mongols or the Ilkhans.[29] How could a prince preserve his kingdom? What advantages could a local ruler derive from his close collaboration with the Mongol elites? What ties did local leaders maintain with the *Ordu*? Without addressing these issues, it is difficult to gain a clear picture of how Mongol rule was exercised in each and every Iranian province as well as throughout the country as a whole. It is also hard to assess how the Mongol system worked in the semi-autonomous regions, from the conquest of eastern Iran until the moment when the original Mongol power turned into an Iranized power during the last two decades of the thirteenth and early fourteenth centuries. Did the conversion of the Ilkhans to Islam change the behavior of the *Ordu* toward the Muslim populations? Did the Mongol administration change its practices accordingly? This issue is particularly important with regard to the collection of taxes and the status of land, compared with the beginning of the Ilkhanid period when Iran was considered an occupied country to be exploited for the benefit of the imperial family and the *noyans*. Indeed, after passing under direct Mongol domination, the conquered regions, according to a steppe tradition, were deemed to be an encampment (*yurt*) of the imperial family, that is, pasture lands for grazing livestock.[30]

In the province of Fārs, whose subjugation was not directly impacted by the Mongol conquest or the massive tribal influx, its lands remained untouched. It benefited from an exceptional status compared with the regions in which the Mongol tribes were widely settled such as Anatolia, Khurasan, and Azerbaijan, in which six hundred kilometers of land from Sulṭāniyya to Mūghān had been turned into summer pastures (*yaylāq*) and winter pastures (*qīshlāq*).[31] The goal of this work is to examine the modalities of Mongol rule in Fārs, starting with the first appearance of Chinggis Khan's army in eastern Iran and continuing until twenty years after the disintegration of the Ilkhanate following the death of Abū Sa'īd in 736/1335.

In two articles, Ann Lambton traced the administrative and fiscal history of Fārs and Kirmān up to the death of Abū Sa'īd, although she simply followed the course of events, with her study reflecting the somewhat confused nature of the sources.[32] In his work on the Mongols in Iran in the thirteenth century, George Lane devoted a few pages to the history of Shiraz under the Salghurids, but he failed to emphasize the different stages marking the Ilkhans' gradual encroachment on the province.[33] In his 2015 monograph, *The Population of Fārs against the Mongols*, 'Abd al-Rasūl Khayrāndīsh examined the confrontation between the Mongols and the local dynasties. He essentially traces the chronology of events from the reign of Salghurid atabek Sa'd b. Zangī until the end of the reign of Shaykh Abū Isḥāq Īnjū and the capture of Shiraz by the Muzaffarids, although he fails to consider the type of sources.[34] Therefore, his analysis does not depict the real role of the Mongol officials when confronted with the corruption of the local Iranian staff in Fārs.

The Mongol rule over Fārs, as I will argue, was mainly exercised in the domain of taxation. The wealth of this region aroused the envy of the Mongolian political authorities, who sought by all means to bring the taxes levied there into the Ilkhans' coffers, although they were far from successful in their efforts. This research involves establishing the chronology of events, but, above all, unraveling the complex relationships between the different players, both locally and in the *Ordu*. It is thus primarily a study of human relations that will shed light on the evolution of Fārs during this period. The official chronicler, often an official of the *Dīvān* and writing from the point of view of the *Ordu*, does not have the same interpretation of events as the local chronicler, whose objective is to showcase his region by recounting its glorious past. It is therefore necessary to read between the lines of the accounts that reflect the chronicler's own vision of how history unfolds.

1

Notes on the Sources

> Medieval historiography offers
> an excellent subject for
> investigating the function
> of the past in medieval
> political life, for few complex
> societies [...] in accordance
> with their vision of history.[1]

Regarding the history of Ilkhanid Iran, a multitude of varied narrative sources are written in various languages, which is not the case for the history of the Golden Horde based in the Pontic-Caspian steppe and the Chaghatayid Khanate in Central Asia. Ilkhanid historiography is also characterized by the influence of Firdawsī's *Shāh-nāma* on historians who penned their chronicles in verse. Despite this abundance of sources, any historian of the Ilkhanid period must overcome several methodological challenges. First, almost all the available sources are external to the Mongol culture, because very few texts were written by the Mongols themselves. The information comes from the conquered peoples or from the Mongols' enemies like the Mamluks of Egypt and Syria. Second, although the historiography of the Mongol era is one of the richest epochs, much of it was written by those holding high positions in the Ilkhanid state and closely associated with the ruling power. Their writings thus fall into the category of official history. Finally, the historian of this period is confronted with another problem: the gap between the rich historiography of the first decades of the Mongol Empire and the relative scarcity of sources available to study the collapse of the Persian Ilkhanate.

Most of the time, the narrative sources are evaluated according to either literary criteria (chronography, dynastic history, biographical dictionary, historical geography, and so on) or linguistic criteria. The classification by genre is spurious and artificial, because many sources can be categorized into several genres. I will thus adopt a different sort of classification, being well aware of the limits of any attempt to fit historical sources into specific categories. Since the objective here is to study the Mongol administrative system and the fiscal policies implemented by the political authorities to dominate Fārs, it is necessary to simultaneously use the sources centered on the Mongol court, the *Ordu*, as well as the local sources centered on the princely courts.

The sources centered on the *Ordu* inform us about the sovereign and his entourage, the various court intrigues, and the military advances of the armies, while the local sources elucidate and enlarge the information drawn from the palace-centered historiography. The sources from the central power can themselves be divided into two more or less distinct groups. On the one hand, a number of major primary texts belong to the official or semi-official historiography, while on the other, there are works composed by people of lesser political status, some of whom held administrative positions within the state apparatus, or by authors postdating the Ilkhanid period. The *Ordu*-focused sources can thus be supplemented by local historiography, although it is hard to identify the texts that may be regarded as regional history. The works usually placed in this category are of a diverse nature and character. By contrast, several texts classified under the heading "general histories" prove to be valuable sources of local history. In some cases, as will be seen, there is a fine line between local history, often largely based on biographical data, and general history, which concerns a chronological record of events. I also have tried to include texts whose scope extends far beyond the boundaries of southern Iran while belonging to the genre of local historiography because of their wealth of information regarding the local dynasties of this area.

Official Historiography

In his work on the writing of history in the Medieval Latin West, Bernard Guénée made it clear that the princes of the Middle Ages were deeply aware of the weight of history. They were exceedingly careful to compose "historical works that, while recounting the recent past, were to present the most favorable image of their reign."[2] The emergence of official history in the West formed part of a long process shaped by the development of bureaucracy, and this development allowed history to gradually gain its autonomy from theology and law. History thus became the auxiliary of power. In Iran, we can observe a similar trend during the Ilkhanid period, albeit much more tenuous, with the historiography written by the staff of the chancellery. Dorothea Krawulsky describes this type of historiography as "offizielle dynastische Geschichtssreibung der Mongolenherrschaft."[3]

Although the Mongols established a historiographical tradition, only a few texts have survived in their original form. *The Secret History of the Mongols* was completed during "Year 1 of the Rat," the date that corresponds to the years 1228, 1240, 1252, or 1264.[4] The author is unknown, but according to Igor de Rachewiltz, *The Secret History of the Mongols* may have been written by a group of people or by a single narrator who recited the events to a secretary.[5] The text lies at the crossroads of several genres. First, it is a tribal history that resembles an epic by retelling the deeds of the great ancestors. This is the only text that informs us about the early institutions of the empire established by Chinggis Khan: the organization of the army, administrative and legal system, and various regulations. In this sense, we may consider *The Secret History* to be part of the official historiography. Subsequently, the successors of the Great Qa'an relied on these institutions to establish administrative bodies in different parts of the empire as well as in their vassal states. These institutions were sometimes adapted according to existing practices, hence the importance of *The Secret History* when studying the administrative system in Iran.

During this period, two figures came to dominate the historiographical production in the Persian language: 'Aṭā' Malik Juvaynī (d. 681/1283) and Rashīd al-Dīn (d. 718/1318). 'Aṭā' Malik Juvaynī was a member of a family that had held important administrative positions since the middle of the twelfth century. His father, Bahā' al-Dīn, for example, had served the Khwārazmshāhs. 'Aṭā' Malik Juvaynī undertook two trips to Qaraqorum long before Hülegü's arrival in Iran, and then in late 1255, he entered the service of Hülegü. After the capture of Baghdad, the Ilkhan entrusted him with the government of the territories administered by the Caliph: ʿIrāq-i ʿarab, Lower Mesopotamia, and Khūzistān. He held this position for over twenty years. His visits to Mongolia as well as his function as governor, which required him to travel throughout the empire, give an undeniable value to his work, *Tārīkh-i jahāngushā*, completed around 1260. ʿAṭā' Malik Juvaynī can thus hardly be considered an independent historian. His links with the Mongol Empire drew criticism in the nineteenth century. D'Ohsson accused him of flattery toward his masters, an accusation often leveled against him. However, this condemnation is too severe, as *Tārīkh-i jahāngushā* is indeed a reliable work. In fact, ʿAṭā' Malik Juvaynī tends to criticize the Mongols but implicitly. He quotes a verse in Arabic from the poet ʿAmr b. al-Hudhayl al-ʿAbdī: "The pedigrees of people such as were handed down of yore cannot be compared with the pedigrees that have grown with the grass."[6] He attacks opportunist officials, whether Mongols or Persians, with ruthless irony: "Every hireling has become a minister, every knave a vizier and every unfortunate a secretary …, every carpet-spreader a person of consequence …; every valet a learned scholar; every camel-driver elegant from much riches."[7] This statement, embellished with quotes from poetry, the Qur'ān, and hadiths, aimed to deliver a culturally coded and incomprehensible message to the Mongol court. This work is the product of its time, and although it is necessary to consider the perspective of the author, it should be recognized as a major source on the period, particularly with regard to the institutions and the progressive implementation of the administrative system in the provinces of the Mongol Empire.

Rashīd al-Dīn, author of the *Jāmiʿ al-tawārīkh*, is the second great figure of Ilkhanid historiography.[8] He is the true official historian of the Ilkhans. Commissioned by the ruling power, the *Jāmiʿ al-tawārīkh* corresponds well to Bernard Guénée's definition of official history. Rashīd al-Dīn writes in the introduction:

> What occurrence has ever been more memorable than the birth of the dynasty of Chinggis Khan …, who subjugated the many kingdoms of the world, conquered and destroyed a host of unruly peoples? … He gave the [whole] world one face, and the same feelings to all hearts; he purified the territories of the Empire, in delivering them from the domination of perverse usurpers and the oppression of proud tyrants.[9]

This vast historiographical undertaking was carried out under the direction of Rashīd al-Dīn, who collected the Persian translations made by his associates from various languages. He also used oral sources. One of his main colleagues who provided him with information about the Mongols and Turks was Bolad Chingsang. After starting his career in China in the service of Qubilai, he was appointed as ambassador and political adviser of the Great Qa'an and sent to Iran where he spent twenty-eight years.[10] Given Rashīd al-Dīn's status in the Ilkhanid state apparatus, he was in a good position to obtain information. The *Jāmi' al-tawārīkh* is therefore a unique authority, especially for the reign of Ghazan Khan.

The *Jāmi' al-tawārīkh* is a source of primary importance on Mongol history for the periods well before the time of Rashīd al-Dīn. According to his own testimony, Rashīd al-Dīn drew from Mongol sources preserved as separate fragments in the treasury of the Ilkhans, supposedly a lost chronicle of the history of the Mongols written in Uighur-Mongol script.[11] These fragments were compiled and referred to as *Altan debter*, the "Golden Records."[12] It was Bolad Chingsang, "the acknowledged expert on Mongolian tradition,"[13] who provided Rashīd al-Dīn with information about the tribes. This part of the *Jāmi' al-tawārīkh* is extremely important, because it determines the tribes and clans or sub-clans of the Mongol *noyans* who played a role in Iran. A comparison with the Chinese use of these Mongolian materials reveals that the Persian version preserves the original information with great exactitude. The *Jāmi' al-tawārīkh*, like *The Secret History*, provides a Mongolian perspective of events; as such, it is a source of primary importance.

Another major source for the history of the Ilkhans is in Syriac, *Maktbānūt zabnē* (usually termed *Chronicon syriacum*), written by Bar Hebræus (d. 1286). In 1264, Bar Hebræus was appointed as the head of the Jacobite Church for the eastern countries under Mongol rule. For twenty-two years, his professional activities led him to travel between Iraq and Azerbaijan, mostly to Marāgha, the capital of the Ilkhans. As a representative of Jacobite Christians in the Persian Ilkhanate, Bar Hebræus was linked to political power. He thus had access to the Ilkhans' library and used its resources to write the *Chronicon syriacum*. However, he cannot be recognized as an official historian of the Ilkhans in the same way as Rashīd al-Dīn was, even though his work, *Chronicon syriacum*, is to some extent a semi-official history. After the death of Hülegü, Bar Hebræus wrote: "The wisdom of this man, and his greatness of soul, and his wonderful actions are incomparable."[14] He mostly viewed the Mongol authorities in a positive light, and the early Ilkhanid era is presented as a golden age for the Syriac communities of the Mongol Empire.

The contents of the book are not all of equal importance. Bar Hebræus relies on Juvaynī to recount non-contemporary events such as the conquest of Chinggis Khan, the fall of the Khwārazmshāh dynasty, and the destruction of the Ismāʿīlī fortresses.[15] However, when it comes to the events that he witnessed firsthand or in which he participated, he presents original information, notably with regard to the *Ordu* and the power struggles between various contenders for the throne. His account is even more significant, because it reflects the point of view of a Christian prelate in contact with the Mongol authorities. To a certain extent, Bar Hebræus's *Chronicon syriacum* compensates for the lack of Mongol sources. Compared with the Islamic sources, there is less doubt about the reliability of this work regarding the life and culture of the Mongols.

Non-official Historiography

A number of texts written during the Ilkhanid period as well as the later historiography—especially that of the Timurid Empire, which is essential for retracing the history of Abū Saʿīd's reign and the collapse of the Ilkhanate in Persia—fall into this category. Nāṣir al-Dīn Bayḍāvī's *Niẓām al-tawārīkh* is the only extant chronicle written between the composition of the two great historiographical monuments, namely Juvaynī's *Tārīkh-i jahāngushā* and Rashīd al-Dīn's *Jāmiʿ al-tawārīkh*. The text was probably penned between 670/1271 and 674/1275.[16] Bayḍāvī provides some information about the Salghurids that is not found in other sources. He clarifies certain episodes in the history of this dynasty, notably during the fratricidal power struggles. This relatively short text, of which numerous surviving manuscripts attest to its popularity, also has a cultural value.[17] Bayḍavī emphasizes the history of his home province of Fārs, which he considers to be the center of the First Persian Empire. He believes that the "land of Iran" (*Irān-zamīn*) extends between the Euphrates and the Oxus. Composed thanks to the patronage of the minister Shams al-Dīn Muḥammad Juvaynī, the *Niẓām al-tawārīkh* supports the efforts of the Juvaynīs to encourage the Mongol authorities to adopt the culture and traditions of their Persian subjects. It is interesting to note that Bayḍāvī introduces the Mongols as the ninth Iranian dynasty, just after the Khwārazmshāhs. The *Niẓām al-tawārīkh* is Bayḍavī's only work written in Persian, which is an implicit way of linking language to Iranian identity.

The history of Öljeitü's reign is well documented in Abū l-Qāsim Qāshānī's *Tārīkh-i Ūljāytū*. Overloaded with dates, the text presents events in a strictly chronological order, year by year, month by month, and often day by day in the form of a real diary. Qāshānī has nevertheless been criticized for his lack of rigor and numerous errors. Despite these flaws, *Tārīkh-i Ūljāytū* is an important source of information.[18] The text is also valuable in terms of cultural history. According to Thomas Allsen, the *Tārīkh-i Ūljāytū* resembles an official Chinese historiography.[19] He explains that the data collection methods used historically in China, where data were preserved in several stages, had an influence on some authors of the Ilkhanid era and even those of the later periods. Thomas Allsen points out that Rashīd al-Dīn seems to have written his history of the Ilkhans, especially the later ones, based on a text resembling a court diary.[20] Qāshānī seems to have been inspired by the methods of Chinese historiography with which he undoubtedly became familiar during his collaboration with Rashīd al-Dīn.

Originally from a *mustawfī* family, Ḥamd Allāh Mustawfī Qazvīnī (d. 740/1349) was appointed superintendent of finance by Rashīd al-Dīn and retained this position during the reign of Abū Sa'īd. He is the author of a general survey of Islamic history, *Tārīkh-i guzīda*, completed in 730/1330 and dedicated to Rashīd al-Dīn's son, Ghiyāth al-Dīn Muḥammad Rashīdī.[21] Charles Melville argues that the survey is a concise version of Mustawfī Qazvīnī's earlier historical works, particularly his *Ẓafar-nāma*, a voluminous versified chronicle that mimics Firdawsī's *Shāh-nāma*. Zayn al-Dīn, son of Mustawfī Qazvīnī, composed the *Dhayl-i Tārīkh-i guzīda*, which covers the period from 742–94 to 1341–91 and is a sequel to the *Ẓafar-nāma*.[22] It contains information not found in other sources, especially about the upheavals in Fārs at the time of the conflicts between the Injuids and the Chupanids.[23]

The *Tārīkh-i Shaykh Ūvays* by Abū Bakr Quṭbī Aharī, whose account ends in 760/1359, is a very useful source, since it reflects the perspective of the Jalayirid dynasty of Baghdad, which was an ally of the Injuids. It also features original information compared with other sources. The author portrays the reign of Ghazan Khan as the beginning of a period of peace that culminated under Abū Saʿīd: "The time of his government was the best period of the domination of the Mongols."[24] Under Rashīd al-Dīn's influence, these historians echo the idea that Ghazan's conversion to Islam marked a real shift in Ilkhanid history.

The historical *Shāh-nāma* can also be considered an unofficial historiography. According to Bert Fragner, the *Shāh-nāma* was a factor contributing to the Mongol's integration into Iranian culture through the practice of "*Shāh-nāma-navīsī*."[25] Despite their undeniable historical value, the versified chronicles have, with a few exceptions, long been ignored.[26] Nowadays, many researchers are using these texts on equal terms with other sources. Although these versified chronicles are mainly centered on the central power, they also include information about the relatively independent provinces like Fārs. The *Daftar-i Dilgushā* by Ṣāḥib Shabānkāra'ī, written c. 720/1320 and covering the history of the Shabānkāra down to the Mongol invasion led by Hülegü, provides some information about the history of the princedom.[27] The *Shāh-nāma-i Chingīzī* by Sham al-Dīn Kāshānī, which was commissioned by Ghazan Khan, relies on the historical facts of Rashīd al-Dīn's *Jāmiʿ al-tawārīkh* while deriving his stylistic inspiration from Firdawsī.[28] The work was begun during the reign of Ghazan Khan but finished under his successor Öljeitü. The *Ghāzān-nāma*, composed by Nūr al-Dīn Muḥammad Azhdarī between 758/1357 and 763/1362 after the fall of the Ilkhans, is explicitly intended as a continuation of Firdawsī's *Shāh-nāma*.[29] It is dedicated to the Jalayirid sultan Shaykh Ūvays (r. 757–76/1356–74). Nūr al-Dīn al-Azhdarī's goal is to present Ghazan Khan as the model for Shaykh Ūvays to follow, thus marking the continuity between the two reigns.

Local Historiography

Iran's geographic and ethnic diversity as well as its propensity for self-governing local powers gave rise to a key feature of Persian historiography, namely "local histories."[30] In 2016, Mimi Hanaoka designated Persian local historiography as "histories from the peripheries."[31] Since the tenth century, works of this type had been written in Iran, with descriptions of a topographical nature, biographies of scholars, particularly those who became the glory of their city or region, and elements of political history.[32] This local Persian historiography is also marked by its pre-Islamic heritage, which arouses a strong sense of national identity among the authors. Whether intentionally or not, local histories are a means of reacting to centralization. Regional historiography is a true "mirror of the living structures of past Iranian societies."[33] Local historiography falls more or less into two groups. There are, on the one hand, texts focusing on the history of a particular region or city since its foundation until the time of the author and, on the other, texts devoted to the history of local dynasties.

The local histories often express the patriotism of their authors. This is the case with the *Shīrāz-nāma*, a history of Shiraz completed in 744/1343–4 by Muʿīn al-Dīn Abū l-ʿAbbās Aḥmad Shīrāzī, also known as Ibn Zarkūb.[34] This work comprises three parts that are characteristic of the historical and geographical writings from the ninth to the twelfth centuries. In the first part, Ibn Zarkūb praises the merits and virtues (*faḍā'il*) of the city and narrates the legends associated with its foundation.[35] While most local history writers focused on ancient Iran, Ibn Zarkūb started the second part of his book with the history of the dynasties that had ruled Shiraz since the Buyids, ending with the reign of Jamāl al-Dīn Shaykh Abū Isḥāq Īnjū. In the third part, the author collects numerous accounts relating to the shaykhs and other famous inhabitants of the city. These accounts are organized, as in early Arabic biographical dictionaries, in "successive layers" (*ṭabaqa*).[36] The *Shīrāz-nāma* has a strong regional identity, committed to drawing attention to the local dynasties that made the city proud. At the beginning of the account of the reign of Shaykh Abū Isḥāq Īnjū, Ibn Zarkūb claims that he wrote a two-volume history about the reign of this prince (*Kitāb-i Tārīkh-nāma*), although the text did not reach us.[37] The *Shīrāz-nāma* is an important source, although it should be taken with some caution on account of its "pro-Injuid" stance. Furthermore, as Ibn Zarkūb was not a professional historian, there are many errors in the dates mentioned in his text.

The *Shadd al-izār* by Muʿīn al-Dīn Abū l-Qāsim Junayd Shīrāzī is also a valuable local source, as it contains the biographies of more than three hundred figures buried in the cemeteries of Shiraz.[38] Like Ibn Zarkūb, the author belonged to one of the most influential families of Shiraz, the Bāgh-i Naw'īs. The apologetic character of the work is undeniable. The biographical sketches are quite stereotypical, as though reflecting the image of a society in which negative character traits should be omitted. Muʿīn al-Dīn Junayd Shīrāzī's remarks accompanied by his moral reflections call for caution, although the individual biographical data such as the origin, education, travels, and religious and social activities of the city's elites allow us to retrace to a certain extent their religious, social, or political roles. Like Ibn Zarkūb, the author of *Shadd al-izār* was not a historian, and the book has numerous shortcomings. However, there is no equivalent source: in addition to its biographical sketches, the text contains a great deal of information about Fārs and the topography of Shiraz.

Three histories of Yazd are also valuable on account of the biographical information relating to some individuals who worked in the administration of Fārs. The first is entitled *Tārīkh-i Yazd* composed by Muḥammad b. Ḥasan Jaʿfarī in the mid-fifteenth century and dedicated to the vizier in the local Timurid administration, Ḍiyāʾ al-Dīn Masʿūd.[39] The second is the *Tārīkh-i jadīd-i Yazd* by Aḥmad b. Ḥusayn ʿAlī Kātib, composed no later than 872/1467–8.[40] The final work is Muḥammad Mufīd Mustawfī Bāfqī's *Jāmiʿ-i mufīdī* completed in 1090/1679–80 and dedicated to the Safavid monarch Shāh Sulaymān (r. 1077–1105/1666–94).[41] This local Yazdi historiography seeks to portray the city as a center of religious education. In the *Tārīkh-i jadīd-i Yazd*, Aḥmad b. Ḥusayn ʿAlī Kātib believes that the central role played by piety and religion in the history of Yazd as well as its virtuous rulers largely contributed to the prosperity of the city.[42]

Fārs did not produce its own local dynastic historiography. Instead, for the Ilkhanid period, Kirmān is endowed with four historical works of this type, two of which are devoted to the history of the Qutlughkhanids and the other two to the Muzaffarids. An anonymous work entitled *Tārīkh-i Shāhī* was written at the request of the princess Ṣafvat al-Dīn Pādishāh Khātūn, the daughter of Terken Khātūn, also known as Qutlugh Terken. The first part of the *Tārīkh-i Shāhī* is devoted to issues of government ethics, while the second part retraces the history of the Qutlughkhanids, especially at the time of Qutlugh Terken, whose reign was deemed as the golden age of the dynasty. The *Tārīkh-i Shāhī* includes original information on certain events or people of Fārs. Another history of the Qutlughkhanids, the *Simṭ al-ʿulā*, was composed a short time later by Nāṣir al-Dīn Munshī Kirmānī. In 693/1294, the author was the head of *dīvān-i rasāʾil* of Ṣafvat al-Dīn Pādishāh Khātūn. In 715/1315–16, Nāṣir al-Dīn

Munshī Kirmānī started writing the *Simṭ al-ʻulā* and finished it the following year, dedicating it to the great Mongol *noyan*, Isan Qutlugh. By means of his position in the Qutlughkhanid chancellery, Nāṣir al-Dīn Munshī Kirmānī had access to documents on the functioning of the Kirmān administration. He was thus able to enrich the historical material of his book.

Two monographs on the history of Muzaffarids provide details about the numerous conflicts between Shaykh Abū Isḥāq Īnjū and Mubāriz al-Dīn Muḥammad as well as between the different members of the Muzaffarid royal family. They were written by religious scholars and members of the entourage of Jalāl al-Dīn Shāh Shujāʻ, who became the prince of Shiraz following the deposition of his father, Mubāriz al-Dīn Muḥammad. The *Mavāhib-i ilāhī dar tārīkh-i Āl-i Muẓaffar* (c. 767/1366) was written by Muʻīn al-Dīn Yazdī (d. 789/1387). Written in a flowery style characteristic of the period, the work ends with an account of the battle between Jalāl al-Dīn Shāh Shujāʻ and his brother, Maḥmūd Shāh, in Shiraz in Dhū l-Qaʻda 767/July–August 1366. Maḥmūd Kutubī began to write a new history of the dynasty entitled *Tārīkh-i Āl-i Muẓaffar*,[43] because he thought that the *Mavāhib-i ilāhī* was written in incomprehensible language.[44] As Maḥmūd Kutubī was close to the princes whose reign he describes, his account sometimes lacks objectivity and presents events from the Muzaffarid point of view. However, compared with other local histories, it provides additional insights into the rivalry between Fārs and Kirmān.

A number of works whose scope extends beyond the boundaries of southern Iran are true local histories of Fārs and Kirmān. Their significance lies mostly in their details regarding the history of the dynasties and their administration of these provinces. Shihāb al-Dīn ʻAbd Allāh Shīrāzī (d. 735/1334), better known as Vaṣṣāf-i Ḥaḍrat "Panegyrist of his Majesty," is the author of a five-part history of the Mongols, the *Tajziyat al-amṣār va tazjiyat al-aʻṣār*.[45] The work is conceived by its author as a continuation of Juvaynī's *Tārīkh-i jahāngushā*.[46] Known by the title *Tārīkh-i Vaṣṣāf*, the text was held in high esteem on account of its literary value, which attracted a large audience compared with historical works.[47] As an official in the Ilkhanid government, Vaṣṣāf was a *mustawfī* in Fārs under Rashīd al-Dīn's patronage and later under that of his son, Ghiyāth al-Dīn Muḥammad Rashīdī. For most of his life, he resided in his native Shiraz, and his pride for the region is all too manifest. Vaṣṣāf's perspective is that of a local historian of southern Iran. He includes important passages about the local dynasties of southern Iran (Fārs and Kirmān), which are of unquestionable value. Vaṣṣāf recognizes the competence of the Mongol officials in the running of state affairs, meaning that his work can be viewed as an "official" history to some degree.

Muḥammad Shabānkāra'ī is the author of a universal history, *Majmaʿ al-ansāb*, of which several copies exist.[48] The author is known only through the prefaces to his work.[49] During the reign of Abū Saʿīd, he sought the patronage of Ghiyāth al-Dīn Muḥammad Rashīdī and sent him a *qaṣīda* every year. He did not reside in the Mongol *Ordu* but probably frequented the court of the last princes of Īj, the Shabānkāra'ī, whose dynasty survived until 1340. Therefore, the prose work *Majmaʿ al-ansāb* "smells sweetly Persian, unlike that of Vaṣṣāf, which is penned by an Arabomaniac *kātib*."[50] Shabānkāra'ī is the first historian to include chapters on the local dynasties of southern Iran in a universal history. As such, the work should also be regarded as a source of local history that provides an eyewitness account of the Ilkhanid period.

The historian of Herat, Ḥāfiẓ-i Abrū (d. 833/1430), provides unique information about Fārs in several of his works. His historical geography is known by the name given by scholars: *Jughrāfiyā-i Ḥāfiẓ-i Abrū*.[51] The text was commissioned by Shāh Rukh in 817/1414. According to the author, he relied on the *Kitāb Masālik wa-l-mamālik* by Ibn Khurdādhbih and the *Ṣuwar al-aqālim* by a certain Muḥammad b. Yahyā, two works that have not reached us.[52] The *Jughrāfiyā-i Ḥāfiẓ-i Abrū* differs from its Arab counterparts because of its lengthy excursus on the history of southern Iran and Khurasan. This valuable source contains original information on the political history of Fārs. Ḥāfiẓ-i Abrū is partly inspired by the historical writings of Mustawfī Qazvīnī, whose son, Zayn al-Dīn, shared the information with him, as well as Shabānkāra'ī's *Majmaʿ al-ansāb*.

In the early fifteenth century, Muʿīn al-Dīn Naṭanzī, another chronicler residing in Fārs, wrote a universal story, the *Muntakhab al-tawārīkh*, in which he devoted a large part to the Lur dynasties, Shabānkāra, Shiraz, and Hormuz following the example of Muḥammad Shabānkāra'ī. For the parts common to both authors, Naṭanzī's account is less comprehensive and sometimes differs from the *Majmaʿ al-ansāb*. The author is often lacking in rigor, and errors in dates and filiations are frequent. However, the work is an interesting source for the study of the southern provinces, particularly because the author takes a different historiographical perspective that diverges from the palace-centered view.

Historical Geography and Biographical Dictionaries

The works of geography and historical topography as well as the travel accounts provide relevant information on towns and villages as well as the economy, trade, production, taxation, and so on. Yāqūt's dictionary of historical geography, the *Muʿjam al-buldān*, written in 623/1225, is useful for identifying toponyms, especially since the data are arranged alphabetically. Pertinent information is also found in the *Nuzhat al-qulūb* (740/1340), an historical geography composed by Ḥamd Allāh Mustawfī Qazvīnī.[53] He collected material from ancient Arab geographers and Ibn Balkhī's *Fārs-nāma*. His account is of great interest for the study of the Ilkhanid period. As he was a tax collector, his account is a fundamental source for understanding the taxes levied in various regions of the empire.

The *Riḥla* of Ibn Baṭṭūṭa, who traveled all over the Muslim world between 1325 and 1354, is another important source of political and cultural history, although it should be used with caution. While travel writings draw from the experience of a real journey, they also partly take their inspiration from works of fiction. The *Riḥla* is a rich and reliable source on various aspects of Islamic civilization, although it contains contradictions and inconsistencies, especially in relation to the dates and some individuals. In addition, the edifying nature of several accounts is beyond doubt, as evidenced by the stories regarding the shaykhs. Ibn Baṭṭūṭa vividly describes his stay in Shiraz, conveying the sociability of the city and the population's daily life. In certain ways, the *Riḥla* resembles hagiographic literature.

Any historian of Mongol Iran encounters challenges when reconstructing the careers of lower-ranking officials as opposed to ministers in the service of the central power. Their names sometimes appear in the sources but often swiftly disappear. These officials, who held political office in Iranian provinces, are rarely mentioned in the Arab biographical dictionaries. In this respect, the *Talkhīṣ majmaʿ al-ādāb fī muʿjam al-alqāb* by ʿAbd al-Razzāq

Ibn al-Fuwaṭī (642–723/1244–1323) is an exception. He frequented the main centers of knowledge in Mongol Iran, Marāgha, and Baghdad and had ties to the Mongol court. Based on his own testimony, he wrote biographies about the main political and intellectual elites of his time. The *Dastūr al-vuzarā'* by Khwāndmīr is also of great interest, as it contains remarks about some Persian ministers at the service of local dynasties. Lastly, the *Mujmal* of Faṣīḥ Aḥmad Khwāfī, written around 1375, is a year-by-year summary of the main events such as enthronement of sovereigns, political assassinations, and deaths of important figures. This relatively reliable text can usefully help distinguish between different dates given by other sources.

In the context of this research on Fārs, the Arabic biographical dictionaries are valuable for reconstructing the careers of religious authorities who fulfilled social or even political functions in Fārs. However, these dictionaries, most often compiled by people from the religious communities themselves, are mainly concerned with religious education and activities as well as the piety of the figures in question. They thus overlook many aspects of a political and economic nature. It is therefore essential to compare these narrative sources with the information found in other textual sources, which, to a certain extent, are similar to archival documents. In addition to historiographical sources, I draw on chancellery documents, letters, as well as epigraphical and numismatic material, now made accessible through their publication.

Hagiographic Sources

Hagiographic literature may be defined as a biographical genre devoted to an individual who enjoys the status of "holy man."[54] These works are composed of anecdotes, which the authors obtained from the oral tradition that was in constant evolution. The emphasis placed on miraculous deeds and the general lack of chronological data, which are distinctive characteristics of this inspirational literature, present considerable problems for the historian. While it is true that hagiographic sources should be used with extreme caution for the reconstruction of historical events, they remain valuable in terms of social and cultural history. As a pioneer in this field, Jean Aubin noted in 1956 that it was necessary to have recourse to a larger documentation than that generally used by historians.[55] Some sixty years ago, he realized that the life of a holy man could be a good document for local history despite the flaws inherent in this literary genre. He believed that "the hagiographic text deals with both the history of mysticism and the material and psychological history of societies."[56] Historical facts, according to Jean Aubin, are lived facts, and thus a rich and evolving imaginative life coexists with minor events collected by scholars from the pages of a few chronicles.[57]

In hagiographic sources, some notions about social life are given from a perspective that differs from that of the official chroniclers, thus throwing light on the psychological environment. This edifying literature is a living source from which historians of Iranian societies may draw. In his book on the shaykhs of Bam in the Timurid era, Jean Aubin shares his thoughts about the psychological aspects of an historical situation of which he outlined the framework.[58] He shows sympathy for the people struck by immense suffering and caught in the turmoil of events beyond their control. Based on these hagiographic texts, Jean Aubin wrote a regional monograph on the social life, economy, settlements, and tribal history of the province. He supplemented this material with other sources such as chronicles, geographical and literary sources, and even archival documents.

Today, historians use hagiographic literature as an historical source with its own specificity. Drawing on a wide range of documents, including hagiographic texts, Shivan Mahendrarajah explored the history of Aḥmad-i Jām's shrine over a long period spanning from Mongol domination to the aftermath of the Iranian revolution in 1979.[59] More recently, in my research on historical and hagiographic sources, I studied the spiritual and political role of Sufi shaykhs in Fārs between the tenth and fifteenth centuries.[60] A number of hagiographic texts are available for Ilkhanid Fārs, some of which remain unpublished. Despite the edifying aspect of these accounts, we will see that the lives of holy men shed light on the way in which political events were perceived by the suffering population, as the voices of ordinary people can be heard in these hagiographic documents. The names of several political actors in Ilkhanid Fārs are also mentioned in the hagiographic texts. Edifying literature complements the chronicles and local histories, as it points out the sociopolitical influence exerted by spiritual masters on the great leaders of this world.

2

Establishing and Governing an Empire

> Even Alexander [the Great] who all
> sources agree in saying was the
> ruler of the world, did not
> come to dominate it so rapidly …
> But in just one year they [the Mongols]
> seized the most populous …
> the best cultivated part of the earth.[1]

The Mongol conquest led to the large-scale displacement of the population living in the area that came under Mongol rule, a kind of *Volkerwanderung* according to Thomas Allsen.[2] Russian soldiers from the western borders of the empire were sent to serve in China, while Chinese officials were transferred to its western parts. Peasants and ordinary townspeople also fled the invasion, taking refuge in places where they felt safe. In pursuing their imperial goals, the Chinggisids gradually turned into "herders of human beings,"[3] whose human herds were heterogeneous and changed substantially on account of their displacement. As a result, the empire created by Chinggis Khan was in perpetual change.

At the outset, the Mongols were not prepared to run such a vast empire.[4] In his article "Who ran the Mongol Empire?" published in 1982, David Morgan questioned how the Mongols had managed to control this immense territory that had recently come under their rule.[5] He saw three possibilities. First, the Mongols were quite capable of ruling according to the steppe traditions. Second, they were able to draw on the ruling experience of the Turko-Mongols, such as the Uighurs who had reigned in Mongolia[6] and the Qara Khitai who had dominated Central Asia until the Mongol conquest in 1218.[7] Finally, the Mongols had the advantage of maintaining the administrative structures of their conquered lands. It seems that the Mongol conquerors ran their empire by keeping the nomadic traditions of the steppe while drawing on the administrative skills learned from the Turko-Mongols. Nevertheless, it is not possible to speak of administrative continuity in countries with long-standing administrative traditions such as China and Iran.

The Mongols ruled the provinces of their empire through foreign governors. As they were numerically inferior to the rest of the population, they feared the resistance of the local people. After conquering northern China, for example, Chinggis Khan appointed a governor from Khwārazm, Maḥmūd Yalavach.[8] To govern the province of Bukhara, the first region of eastern Iran to be administered directly by the Mongols from 1220 onward,[9] the Great Khan sent two Kitan officials, Yelü Ahai[10] and his son Yelü Mensü-kü.[11] Both bore the Chinese title of "Great Preceptor" (*t'ai-shih*).[12] The practice of appointing governors of foreign origin to rule provinces was systematic in Yüan China. To maintain their political dominance, the Mongols divided the population of the empire into four ethnic groups: Mongols, people from Central Asia, northern Chinese, and southern Chinese. Recruitment to the administrative service and subsequent promotions were made according to these four groups.[13] The reason why the Mongols came to successfully dominate such a vast empire lies in the fact that they willingly used and adapted the institutions and administrative practices of their Chinese and Muslim subjects. In short, this way of governing gave rise to an imperial culture that blended Mongol social and cultural norms with the traditions and practices of the conquered peoples and even foreign elements imported by the Mongols.[14]

Legal and Administrative Foundations of the Great Mongol State (1220–58)

As soon as the empire was founded by Chinggis Khan, the Mongols established a new system to efficiently exploit the resources of the newly conquered territories. *The Secret History of the Mongols* describes the *quriltai* of 1206—during which Chinggis Khan was proclaimed Great Khan and founded the "great Mongol state" (*yeke monggol ulus*)—and bears witness to his concerns about managing his subjects.[15] Chinggis Khan nominated his stepbrother, Shigi Qutugu, as the supreme judge of the entire empire,[16] putting him in charge of judicial affairs and the sharing out of the subject peoples among the members of the imperial family.[17] He ordered Shigi Qutugu to write "in a blue-script register all decisions about the distribution and about the juridical matters of the entire population, make it into a book. Until the offspring of my offspring, let no one alter any of the blue writing that Šigi Qutugu, after deciding in accordance with me, shall make into a book with white paper."[18] After conquering the Muslim lands of eastern Iran, Chinggis Khan realized that to govern the sedentary populations of his empire, he needed people who were knowledgeable "about the laws and customs of cities."[19] *The Secret History of the Mongols* asserts that the Mongols were eager to invest in administration, although, considering themselves a "nation in arms," they did not distinguish between civil and military administration.[20]

In all modern states, the population census is an important means of social control and resource mobilization. In the Mongol Empire, it became one of the major institutions for exploiting its subjects, whether nomadic or sedentary, urban or rural dwellers.[21] Ögödei Qa'an followed the example of Chinggis Khan, although it was from 1252 onward under Möngke Qa'an that censuses were systematically made and that a centralized administrative structure was put in place to properly exploit the subjects, while taking care not to exhaust the resources of the empire. In Persian and Syriac sources, Möngke is presented as an expert in administration. Bar Hebræus recounts how he was chosen as Great Qa'an. Batu, the Jochid Khan, says: "With the exception of Möngke, I cannot see any man of us who is capable of ruling rightly a great kingdom like this."[22] Möngke Qa'an ascended to the Mongol throne on Ṣafar 20, 650/May 2, 1252, and drew inspiration from the advice of the *noyan* Arghun Aqa, who was a Mongol of the Oirat tribe and the first Mongol administrator of pre-Ilkhanid Iran. Thanks to his knowledge of Uighur script, he was employed as one of the *bitikchi* in the court of Ögödei Qa'an. He was later sent as *basqaq* to Khurasan, before being appointed as governor of the western territories extending from the Oxus to Rūm in 641/1243–4. He was granted the title of governor of the empire of the great Mongols (*ulugh manqul ulus bek*).[23] He had sufficient experience allowing him to govern the sedentary populations.

In the mid-thirteenth century, the fiscal system consisted of a combination of traditional local taxes based on the Chinese, Turkic, or Muslim systems among others as well as new taxes introduced by the Mongols.[24] The *noyans* committed numerous abuses for their own personal gain. Taxes were high and levied two or three times a year or collected two or three years in advance.[25] To avoid the economic collapse of the empire, Möngke Qa'an instituted several reforms. Two types of taxes were applied: a kind of Mongol tribute paid by adult males and traditional taxes on agricultural income (from which nomads were exempt) as well as taxes on trade.[26] He limited the right of requisition of the Mongol envoys, the *ilchis*, and prohibited tax collectors from committing abuses during tax collection.[27] To restore economic activities in the devastated territories, he also introduced measures to reduce forced labor and to ease the burden on the postal network, the *yam*.[28] The implementation of all these reforms required a centralized and efficient administrative system.

Möngke Qa'an established a central secretariat in Mongolia whose chief official was a Mongol Jalayirid, Menggeser.[29] Like Shigi Qutugu, he was a supreme judge (*yeke yarghuchi*), chief administrator in charge of the security of the Great Qa'an, and the "great chancellor" (Mongolian, *chingsang*).[30] Menggeser acted as the Qa'an's chief adviser. Under Menggeser was another official, Bulghai, a Nestorian Kereit, who was a *bitikchi* of Chinggis Khan and whose family had served Tolui. Bulghai oversaw secretaries and chamberlains and headed the office that was in charge of foreigners in the service of the Mongols.[31]

Under the central secretariat, regional secretariats had to govern the sedentary populations across the empire. These secretariats were found in northern China, Turkistan, and Iran. In the Chinese sources, the regional secretariats are referred to as "mobile secretariats."[32] Paul Buell considers these regional administrations to be "joint satellite administrations,"[33] namely the satellites of the central secretariat. The staff in the regional secretariats worked with the imperial agents of the Great Qa'an. The regional administrations represented the interests of the imperial class as well as those of the tributary princely houses and local elites.

In Iran, the regional secretariat was in Ṭūs, Khurasan, headed by Arghun Aqa who had governed the province since 1243–4. He was assisted by the representatives of Möngke, Hülegü, Arigh Böke, and Batu. As regional governor, he took charge of imposing and collecting taxes in the territories under his rule. Each governor had many staff recruited from the local population. The political positions traditionally belonged to the "people of the pen," who were competent in administrative skills. In Iran, the great families of divanians supplied civil servants to the Mongol administration, even before the arrival of Hülegü. To acquire a position in the state apparatus, they established contacts with the Great Qa'an Ögödei and traveled to Mongolia.[34] 'Aṭā' Malik Juvaynī, who descended from a divanian family that had held high office under the Saljuqs and the Khwārazmshāhs, stayed in Mongolia for two periods: under Ögödei from 1249 to 1251 and then after Möngke's enthronement from 1251 to 1253. Therefore, when Arghun Aqa was appointed governor of Khurasan, 'Aṭā' Malik Juvaynī and his brother, Shams al-Dīn Muḥammad, joined him as his advisers. Arghun Aqa appointed a Khwārazmian, a certain Fakhr al-Dīn, as *ulugh bitikchi*. After his death, his son Ḥusām al-Dīn succeeded him.[35]

The central secretariat backed by a dual civil and military administration ran the provinces.[36] After the conquest of eastern Iran in 1230–1, Ögödei ordered Chormaqan Qorchi to stay there as commander-in-chief (*tammachi*) of the Mongol forces.[37] Similarly, after the conquest of Qipchāq and the Russian territories in 1237–40, Ögödei nominated his *darughachis* and *tammachis* to manage the populations of the main cities.[38] The *darughachis* resided at the court of the tributary states and acted as representatives of the Great Qa'an.[39] They were all Mongols or Asian Turks who had troops at their command to reinforce their authority. They had various functions: tax and tribute collection, supervision of *yam*, population census, and maintaining peace. No document from a vassal court was valid without being authenticated by the seal of a *darughachi*.[40] He monitored the activities of the administrative staff serving the local rulers so that the Great Qa'an along with his central secretariat and liaison officers could establish a permanent surveillance over the semi-autonomous states. Quṭb al-Dīn Muḥammad, the ruler of Kirmān, had picked his local staff from among the Muslim men of letters who had served before him, although five *darughachis*, all Mongols and Turks, joined them at the behest of the Mongols to monitor and report the activities of the local officials to the Great Qa'an.[41] As a result, to better control the semi-autonomous states, the Mongols set up a dual administrative system composed of both local and Mongol—or at least nonindigenous—staff.

Administrative Breakdown under the Ilkhans (1258–1336)

After the fall of Baghdad, Hülegü set up his camp in Marāgha, which became his capital. Consequently, Iran was governed by a non-Muslim power until the official conversion of Ghazan Khan to Islam in 694/1295. For nearly forty years, the Persian elites had no choice but to serve and collaborate with their new masters who, though tolerant in religious matters, had a conception of power and an attitude quite foreign to Persian culture. Administrative skills traditionally had passed down from generation to generation within large Iranian families of divanians or small groups of elites. The divanians guaranteed the continuity of the administrative traditions, while preserving the cultural foundations of Iranian society. The best example is Niẓām al-Mulk under the Saljuqs, not to mention Shams al-Dīn Muḥammad Juvaynī and Rashīd al-Dīn during the Ilkhanid period.

In Mongol Iran, new social classes rapidly emerged on the political scene such as Jewish civil servants who, before entering the administrative service, treated and healed the Ilkhans. Qāshānī mentions the appointment of a Jew, a certain Najīb al-Dawla, as *ḥākim* of Nawbanjān. He arrived at the *Ordu* of Öljeitü in Ramaḍān 705/March–April 1306 along with a group of Jewish physicians. The appointment of a Jewish governor at this time indicates that the Jewish community, which had played an important role in the early Ilkhanid administration, was still dominant.[42] Another population group, that of the newly wealthy, achieved a rise in status, like Öljeitü's minister Tāj al-Dīn 'Alī Shāh, who demonstrated how an individual could rise in politics without any particular administrative ability. Tāj al-Dīn 'Alī Shāh started out as a "royal merchant" (*ortaq*) of the *Ordu*. In 709/1311, he became the only Ilkhanid vizier not coming from a divanian family or a Jewish background.[43] There were also great wealthy merchants to whom the Ilkhans entrusted administrative affairs such as Jamāl al-Dīn Ibrāhīm Ṭībī in Fārs. Proximity to the Ilkhan or a *noyan* or even personal fortune paved the way for a career in the administration. However, the function of *ṣāḥib-dīvān* (minister of finance, *vazīr-i māliyāt*),[44] as shown by Jean Aubin in his book *Émirs mongols et vizirs persans*, was not without danger. It is mentioned that only one of the viziers of the Ilkhans died of natural causes. And apparently Tāj al-Dīn 'Alī Shāh died in June 1324 after the fear of death overcame him: summoned to render his account, he fell ill for a few days and died shortly afterward.[45]

The period of Mongol domination in Iran marked a break in the administrative functioning of the state. Indeed, the Ilkhanid state was a dual administrative system—Mongol with Mongol officials and Iranian with the divanian officials—like that established in the semi-autonomous tributary states of Fārs and Kirmān.[46] The most important administrative disruption under the Mongols was related to the function of vizier,[47] who ceased to be the prime minister who oversaw all state affairs. In his study on the Mongols of Iran, Bertold Spuler makes a list of those whom he considered "prime ministers." They held this office between 1260 and 1340 under various titles: *vazīr, ṣāḥib-dīvān, nā'ib, khāzindār,* and *umūr-i dīvānī.*[48] This list includes Persians of course, but it also features Mongols who were mostly military officers: Sughunchaq Noyan, Buqa, Sikpur Noyan, Nawrūz, and his brother, Ḥājjī Narīn. The Persian vizier acted in accordance with the Mongol officials. After being the deputy (*nā'ib*) of Sughunchaq Noyan, Shams al-Dīn Muḥammad Juvaynī was for a few months until his execution in 1284 the *nā'ib* of Buqa, who was the chief minister. As the mastermind of Arghun's victory over Aḥmad Tegüder, Buqa was appointed to this position by the new Ilkhan in recognition of services rendered. He then became a dominant figure in the empire.[49] The account of Bar Hebraeus, the great head of the Jacobite Christians in the Persian Ilkhanate, is significant in this respect:

> After the kingdom of Arghun, the son of Abaqa, was established, Buqa, the treasurer who had been the cause of the saving of Arghun from Aḥmad, as has been shown above, prospered exceedingly, and he became so high and mighty in the kingdom that even the princes and princesses, and the sons-in-law and the daughters-in-law, and the captains of the armies of the Mongols, used to come and submit to him, and stand at his gate and beg stipends from him.[50]

In the Ilkhanid era, it seems that the power of the vizier was essentially limited to taxes and state finances. However, the prime minister was not always the chief financial officer, as was the case under the Saljuqs. Sometimes the function of the minister of finances was distinct from that of the vizier and held by a deputy vizier. In 678/1279, for example, Majd al-Mulk Yazdī occupied the function of *mushrif al-mamālīk* alongside Shams al-Dīn Muḥammad Juvaynī, who became *ṣāḥib-dīvān* to Hülegü. Majd al-Mulk Yazdī signed documents on the left, while Shams al-Dīn Muḥammad Juvaynī did them on the right.[51] This diluting of power was not permanent, as sometimes a vizier was attributed a broad range of powers. Everything depended on the Ilkhan's confidence in his vizier and the latter's good relationship with the Mongol official who assisted him, which was based on their common interests.

The dual system that prevailed during the early decades of the Mongol period is difficult to evaluate, because the Ilkhans, unlike Möngke, did not set up clear administrative procedures. The titles and functions of the officials were not clearly distinguished. This dual administration led to animosity and jealousy between the officials in charge, particularly when they were both Persians. The latent hostility between Shams al-Dīn Muḥammad Juvaynī and Majd al-Mulk Yazdī is a well-known example.[52] The collaboration between a Persian divanian and a Mongol *noyan* seemed to work better, for example, the mutual understanding between Shams al-Dīn Muḥammad Juvaynī and Sughunchaq Noyan or between Ṣadr al-Dīn Aḥmad Khālidī Zanjānī and Ṭaghachar Noyan.[53]

With its *bitikchis*, *darughas*, and *yarghuchis*, the Mongol administration interfered in all affairs of the Persian chancellery. With the notorious exception of Shams al-Dīn Muḥammad Juvaynī, the viziers could not gain access to the Ilkhan unless they were presented by a *noyan*. It is necessary to define the exact meaning of several terms widely used in the Persian sources from this period in relation to civil servants, mainly in the local administration. Just as the high civil administration remained in the hands of the Persian divanians—most often in association with a *noyan*—at a lower level, the Mongols appointed local civil servants, generally referred to as *mulūk*. Behind this term lies a diversity of social realities. Some *mulūk* found a place in the administration and were sometimes promoted to high ranks, while the term also denoted village noblemen without much power or future, not to mention the princes who retained relative autonomy in Fārs, Shabānkāra, Kirmān, and the Caspian provinces. In fact, the Ilkhanid government entrusted the local administration to these *mulūk*, hence the title *ḥākim* given to them in the sources.[54]

The term *ḥākim* is usually translated as "governor," although the translation is not accurate. The governors were rather the Mongol *amīrs* whose Persian high officials were the *nuvvāb*. In Baghdad, 'Aṭā' Malik Juvaynī was the *nā'ib* to Sughunchaq Noyan, the titular governor.[55] The term can also be used in a collective sense. The term "*ḥukkām* of Fārs" refers to the agents who were the "administrative officials of the province" instead of the "local governors" and who had less power than the governors. The *ḥukkām* of Shiraz were mere fiscal agents, while the divanians mentioned in the chronicles as provincial "governors" (without giving any precise date) were administrators for a certain period. Moreover, in the border provinces from Khurasan to Anatolia, the civil and fiscal administrations worked together with a military government. In Diyar Bakr, Raḍī al-Dīn Bābā Iftikhārī Qazvīnī and Jalāl al-Dīn Ṭūra'ī Khutanī shared their function of *ḥākim*, while the *noyan* Durbai, a Tartar, was a military governor there.[56] Finally, the entire state apparatus was headed by one or more *amīr-i buzurg* who assisted the Ilkhan in running state affairs. This administrative system was rendered more flexible in the late thirteenth century when the Ilkhans, who had endured several challenges from the *noyans*, sought to redefine their legitimacy based on Islamic principles.

Destructive Impact of the *Ordu*

During the Persian Ilkhanate, politics was decided in tents. Therefore, the history of Iranian society under Mongol rule is first and foremost the history of the *Ordu* of the Ilkhans and the great Mongol *noyans*. They surrounded and dominated the sovereign or sometimes even stood up against him. They constantly interfered in the affairs of state. The *noyans* lived in the *Ordu* together with their relatives in a broader group comprised of physicians and astrologers, Jews, and Christians. The upper classes of Iranian society in turn held different positions vis-à-vis the Mongol *noyans*. In the upper levels of the administration, some people were less willing to comply with the *noyans*. There were also Sufi masters, whose followers were the *noyans*. Ilkhanid Iran has long seduced our imagination on account of its religious eclecticism and its openness to the West, although this eclecticism by no means excluded the Muslim elites, whether at the central or local levels. They retained their prestige and influence, which had been acquired over several generations, particularly the sayyids, the descendants of Prophet Muḥammad.

Great careers could be made at the *Ordu* of the Ilkhan or even at a distance provided that the individuals had influential supporters or well-placed relatives, as we will see for those seeking administrative responsibilities in Fārs. The *Ordu* was a place where nobles came to gain the support of a Mongol *noyan*, who could grant them access to the Ilkhan. If an Iranian were appointed as a *nā'ib* to a *noyan* or to a Mongol princess, this marked the beginning of his political career. The *Ordu* was also a place of intrigues for the nobles working in the semi-autonomous courts, as they would not hesitate to bring down one rival or another to obtain lucrative administrative positions. In short, fortunes could be made and lost in the *Ordu*. As a consequence, it could have a destructive effect on the economy of the empire.

Due to the mismanagement of the *Ordu*, the state coffers were always empty. The taxation system was not well managed, and many officials arbitrarily levied taxes on people for their own profit.[57] Describing the taxes imposed on Dār al-mulk-i Shīrāz under Salghurid atabek Sa'd, Vaṣṣāf speaks of "*qufchūr-i mawāshī*,"[58] a tax on sheep. Even though Fārs was not yet under Mongol domination, Vaṣṣāf's use of the Mongol term *qubchūr* to refer to taxation was a symbol of Mongol oppression.[59]

The Mongol envoys, the *ilchis*, arrived accompanied by five hundred or a thousand horsemen. They stayed for several months in the provinces, seized the cattle of peasants, and made all kinds of requisitions. The local inhabitants were forced to house them and meet their needs, paying additional expenses on top of their daily living costs.[60] In this respect, the Persian *ḥukkām*, who likewise moved with their numerous attendants between the provinces and the *Ordu*, were no less trouble than the Mongol envoys. Like the *ilchis*, they made excessive demands on the local population.

Land Status and Insecurity of Property Titles

The Mongol period marks a rupture in terms of land status.[61] There was a noticeable increase in imperial assets. After the Mongol conquest, some lands were recognized as the private property of the royal family (*injü*), while others were allocated to the *noyans* or people close to the imperial family.

The conquered lands were divided into *dalay* and *injü*. The term *dalay* originally referred to the subjects of the Great Qa'an but later applied to the lands belonging to him.[62] Similarly, the term *injü* first designated the people whom the Great Qa'an had given as an appanage to his relatives, and then by extension, the land granted as an appanage. The term *dalay* was rarely employed in the Persian sources, while the term *injü* was widely used during the Ilkhanid period.[63] Most often, it referred to both the subjects of the Ilkhan and the imperial lands,[64] although it did not always have the same meaning throughout the period and in the different regions of the Ilkhanate. Writing in the fourteenth century, Shabānkāra'ī maintains that the *injü* of Fārs was the property of the sovereign and belonged to the *Dīvān* (*māl-i khāṣṣ-i pādishāh va amlāk-i dīvān*).[65] The private property of the Ilkhans, the *injü* lands, as well as the *dīvānī* properties were constituted by either the legal confiscation of abandoned lands or the spoliation of properties belonging to local princes or private landlords. Nevertheless, the distinction between these two types of land is not clear. It seems that the Ilkhans added certain domains that had formerly belonged to the state to the imperial lands. Private properties or *milkī* could at any time be confiscated and become *injü*.[66] Rashīd al-Dīn, for example, ordered the confiscation of Sharaf al-Dīn Muẓaffar's properties in the Yazd region in favor of the *Dīvān*. He was the father of Mubāriz al-Dīn Muḥammad, who later founded the Muzaffarid dynasty in Fārs. Eventually, after spending two years at the *Ordu*, Sharaf al-Dīn Muẓaffar managed to recover his property.[67]

Persian high officials also built up massive fortunes in property, often spread across several provinces. In fact, after obtaining a key position in the central power, the Persian divanians carved out large estates for themselves by monopolizing the best lands. The Juvaynīs possessed many villages in the southern and western provinces of the Ilkhanate, while Rashīd al-Dīn acquired land in the Yazd region[68] and Azerbaijan.[69] However, one property acquired by a high-ranking official when he had the favor of the Ilkhans was brutally seized after his fall from grace. The downfall of the Juvaynīs in 1284 was succeeded by the confiscation of all their property for the benefit of the Ilkhans' *injü*. Vaṣṣāf designated this land using the term *īnjū-i ṣāḥibī*.[70] The tax collecting measures taken by Ghazan and Rashīd al-Dīn aimed to ensure security of the peasants and profits for their masters. However, Ghazan's reforms aimed at protecting private property did not prevent abuses.[71] At the end of Öljeitü's reign, the powerful Amīr Chūpān—whom Jean Aubin described as one of the "leaders of the Mongol noblemen's opposition against the influence of Persian bureaucracy"—claimed, in the name of the *yasa*, all the properties that were apparently inherited by a certain princess Nāz Khātūn. She was part of the booty of Amīr Chūpān's father when he accompanied Hülegü on his march to Baghdad. Since this land usurpation was contrary to *sharīʿa* law, the minister Tāj al-Dīn ʿAlī Shāh offered Nāz Khātūn a province in Anatolia in exchange for her inheritance rights.[72] In terms of land ownership, at a time when the Ilkhan reigned as a Muslim sultan, the *yasa*'s principles no longer took precedence over the *sharīʿa*, unlike at the beginning of the Ilkhanid period.

It has often been claimed that the Ilkhans had no interest in state affairs. This was undoubtedly true for some of the Ilkhans, the best example of whom was Gaikhatu who handed power over to his confidant, Ṣadr al-Dīn Aḥmad Khālidī Zanjānī. However, the Ilkhans generally manifested the concerns of true statesmen, albeit in rather awkward ways. They were subject to diverse influences, sometimes leading them to create incoherent policies such as those advocated by Aḥmad Tegüder in Fārs.

The *Ordu* was a mobile city as well as the administrative center of the empire.[73] Ibn Baṭṭūṭa, who traveled to Iran during the reign of Sultan Abū Saʿīd, indicated that the viziers and secretaries followed the Ilkhan wherever he went. The civil servants of the administration thus remained permanently in the entourage of the sovereign.[74] Indeed, the long-held conception that the Mongols were not actively engaged in the administration but rather left state affairs in the hands of Persian officials is far from reality. According to David Morgan, such an empire could not have continued over a lengthy period of time by its military might alone, and its collaboration with administrative machinery was already in place.[75] Since our knowledge mainly depends on Persian sources, which should be treated with much caution, we have a somewhat distorted idea of how Mongol domination was exercised in Iran, both from the center power and in the local regions. The Mongol domination over Fārs was not only managed by incompetent Mongol officials whose mistakes had to be corrected by Persian divanians. On the contrary, as we will see, many Mongol or Turko-Mongol administrators were required to correct the administrative disorder created by Persian civil servants. Samaghar Noyan, for example, is described as "a righteous *amīr* and a perfect *yarghuchi*" who opposed the actions of Fakhr al-Dīn Mustawfī Qazvīnī in Anatolia.[76] And Vaṣṣāf, who was not a complacent observer, repeatedly observed this trend in Fārs.

3

Competent Governance under Abū Bakr Salghur

The sources diverge regarding the tribal affiliation of the Salghurid dynasty. In Rashīd al-Dīn's *Jāmiʿ al-tawārīkh*, the history of the Salghurids only appears in three manuscripts in a section about the Oghuz Turks. For Stefan Kamola, they were described here as part of the collective identity of the Oghuz Turks, mentioned in Maḥmūd Kāshgharī's *Compendium of the Turkic Dialects* in the eleventh century.[1] The Salghurids emerged as a line of atabeks appointed by the Saljuqs. The first atabek, Faḍluyya of the Shabānkāra, was appointed by Alp Arslan in 1066, although neither he nor any of his successors could have been affiliated with the Salghurid clan. It is thus unknown how the name Salghur was associated with this dynasty in Fārs. Indeed, they participated in the Saljuq invasion of the Bilād al-Rūm in the late eleventh century.[2] Subsequently, they took advantage of the fall of the Saljuq sultans to create an autonomous dynasty in Fārs.

Establishment of the Salghurids in Shiraz

In reports of the bygone emperors, it's told
That when Takla ascended the throne of Zangī,
None in his age did suffer from another:
Priority was his, even if for this alone![3]

Muẓaffar al-Dīn Sunqur b. Mawdūd (r. 543–56/1148–61)[4] seized power shortly after the execution of the atabek Boz Aba, the last Saljuq atabek of Fārs, in 542/1147.[5] Zangī b. Mawdūd (r. 556–70/1161–75),[6] Muẓaffar al-Dīn Sunqur's brother, succeeded him after crushing his family rivals and then adopted the title of Muẓaffar al-Dīn.[7] Vaṣṣāf praised him as an "enlightened and wise king."[8] Zangī acknowledged Saljuq suzerainty, although his allegiance to the sultans fluctuated with the political climate. Indeed, Fārs suffered from all the conflicts affecting Zangī's reign, but his many pious works in Shiraz would have ensured his support of the population.[9]

After the death of Zangī b. Mawdūd, Tekla (r. 570–90/1175–94), one of his five sons, inherited the crown and the throne (*vārith-i tāj va takht*).[10] According to Bayḍavī, he was designated as heir to the throne before his father's death.[11] In 574/1179–80, at the start of his reign, he was attacked by the atabek of Azerbaijan, Muḥammad Pahlavān.[12] Then in 577/1182–3, Tekla was forced to repel his cousin, Tughril b. Sunqur, who tried to seize power. The sources do not agree on the reasons for this rivalry.[13] According to Bayḍavī's *Niẓām al-tawārīkh*, Tekla finally managed to eliminate Tughril in 577/1181–2.[14] This may quite possibly be the true version of events, since Bayḍavī's chronicle, which featured original information, is a reliable source for this period in the history of Fārs.[15]

Hagiography, as previously mentioned, provides a perspective that is absent from historiography.[16] Hagiographic sources often record the memory of events that directly impacted civilian populations, as is the case with the conflicts between the members of the Salghurid family. This is echoed in the *Tuḥfat ahl al-ʿirfān*, the life of Rūzbihān Balqī, the holy man of Shiraz. According to the hagiographer, during the riots occurring in Shiraz following the uprising of "certain members of Āl-i Salghur against the atabek Tekla,"[17] the latter asked Rūzbihān for help, who said to him: "Go Tekla, God has told me that this ruler will not take over the city."[18] The planned battlefield was a plain in the vicinity of Shiraz. The atabek ordered that the earth be plowed and soaked with water. On arrival, the opposing army became bogged down, with the horsemen and their horses falling down. The small army of Shiraz arrived and only had to capture them.[19] In this real historical episode, the spiritual power of Rūzbihān and the political power of the Tekla are complementary, together solving the difficulties faced by the atabek and the people of Shiraz. Although the hagiographer's primary focus is Rūzbihān, the presence of these stories shows that these political conflicts caused suffering to the inhabitants of the city.

After the death of Tekla in 590/1194, his younger brother, ʿIzz al-Dīn Saʿd b. Zangī, succeeded him. He too was compelled to fend off Tughril b. Sunqur who sought to seize power once again.[20] ʿIzz al-Dīn Saʿd was the first important ruler of the dynasty. He managed to appease the Shabānkāra tribes for a certain time, although they subsequently blocked the Salghurids' advance to the east in the reign.[21] ʿIzz al-Dīn Saʿd pursued a policy of expansion far beyond Fārs.[22] The political agenda of most of the rulers of the province should be analyzed in terms of regional competition. ʿIzz al-Dīn Saʿd seized the strategic point of Sīrjān, a town located on the main road between Yazd and Hormuz and at the crossroads of the Shiraz-Kirmān route.[23] He led a campaign in Kirmān to annex it to the Salghurid territories and then captured Isfahan in 614/1217–18.[24] In the same year, he sought to extend his influence northward to Jibāl but came up against ʿAlāʾ al-Dīn Muḥammad Khwārazmshāh,[25] who took him prisoner.[26] ʿIzz al-Dīn Saʿd remained in captivity in Hamadān until he agreed to pay an annual tribute equivalent to one-third of the province's income.[27] He also gave his daughter, Malika Khātūn, in marriage to one of the sons of ʿAlāʾ al-Dīn Muḥammad.[28] In the absence of ʿIzz al-Dīn Saʿd, his son Abū Bakr gained power in Shiraz, although he refused to open the city gates for his father when he returned from captivity; instead, it was the inhabitants of Shiraz who let ʿIzz al-Dīn Saʿd enter the town at night, thus indicating the level of his popular support. Abū Bakr was imprisoned in the fortress of Iṣṭakhr.[29] After the death of ʿIzz al-Dīn Saʿd in 628/1230, Abū Bakr succeeded him and inherited a prosperous kingdom. He continued the expansion policy of his father but was the first ruler of Fārs to encounter the Mongol domination in the province.

Abū Bakr's Territorial Expansion in the Persian Gulf

> The wolves having shut their claws …
> Whence this calm, I asked someone;
> Look how ignorant you are, he replied.
> That is how it was then you saw
> a world full of turmoil and horror.

Thus it is now render the just Sultan
Atabak Abubakr ibn Sa'd Zangi.[30]

In the above citation, Sa'dī, the famous poet of Shiraz, cites the reasons of Abū Bakr's return to his homeland after many years of wandering, notably motivated by the return of stability in the region after a period of anarchy following the irruption of the Mongols in Iran.[31] During his long reign, Abū Bakr strove to ensure political stability and prosperity of his kingdom.[32] The principality of Shabānkāra and the empire of Khwārazmshāh, of which the Salghurids were tributaries, did not allow him to pursue his territorial expansion across the continent. Abū Bakr therefore ensured a stable and abundant income for the province by implementing a policy of domination over the major ports of the Persian Gulf. In Muḥarram 628/November 1230, he occupied the island of Qays,[33] which, after the decline of Sīrāf in 367/977,[34] had become the primary center for trade with India and the Far East.[35] For the products transported through Qays, Shiraz was the main stopover.[36] In Dhū l-Ḥijja 633/August 1235, Abū Bakr captured Baḥrayn, which controlled the Hedjaz road, allowing him to derive significant income.[37] Along with Ma'bar and Ceylon, Qays and Baḥrayn were the most famous places for pearl fishing.[38] Abū Bakr then turned his attention to the port of Qaṭīf[39] in the Arab continent. Tārūt castle located on a small island close to Qaṭīf fell first to the troops of the atabek in the spring of 641/1244.[40] During the battle, a Bedouin leader was killed, which caused unrest among the Arab tribes. As Abū Bakr's hold over Qaṭīf thus remained precarious, he dispatched troops to remain there on the ground. Abū Bakr nevertheless decided to ally with the Bedouins.[41] Each year, he paid their leaders and dignitaries a sum of twelve thousand Egyptian dinars at the time of the date harvest. The Bedouins regarded the payment as compensation for the Salghurid presence in the region and thus stopped the unrest.[42]

On the island of Qays, the atabek appointed trusted officials and an elite garrison (*lashkar-i guzīda*) made up of Turks, Lurs, Kurds, and "people from the coast" (*savāḥil-nishīnān*). On the island, Abū Bakr amassed all the supplies, weapons, and equipment necessary for the ships.[43] These measures were aimed at preventing the prince of Hormuz, Maḥmūd Qalhātī, from capturing Qays.[44] The fame of the atabek Abū Bakr soon spread as far as India among the communities of Persian and Arab merchants settled in Indian ports. These merchant colonies sometimes recognized the nominal authority of the Muslim princes who ruled the opposite shore of the Arabian Sea. With the authorization of their local non-Muslim rulers, the rich merchants built mosques on the Indian shores. The names of these princes were then mentioned in the *khuṭba* during Friday prayer: the atabek Abū Bakr[45] in the thirteenth century and the prince Hormuz Sayf al-Dīn in the fifteenth century might thus have been mentioned in those distant mosques.[46] The merchants had shared interests that bound them to the prevailing political power of the Persian Gulf area,[47] although this did not impact the political status of the city where the *khaṭīb* officiated. These great merchants in international trade most certainly contributed to the prosperity of Abū Bakr's kingdom: "People flocked from everywhere, the markets and streets [of Shiraz] were congested with the crowd that thronged there," as expressed by Mu'īn al-Dīn Junayd Shīrāzī, the author of *Shadd al-izār*, in a biographical record about the atabek.[48]

Autonomy in Exchange for Allegiance to the Great Qa'an

That Sa'dī, who carried off the ball of rhetoric,
Lived in the days of Bū Bakr Ibn-i Sa'd;
Fittingly, I make much of his age,
Even as did the Master of the era of Nūshīn-Ravān;
World's Guardian, Nourisher of the Faith, Just Ruler:
Bū Bakr's like since 'Umar's time has not appeared.[49]

The conquest of eastern Iran by the troops of Chinggis Khan, whose indirect consequences were felt later in southern Iran, had aroused Abū Bakr's fear. However, the ideology of conquest, which distinguished between subjugated peoples (*il*) who were spared and rebellious peoples (*bulgha*) who were punished, was not foreign to him. Out of prudence, Abū Bakr thus decided to preserve peace in the region and to pledge allegiance to Ögödei Qa'an. He sent his nephew Tahamtan to offer him his submission, and in turn, Ögödei confirmed Abū Bakr's position and bestowed on him the title of Qutlugh Khan ("Fortunate Khan").[50] Every year thereafter, he sent his son and future heir, the prince Sa'd, to the Mongol court with a tribute of one thousand dinars of gold.[51] The amount paid was only a small fraction of his budget, equivalent to the income of the smallest district of Shiraz. He also added pearls and gifts to the tribute as well as other goods much sought after by the Mongols. According to Vaṣṣāf, the atabek Abū Bakr had secured many resources that allowed him to accumulate money in his treasury.[52] At this period, Fārs was one of the most prosperous provinces of Iran thanks to its trade activities and agricultural production.[53]

During the last years of his reign, Abū Bakr witnessed the arrival of Hülegü in Iran. The abolition of the Abbasid Caliphate was viewed as a tragedy in the Muslim world. Sa'dī composed an elegy in which he declared:

> The heavens would be right to weep down blood full,
> For the fall of the realm of Musta'sim commander of the faith full.[54]

A coin minted around 656–8, probably in Shiraz, featuring the names of Möngke Qa'an and Abū Bakr shows the decline of the Salghurids' position. It lacks the titles of both the Salghurids and their seal (*tamgha*).[55] However, due to his political skill, Abū Bakr managed to prevent the destruction of the Qal'a-i Safīd, one of the impregnable fortresses of Iran located in the region of Nawbanjān, north of Shiraz.[56] An order was given and enforced by a *yarligh* authorizing the destruction of all fortresses in the region of Shiraz, although an exception was made for the Qal'a-i Safīd. Irrigated by mountain streams, cereals were grown there, along with fruits, especially figs.[57] The place was only accessible along a narrow path on which a single horseman could pass.[58] This is why the atabek Abū Bakr had deposited his personal treasure in this fortress and assigned trusted people to guard it. Each year, part of the grain harvest produced on the lands around the fortress was set aside, while the rest was used to pay the soldiers.[59] Nawbanjān was the market town of the Qal'a-i Safīd. The sources do not specify the reasons why Abū Bakr appealed to prevent the destruction of the fortress, although he probably made the Mongols understand the strategic importance of the site for observing and controlling the Shiraz-Arrajān road. In 795/1393, after capturing this fortress, Tamerlane was able to subjugate all the princes of the region.[60]

Abū Bakr took care to accommodate the Mongol officials sent to Shiraz to collect taxes outside the city. By limiting contact between Mongol tax collectors and townspeople, Abū Bakr intended to prevent any incidents that might have escalated into a massacre.[61] For the same reason, he established the seat of his own government outside the city near the encampment (*lashkargāh*) of the Mongol tax collectors in a garden called Bāgh-i Fīrūzī, which was especially set up as the residence of the high dignitaries of the administration. Every morning, these dignitaries were escorted by soldiers to the camp of the Mongol officials to settle government business.

Thanks to his skillful policy toward Hülegü, Abū Bakr managed to preserve his autonomy in Fārs, but the upkeep of the *amīrs* and Mongol officials in the region as well as the increasing demands of the *Ordu* weighed heavily on the finances of the atabek. According to Vaṣṣāf, the kingdom's revenues were no longer sufficient to satisfy both the demands of the Mongol authorities and the needs of the local administration, including the payment of salaries to the army. Increasing the income of the *dīvān-i atābakī* thus seemed inevitable.[62]

Establishment of a New Fiscal Policy

Vaṣṣāf's testimony is the best source on taxation in Fārs. At the time of the atabek Sa'd, Abū Bakr's father, tax levies did not weigh heavily on the population. Property and water taxes were not levied, while the amount of taxes on crops and fruit trees cultivated in districts outside Shiraz as well as on livestock was not fixed in advance,[63] as it depended on the annual income derived therefrom. Regarding the lands belonging to the *dīvān-i atābakī*, which were cultivated by wage-earning peasants, the *dīvān* provided the seed and salary advances to the peasants. The atabek kept only half of the income.[64]

Abū Bakr was compelled to make a reform to raise taxes. He appealed to 'Imād al-Dīn Mīrāthī, a religious scholar from 'Irāq-i 'arab,[65] who was in charge of drafting the correspondence of the Abū Bakr's *dīvān*.[66] According to Ibn Zarkūb, the author of the *Shīrāz-nāma*, 'Imād al-Dīn Mīrāthī had versified his correspondence with Khwāja 'Amīd al-Dīn Abū Naṣr Abzarī, the atabek Sa'd's minister. Thus, when Abū Bakr appealed to him, he had already been communicating with the circles of the Salghurid administration for a long time.[67] 'Imād al-Dīn Mīrāthī justified the tax increase by claiming that religious law made it possible for those in power to ask the wealthy for help, by persuasion or by force, to protect Muslims and the borders of Islam.[68] He therefore found a religious justification for the tax increase. The reform was known as *mīrāthī*, after the name of its initiator. A tax was levied on goods entering Shiraz: 10 percent of the value was paid on each head of horse, camel, donkey, and cow as well as on all foodstuffs except for barley and wheat.[69] Half of the income came from the irrigated lands cultivated by peasants, landowners, families of notables, or tribes. A tax was also levied on grain lands and fruit trees depending on the area and production. Extortion was common in the wealthy villages north of Shiraz, which produced the food needed to feed the city's population.[70]

Abū Bakr further increased his resources by seizing the estates and properties (*amlāk va amvāl*) of landowners. He dismissed the *qāḍī al-quḍāt* Sayyid ʿIzz al-Dīn ʿAlavī and nominated Majd al-Dīn Ismāʿīl Fālī in his place. Originally from Fāl, a renowned intellectual and religious center, this newcomer belonged to a famous family of qadis whose members had held this position in Fārs for several generations. In an edifying biography of the qadi in *Shadd al-izār*, Majd al-Dīn Ismāʿīl Fālī is portrayed as a man of great piety, who practiced asceticism and lived in service to God. He was portrayed as a man of great integrity who derived his livelihood from his lawful possessions in Sīrāf and who did not accept anything from the Treasury (*bayt al-māl*).[71] The portrait of Majd al-Dīn Ismāʿīl painted by the author of *Shadd al-izār* is in contradiction with the person whom Abū Bakr appointed to office. Following the dismissal of Sayyid ʿIzz al-Dīn ʿAlavī, he was in charge of the administration of private properties in Fārs.[72] Majd al-Dīn Ismāʿīl was ordered to investigate titles of ownership. Anyone without a title proving that their property had belonged to their family for at least fifty years had it confiscated.[73] Thus, all the lands in the warm regions (*garmsīr*), which had evaded the control of the *dīvān* of Shiraz since the fall of the Buyid dynasty, were proclaimed as the territory of the *dīvān-i atābakī*.[74] The disorder that had reigned in the region following the fall of the Saljuqs facilitated the rise of the Shabānkāra tribes, leading some local elites to take advantage of the situation and seize lands belonging to the *dīvān* of Shiraz. The sources are not sufficiently precise about these circumstances. The Ilkhans later sought to recover the lands that had belonged to the *dīvān* of the atabeks, which was a pretext for sending many officials to Fārs, especially during the reign of Arghun. Here, the role played by religious scholars in tax matters should be underlined. In a way, their status gave legitimacy to the measures taken by the authorities, even though these measures were not necessarily lawful in the eyes of the population.

Abū Bakr, a Ruler Concerned about His Power

The *Shadd al-izār* provides a biographical sketch of the atabek Abū Bakr, who is portrayed as a just ruler with scrupulous respect for the *sharīʿa*. He frequented the *khānaqāhs* of Shiraz and took part in sessions of *dhikr*. The pious foundations that he established in Fārs attest to his desire to strengthen the religious structures of society.[75] According to *Shadd al-izār*, Faqīh Ṣāʾin al-Dīn Ḥusayn b. Muḥammad b. Salmān, a member of a renowned family of devotees of Shiraz who avoided any contact with political men, praised the atabek Abū Bakr and described him as an ascetic.[76] However, Faqīh Ṣāʾin al-Dīn Ḥusayn refused the gifts of sultans and governors: "Do not go to their doors, he said, whoever accepts a single drop of water from them, his lips will burn sooner or later."[77] The famous preacher of Shiraz, Rukn al-Dīn Abū Muḥammad Manṣūr, known as Rāstgūy,[78] might have written *duʿāʾ* for him.[79] According to Vaṣṣāf, Abū Bakr sought the company of the ascetics and pious men of Shiraz rather than that of the *ʿulamāʾ*.[80] He affectionately received Sufi shaykhs and enjoyed their blessings. He appointed as *qaḍī al-quḍāt* a certain Jamāl al-Dīn Miṣrī who had arrived in Shiraz wearing the *khirqa*.[81]

Despite his strong respect for the *sharīʿa*, Abū Bakr was always tolerant toward noblemen. Vaṣṣāf describes that during the *bazm*, he did not prohibit the *amīrs* and the great men of the kingdom from listening to music and drinking wine.[82] Abū Bakr was a devout Muslim, but he was wary about controlling all affairs in his kingdom. After his accession to power, Abū Bakr dismissed his father's former minister Khwāja ʿAmīd al-Dīn Abzarī[83] and had him imprisoned at Qalʿa-i Ushkūnvān along with his son, Tāj al-Dīn Muḥammad.[84] Khwāja ʿAmīd al-Dīn Abzarī was in constant correspondence with the Caliph's *dīvān* before the fall of Baghdad.[85] He was also sent as an envoy to the court of Khwārazmshāh.[86] Accused of spying for the latter court during the reign of Saʿd b. Zangī, Khwāja ʿAmīd al-Dīn Abzarī was executed on the order of Abū Bakr, who had found a political justification for his eradication.[87]

The atabek personally supervised the finances of the province,[88] thus depriving his ministers and representatives of any freedom of action.[89] As his minister, he had appointed Amīr Fakhr al-Dīn Abū Bakr, a man of humble origin.[90] Indeed, Fakhr al-Dīn Abū Bakr's father had brought vegetables to the kitchen of the atabek, who then took on the young boy as one of the servants in the kitchen. Impressed by Fakhr al-Dīn Abū Bakr's intelligence, the atabek subsequently entrusted him with the guarding of the treasury, and gradually, his position improved to the extent that he was accepted into the administration.[91] However, the sources did not mention any of his possible actions as minister. In return, Amīr Fakhr al-Dīn Abū Bakr was described as generous toward imams and men of honor. During his time in office, he managed to become considerably wealthy. At the time of Vaṣṣāf's writing, the annual income from the assets that Amīr Fakhr al-Dīn Abū Bakr had placed in *waqf* amounted to more than thirty thousand gold dinars, "despite the plunder by his children and foreigners."[92] Through the term foreigners, Vaṣṣāf means the Mongols. The *waqf* system made it possible to exercise control over assets and to continue to benefit from them, since the founder and his heirs were its administrators.[93] It was thus a relatively safe investment, even if the assets placed in *waqf* risked being looted. However, the risks involved in investments in pious endowments were less than those relating to international trade. Atabek Abū Bakr closely monitored the activities of the wealthy and indeed anyone with influence in Shiraz. For a man as suspicious as Abū Bakr, the large families of sayyids represented a potential danger. As descendants of the Prophet, the sayyids enjoyed considerable status among the population of Shiraz. The great families of sayyids were actively engaged in religious patronage through their pious deeds. They also redistributed part of their income to the poor, which further strengthened their influence in society. When Abū Bakr deposed 'Izz al-Dīn 'Alavī in favor of Majd al-Dīn Ismā'īl, his possessions were confiscated on the grounds that the sayyids could constitute an influential group in Shiraz, capable of seizing power.[94]

Abū Bakr had a complex personality. Though tolerant toward the *amīrs* in religious matters, he did not hesitate to repress any ideas that deviated too far from religious orthodoxy, which could spread throughout society and undermine the morals of the population, or in other words, his power. He thus expelled a group of individuals from Shiraz on the pretext that they were teaching philosophical sciences (*'ulūm-i ḥikma*), which he deemed contrary to the *sunna* of the Prophet. He believed that their teachings risked misleading the people of Shiraz.[95] For Vaṣṣāf, the atabek's contradictory attitude was motivated by his passion for property and power. Abū Bakr nevertheless left behind him the memory of a just ruler concerned about the well-being of his subjects. His good administration of the province's internal affairs and his prudence and skillful engagement with regard to Mongol power brought peace to his kingdom. He died peacefully on Jumādā II 5, 658/May 18, 1260, and left a prosperous province to his successors. Thanks to his cooperation with Ögödei and then with Hülegü, he managed to protect his kingdom from brutal Mongol invasions unlike elsewhere in the region. Nevertheless, the political errors committed by his successors led to Fārs being brought under the direct control of the Ilkhans.

4

Progressive Administrative Control of the Ilkhans over Fārs

Atabek Abū Bakr's good governance of Fārs ended with his death after a reign of thirty-six years. His death led to a serious dynastic crisis that increased the influence of the Mongols in the region. Within less than three years, several young princes, all unprepared to rule, successively took the throne. Their poor governance, combined with intrigues and murders within the Salghurid family, brought great instability to Shiraz and reduced the autonomy of Fārs.

Ineptitude of Abū Bakr's Successors

> Sa'd … the majestic Shāhanshāh …,
> lord of the kings of Arabia and Persia,
> the Sultān of the land and the sea,
> the heir of the kingdom of Salomon.[1]

Abū Bakr's son, the young prince Sa'd, learned of his father's death when returning from a mission to the court of Hülegü.[2] He was immediately enthroned, and a coin and seal were minted in his name. But shortly afterward, he fell seriously ill and died twelve days later in Ṭabartū at the age of thirty-seven.[3] The power was then transferred to Sa'd's widow, Terken Khātūn, of the atabek family of Yazd.[4] Amīr Fakhr al-Dīn Abū Bakr, the former minister to atabek Abū Bakr, came to offer his services.[5] This man of low status had acquired enormous wealth while serving the atabek. His fortune, accumulated in pious charitable foundations, ensured his influential position among the population of Shiraz. This probably explains why Terken Khātūn had him assassinated.[6] At the time of his death, Amīr Fakhr al-Dīn Abū Bakr probably tore up the map of the forts where the treasures of the atabeks had been hidden. As his replacement, Terken Khātūn appointed Khwāja Niẓām al-Dīn Abū Bakr, a noble man from Shiraz.[7] Just as the atabek Abū Bakr had sent his nephew Tahamtan to Ögödei to offer his allegiance, Terken Khātūn sent his new minister to Hülegü to pledge his loyalty to him.[8] In return, she received a *yarligh* of investiture in the name of the atabek's twelve-year-old son, Muḥammad, who was bestowed with the title of Sulṭān ʿAḍūd al-Dīn.[9] Terken Khātūn also promised the hand of her daughter, Abish Khātūn, in marriage to Mengü Temür, one of Hülegü's sons.[10] Even though the marriage of a Muslim woman with a non-Muslim was contrary to Islamic law, Terken Khātūn intended to consolidate her position at the *Ordu* by means of matrimonial ties between Mongols and Salghurids. Unfortunately, the young prince Muḥammad died in an accident just two years and seven months later in 660/1262.[11] He fell from a roof, and according to Shabānkāraʾī, it was his own mother who pushed him.[12] Mourning rituals were held in Shiraz and Kirmān, because the reign of Muḥammad had raised hopes of a rapprochement between the two provinces, which were both ruled at the time by two women of the same name, Terken Khātūn.[13]

The people of Shiraz disliked Terken Khātūn, because she had raided the treasure amassed by Abū Bakr for her own benefit. According to Vaṣṣāf, the townspeople regretted that the marriage between Saʿd and Terken Khātūn took place at an ominous time, as it coincided with the fall of the Abbasid Caliphate.[14] Rumors also circulated about a love affair between Terken Khātūn and a certain Shams al-Dīn Miyāq, a man of incomparable beauty who was a member of the Turkic *ghulāms* of her husband.[15] The Shirazis became fed up with Terken Khātūn's intrigues, her political course, and her personal conduct.

Since the atabek Saʿd b. Abū Bakr had no other heir, Terken Khātūn, after the period of mourning, took counsel to find a successor for her deceased son Muḥammad. Abū Bakr's nephew, Muḥammad Shāh b. Salghur Shāh, was chosen.[16] Muḥammad Shāh had participated in the capture of Baghdad alongside Hülegü, who had directly witnessed his bravery.[17] He was thus a man whom the Ilkhan would recognize as the ruler of Fārs. Terken Khātūn, who had hoped to increase her influence in Fārs, gave him her daughter, Bībī Salgham, in marriage.[18] However, "such promise was not to raise the House of Salghur from the decline that had set in since the demise of Abū Bakr." Muḥammad

Shāh's accession was viewed by the chief *qāḍī* "as God's retribution (*qiṣāṣ*) for unspecified transgressions visited upon atabek Abū Bakr and his heirs."[19]

Muḥammad Shāh proved unfit to exercise power. Vaṣṣāf scorns his carefree life and his brutalness toward his entourage.[20] "He spent the days of his sultanate in debauchery, epicurean indulgences and pleasure-seeking," says Ibn Zarkūb.[21] His reign lasted only eight months. Terken Khātūn had him arrested by the *amīrs* who supported her, namely the Shūls and the Turkmens. She then had him taken to Hülegü after denouncing his inability to rule.[22] As the Ilkhan still had a favorable opinion of his former comrade in arms and drinking associate, he was pardoned and remained at the Ilkhan's court. However, when news of an uprising in Fārs reached the *Ordu*, Hülegü had him executed on Ramaḍān 10, 661/July–August 1263.[23]

Subsequently, Terken Khātūn released Saljūq Shāh, a brother of Muḥammad Shāh, from prison and pushed him to the throne.[24] When passing his days in drunken orgies, the young Muḥammad Shāh suspected that his brother would seize power and thus had him locked up in the fortress of Iṣṭakhr.[25] From prison, Saljūq Shāh wrote an appeal for his release:

> My chains are long and may pain and sorrow are deep.
> Your pleasure and music lofty.
> Rely neither on this depth nor that height.
> For destiny has a thousand tricks up its sleeve.[26]

Muḥammad Shāh ignored his plea, and Saljūq Shāh remained deliberately forgotten in the fortress. Vaṣṣāf gives detailed information about the personality of Saljūq Shāh, whom he describes as an educated (*adīb*) and good-looking prince. He says that day and night, he spent his time leading a merry life, playing the *ney*, and drinking wine in an old palace called Ṣabūḥābād, located to the north of Shiraz.[27]

Once on the throne of Shiraz, Saljūq Shāh began by removing some of the *amīrs* whom he deemed too powerful. He married Terken Khātūn to prevent her from plotting schemes and intrigues against him.[28] Later, during an excessive drinking spree, he had her beheaded by a Turkic slave. Terken Khātūn's bloody end is widely reported in the sources.[29]

This event would probably have had no repercussions in the *Ordu* if Saljūq Shāh had left it at that. After the assassination of Terken Khātūn, the Mongol *basqaqs*, Qutlugh Bitikchi and Oghul Beg, fled Shiraz out of fear and traveled to Tabriz. Saljūq Shāh pursued them and personally killed Oghul Beg.[30] His men and the people (*'āmma*) of Shiraz attacked and set fire to the pavilions of Mongol officials located outside the city. Mongol women and children were among the victims.[31] These events undoubtedly bear witness to the people's desire to seek revenge against the Mongol presence in the region, although the real reason why Saljūq Shāh rebelled against the Ilkhanid authorities is not clear. According to the Mamluk sources, during the reign of Saljūq Shāh, Sultan Baybars wrote "to the king (*malik*) of Shiraz, to the king of the Lurs and to the Arab tribes of Khafāja" to encourage them to rebel against Hülegü.[32] In 662/1263–4, a group of commanders from Shiraz fled to Egypt and entered the service of Sultan Baybars.[33] However, it is difficult to admit that Saljūq Shāh attacked the Mongol tax collectors at the instigation of Baybars. His immense popularity in Shiraz was probably because he embodied the spirit of resistance against the Mongols.

These events were reported to the *Ordu* by Shams al-Dīn Miyāq,[34] who quite possibly denounced Saljūq Shāh to avenge the assassination of Terken Khātūn with whom he had a love affair. These issues provided sufficient motive for the Mongols to send troops to Fārs. Hülegü sent an army against Saljūq Shāh, led by a level-headed general, Altaju Noyan.[35] The rulers whose power was recognized by the Ilkhans were forced to side with the Mongol troops, not only for the conquest of new territories but also in the case of disturbances and rebellions in the subjugated regions. Altaju thus called in additional troops from Isfahan, Lār, Yazd, Kirmān, and Īj. The tributary rulers were required to provide military support to the Mongols, but several members of this military coalition had personal reasons for participating in the campaign. The late Terken Khātūn was the sister of the atabek of Yazd, 'Alā' al-Dawla, while family and matrimonial ties united the Qutlughkhanids of Kirmān to the Salghurids. At Īj, the rulers of Shabānkāra claimed independence from Shiraz and blocked the eastward thrust of the Salghurids. This coalition was led by 'Aḍud al-Dīn Amīr Ḥājjī, *amīr-i buzurg* of Kirmān,[36] 'Alā' al-Dawla, the atabek of Yazd, and Niẓām al-Dīn Ḥasan, the king of Shabānkāra.[37]

After arriving in Isfahan, Altaju sent an *ilchi* to negotiate with Saljūq Shāh, but he escaped.[38] The general Altaju then gathered the Mongol forces and his allies in the city. Meanwhile, Saljūq Shāh fled in the direction of Jīrūft,[39] accompanied by his army that had joined the Shūls, the traditional allies of the Salghurids, and by troops from Lār, whose commander had decided not to join the Mongol forces. The principality of Lār was ruled by a princely family, the Gurgīn-Milādīs, whose origins could be traced back to the pre-Islamic period by several legendary accounts. The governments of Lār and Shiraz had shared trade interests, because one of the main routes to the islands of the Persian Gulf passed through Lār.[40] Arriving in Jīrūft, Saljūq Shāh is said to have killed the Mongol *basqaq* and replaced him with one of his servants.[41] Although this information is unlikely true, it testifies to the image that Saljūq Shāh crafted for himself in the local Persian sources. As the balance of power was not in his favor, Saljūq Shāh decided to seek refuge in Kāzarūn.[42]

The news of the Mongols' attack on Fārs instilled fear in the people of Shiraz. Muqarrab al-Dīn Abū l-Mafākhir Mas'ūd, Abū Bakr's former minister, along with the qadis, the officials of the *dīvān-i atābakī*, and the dignitaries of the city traveled to Altaju.[43] They held the Qur'ān in their hands as a sign of surrender.[44] Altaju welcomed them and banned his troops from massacring and pillaging the city. He headed southward to the coast to capture Saljūq Shāh who finally opposed the Mongol army at Kāzarūn. The Iranian military contingents joined the Mongol army and were the bravest in battle. Saljūq Shāh nevertheless slew Niẓām al-Dīn Ḥasan, the king of Shabānkāra, with his own hands,[45] while 'Alā' al-Dawla, the atabek de Yazd, died from his wounds.[46] Hunted down by the Mongols, Saljūq Shāh fled with those still faithful to him and took refuge in the shrine of Shaykh Murshid al-Dīn Abū Isḥāq, the famous Sufi holy man of Kāzarūn.[47] Mongol troops surrounded the mosque where the tomb was located. According to *Tārīkh-i Shāhī*, "with an army like an iron mountain (*kūh-i āhin*) and a billowing sea (*daryā'i mawj*) in two days had Kāzarūn's Friday Mosque besieged."[48] Popular rumor attributed miraculous virtues to the shrine of the shaykh, narrating, for example, that Saljūq Shāh threw a piece of stone taken from the tomb to obtain the shaykh's intercession. But no such miracle happened.[49] The Mongols killed many of Saljūq Shāh's followers and inhabitants of Kāzarūn.[50] Saljūq Shāh managed to escape but was finally captured and killed at the foot of the Qal'a-i Safīd fortress at the end of the year 662/December 1263 after a reign of just seven months.[51]

Altaju dismissed the military contingents who had reinforced the Mongol troops. He appointed a *basqaq* in Shiraz and returned to Hülegü. He refused to listen to the advice of his companion, Damür Temür, to order the massacre of the city's entire population. But he fell victim to his own indulgence sometime later.[52] On the news of new troubles in the province, he received seventeen strokes of cane for not massacring the population.[53]

About a year later, a millenarian uprising broke out in Fārs, described in detail by Vaṣṣāf. This popular uprising occurred at the instigation of a certain Qāḍī Sharaf al-Dīn Ibrāhīm, a Shirazi of noble origin and renowned piety. After settling for a time in Khurasan, he returned to Fārs, gathering disgruntled and devoted people along the way. The atrocities of the Mongol authorities, which he had directly witnessed, had undoubtedly troubled his devout spirit. He thus proclaimed himself the Mahdi, the expected one.[54] People declared that he had the gift of reading hearts.[55] He claimed to have the miraculous ability to clothe horsemen in armor and provide them with weapons. Vaṣṣāf wrote that people let themselves be deceived by him.[56] The material devastation caused by the Mongol domination had plunged the populations into moral despair. Popular belief at the time associated the rule of justice in this world with the intervention of supernatural forces. People from all walks of life lived with this expectation. In *Kitāb al-Insān al-kāmil* ("The Book of the Perfect Man"), 'Azīz al-Dīn Nasafī blamed his Sufi mentor in Baḥrābād, Sa'd al-Dīn Ḥamū'ī (d. 649/1252), because he had affirmed that there were only twelve *awliyā'* in the Muslim community, the twelfth being the "Master of the Time" (*ṣāḥib al-zamān*). According to Nasafī, such words misled the population. He said he had met many people in Khurasan, Kirmān, and Fārs proclaiming: "The promised Master of the Time is me!"[57] Although Turkmens joined Qāḍī Sharaf al-Dīn Ibrāhīm, the common people who had gathered around him failed to form a formidable army.[58] In Rajab 663/April–May 1265,[59] as he approached Shiraz, his disorganized band was overwhelmed in the Pul-i Kuvār by the military detachments of the Mongolian *basqaqs* and Kelja, the representative of the atabeks' *dīvān*.[60] Qāḍī Sharaf al-Dīn Ibrāhīm was executed along with Shams al-Dīn 'Umar Mashhadī Ṣalī,[61] a great preacher in Shiraz followed by both elite and common people (*al-khawāṣṣ wa al-'awāmm*).[62] In other words, this preacher had a significant influence over the entire population of the city. Shams al-Dīn 'Umar probably showed interest in the millenarian ideas of Qāḍī Sharaf al-Dīn Ibrāhīm, considered subversive by the authorities. This minor victory nevertheless saved Fārs from greater disaster, as Hülegü was about to send a powerful Mongol army to the region. After learning that order had been restored with the help of the Shirazis, the Ilkhan no longer pursued this strategy.[63]

The disastrous policies of Terken Khātūn, the incapacity of the atabeks, and the subsequent crowning of a young princess (discussed below) created great political instability in Shiraz and Fārs in less than three years. According to Vaṣṣāf who lamented the powerlessness of his compatriots to resist the Mongols, Fārs would inevitably fall into "the hands of the foreigners (*bīgānagān*)." The example of Saljūq Shāh, a hero who dared to fight against the Mongol emprise, had been a disaster. However, the repression led by Mongol officials was not the main cause behind the Ilkhanids' gradual takeover of the region and its coveted economic resources; instead, it was the intrigues of the Persian nobility.

Two Capable Turko-Mongol Administrators

What was the status of Fārs after the death of Saljūq Shāh? Nominally, the Salghurid dynasty was still in power, but it was now embodied by two very young princesses, Bībī Salgham and Abish Khātūn,[64] both daughters of Terken Khātūn.[65] As heirs to the throne of Fārs, they had the traditional tribal support of the Shūls and the Turkmens. The Ilkhans, who were by no means interested in directly managing their provinces, promoted dynastic continuity in the province, as they had done elsewhere.

Immediately after the killing of Saljūq Shāh, they placed on the throne Abish Khātūn, who was no more than four or five years old.[66] The *khuṭba* was pronounced, and coins were minted in her name in Shiraz. On the first coinage issued in the name of Abish Khātūn probably in 663/1264–5, she bears the title "The Eminent Queen" (*al-malika al-mu'aẓẓama*). The mention of her name and title indicates her distinguished and elevated position in the Mongol Empire.[67] The Salghurid administration remained in place in an autonomous capacity under the leadership of Kelja, who had fought Qāḍī Sharaf al-Dīn Ibrāhīm alongside the Mongols. However, this system could no longer work, since Abish Khātūn was a child. From then on, the Mongol emissaries responsible for collecting taxes succeeded one another in Shiraz.

The decisions taken by the Ilkhan and his entourage illustrate the inefficiency of the Salghurid administration.

Inkianu: A Competent Turkish Administrator and Victim of *Ordu* Intrigues

Throne, fortune, high command, dominion,
—all these things, are nothings,
since they pass away: far better than
some palace daubed in gold
is the memorial of a goodly name.[68]

At the beginning of the year 665/October 1266, Abaqa, who had succeeded Hülegü in 663/1265, sent Damür Temür to Fārs. He was already familiar with the region as he had first traveled there in the company of Altaju at the time of Saljūq Shāh's revolt. He was accompanied by a secretary, a certain Shādī Bitikchi.[69] They were in charge of the annual tax collection.[70] However, in the absence of a real governor, it was unclear how to proceed, and much confusion reigned.[71] In 667/1268–9, the Ilkhan decided to appoint Inkianu as governor, granting him full powers (*ḥukūmat-i kullī*).[72] Vaṣṣāf held him in high esteem, describing him as a judicious and shrewd, very strict, but just and wise Turk.[73] Shortly after his arrival in Shiraz, Inkianu restored the administrative structure by appointing competent officials. He provided adequate allowances to tax collectors, their agents, and their secretaries. To bring taxes into the coffers of the *Dīvān* and eliminate widespread corruption, he ensured that the tax collectors acted with justice or be subject to severe punishment or death.[74] His strict administration earned him the hostility of several officials whose opportunities for self-enrichment had been limited.

After the arrest and beheading of Kelja, the representative of Abish Khātūn's *dīvān* who had organized a revolt against him, Inkianu fell victim to a group of local notables.[75] Dissatisfied with his modifications, some Persian officials changed their attitude toward him. They went to the *Ordu* to denounce Inkianu's actions, asserting that he aimed to seize power in Fārs. According to these notables, during his tenure, Inkianu had minted coins with a "sign written in Khiṭā'ī script along the base under the name of the Pādishāh."[76] In support of their attacks, they produced a document, which recorded everything that Inkianu had confiscated in Shiraz and the province. According to his accusers, this had been committed for his own personal gain and for that of his family. They also had appended to this document any spending deemed irregular.[77] Abaqa subsequently ordered Inkianu to appear at the *yarghu*, where he justified his actions by saying that he had increased the volume of revenue collected in Fārs.[78] His skillful words saved his life, but he was dismissed from political office and sent to Qubilai in China. For the Ilkhan, this exile was a punishment intended to cleanse him of his misdeeds, and if he returned safely, after enduring the hardships of the journey, he would be entitled to a high position.[79]

Little is known about Inkianu who is praised as a just *amīr* in the *Tārīkh-i Vaṣṣāf* on the occasion of his stay in Shiraz as well as in Sa'dī's poetry. He seems to have been one of the fighters who had accompanied Hülegü in his military campaigns. According to Shams al-Dīn Kāshānī's *Shahānshāh-i Tchingīzī*, after his conquests, the Ilkhan granted him the district (*vilāyat*) of Shiraz.[80] If this information is correct, it seems that Inkianu was already involved in the collection of taxes in Fārs before Abaqa sent him to restore the fiscal situation in the province.

The inefficiency of the Ilkhan in the administration of the region was not due to his administrative ineptitude. It was rather the consequence of intrigues, as the local notables endeavored to defend their personal interests at the court of the Ilkhan. The *Ordu* was a place where even competent officials could be toppled by unfounded accusations or a network of conspiring subordinates. Inkianu was certainly an example. This was one of the main characteristics of the administration's functioning at both the central and local levels throughout the Ilkhanid period.

Rigorous Administration of the Mongol Sughunchaq Noyan

Inkianu was succeeded by Sughunchaq Noyan, an *amīr* of the Chinggisid nobility.[81] From 653/1256, he had been one of Hülegü's most trusted men.[82] He had joined him in the conquest of Iran and then in the campaigns of Iraq and Syria.[83] He was also the Ilkhan's confidant and his envoy to Berke Khan.[84] After the conquest of Baghdad, he was responsible for providing an inventory of the Caliph's property.[85] The career of Sughunchaq Noyan is typical of the great Mongol *noyans* who, thanks to their skills as military leaders and administrators, assisted the Ilkhans. He was further promoted during the reign of Abaqa, becoming one of the great *amīrs* of his entourage. He then became his lieutenant and governor with full powers (*ḥākim-i muṭlaq*), particularly for Baghdad and Fārs.[86]

In 670/1271–2, Sughunchaq Noyan arrived in Shiraz, accompanied by Khwāja Shams al-Dīn Ḥusayn 'Alkānī, as *ulugh bitikchi*. He was in charge of monitoring the "accounts and abuse."[87] According to Vaṣṣāf, he put the affairs into order in a competent and fair manner.[88] Once informed of the circumstances, Sughunchaq Noyan decided that from the beginning of the year 671/1271–2, Fārs would be divided up into tax districts (*bulūk*).[89] Each *bulūk* was leased to local notables, who were responsible for fulfilling their tax obligations and maintaining order in their constituencies. Sayyid 'Imād al-Dīn Abū Yu'lā took charge of the financial management (as a tax farmer) of one of the *bulūk*.[90] Muḥammad Beg, Tutiyaq, and Bulughan[91] were appointed as *basqaqs*. Bulughan was also the governor of Shiraz and had a military status.[92] The *basqaqs* were accompanied by small military detachments that assisted them in the tax districts.[93] By dividing Fārs into several *bulūk*, Sughunchaq Noyan wanted to ensure that no single notable was capable of opposing the tax collection.

Sughunchaq Noyan was also commissioned to quash any attempt at rebellion in the province. To ensure its stable income, the atabek Abū Bakr had brought under his control the islands of the Persian Gulf, which were important strategic points in foreign trade. The prince of Hormuz, Maḥmūd Qalhātī, never attempted to seize Qays, because Abū Bakr had established a strong military garrison there. At the start of the year 671/summer 1271, however, being aware of the weak political authority in Shiraz, Maḥmūd Qalhātī tried to seize the island.[94] Sughunchaq Noyan assembled a fleet at Sīrāf and gathered the Mongol and Muslim armies to repel Maḥmūd Qalhātī. Part of his fleet consisted of boats from Baḥrayn and the neighboring coasts. The Mongol *noyan* captured Qays in the spring of 672/1272–3, pursuing Maḥmūd Qalhātī as far as Qalhāt.[95] Sughunchaq Noyan and Shams al-Dīn Muḥammad Juvaynī engaged in trade in Hormuz. In a biography about the great merchant Jamāl al-Dīn Ibrāhīm Ṭībī, Ibn al-Suqā'ī said that the *ṣāḥib-dīvān*, Shams al-Dīn

Muḥammad Juvaynī, and the account manager (*mustawfī*), Sughunchaq Noyan, entrusted Jamāl al-Dīn Ibrāhīm Ṭībī with goods worth sixty thousand dinars.[96] The Mongol *amīr*'s desire to keep Qays was likely motivated by their own vested interest in the islands.

After accomplishing his mission, Sughunchaq Noyan returned to Shiraz and collected the tax income for the previous two years. He returned to the *Ordu* accompanied by Abish Khātūn, then aged about fifteen years, to confirm her marriage with Mengü Temür.[97] As previously mentioned, when Abish Khātūn was a child, her mother Terken Khātūn had promised her to Hülegü's son. As dowry, she brought with her the possessions of the Salghurids in Shiraz as well as part of the annual taxes collected in the city: two-thirds of the annual revenue of the Fīrūzī and Nawrūzī gardens and the markets as well as eighty thousand dinars from one-sixth of the Salghurid estates. As a Mongolian princess by her marriage to a prince of imperial blood, Abish Khātūn was granted a pension of one hundred thousand dinars.[98] As the main wife of Mengü Temür, she remained with her mother-in-law, Öljei Khātūn, until she was appointed governor of Fārs in 682/1283–4 by the Ilkhan Aḥmad Tegüder.[99]

After Sughunchaq Noyan returned to Tabriz, tax collection in Fārs became more chaotic. For a few years, a rich Yazdī merchant was in charge of taxes, but this ended in disaster.[100] The tax farm system allowed officials to misappropriate taxes for their own benefit. Vaṣṣāf denounces the gifts presented to the Mongol *noyans* as well as the bribes (*bakhshish*) paid to the officials in charge of collecting taxes. These abuses were such that in 679/1280, a *yarligh* from Abaqa sent Sughunchaq Noyan for a second time to Fārs to verify the tax registers (*taḥqīq-i muḥāsalāt*), collect any arrears, and repress "the tyranny of the tyrants" (*ẓulm-i ẓālimān*).[101] According to Ḥāfiẓ-i Abrū, who, like Vaṣṣāf, presents Sughunchaq Noyan as a just and wise *amīr* (*amīrī ʿādil va zīrak*), he managed to carry out this task with fairness.[102] Sughunchaq Noyan checked the accounts of the farmers (*arbāb-i bulūkāt*) and, after realizing that they had not paid all the collected tax to the *Ordu*, he decided to repeal the tax farm system.[103] He appointed Khwāja Niẓām al-Dīn Vazīr, the farmer whose district was relatively prosperous, as the only official in charge of tax collection. According to Vaṣṣāf, Khwāja Niẓām al-Dīn Vazīr had not siphoned off the state revenues (*māl-i dīvānī*) as much as the other farmers had. He was subsequently the sole person responsible for collecting taxes from all the *bulūk* of Fārs.[104] Sughunchaq Noyan had a group of Mongol officials banished from the region, because they had presumably colluded with the farmers who had embezzled the taxes.[105] After accomplishing his mission, he returned to the *Ordu*, taking with him those previously responsible for collecting taxes so that they would pay the arrears to the treasury.[106] Sughunchaq Noyan's lenience toward the farmers was mainly because the Ilkhan had no other choice but to rely on the local intermediaries for tax collection.

Sughunchaq Noyan's favor to Khwāja Niẓām al-Dīn Vazīr infuriated the dispossessed farmers and wealthy families, two extremely influential groups. Among them, Sayyid 'Imād al-Dīn Abū Yu'lā and Shams al-Dīn Malik formed an alliance and traveled together to Tabriz.[107] Familiar with the court of the Ilkhan, Sayyid 'Imād al-Dīn Abū Yu'lā had several supporters there and knew that his words would be heeded. He obtained an audience from Buqa,[108] a Jalayirid of the Oirat clan. As the son of an archer in the Imperial Guard, Buqa had been orphaned at a young age. After the death of his father, he was brought up in the house of Abaqa and thus became close to the Ilkhan. He later embarked on a career in the treasury. Sayyid 'Imād al-Dīn Abū Yu'lā and Shams al-Dīn Malik denounced Sughunchaq Noyan's supposed wrongdoing to Buqa. The latter sent them to Abaqa who "poured wine for them with his own hand."[109] Sayyid 'Imād al-Dīn Abū Yu'lā and Shams al-Dīn Malik made a strong case against Sughunchaq Noyan and Khwāja Niẓām al-Dīn Vazīr, thus persuading the Ilkhan. Although Sughunchaq Noyan and Khwāja Niẓām al-Dīn Vazīr fell into disgrace, they nevertheless received privileges, with the Ilkhan issuing edicts (*yarligh*) and tablets of authority (*paiza*) for them.[110] Abaqa sent another high-ranking *noyan*, a certain Ṭaghachar Noyan, to Shiraz.[111] He was accompanied by an administrative secretary, the future minister Ṣadr al-Dīn Aḥmad Khālidī Zanjānī.[112] From a qadi family, he was part of the elite of Qazvīn where people had realized the benefit of learning Mongolian. As a young man, Ṣadr al-Dīn Aḥmad Khālidī Zanjānī entered the service of Ṭaghachar Noyan as his adviser.[113] According to Jean Aubin, he was "the best example of the loyalty of interest that bound a *noyan* and a divanian together."[114] Ṭaghachar Noyan entrusted the administration of Fārs to Qavām al-Dīn Bukhārī and Sayf al-Dīn Yūsuf. Shams al-Dīn Malik, the farmer who had instigated the downfall of Sughunchaq Noyan, governed for a year with their assistance, while the

Mongol Bulughan continued to exercise his office of *basqaq*, as in the past.[115] Ṭaghachar Noyan and Ṣadr al-Dīn Aḥmad Khālidī Zanjānī were in charge of collecting unpaid taxes (*baqāya*).[116] Assisted by Sayyid ʿImād al-Dīn Abū Yuʿlā and Shams al-Dīn Malik, they examined the accounts of the farmers. Unsurprisingly, they began by reviewing the accounts of those whose downfall they desired. Khwāja Niẓām al-Dīn Vazīr was compelled to pay to the treasury two hundred tomans[117] as illicit profits in addition to regular taxes.[118] He was imprisoned in Shiraz in the house of Sayyid ʿImād al-Dīn Abū Yuʿlā.[119]

For about two decades, the Ilkhans pursued a failed policy in Fārs. Their attempts to maintain the dynastic tradition through the young princess Abish Khātūn ended in complete fiasco because of the inability of the Salghurid chancellery's officials. Despite their competence, the Mongol and Turkic *amīrs* sent to the province to put its fiscal affairs into order constantly clashed with local officials and failed to achieve their goal. They all fell victim of Persian dignitaries, who conspired with influential figures close to the Ilkhan at the *Ordu* for their own benefit. This recurrent problem illustrates the difficulties of the Ilkhans to fiscally control a region where they lacked trustworthy people to collect taxes on their behalf.

Consequences in Shiraz of Political Instability at the *Ordu*

Abaqa died on Dhū l-Ḥijja 20, 680/April 1, 1282, just a few months after these events took place in Hamadān. Instead of his son, Arghun, he was succeeded by Aḥmad Tegüder, who had the support of the most influential *amīrs* of the time as well as the Juvaynīs.[120] Immediately after the enthronement of Aḥmad Tegüder, Arghun dispatched his envoys to inform the new Ilkhan that the throne was his hereditary birthright and could not be decided by the *quriltai*, which had secured the Hülegüid Crown for Aḥmad:

> Now that Abaqa has left this world,
> For that place of goodly happiness,
> His throne went to his beautiful son.[121]

Aḥmad Tegüder's accession to power challenged the policies of the *Ordu*: various Mongol and Iranian officials thus tried to take advantage of this new situation. The political stance taken by Aḥmad Tegüder in Fārs suggests that he was influenced by these numerous factions.

The Mongol Bulughan Resists Aḥmad Tegüder

The new Ilkhan could not rally all the Mongols, because some of them reproached him for converting to Islam.[122] It was not clear whether he would be able to hold on to power for a long time. Bulughan, the head of the Mongol administration in Fārs, and his *nökers*, Qavām al-Dīn Bukhārī and Sayf al-Dīn Yūsuf, did not take a stance and did not support Aḥmad Tegüder. Bulughan released the former farmer, Khwāja Niẓām al-Dīn Vazīr, who had the support of certain Shiraz notables. With the support of the latter as well as the Mongol *amīrs* in the region, who looked after their personal interests in the fiscal affairs of Fārs, Bulughan practiced an evasive policy, delaying the *ilchis* who came to claim the taxes.[123] He used the sums destined for the tax collectors to strengthen his position in Fārs by subordinating a number of people. For a year, taxes were not paid to the *Dīvān* of the Ilkhan. He made contact with Arghun, who had launched a rebellion against Aḥmad Tegüder in Khurasan, offering him "a look at Fārs" in exchange for an army.[124] Meanwhile, Sayyid ʿImād al-Dīn Abū Yuʿlā became involved in the intrigues against Bulughan in the *Ordu*. In a letter sent by the *ṣāḥib-dīvān* Shams al-Dīn Muḥammad Juvaynī to Shiraz, dated the end of Dhū l-Ḥījja in the year of the sheep (late March 1283), he warned the tribal chiefs of Fārs against the policy of Bulughan and his *nökers*, who supported Arghun. Shams al-Dīn Muḥammad Juvaynī said that they intended "to take the wives and children of the Muslims captive to the Mongols."[125] Immediately, the *amīrs* of Kirmān, Shabānkāra, Lur-i Buzurg, and Lur-i Kuchik, the traditional rivals of Shiraz, sent emissaries to the *Ordu* asking for permission to attack Bulughan and his allies. The Ilkhan refused, instead inviting them to follow the path of righteousness (*ṣirāṭ-i mustaqīm*).[126]

As Aḥmad Tegüder's words did not change Bulughan's mind, the Ilkhan then appointed Ṭash Mengü as general administrator (*ḥākim-i kullī*) of Shiraz with the order to dismiss Bulughan and confiscate his property.[127] The atabek of Yazd, Yūsuf Shāh, was to provide him with military assistance if necessary. Bulughan sent a mob (*ʿawāmm al-nās va-l-rijāla*) to attack the house of

Ḥusām al-Dīn Muḥammad, who was the representative of the supreme *dīvān* of Ṭash Mengü.[128] Ḥusām al-Dīn Muḥammad was taken captive to Bulughan and was executed on his order. Aware that he was unable to resist Ṭash Mengü, Bulughan fled to Khurasan with Qavām al-Dīn Bukhārī, Sayf al-Dīn Yūsuf, and the rest of his retinue. He took with him as many treasures as possible.[129] The *basqaqs* and the tribal chiefs immediately came to the service of Ṭash Mengü, who seized Bulughan's possessions and the vast wealth that he had accumulated in less than a year.[130]

While the purpose of hagiographic literature is to trace the career of a holy man, it also tells how ordinary people saw political events. Although not viewed positively by historians, Bulughan is the subject of an edifying tale in the life of Rūzbihān Baqlī, the famous Sufi master of Shiraz. One day, Bulughan went hunting with a town dignitary. The story begins with the account of a Mongol *amīr* who had been in disbelief (*kufr*) and ignorance (*ḍalālat*) for many years. During the hunting party, Bulughan asked his companion about Shaykh Ṣadr al-Dīn Ibrāhīm.[131] The man praised all the shaykh's qualities to such an extent that the *amīr* in Shiraz demanded to meet him. Bulughan told his hunting companion that he had dreamed of a Sufi master who had asked him to convert to Islam. Ṣadr al-Dīn Ibrāhīm was invited to the house of the Mongol official, who uttered as soon as he saw him: "This shaykh is the one who asked me to become a Muslim." Ṣadr al-Dīn Ibrāhīm made him pronounce the Muslim profession of faith. According to a common feature of hagiographic literature, Ṣadr al-Dīn Ibrāhīm made several invocations, and more than seventy Mongols were converted to Islam.[132] While this anecdote aims to draw attention to the Sufi shaykh, it also attests to the esteem held by the Mongol *amīr* in the eyes of the population of Shiraz. Just like Saljūq Shāh, who in 662/1263–4 was praised as a hero for opposing the Ilkhanid power in Fārs, the Mongol Bulughan also embodied the resistance of local power against the *Ordu*.

Faced with difficulties in collecting taxes, Aḥmad Tegüder sought to restore the Salghurid House. In 682/1283–4, he issued a *yarligh* to appoint Abish Khātūn as governor of Fārs instead of Ṭash Mengü who had fled with a vast array of treasures.[133] The people of Shiraz celebrated the return of Abish Khātūn. They closed the markets and decorated their neighborhoods and buildings; musicians even played on the roofs of houses. For a month, Shiraz was immersed in joy.[134] The local feeling of patriotism, which had never ceased in the city, once again came alive in an outburst of rejoicing with the arrival of the Salghurid princess.

Abish Khātūn and the *Injüs* in Fārs

After her appointment to the government of Fārs, Abish Khātūn settled in the house of her ancestors.[135] She appointed Jalāl al-Dīn Arqān, a member of the Salghurid family, as her minister.[136] Khwāja Niẓām al-Dīn Vazīr was also nominated as minister on account of his administrative skills developed over the years.[137] In 678/1279–80, he had taken a position of responsibility in Fārs at the time of Sughunchaq Noyan.[138] Abish Khātūn asked Aḥmad Tegüder that part of the atabeks' former properties, which had been incorporated into the *injü* of the Ilkhans, be returned to the Salghurid crown.[139] With her *ṣāḥib-dīvān*, Khwāja Niẓām al-Dīn Vazīr, it was agreed that all property of the Salghurid crown would be jointly managed by the representatives of both the Salghurids and the Ilkhans. Aḥmad Tegüder granted Abish Khātūn's request and handed over the Ilkhan property that had previously belonged to the atabeks, notably villages, hamlets, irrigated land, water resources, and mills.[140] Vaṣṣāf expresses his fondness for Aḥmad Tegüder—"he was just of heart" (*'ādil-i dil*)[141]—but also states that the Ilkhan was not an expert in the art of administration.[142] To justify this appropriation of *injü* land, Abish Khātūn had argued that she had two children from her imperial marriage with Mengü Temür, namely two daughters, Kürdüchin and Alghanchi.[143] As she had confidence in her family's support in the *Ordu*, Abish Khātūn spent lavishly, particularly to establish pious foundations in Shiraz. By transferring the atabek's crown assets into *waqf*, she thus consolidated her popular support in the city. The income from the pious foundations financed her charitable contributions for the population. Moreover, these foundations were taxed at a lower rate than other properties, and in some cases, they even benefited from tax exemptions by royal decree.[144] As a result, the revenues that the *Dīvān* received in Fārs were diminished significantly.

Abish Khātūn's return to Fārs coincided with severe drought and famine in the province. For three consecutive years, it did not rain, and the price of wheat rose from one hundred to twelve hundred Shirazi dinars for a *kharvār*. Wheat was only available on the black market. So as not to starve, people were forced to eat grasshoppers in spring and to drink the animal blood in fall. At least one hundred thousand people are believed to have died due to the lack of food in the province.[145] However, historical sources do not specify the measures taken by Abish Khātūn and her government to improve the situation.

A year after Abish Khātūn's arrival in Shiraz, in Jumādā 683/July 1284, a clash broke out between Aḥmad Tegüder and Arghun, who seized power with the support of Buqa. Though outwardly aligned with Aḥmad Tegüder, from the outset, Buqa sided with Arghun, who finally triumphed over the forces of the Ilkhan near Qazvīn on Ṣafar 16, 683/May 4, 1284.[146] Aḥmad Tegüder was executed a few months later on Jumādā I 27, 683/August 11, 1284. Arghun was enthroned the next day, although he held a second coronation on Ṣafar 10, 685/April 7, 1286, after his power was confirmed by a *yarligh* of the Great Qa'an Qubilai.

Return to Matters of Sayyid 'Imād al-Dīn Abū Yu'lā

Arghun's enthronement boosted Buqa's power in the political core of the Ilkhanate, and he was endowed with every title "except that of the Khan."[147] Arghun entrusted him with all military and administrative responsibilities of the kingdom. The governors of the regions were not endorsed in their functions without the command and "red seal" (*altamgha*)[148] of Buqa.[149] Indeed, he was the strong man of the government.[150] Buqa was both a great *amīr* with full authority (*ṣāḥib-i ikhtiyār-i mamālik*) and a minister (*ṣāḥib-divān*).[151] This unique position was recognized in his new title, *chingsang*, which was only granted to the most senior members of the Qa'an's secretariat in China. He was a difficult but honest man who oversaw the *yasa*.

Arghun released the *noyans* Ṭaghachar Noyan and Jochi Noyan, who had been imprisoned in Tabriz by Aḥmad Tegüder. Driven by opportunism, Sayyid 'Imād al-Dīn Abū Yu'lā moved closer to Arghun so as to maintain his influence in the *Ordu*. The Ilkhan had realized that 'Imād al-Dīn Abū Yu'lā could serve him in Fārs, because he was a "sayyid from a noble family" and had already shown his loyalty to the Ilkhans. He was subsequently appointed to the government of Shiraz and coastal regions without an associate. The ministry of finances (*dīvān-i istīfā'*), previously held by Sayf al-Dīn Yusūf, who was Bulughan's former *nöker*, was also entrusted to him. The tribal chiefs were under his authority, and he had the power to appoint and remove the *amīrs* of Shiraz. The Mongols Awdamish and Cherik, who had served the new Ilkhan for two years, were sent to Shiraz as *basqaqs*. Arghun summoned Abish Khātūn to Tabriz.[152]

The officials working closely with Abish Khātūn had not forgotten the intrigues plotted by Sayyid 'Imād al-Dīn Abū Yu'lā against Sughunchaq Noyan, which brought about his disgrace. Worried by the news of his return to Fārs, they went to warn Abish Khātūn.[153] Soon after his arrival in Shiraz, Sayyid 'Imād al-Dīn Abū Yu'lā began to examine the accounts of the civil servants. Khwāja Niẓām al-Dīn Vazīr was pilloried.[154] However, Abish Khātūn stubbornly refused to return to the *Ordu*, as she enjoyed the prestige of the Salghurid dynasty and was backed by her supporters, including a group of notables who, out of personal interest, had rallied to Sayyid 'Imād al-Dīn Abū Yu'lā.[155] On Ramaḍān 22, 683/December 2, 1284, at the end of the month of fasting, Sayyid 'Imād al-Dīn Abū Yu'lā marched to the great square of Shiraz with great pomp and accompanied by his retinue. The *amīrs* and important dignitaries of the court offered their services to him, and when the moon of the month of Shawwāl, which heralds the end of Ramaḍān, appeared in the sky, Sayyid 'Imād al-Dīn Abū Yu'lā ordered the end of the fast and led the prayer in the square himself. Abish Khātūn and her officials did not attend this large religious event.[156] The absence of the princess and her entourage at this important religious ceremony sent a clear sign that the Salghurid court did not like Sayyid 'Imād al-Dīn Abū Yu'lā.

Boldness of the Mongolian Princess

Sayyid 'Imād al-Dīn Abū Yu'lā had acted without respect toward the young princess, failing to pay her a visit at the palace.[157] Abish Khātūn reminded him that he was one of the servants of the court (*bandagān-i dargāh*).[158] She began to plot against him with her followers, accusing him of corruption and tyranny toward the population. A death sentence was pronounced and signed by several notables and imams of the city, but they had to wait for the right opportunity to implement their decision.[159] However, the conspirators, being unfamiliar with Mongol customs, were not aware of the dangerous consequences of their judgment, as this act was a clear violation of the *yasa*. Abish Khātūn probably thought she was protected by reason of her marriage to Mengü Temür.

News meanwhile came from Kirmān that an army of Negüderis had been seen moving from Sīstān.[160] Sayyid ʿImād al-Dīn Abū Yuʿlā told Abish Khātūn that he would lead the troops to the border while she should travel to Qalʿa-i Iṣṭakhr to remain in safety.[161] Abish Khātūn was furious, as she believed that he wanted her imprisoned. She thus found the right opportunity to have him assassinated by his supporters: Sayyid ʿImād al-Dīn Abū Yuʿlā was stabbed and beheaded on Shawwāl 21, 683/December 31, 1284, just a month after his arrival in Shiraz.[162] The conspirators looted his house and joyously paraded his head throughout the city to the sound of drums, while congratulating themselves. A learned man from the city recited a quatrain at the foot of Abish Khātūn's throne:

> Ô Shāh, may your visage out of joy be [glowing] like rubies,
> May your throne be above the highest heaven,
> Every head that is not your wish or accordance with your desire,
> May it be bodiless like the head of ʿImād Abū Yuʿlā.[163]

Sayyid ʿImād al-Dīn Abū Yuʿlā's nephew, Sayyid Jamāl al-Dīn Muḥammad, was also executed the following night. His body was never found. The assassins paid *bakhshish* to the Mongol *basqaqs*, Awdamish and Cherik, to stop them from reporting the news.[164] Worried about the situation, Abish Khātūn's minister, Khwāja Niẓām al-Dīn Vazīr, had taken refuge in Yazd, even before the assassination of Sayyid ʿImād al-Dīn Abū Yuʿlā.[165]

Abish Khātūn regained power in Shiraz, while Sayyid ʿImād al-Dīn Abū Yuʿlā's young son fled to the *Ordu*.[166] Buqa was enraged by the account of events and asked Arghun to punish the princess for her clear infraction of the *yasa*. Arghun sent a message to Öljei Khātūn, Abish Khātūn's mother-in-law, saying that she had overstepped the *yasa* by killing an official and should appear at the *yarghu*. He sent an *ilchi* to Shiraz with an order to take Abish Khātūn to Tabriz.[167] Not only did the young princess not comply, but she offered the emissary gifts for the Mongol *amīrs* and princesses in the hope that they would come to her aid.[168] This behavior only infuriated Arghun and Buqa even more. The Ilkhan then dispatched to Shiraz the *yarghuchi*

Tuladay and Ḥusām al-Dīn 'Umar Shīrzādī Qazvīnī,[169] a relative of Buqa, to investigate the murder of Sayyid 'Imād al-Dīn Abū Yu'lā and his nephew. The pair tortured officials but treated Abish Khātūn with respect because she was the "Khan's wife" (*'arūs-i khān*).[170] The princess was finally compelled to travel to Tabriz to appear in the *yarghu*; she was accompanied by Jalāl al-Dīn Arqān, the representative of her *dīvān*, and a group of *amīrs* and tax collectors from Shiraz.[171] Öljei Khātūn spoke up again on behalf of Abish Khātūn, whose rank prohibited her from being put on trial alongside her inferiors (*zīrdastī*). Qavām al-Dīn Bukhārī, Sayf al-Dīn Yūsuf, and Shams al-Dīn Ḥusayn 'Alkānī were beaten under the watchful eye of Sayyid 'Imād al-Dīn Abū Yu'lā's servants who counted the blows, although they refused to confess. After just three strokes of cane, however, the Salghurid Jalāl al-Dīn Arqān confessed that they were all the accomplices of Abish Khātūn. Unfortunately, his confession did not save his life, as he was executed shortly afterward. Meanwhile, the administrators were temporarily spared because they were in charge of tax collection and had pledged to increase levies.[172]

Abish Khātūn and her accomplices were condemned to pay the annual sum of five hundred thousand dinars to the children of Sayyid 'Imād al-Dīn Abū Yu'lā and two hundred thousand dinars to his nephew's children.[173] As a result of her mistreatment, Abish Khātūn died the following year in 685/1286–7 at the age of twenty-six.[174] Though a Muslim, Abish Khātūn was buried according to Mongol custom in Charāndāb-i Tabrīz. As the wife of a Mongol blood prince, she was buried with gold and silver vessels filled with wine.[175] The Islamic rules of succession were not respected in her case. In accordance with the *yasa*, the lands that she had inherited were divided into four shares: two parts were bequeathed to her daughters, Kürdüchin and Alghanchi, one part went to her servants, and the last part was given to Taichu, the son of her husband Mengü Temür's other wife. The sum of hundred thousand dinars that Hülegü had granted her from the taxes of Shiraz at the time of her marriage was also shared between her heirs.[176] The people of Shiraz were so attached to the princess Abish Khātūn that when the news of her death reached the city, the inhabitants were struck by grief. Public lamentations were held in mosques for three days.[177]

The Shirazis were incredibly attached to the Salghurid rulers who, despite their Turkic origin, were considered the heirs of Fārs. Through poetry, the royal past of the province was made tangible. Saʿd b. Zangī and his son, Abū Bakr, were given the title "inheritor of the Salomon throne," while Saʿdī hails Abū Bakr as Solomon's "deputy" (*qā'im-i maqam*) in his *Gūlistān*.[178] After Abish Khātūn's death, Vaṣṣāf composed an elegy in her honor:

> If the throne brought fortune, why would a monarch abandon it,
> If the crown was an eye, it would weep for Abish.
> Alas! The heiress of Solomon's kingdom has gone to the grave!
> Where is Solomon, to weep for his fair Balqīs?[179]

The disorder sparked by the succession crisis in the aftermath of Abū Bakr's death persisted throughout the regency of Terken Khātūn and then continued with varying degrees of violence for more than twenty years. During this period, the lack of cooperation between the various Salghurid atabeks and the Ilkhanid authorities as well as the intrigues of local officials led the Mongols to progressively tighten their grip on the region over time.

5

Ilkhanid Policy in Fārs

According to Vaṣṣāf, Abish Khātūn's enthronement, even more so than her marriage to the Mongol prince Mengü Temür or her death, marked the province's fall into the hands of foreigners.[1] Just as Terken Khātūn's two daughters, Bībī Salgham and Abish Khātūn, were the only representatives of the Salghurid House after Saljūq Shāh's death, the two very young princesses Kürdüchin and Alghanchi were the only surviving children of the late princess Abish Khātūn. The girls were far too young to rule. In the absence of a strong local authority, the Ilkhans had no choice but to intervene directly in the administration of the province. Arghun's objective was to reconquer the territories that the Mongols had lost following the illogical administrative strategy of Aḥmad Tegüder, especially since tax revenues were necessary to meet the expenses of the Mongol *amīrs* and princesses.

Arghun and the Crown Lands

By seizing private property or land belonging to the Salghurid crown, part of the territory of Fārs became incorporated into the imperial family's *injü*.[2] We previously saw how Abish Khātūn managed to reclaim her ancestral lands (*amlāk-i atabākī*) that had been included in the Ilkhans' *injü*. Such land usurpation, however, was not specific to the Ilkhans. The atabek Abū Bakr had also seized property from individual owners, taking over land that had previously belonged to the Sayyid families of Shiraz.

During Abaqa's reign, an initial attempt was made to reclaim the lands seized by the atabek Abū Bakr. Sayyid Fakhr al-Dīn Ḥasan Shīrāzī, who frequented the circles of the *Ordu*, sought to add to the *injü* the domains that his ancestors had acquired from the Buyid ʿAḍud al-Dawla Fanā Khusraw but that Abū Bakr had later seized. Abaqa thus dispatched Sayyid Fakhr al-Dīn Ḥasan Shīrāzī to Fārs. The *basqaqs* who stayed in Shiraz were opposed to the restitution of these lands, undoubtedly because of their vested interest in them. Sayyid Fakhr al-Dīn Ḥasan Shīrāzī thus returned empty-handed to the *Ordu* but remained determined until Arghun became Ilkhan.[3] We may speculate as to why Sayyid Fakhr al-Dīn Ḥasan Shīrāzī sought to add these properties to the Ilkhans' *injü* rather than to return them to his own family. He no doubt wanted to consolidate his position at court to gain advantages and perhaps an administrative position in Fārs.

This property issue was one of the reasons explaining the deterioration of relations between Arghun and Buqa. The Ilkhan believed that the Ilkhanate's revenues, pastures, and people were the heredity property of the Hülegüid family, particularly the descendants of Abaqa.[4] Arghun summoned Sayyid Fakhr al-Dīn Ḥasan Shīrāzī as well as the notables and tax collectors of Shiraz who resided in the *Ordu*. He ordered them to recover these properties. Buqa nevertheless disagreed as to whether these lands should be included in the Ilkhans' *injü*. In his view, the *Dīvān* already collected the tax revenues from Fārs, thus making little difference as to whether they were collected from the public (*dalāy*) or royal (*khāṣṣ*) treasury.[5] Additionally, these areas had been held by different landowners for generations. Buqa believed that this land confiscation would only create chaos in the area. Arghun nevertheless disagreed, believing that if these lands were integrated into the royal *injü*, he would have an independent source of revenue. Despite the fact that Arghun had granted full administrative authority to Buqa, he handed over control of all the *injü* lands to Ṭaghachar Noyan.[6] In 685/1286–7, he sent Sayyid Fakhr al-Dīn Ḥasan Shīrāzī along with Yul Qutlugh, a son of the Mongol administrator Arghun Aqa, to take possession of the *injü* lands of Fārs.[7] No landlord could produce the religious (*sharʿī*) or customary (*ʿurfī*) legal documents proving that he was the true owner of his land. According to Vaṣṣāf, a quarter of all villages, farms, gardens, irrigation systems, water resources, and mills were arbitrarily bound to the *Dīvān*.[8] In this manner, Yul Qutlugh and Sayyid Fakhr al-Dīn Ḥasan Shīrāzī expropriated properties from owners who had held them for a century.[9] Following Arghun's incorporation of these vast tracts of land into the Ilkhanid domains, the *Dīvān* received six hundred thousand dinars from these properties at the time of Vaṣṣāf.[10]

Buqa's favor with Arghun continued to wane, as the latter turned his attention toward the *amīr* Ṭughan Taraqay, who had settled in Qūhistān, hence his name, Ṭughan Qūhistānī.[11] He was an ally of Shiraz's tax farmers, who had been waiting in the *Ordu* for the settlement of their accounts since Abish Khātūn's affair with the assassination of Sayyid 'Imād al-Dīn Abū Yu'lā.[12] Thanks to Ṭughan Qūhistānī, they were assigned the tax farm of the entire Fārs, land and sea (*barr va baḥr*), in exchange for returning the sum of five hundred tomans in five-year arrears to the treasury. If they failed to do so, they were threatened with prosecution in the *yarghu*.[13] The commissioners in charge of recovering the taxes, Sarban and Joshi Noyan, were from the opposing faction to Buqa. They traveled together to Shiraz. Fakhr al-Dīn Mubārak Shāh, Ṭughan Qūhistānī's representative and secretary, was also present on the journey.[14] The Fārs population unsuccessfully tried to raise the requested amounts. Sarban and Joshi Noyan returned to Tabriz, thus leaving Fakhr al-Dīn Mubārak Shāh to collect new sums, although the population could not afford to pay them. Since the Shiraz tax collectors were unable to collect the amounts demanded by the central government, their mission was deemed a failure. This nevertheless marked a turning point in Ṭughan Qūhistānī's rivalry with Buqa, whose influence had aroused the hatred of other great *amīrs*. Ṭughan Qūhistānī headed coalition that had formed against Buqa and that would eventually prove fatal to the latter.

Ḥusām al-Dīn 'Umar Shīrzādī embodies the Persian divanian of the era, as his professional success was dependent on the backing of a Mongol protector. He entered politics as Buqa's *nā'ib* and then became a great *amīr* of the Ilkhanate during the early years of Arghun's reign. Buqa had sent Ḥusām al-Dīn 'Umar Shīrzādī to investigate the murder of Sayyid 'Imād al-Dīn Abū Yu'lā in 683/1284. For a while, Ḥusām al-Dīn 'Umar Shīrzādī was in charge of tax collection in Fārs, but during this period, he illicitly acquired large sums of money. According to Vaṣṣāf, he engaged in torture and money extortion that left a painful memory in the region.[15] Ḥusām al-Dīn 'Umar Shīrzādī thus fell into disgrace with his protector Buqa. Sarban and Joshi, the Ilkhan's informants in Fārs, accused Ḥusām al-Dīn 'Umar Shīrzādī of being in debt to the amount of 150 tomans for his mission to Shiraz. This settling of scores at the *Ordu* nevertheless had a devastating impact on the provinces.

Arghun's New *Dīvān* Team: Repercussions in Fārs

Following his disagreement with Arghun, Buqa lost his standing with the Ilkhan and thus his political influence. His relatives and representatives were ousted from their positions.[16] Buqa then orchestrated a plot, partly motivated by his alignment with the Jalayrid tribe, to put on the throne a certain Jushkab Oghul, a puppet prince descended from Hülegü who was governor of Diyar Bakr.[17] Buqa promised him the throne, although Jushkab Oghul betrayed him, resulting in the arrest and execution of Buqa in Dhū l-Ḥijja 687/January 1289.[18]

After Buqa's revolt, Arghun overthrew the hierarchy by giving the *Dīvān* supremacy over the *noyans*.[19] Arghun changed the administrative officials appointed by his former ally. Sharaf al-Dīn Simnānī became 'Irāq-i 'arab's *ṣāḥib-dīvān*.[20] In Jumādā II 688/June 1289, Sa'd al-Dawla, a Jewish physician who had cured Arghun, acceded to the position of general administrator of the empire.[21] Ordo Qiya accompanied him as financial controller.[22] The latter was one of the great Mongol *noyans* who was sent by Arghun to inform the court of Qubilai about his enthronement. On his return to Tabriz, Ordo Qiya became the military adviser of the Ilkhan. As was customary, Sa'd al-Dawla surrounded himself with Mongol protectors. He also took Ordo Qiya, Joshi Noyan, and a certain Quchan as his representatives.[23]

Holding Sa'd al-Dawla in high esteem, Vaṣṣāf writes that he honestly collected taxes in Baghdad and brought large sums to the treasury in a very short space of time.[24] Sa'd al-Dawla's priority was to resolve the tax issue in Fārs, because the *Dīvān* was faced with a lack of financial resources. On Sha'bān 7, 688/August 26, 1289, he appointed his son, Shams al-Dawla,[25] as the administrator of Shiraz. He traveled to Fārs accompanied by Joshi Noyan and 'Izz al-Dīn Muẓaffar b. Muḥammad.[26] The latter came from a family of administrators; his grandfather, 'Amīd al-Dīn Abū Naṣr Abzarī, was a minister to the Salghurid atabek Sa'd b. Zangī. The administrators (*ḥukkām*) in Fārs came to meet Shams al-Dīn Ḥusayn 'Alkānī and presented them with gifts to win their favor.[27] However, a few months later, they fell prey to the arbitrary nature of Ilkhanid power. Fakhr al-Dīn Mubārak Shāh, Majd al-Dīn Rūmī, Shams al-Dīn Ḥusayn ʻAlkānī, and his son were all put to death,[28] after being accused of committing errors in the management of the province's financial affairs.[29] Sayf al-Dīn Yūsuf and Khwāja Niẓām al-Dīn Vazīr, Abish Khātūn's former minister, were able to save their lives once again by adding an additional hundred tomans to the amount owed to the treasury.[30] Fearing a similar outcome to what happened to the *ḥukkām*, tax collecting officials immediately placed themselves at the service of Joshi Noyan. They compiled a thorough inventory of the possessions of the landed aristocracy and common peasants. Money was extorted from large landowners, while fines were levied on the general public. These measures yielded five tomans to the *Dīvān*.[31] Joshi Noyan had the list of crown assets in each district drawn up: villages, cultivated land, water resources, waterwheels, mills, and irrigated land. Fruit trees, vines, and young plantations were counted, as were willows, plane trees, and junipers; in other words, anything that might be taxed.[32] Despite putting the population under immense financial strain, Sayf al-Dīn Yūsuf and Khwāja Niẓām al-Dīn Vazīr failed to raise the promised amounts. On Rabīʻ II 19, 689/May 1, 1290, Joshi Noyan had them beheaded for breaking their promises. Their heads were hanged from the gate of Shiraz to serve as a lesson for others.[33]

Shams al-Dawla ruled Shiraz until the death of Arghun on Rabīʻ I 7, 690/ March 10, 1291. Vaṣṣāf stresses his honesty, claiming that "despite being Jewish," Shams al-Dawla was well respected by those in religious circles in Shiraz. This respect ensured that the Jews in the city remained safe from the pogroms taking place throughout Iran following the execution of his father Saʻd al-Dawla, who had fallen prey to the retaliation of the *noyans* led by Ṭaghachar Noyan and Ṭughan Qūhistānī. Indeed, Saʻd al-Dawla was held responsible for the illness that killed Arghun. His protector Ordo Qiya and many of his allies suffered the same fate.[34]

Arghun's reign was undoubtedly one of the most difficult periods for the peasants of Fārs, because tax collectors, whether Mongolian or Persian, engaged in extortion during tax collections despite Shams al-Dawla's strict administrative approach. Furthermore, years of drought, locust infestations, and instability perpetuated by the raids of the Negüderis had significantly damaged the agricultural resources of Fārs.

Persistent Difficulties in Tax Collection in the Gaikhatu Era

Arghun's death gave rise to a new power struggle in the imperial family between Arghun's brother, Gaikhatu, and Hülegü's grandson, Baidu. Gaikhatu momentarily prevailed. He appointed Ṣadr al-Dīn Aḥmad Khālidī Zanjānī as vizier and great *amīr*. The latter held the golden seal (*altun tamgha*). As *amīr*, he received the horse's tail standard and the great drum (*tūq va kūrga*) in addition to the command of a force of ten thousand men. Gaikhatu conferred on him the title of "President of the World" (*ṣadr-i jahān*).[35] Coming from a family of qadis from Qazvīn, Ṣadr al-Dīn Aḥmad Khālidī Zanjānī had assisted Ṭaghachar Noyan when he was in charge of the management of the *injü* in Fārs. Ṣadr al-Dīn Aḥmad Khālidī Zanjānī had demonstrated his ability to restore these lands. He took over the management of *injü* property from Ṭaghachar Noyan and entrusted it jointly to Ḥasan and Taichu, two nephews of Aq Buqa, although they were dismissed sometime later.[36]

When the administration of the region was entrusted to Shams al-Dawla in 688/1289, ʿIzz al-Dīn Muẓaffar b. Muḥammad took part in the usurpation of lands in Fārs. Like many other Iranian notables, he tried to protect his position by staying in Tabriz for extended periods, and as a result of his proximity to central power, he obtained lucrative administrative positions. Despite the changes that had occurred in the *Ordu* following the fall of Saʿd al-Dawla, ʿIzz al-Dīn Muẓaffar still actively participated in Ilkhanid politics in the province. Thanks to his friendship with the new minister Ṣadr al-Dīn Aḥmad Khālidī Zanjānī, ʿIzz al-Dīn Muẓaffar became his close collaborator in the administrative affairs of Fārs. The minister granted him the title of ʿAmīd al-Mulk and entrusted him with the administration of the entire province.[37] According to a long-standing custom, ʿIzz al-Dīn Muẓaffar stayed in court while his local correspondents took charge of collecting funds for the Ilkhan's treasury.

However, this policy based on the direct administration of Fārs by Mongol officials, who were supposed to work closely with local notables, failed once more. Ilkhanid officials went back to the farming system to collect taxes. Despite its drawbacks, the tax farming system was easier for the Ilkhans to manage. On several occasions, they entrusted the tax farming to eminent Muslim merchants.

Mongols and Trade

According to research on the emergence of nomadic empires, the alliance between a charismatic clan and major traders favored the expansion of nomadic states, thus allowing them to exercise political control through trade networks.[38] Two types of merchants existed in the Mongol Empire: private merchants who used their own capital and merchants who traded with capital entrusted to them by an imperial prince or princess or by a high court official. These merchants were called *ortoq*,[39] a term of Turkic origin that means "partner."[40] Their existence was first observed in Eurasia, while their activities in Yüan China are also well attested in the Chinese sources.

As evidenced by observers sent to Mongolia by the Sung dynasty, the influence of merchants grew under Ögödei. According to an envoy who arrived in Qaraqorum in 1234, the emperor, princes, princesses, and their families entrusted their wealth to the Muslim merchants to make it productive.[41] These imperial merchants also falsely accused the local populations of stealing the goods that they were transporting through the provinces; they would then demand their payment. Many travelers described how this behavior spread throughout the empire and became institutionalized.[42] Muslim merchants realized that they too could profit from this situation. Consequently, Möngke attempted to subjugate the merchants to the central government in an effort to put an end to these abuses. Merchants were barred from using the *yam* or horses from the official postal network, their income was restricted, and they had to pay taxes like the rest of the empire's subjects.[43]

Like the Qa'ans in China, the Ilkhans showed a genuine interest in trade. After the fall and looting of Baghdad, Hülegü appointed a certain ʿAlī Bahādụr as *shiḥna*, who was given the task of rebuilding the city and restoring prosperity to its merchants.[44] In 1265–6, Abaqa issued a *yarligh* addressed to his financial secretary, in which he stated that his father and ancestors held the *ortoqs* in high esteem. Abaqa instructed his officials not to obstruct the commercial activities of merchants, who used a portion of their earnings to convert arid land into fertile soil.[45]

The Mongols' fascination with merchants was not limited to their commercial activities. The great merchants were capable of managing large sums of money, as they were literate and fluent in several languages. The Ilkhans quickly realized that such skills could be exploited in their administrative system, not to mention their wealth and social standing. For this reason, the Ilkhans gave them various responsibilities to manage tax affairs and even perform diplomatic missions. According to the sources, two great international merchants with commercial interests in the Far East were active in Fārs. Abaqa thus appointed Khwāja Shams al-Dīn Muḥammad b. Malik Tāzīgū in 676/1277–8 as the only tax farmer of the province (*ṣāḥib-i muqāṭaʿa*).[46] Over two decades later, in early 692/late 1292, Gaikhatu appointed Jamāl al-Dīn Ibrāhīm Ṭībī, another great merchant, to manage tax collection in Fārs.

Khwāja Shams al-Dīn Muḥammad b. Malik Tāzīgū was a wealthy Yazdī merchant who traded with India and China.[47] As a representative of minister Shams al-Dīn Muḥammad Juvaynī in Yazd, he played an important role in the Ilkhanid administration. Indeed, the minister had entrusted him with constructing a large complex of charitable buildings in the city, which included a hospital, pharmacy, asylum for the mentally ill, as well as a mosque and madrasa. The construction of these buildings was completed in 666/1267–8.[48] Ḥāfiẓ-i Abrū describes Khwāja Shams al-Dīn Muḥammad b. Malik Tāzīgū as one of the wealthiest people in Fārs.[49] His career was nevertheless brief. District tax collectors who had to pay him the amount owed to the *Ordu* failed to fulfill their obligation. As a result, he was compelled to pay the sums out of his own pocket. He ended up losing all his possessions, and just three years after his appointment to tax farming in Fārs, he was living in poverty.[50]

It is difficult to accurately describe Khwāja Shams al-Dīn Muḥammad b. Malik Tāzīgū's function as tax farmer, because the sources contain very little information. One incident from his military career is comparatively well documented. During the winter of 677/1278–9, a courier from Kirmān arrived to announce that a thousand Negüderi horsemen were on their way to Fārs.[51] Shams al-Dīn Muḥammad b. Malik Tāzīgū, along with the *umarāʾ* of Fārs, immediately mustered an army composed of Shūls, Turkmens, and Kurds.[52] The two opposing sides clashed near Tang-i Shikam. The Mongol *basqaqs* and the *amīrs*, who were all drunk, destroyed the bridge while crossing the river. Shams al-Dīn Muḥammad b. Malik Tāzīgū and Bulughan, the Mongol governor of Shiraz, fled for their lives.[53] The Negüderis plundered the wealthy villages surrounding the city and kidnapped children.[54] A few years later, the Negüderis raided Fārs, thus devastating the hot regions (*garmsīr*) and coastal regions (*savāḥīl*). A large portion of Shams al-Dīn Muḥammad b. Malik Tāzīgū's wealth was derived from the camel trade; Negüderis' raids undoubtedly dealt him a significant blow, because they took away around one hundred and twenty thousand camels.[55] This figure is most certainly exaggerated, although it indicates the fame of this great and affluent merchant. He had established numerous *awqāfs*, no doubt in an unsuccessful attempt to safeguard his fortune.

Jamāl al-Dīn Ibrāhīm b. Muḥammad Ṭībī Sawāmilī's career is better attested in the sources. Gaikhatu honored him with the title "King of Islam" (*malik al-islām*) and bestowed high distinctions on him.[56] Jamāl al-Dīn Ibrāhīm's father from Ṭīb in southern Iraq[57] sold thin-necked copper bowls (*sawāmil*), from where his name is derived.[58] His son, Jamāl al-Dīn Ibrāhīm, frequently visited pearl fisheries and started out as a simple pearl piercer. He then engaged in commercial activities with the Far East, eventually accumulating an enormous fortune. When he settled in Fārs, he was without a doubt the richest merchant operating in the seas of India. Ibn al-ʿImād, the author of *Shadharāt al-dhahab*, described him as the "chief of traders" (*ra'īs al-tujjār*).[59] According to Ḥāfiẓ-i Abrū, at any one time, he had a hundred ships in motion, which was quite a sizable number.[60] Of all the provinces of the Ilkhanate, Fārs had the third highest annual income, with the majority of this income coming from Indo-Persian trade.[61]

One of Malik al-Islām's brothers, Taqī al-Dīn, bore the title of Marzubān al-Hind.[62] He was minister to the Pandya princes who reigned in the far south of India. Taqī al-Dīn's influence in Kayāl, Patān, and Malipatān grew further when he acquired the trading monopoly of these three free ports on the Maʿbar coast, which was a stopover route to China.[63] In these ports, the Friday prayer was said in his name.[64] The two brothers thus almost exclusively controlled trade to India and the Far East. According to Vaṣṣāf, when goods from the Far East and India arrived, Taqī al-Dīn's agents reserved what was of interest to Malik al-Islām Jamāl al-Dīn Ibrāhīm before allowing the other merchants to engage in transactions. The goods reserved for his brother were shipped to Qays by his own ships. Again, Malik al-Islām's representatives were given preference over other merchants when choosing products, especially fabrics.

Malik al-Islām made the island of Qays his center of power. It thus became the great trading post of the Persian Gulf. He traded extensively in horses with India, where Arab and Persian horses were highly valued. Every year, he sent 1,400 horses from his personal stud farms. Jamāl al-Dīn Ibrāhīm also owned stud farms in Qaṭīf, Laḥsa, Baḥrayn, Qalhāt, and Hormuz, regions that were included in the economic domain of Qays.[65] Furthermore, the island protected him from the whims of the Mongol *Ordu*, of which he was rightfully wary, as we will see.

Gaikhatu entrusted Malik al-Islām Jamāl al-Dīn Ibrāhīm with the management of the *injü* domains of Fārs for four years, requiring him to pay to the Ilkhan an annual sum of one thousand tomans while giving him an allowance of 114 tomans for his personal expenses.[66] Of course, the outward appearances of Salghurid power were preserved. The young princess Kürdüchin, who was the daughter of Abish Khātūn and Mengü Temür, was considered the heiress of the "Kingdom of Solomon" (*mulk-i Sulaymān*),[67] and the beating of the drum continued in front of the atabeks' palace.[68] According to the historian Rashīd al-Dīn, the function of *malik* in Shiraz had since passed into the hands of the *ortoqs*.[69]

Jamāl al-Dīn Ibrāhīm had amassed a substantial fortune through his successful commercial activities. His representatives at the *Ordu* paid in advance the sums due for the coming year; they also added other gifts for the Ilkhan and his retinue as well as the Mongol princesses and *amīrs*. By doing so, Malik al-Islām hoped that he would be able to prevent the comings and goings of the *ilchis* in the province during tax collection. He obtained a *yarligh* from Gaikhatu, forbidding the *basqaqs* and *ilchis* from venturing into the areas where he owned tax farms. All these Mongol envoys lived at the expense of the locals. Malik al-Islām took this measure seriously so as to safeguard the population from abuse and violence.

Nevertheless, these measures were not heeded for long. ʿIzz al-Dīn Muẓaffar, a protégé of Ṣadr al-Dīn Aḥmad Khālidī Zanjānī, who was his collaborator in overseeing the financial affairs of Fārs, plotted against Malik al-Islām in the *Ordu*. ʿIzz al-Dīn Muẓaffar was from the district of Fāl, which rivaled Qays. Conflicts of interest in the area thus served as the basis for animosity between the two men.[70] Since ʿIzz al-Dīn Muẓaffar was in charge of the region's taxes in the *Ordu*, he was able to divert for his own benefit more than three hundred tomans from the legal taxes paid over the course of three years.[71] An *ilchi* was dispatched to Shiraz, demanding that one hundred tomans in gold and five thousand *mans* worth of pearls be paid in full within ten days in order to settle the arrears of a *muqāṭaʿa* for which Malik al-Islām was responsible in the coastal region. The wealthy merchant gave thirty thousand tomans from his personal fortune, but in the meantime, a second *yarligh* arrived and abruptly canceled the initial demand.[72] In 693/1294, Malik al-Islām had no choice but to go to the *Ordu* to protect his fortune and foil any new intrigues of ʿIzz al-Dīn Muẓaffar. Nevertheless, due to his wealth, he offered large sums of money to obtain a new tax farm for Fārs and the coastal regions.

Gaikhatu's extravagance and reckless spending, along with the largesse of his minister, had driven the state's finances to the brink of bankruptcy. He looked for a solution to rectify the situation. At the instigation of Ṣadr al-Dīn Aḥmad Khālidī Zanjānī, in 693/1294, Gaikhatu adopted paper money based on the Chinese model, the *chāv*. Gold and silver coins were replaced by this new currency, but due to the population's lack of confidence in it, it became a total failure within a few months.[73] This economic disaster was compounded by an epidemic that broke out after Arghun's death, destroying herds in Baghdad, Mosul, Diyar Bakr, and Khurasan.[74] Gaikhatu's power was considerably weakened. Baidu took advantage and rebelled against him. Rival armies clashed near Hamadān. Ṭaghachar Noyan, whom Gaikhatu had sent to suppress the revolt, sided with Baidu. Gaikhatu was thus forced to retreat to Tabriz where he was captured and executed on Jumādā I 6, 694/March 24, 1295.[75]

At the time of Baidu's revolt against Gaikhatu, Malik al-Islām was staying in the *Ordu* for a year. From the new Ilkhan, he later obtained the tax farming of Fārs, including its coastal regions, based on the same agreement that he had signed under Gaikhatu.[76] Baidu appointed Qunchuqbal, Abatay Noyan's grandson,[77] to the administration of Fārs and Shabānkāra.[78] He sent the *ilchīs* to Shiraz with the order to arrest ʿIzz al-Dīn Muẓaffar and the Mongol *basqaq*, a certain Qurumishi.[79] Malik al-Islām's enemies, who had seized his property in his absence, were subsequently apprehended.[80] Nevertheless, the financial situation of the Ilkhans remained precarious, as the treasury was completely empty. Baidu's power was uncertain and threatened by Ghazan, Arghun's son and an ally of Amīr Nawrūz.[81]

Ghazan's Administration in Fārs

Ghazan's image as a great statesman, the founder of the Islamic Ilkhanate, and the author of various reforms designed to free Muslim populations from the yoke of the Mongols was first portrayed by Rashīd al-Dīn, who became the *éminence grise* of the new Ilkhan from 697/1298. Prior to this time, this image was not at all discernible. It is important to recall the circumstances surrounding Ghazan's enthronement, because they had an important impact on the fiscal administration of Fārs.

Ghazan was born on Rabīʿ I 29, 670/November 5, 1271. At the beginning of his reign, his father Arghun had appointed him governor of Khurasan and Māzandarān. This appointment indicated Arghun's intention to designate him as his successor. According to Rashīd al-Dīn, he acted as his deputy (*qā'im-i maqām*) in the region.[82] Numismatics supports this evidence, as Ghazan's name appears next to that of his father on coins minted in 1288, 1289, and 1291.[83] As early as 688/1289, he faced an almost five-year revolt led by Amīr Nawrūz, Arghun Aqa's son. The two men reconciled following Gaikhatu's removal by Baidu in Jumādā I 694/March 1295. The young prince Ghazan was without great ambition at that time, instead preferring hunting and worldly pleasures. Nawrūz sought to push him to the throne, confident that he would be able to hold on to the reins of power. At his instigation, Ghazan converted to Islam to rally the Mongol *amīrs* of Baidu's army who had become Muslims.[84]

Ghazan and Nawrūz joined forces against Baidu in Khurasan and marched to the city of Ray. Nawrūz was undoubtedly the mastermind behind the victory, with Ṣadr al-Dīn Aḥmad Khālidī Zanjānī by his side. The latter's presence was necessary to join forces with Ṭaghachar Noyan whose subsequent betrayal of Baidu was a crucial element in their victory.[85] Ṭaghachar Noyan's defection prompted others to defect, and overnight Baidu was left without troops.[86] Nawrūz pursued him, and he was beheaded on Dhū l-Qa'da 23, 694/October 4, 1295, in Tabriz.[87] Ghazan was enthroned on Dhū l-Ḥijja 29, 694/November 9, 1295. The new Ilkhan took the title of "King of Islam" (*pādishāh al-islām*).[88] Nawrūz, the real victor and mastermind behind Ghazan's ascension to power, imposed his strategy of Islamization and his choice of men.[89] In a *yarligh*, he was promoted to lieutenant general with complete control over the Ilkhanate as well as unlimited vizierate authority and command of the armed forces.[90]

Ghazan retired to his winter headquarters in Mūghān, while Nawrūz remained in Tabriz. With complete authority, Nawrūz appointed representatives whom he trusted in the provinces and reorganized the chancellery staff.[91] He appointed Jamāl al-Dīn Dastajirdānī to the vizierate, while Nawrūz's brother, Ḥājjī Narin, oversaw him.[92] The latter was responsible for finances (*umūr-i dīvān*) and held the great seal.[93] Nāṣir al-Dīn Saltilmish held the seal of *ṣāḥib-dīvān* and was in charge of signing documents.[94] Sharaf al-Dīn Simnānī was bestowed with the title of great secretary (*ulugh bitikchī*).[95] However, as Jean Aubin noted, this division of duties was ineffective and had a negative impact on the management of the provinces.[96]

Setbacks of Malik al-Islām at the *Ordu*

Shortly after Ghazan's enthronement, the *amīr* Horqudaq was sent as an administrator to Fārs where he stayed for one year[97] to investigate the reasons behind the struggle between 'Izz al-Dīn Muẓaffar and Malik al-Islām.[98] The latter was on a military expedition to Qays (Ramaḍān 695/July 1296) where he had to ward off the prince of Hormuz, Bahā' al-Dīn Ayāz. Upon his return to Shiraz, some *ilchis* arrived carrying a *yarligh*, which requested him to go meet Ghazan.[99] Malik al-Islām threw a lavish party close to the *Ordu* to win over the new Ilkhan's favor. He presented Ghazan with an array of valuable items from India and China, including one hundred geldings, pearls, silks, clothing with gold embroidery, jewels, gold and silver dishes, and precious stones.[100] All these gifts attest to the sheer wealth of Malik al-Islām, who tried to consolidate his position at court where he had spent two years.

As Ghazan had difficulty imposing his power on Nawrūz, he eventually decided to remove this powerful rival and his clan in the summer of 696/1297. The Khālidīs had a hand in his demise, which in turn reinforced their own power.[101] On Muḥarram 1, 696/October 30, 1296, Ṣadr al-Dīn Aḥmad Khālidī Zanjānī acceded to the vizierate for the second time.[102] During his years spent in Tabriz trying to counter 'Izz al-Dīn Muẓaffar's actions, Malik al-Islām had grown close to Ṣadr al-Dīn Aḥmad Khālidī Zanjānī and became his friend. The issue of his dispute with 'Izz al-Dīn Muẓaffar was raised once again. Malik al-Islām was able to respond to 'Izz al-Dīn Muẓaffar's intrigues by presenting the *yarligh* of Arghun, which attested to his expenses. 'Izz al-Dīn Muẓaffar was finally tried in the *yarghu* on Muḥarram 10, 696/November 8, 1296, and executed the following day.[103]

Examining Malik al-Islām's accounts, the investigators of the *Dīvān* discovered that it owed him 170 tomans.[104] He received ʿIrāq-i ʿarab's tax farm for three years along with that of Baṣra and Wāsiṭ, which played an important economic role. He also received the tax farm of the *injü* of Fārs, Shabānkāra, and the coastal regions for a period of ten years. Thus, Malik al-Islām had a vast region under his authority, extending from Baghdad to Shiraz and from Baḥrayn to Qays.[105] Malik al-Islām's financial investment in the *Ordu* to obtain protectors had finally paid off, and his business prospered for a time.

At the end of the year 697/1298, Malik al-Islām was once again summoned to the court of the Ilkhan as part of an investigation conducted on Ghazan's order regarding the management of civil servants and provincial governors (*mulūk-i aṭrāf*).[106] The situation had turned on him. Ṣadr al-Dīn Aḥmad Khālidī Zanjānī had provoked fierce jealousy ever since his initial appointment to the vizierate. After being accused of embezzlement by the Ilkhan representatives, he was executed in Rajab in 697/April–May 1298 despite his convincing defense.[107] Malik al-Islām could thus no longer count on the support of his protector. Local officials claimed that illegal agreements had been made between Malik al-Islām and the ousted minister. Therefore, despite being in Ghazan's favor, Malik al-Islām no longer benefited from the deductions for his personal expenses, with large sums being added to the amount due for the tax farms that he owned. He was forced to pay for these surplus costs out of his personal fortune and had his accounts reexamined. He stayed at the *Ordu* for two more years while incurring enormous expenses. A compromise was finally reached. He was only asked for forty-five tomans from Shiraz's district taxes. He regained the favor of the Ilkhan, who desperately needed his financial assistance, although he declined the new tax farm offered to him.[108]

Division of Fārs into Tax Districts

Ghazan attempted to reform the tax collection methods once again in order to put an end to the exactions of civil servants. Fārs was divided into sixteen tax districts (*bulūk*). From the beginning of the year 698/1299, each *bulūk* was entrusted to a tax farmer for a period of three years. In return, the tax farmer had to pay an annual sum of one thousand tomans to the Ilkhan's treasury. The tax farmers paid in advance an estimated eighty thousand dinars in expenses to cover the wages and pensions of soldiers and second-rank civil servants. These expenses were deducted from the total amount later sent to the *Dīvān*. The tax collectors were not yet allowed to ask peasants for an advance payment. To obtain these farm rents, which had considerable financial benefits, Shiraz's dignitaries clashed with one another in the *Ordu*. A certain Sādaq Tarkhān was appointed *shiḥna* of the region.[109] After surviving the bloody purges that had plagued chancery circles since Aḥmad Tegüder's reign, Sharaf al-Dīn Simnānī was in charge of ensuring that the tax collectors did not oppress peasants.[110] Indeed, the Mongols had every reason to prevent the economic decline of the taxable population, as they desperately needed their taxes. According to Vaṣṣāf, the situation in Shiraz remained excellent for a period of three years.[111]

In 699/1299–1300, following Sa'd al-Dīn Sāvajī's appointment to the position of *ṣāḥib-dīvān* and Rashīd al-Dīn's appointment to the vizierate, new administrative measures were implemented. Civil servants received instructions to avoid abuses when levying taxes.[112] In 702/1302–3, Muḥammad Qushchi went to Fārs to reinvestigate the issue of the *injü* lands in the province and examined the various registers that recorded the status of lands. The *ṣāḥibī* register detailed the lands confiscated from the minister Shams al-Dīn Muḥammad Juvaynī after his execution in 683/1284. The lands acquired by Taichu when he was in charge of the *injü* in the province under Gaikhatu were recorded in the *Taichu* register.[113] The *'aḍudī* register likely contained the list of lands established as *waqf* for the Madrasa-i 'Aḍudiyya, built by Terken Khātūn, Salghurid atabek Sa'd b. Abū Bakr's wife. Vaṣṣāf also refers to a *maqbūlī* register whose origin is unknown.[114] The documents attesting to the transfer of imperial property to private parties were submitted to the court for verification.[115] With three years of taxes paid on their products, the domains that had been improperly added to these registers were recovered and returned to the royal *injü*.[116] Thus, Ghazan added a large portion of Fārs' revenues to the crown property.[117]

Vaṣṣāf significantly downplays the impact of Ghazan's reforms, writing that the tax officials were not only inexperienced but that they also accepted bribes from Persian notables in order to pay less tax to the treasury. Furthermore, because Shiraz was situated far from the court, civil servants were free to engage in extortion, abuse, and over-taxation as they pleased. In addition, there were additional intrigues and ongoing rivalries between prominent local figures.[118] This was typical following the removal of the Salghurid atabeks from the province, which put local Persian officials in charge of tax collection.

The *Dīvān* in Search of Financial Resources

Ghazan died on Shawwāl 11, 703/May 11, 1304, and was succeeded by his brother Öljeitü. The financial situation was dire. The new Ilkhan tried to rely on Malik al-Islām's wealth, thus summoning him to the *Ordu*. He was offered the tax farm of Fārs as well as the administrative affairs of Baghdad, but due to his unfortunate experiences in the past, Malik al-Islām declined and returned to Qays.[119] At the end of 703/1304, 'Izz al-Dīn Qūhadī,[120] an official in Rashīd al-Dīn's entourage, along with a certain Ming Qutlugh moved to Fārs to collect taxes.[121] They demanded nothing in return, as they knew that the imposition of supplementary taxes would only provoke the opposition of inhabitants. The due amounts were noted as arrears. The *basqaqs* were tasked with recovering these sums at a later date.[122] Soon after, the great *amīr* Istifchaq Sukurchi was dispatched to the region to collect the *tabghur*, a special tax for the soldiers manning the empire's borders. Istifchaq Sukurchi and his *nökers* were also in charge of collecting additional levies for princes, princesses, and *amīrs*.[123] The collection of these taxes resulted in a new series of abuses. Local lords (*mulūk*) and administrators (*ḥukkām*) levied an additional one and a half dinar for every six dinars paid for the expenses of the *ilchis* and *basqaqs*. Other taxes were imposed on herds and goods, effectively doubling the amount of the *tabghur*. Even though Rashīd al-Dīn ordered the restitution of these sums, the *ḥukkām* of Shiraz, who personally profited from these taxes, disregarded his directives. Öljeitü himself ordered that the additional taxes be returned to the peasants. Although the sources make no mention of it, it is highly likely that this order was not followed.[124] As can be seen, the *Ordu* failed to manage the province's taxation, because it had no control over the intermediary officials. These circumstances persisted throughout the Ilkhanid era, demonstrating once again the challenges of maintaining administrative and financial dominance in the region.

The Return of the Ṭībī Merchants to the Tax Farm

In 705/1305–6, following unfavorable climatic conditions, harvests were poor, and tax levies were consequently reduced. Öljeitü once again called on Malik al-Islām. A *yarligh* was sent to Qays ordering him to return to Shiraz and take charge of the province's fiscal affairs.[125] Malik al-Islām was ill, likely affected by the death of his son Fakhr al-Dīn Aḥmad at the end of 704/1305 when he returned from China.[126] Malik al-Islām took action to prevent the usurpation of the *amīrs* and *basqaqs* and tried to abolish irregular taxes. He offered advances to peasants and only recorded the amounts due owing to the region's state of ruin. His efforts to redress the situation in the region were interrupted by his death on Jumādā I 21, 706/November 28, 1306.[127]

ʿIzz al-Dīn ʿAbd al-ʿAzīz, one of Malik al-Islām's sons, succeeded him with the tax farming in Fārs. However, around 713/1313–14, he was summoned to the *Ordu* to have his accounts examined.[128] It was discovered that his father owed the *Dīvān* three hundred tomans.[129] ʿIzz al-Dīn ʿAbd al-ʿAzīz was unable to pay this sum, because he lacked his father's financial means. He returned to Shiraz and sought refuge on the coast. Ashtu, the Mongol *basqaq*, pursued him but was unable to apprehend him.[130] ʿIzz al-Dīn ʿAbd al-ʿAzīz managed to maintain his authority over the coastal area for just over a decade.[131] In all likelihood, the Ilkhans did not control the entire province and did not even attempt to do so. The coastal regions presented no significant economic interest to them, because their arid climate made it impossible to grow anything other than dates and wheat. Furthermore, their remoteness and adverse climate did not permit the presence of administrative staff required for the fiscal management of these districts.

When ʿIzz al-Dīn ʿAbd al-ʿAzīz was summoned to Tabriz to have his accounts examined, he also had to explain the murder of his brother-in-law, ʿAbd al-Salām.[132] Before Malik al-Islām's death, ʿAbd al-Salām, who was also a wealthy merchant, had stayed at the *Ordu*. He was later appointed to administer certain regions of Fārs.[133] It is likely that ʿAbd al-Salām and ʿIzz al-Dīn ʿAbd al-ʿAzīz had a conflict of interest, which motivated the latter's decision to poison his rival. ʿAbd al-Salām's son, Zayn al-Dīn, who was at the Ilkhan's court when ʿIzz al-Dīn ʿAbd al-ʿAzīz was convocated, took over his position, which he kept for two years.[134] In 715/1315–16, he was deposed after rejoicing in the disgrace of the *amīr* Tumaq following a disagreement with the minister Tāj al-Dīn ʿAlī Shāh. Zayn al-Dīn would not have survived this situation without the intervention of wealthy and influential court figures.[135] Thereafter, no other merchants were assigned to tax farming in Fārs. The age of the great merchants had passed. Many of them lost their entire fortune after being enticed by the potential profit of such an endeavor, and failing to recognize the risks, they were forced to incur the charges themselves.

A Yazdī Sayyid in Charge of Tax Collection

At the time of the Mongol conquest, the lineages of sayyids were at the summit of Iranian society. Öljeitü appealed to a Ḥusaynī sayyid who was already known in *Ordu* circles. In 716/1316, the Ilkhan made Sayyid ʿAḍud al-Dīn Muḥammad b. Abī Yuʿlā b. Mujtabā responsible for tax collection in Shiraz.[136] Jean Aubin describes him as "a typical specimen of the Iranian Muslim aristocracy at that time."[137] Sayyid ʿAḍud al-Dīn Muḥammad did not refuse public responsibilities or any financial opportunities to increase his wealth. Two Arabic biographical dictionaries have entries on him: Ibn al-Fuwaṭī's *Talkhīṣ* and Ibn Ḥajar al-ʿAsqalānī's *Durar al-kāmina*.[138] While described as a merchant (*tājir*) and a notable (*khwāja*), Sayyid ʿAḍud al-Dīn is presented as a man versed in divine gnosis (*maʿrifa*) who was not interested in worldly goods. His name appears on an attestation verifying the significance of Rashīd al-Dīn's religious work, dated Ramaḍān 21, 706/March 26, 1307, in which he proclaims himself "King of the qadis and the sayyids" (*malik al-quḍāt va-l-sādāt*) of Yazd.[139] When Sayyid ʿAḍud al-Dīn Muḥammad was appointed to Shiraz, he had long frequented the members of Öljeitü's chancellery circles, in particular Rashīd al-Dīn. In 707/1307–8, he obtained the Yazd district tax farm.[140] Shabānkāraʾī presented him as one of the *dīvānī* officials with a high position.[141] However, Sayyid ʿAḍud al-Dīn Muḥammad was probably more interested in Yazd than in Shiraz. Shortly after his appointment in Fārs, Öljeitü died on Ramaḍān 28, 716/December 14, 1316, and the sayyid decided to resign from his position in Shiraz and return to his homeland.[142] However, he soon came into conflict with Mubāriz al-Dīn Muḥammad b. Muẓaffar, whose family had enjoyed even greater prestige at the Ilkhanid court for many years.

Mubāriz al-Dīn Muḥammad's father, Sharaf al-Dīn Amīr Muẓaffar, was from an Arab family in Khwāf in Khurasan, who had emigrated to Yazd before Chinggis Khan's invasion of eastern Iran.[143] Öljeitü promoted him to the position of guardian of the Yazd fortress and protector of the region's roads.[144] In 712/1313, the Ilkhan sent him to quash a revolt by Arab tribes who were looting in Shabānkāra; he was forced to engage in combat.[145] As a reward, he received the government of Yazd but died of illness shortly after on Dhū l-Qa'da 16, 712/March 15, 1313.[146] His son, Mubāriz al-Dīn Muḥammad, went to Tabriz, stayed there four years, and inherited his father's position.[147] In 716/1316–17, Öljeitü granted him the government of Maybud and then appointed him as governor of Yazd.[148] At the beginning of the reign of Abū Sa'īd, who succeeded Öljeitü in Ṣafar 717/April–March 1317,[149] he repelled a raid led by Negüderis on the border of Kirmān. Mubāriz al-Dīn Muḥammad delivered the heads of some dead Negüderis to the newly appointed Ilkhan, who praised him for his bravery.[150] Shortly after his return from the *Ordu*, Mubāriz al-Dīn Muḥammad was confronted with the revolt of Jamāl Lūk, described by Naṭanzī as a highwayman.[151] Like Qāḍī Sharaf al-Dīn Ibrāhīm's movement a few decades earlier, the popular unrest led by Jamāl Lūk likewise ended in failure. However, popular tradition portrayed him as a hero. Ibn Baṭṭūṭa, who recorded the local community's reaction to Jaml Lūk's actions, states that he only attacked those who did not pay the *zakāt*. Toward the end of his life, he repented and devoted himself to asceticism. This devout character was very typical of the time. In fact, Mubāriz al-Dīn Muḥammad, who represented the Ilkhanid authority, crushed Jamāl Lūk and his men on a mission to "clean up the roads."[152] All Mubāriz al-Dīn Muḥammad's brilliant actions earned him the esteem and confidence of the Ilkhan. Consequently, Sayyid 'Aḍud al-Dīn's trip to Tabriz was useless, because Abū Sa'īd refused to allow him to return to Yazd to reestablish the tax farm that he had owned before his appointment to Shiraz. His trip to the Ilkhan's court to plead his case and counter Mubāriz al-Dīn Muḥammad's influence was unsuccessful.[153] However, Sayyid 'Aḍud al-Dīn stayed in favor in the *Ordu*, because he belonged to the powerful landed aristocracy of the descendants of the Prophet. In 728/1328, Abū Sa'īd sent him on a diplomatic mission to the Sultan of Delhi, Muḥammad

Tughluq Shāh (r. 720–5/1320–5).[154] The Ilkhan entrusted him with large sums of money. Sayyid 'Aḍud al-Dīn Muḥammad stayed at the court for three months and offered the Sultan a toman of gold coins as *ṣadaqa* every day.[155]

Like Aḥmad Tegüder before him, Abū Sa'īd appealed to the strong dynastic tradition in Shiraz. At the beginning of 719/1319, an Ilkhan's *yarligh* entrusted the government of the "Kingdom of Solomon," lands and islands, to the Salghurid House. Kürdüchin (d. 738/1337–8),[156] the eldest daughter of Abish Khātūn and Mengü Temür, received a permanent contract (*muqāṭa'a-i abadī*) for the region's tax farm.[157] Vaṣṣāf praises Kürdüchin for her effective administration of local affairs. She took care to uphold the religious foundations laid down by her forefathers, particularly Madrasa-i 'Aḍudiyya, as the *awqāf* had an annual revenue of two hundred thousand dinars.[158] Nevertheless, it is necessary to put into perspective the political role of this Salghurid princess, who primarily served as a patron and did not actually rule the region. The Salghurids' return to power in Fārs was primarily a symbolic act. In fact, the real management of the province's tax affairs was in the hands of its officials, appointed by the Ilkhan to manage the imperial assets (*injü*). After Abū Sa'īd's death, these officials who acted on behalf of the Ilkhan gave rise to the Injuid dynasty, whose name derives from the function that they had exercised since the time of Öljeitü.

Injuids Governors of Shiraz

Unlike most of the great *amīrs*, the Injuids were not of Mongol descent. According to the sources, Sharaf al-Dīn Maḥmūd Shāh Īnjū was a descendant of the famous mystic of Nishapur, Abū 'Alī Daqqāq (d. 405/1014–15). The Injuids enjoyed a close relationship with Amīn al-Dīn Balyānī, the holy man of Kāzarūn, whose ancestors were also from Khurasan.

Ever since Öljeitü's reign, Sharaf al-Dīn Maḥmūd Shāh had been mixing with people connected to the *Ordu*. Thereafter, at the start of Abū Sa'īd's reign, he gained influence, notably through the Chupanid clan. The Ilkhan Abū Sa'īd came to throne at the young age of twelve thanks to the support of the influential Amīr Chūpān.[159] Following Amīr Chūpān's execution in 727/1327,[160] Sharaf al-Dīn Maḥmūd Shāh further strengthened his position and became the great *amīr* of the Ilkhanate (*amīr-i ulūs*). Matrimonial ties connected him with Ghiyāth al-Dīn Muḥammad Rashīdī; his son, Jalāl al-Dīn Masʿūd Shāh, then married one of the minister's daughters.[161] According to Shabānkāraʾī, Sharaf al-Dīn Maḥmūd Shāh and Ghiyāth al-Dīn Muḥammad Rashīdī intended to revive "the Sunna of ʿUmar and the time of Ghazan," thereby giving Abū Saʿīd's reign a luster akin to that of his glorious forefather.[162]

Some authors put a very early date on Sharaf al-Dīn Maḥmūd Shāh's administration of Fārs. The origin of this confusion appears to be the ambiguity surrounding the terms used in the sources to describe Sharaf al-Dīn Maḥmūd Shāh's precise functions in the region. Ibn Zarkūb says that at the beginning of Öljeitü's reign, he took charge of the province of Fārs (*vilāyat-i Fārs mutaṣarruf*).[163] Naṭanzī confirms this information by saying that the government of Fārs (*ḥukūmat-i Fārs*) was entrusted to the Injuids during the reign of Öljeitü.[164] Shabānkāraʾī's account explains the responsibilities of Sharaf al-Dīn Maḥmūd Shāh in Fārs at the time of Öljeitü, stating that he and his brother, Mubārak Shāh, were in charge of managing the *injü* property of Fārs for a long time.[165] Shabānkāraʾī portrays both brothers as competent, just, and fair *amīrs*.[166] He confirms that one brother frequently resided at the *Ordu*, while the other stayed in Fārs to manage its fiscal affairs. At that time, as Shabānkāraʾī claims, tax farming was managed by Malik al-Islām's children, particularly his son ʿIzz al-Dīn ʿAbd al-ʿAzīz.[167]

As shown above, the sources are quite confused on this issue. Shabānkāraʾī is the only one to mention that the tax farm of Fārs was, at least partly, under the jurisdiction of Malik al-Islām's son. This situation was undoubtedly the source of a dispute that broke out between Sharaf al-Dīn Maḥmūd Shāh and ʿIzz al-Dīn ʿAbd al-ʿAzīz. This quarrel stemmed from their conflict of interest in the region. ʿIzz al-Dīn ʿAbd al-ʿAzīz was close to Dimashq Khwāja, the son of the powerful Amīr Chūpān. He distributed pearls and precious stones to princesses and *amīrs* to such an extent that even "the necks of camels were adorned with them."[168] ʿIzz al-Dīn ʿAbd al-ʿAzīz's opponents—or Sharaf al-Dīn Maḥmūd Shāh's supporters—mounted a coup against him, resulting in his execution in Tabriz in Shawwāl 725/early September 1325.[169] In this way, they managed to put their protégé in power in Shiraz.[170] Sharaf al-Dīn Maḥmūd Shāh's career was marked by several stages in Fārs. He effectively became *ḥākim* of the province in 725/1325 after the execution of his rival,

ʿIzz al-Dīn ʿAbd al-ʿAzīz,[171] although he carried out this function via his sons, the elder Jalāl al-Dīn Masʿūd Shāh from 726/1326 to 730/1330 and then the younger Ghiyāth al-Dīn Kaykhusraw from 730/1330 to 736/1335,[172] while he was residing at the *Ordu*. To protect his interests, the administrator of a region never resided there, instead ruling through his representatives so that he could monitor and thwart any court-bound intrigues. However, this practice had unexpected consequences, because it gave local staff significant leeway.

According to the *Shīrāz-nāma*, Abū Saʿīd appointed by royal order one of his protégés, a certain Musāfir Īnāq, as governor of Fārs in 735/1334–5.[173] Persian sources generally date these events to 734/1333–4, which is also confirmed by the Mamluk chronicler al-Muqrī,[174] but, once again, the sources give different versions of the events. Shabānkāra'ī, who favored Sharaf al-Dīn Maḥmūd Shāh, asserts that during a drinking binge, a quarrel broke out between Maḥmūd Shāh's son Masʿūd Shāh and Abū Saʿīd's favorite suitor, Musāfir Īnāq, who ran away and took refuge with the Ilkhan. The Ilkhan blamed Maḥmūd Shāh for his son's mistreatment of his lover: "I have given to you and your sons all Īrān and Tūrān, and still one of yours is rude to me."[175] It is worth noting the reference to the traditional dichotomy in ancient Persia between Īrān, the civilized world, and Tūrān, the world of the steppes. This suggests that the Mongol Abū Saʿīd might have symbolically granted the Injuids authority over the entire Iranian world to demonstrate his attachment to them. This image recalls the twelfth-century poet Sūzanī Samarqandī's panegyric addressed to the Qara Khitai sovereign, Ṭamghach Khan:

> To the king, Īrān returns through acquisition and Tūrān through inheritance. He takes the acquisition with his sword and mount, and the inheritance he takes from Afrāsiyāb.[176]

Other sources agree that Abū Saʿīd removed him from the government of Fārs in favor of Musāfir Īnāq. According to Ḥāfiẓ-i Abrū, Sharaf al-Dīn Maḥmūd Shāh had accrued one hundred tomans of income on his private properties (*amlāk-i khāṣṣ*) in Shiraz, Shabānkāra, and all the territories included in Fārs.[177] Dissatisfied with Abū Saʿīd's new appointment, which deprived him of significant income, Sharaf al-Dīn Maḥmūd Shāh starting plotting in the *Ordu* against Musāfir Īnāq. His son, Jalāl al-Dīn Masʿūd Shāh, and a number of great *amīrs* were among the conspirators.[178] They attacked the house of

Musāfir Īnāq, who managed to flee to the palace of Abū Saʿīd; the conspirators were later captured. The Ilkhan ordered their execution, but following the intervention of the minister Ghiyāth al-Dīn Muḥammad Rashīdī, they were only detained and imprisoned until the end of Abū Saʿīd reign. Sharaf al-Dīn Maḥmūd Shāh, who had been imprisoned at Qalʿa-i Ṭabarak in Isfahan on account of his involvement in the intrigue, was recalled to the *Ordu* where he remained until Abū Saʿīd's death, while his son Jalāl al-Dīn Masʿūd Shāh was sent to Anatolia to Shaykh Ḥasan Buzurg.

A hagiographic version of the conflict appears in the life of Amīn al-Dīn Balyānī. Jalāl al-Dīn Masʿūd Shāh said that when he was at Sulṭāniyya, he joined a group of *amīrs* who revolted against Abū Saʿīd. With a single stroke of his sword, he could have cut down the banner of the Ilkhan who had ordered his execution. Masʿūd Shāh appealed to Shaykh Amīn al-Dīn for help. At this point, Abū Saʿīd's sister also appeared and interceded on his behalf. He was released, and his life was saved thanks to the "spiritual blessing (*baraka*) of Shaykh Amīn al-Dīn."[179] Masʿūd Shāh also said that one day when he was fighting in Anatolia, his horse rushed forward and knocked him to the ground in enemy territory. Once again, he appealed to Shaykh Amīn al-Dīn, who appeared, took the reins of the horse, and led him away from the circle of enemies.[180] Masʿūd Shāh maintained close personal ties with Amīn al-Dīn Balyānī. He claimed that he was the shaykh's disciple "in heart and in soul" by his understanding of the truth (*taḥqīq*), rather than out of imitation (*taqlīd*) or habit (*ʿāda*), in order to bear witness to his charisma (*karāmāt*).[181]

Although these hagiographical texts express the idea of *Sitz im Leben*, many such stories that feature Amīn al-Dīn Balyānī with the Injuids reveal the true intimacy between the shaykh and various members of the dynasty, who appear in several edifying tales as the protégés of Amīn al-Dīn. Like the Injuids, the Balyānīs embodied the national Iranian sentiment. The Injuids received widespread support from the Shirazi population when they were in charge of running Fārs. This was confirmed by the events that occurred in the province following Abū Sa'īd's death in 736/1335.

6

Fārs amid the Rivalries of Chupanids, Injuids, and Muzaffarids

The kingdom without a sultan
became like a body without a soul and
a flock without a shepherd.[1]

The succession crisis that followed Abū Saʿīd's death on Rabīʿ II 13, 736/November 30, 1335, at Qara Bagh sparked a long period of anarchy in Fārs, leading to the fragmentation of the Persian Ilkhanate through factionalism, fratricidal struggles, and many alliances and counter-alliances.[2] Abū Saʿīd's reign had witnessed the rise to power of the great *amīrs*, particularly the Chupanids[3] and the Jalayirids,[4] not to mention the growing influence of certain individuals close to the Ilkhan. After Abū Saʿīd's death, the leaders of these various factions tried to seize power behind the legitimacy of a puppet Ilkhan who maintained the illusion of imperial power.[5] Fārs nevertheless remained largely independent, and despite suffering from poor administrative leadership, it was still one of the richest provinces in Iran. The Chupanids made several attempts to take control of it, but their efforts were thwarted by Shaykh Ḥasan Buzurg Jalāʾir, who instead supported numerous Chupanid dissidents and descendants of the Injuid Sharaf al-Dīn Maḥmūd Shāh.[6]

In historical sources, the description of the events in Fārs between Abū Saʿīd's death in 736/1335 and Jamāl al-Dīn Shaykh Abū Isḥāq Īnjū's execution by the Muẓaffarids in 758/1357 is quite confusing. However, this reflects the chaos that shook the region for two decades owing to the multiple troop movements and recurrent sieges of Shiraz. It is thus challenging to establish the timeline of events with any degree of certainty and to identify the motivations behind the protagonists' continual betrayals and intrigues.

First, the chronology of the events must be determined in order to trace the history of Fārs during this period marked by the collapse of the central power. It is also necessary to understand the factors that prevented Sharaf al-Dīn Maḥmūd Shāh's descendants from retaining power despite their significant interests in the province, their administrative responsibilities spanning nearly three decades, and their considerable support of the population of Shiraz.

At the time of Abū Saʿīd's death, Sharaf al-Dīn Maḥmūd Shāh was in Qara Bagh with three of his sons: Jalāl al-Dīn Masʿūd Shāh, Shams al-Dīn Muḥammad,[7] and Jamāl al-Dīn Shaykh Abū Isḥāq.[8] His youngest son, Ghiyāth al-Dīn Kaykhusraw, was acting as his father's substitute (*qā'im-i maqām*) in Shiraz.[9] Following Sharaf al-Dīn Maḥmūd Shāh's execution at the order of the Ilkhan Arpa Ke'ün in Rajab 736/March 1336, his sons escaped out of fear for the safety of their families.[10] Shams al-Dīn Muḥammad and Jamāl al-Dīn Shaykh Abū Isḥāq sought refuge with Arpa Ke'ün's rival, ʿAlī Pādishāh, the governor of Diyar Bakr,[11] while Jalāl al-Dīn Masʿūd Shāh placed himself under the protection of Shaykh Ḥasan Buzurg in Anatolia.[12] After his victory over ʿAlī Pādishāh in Muḥarram 737/August–September 1336, which established his potential authority over the entire empire, Shaykh Ḥasan Buzurg appointed his protégé Jalāl al-Dīn Masʿūd Shāh to the vizierate. One year later, he was relieved of this duty and appointed as the governor of Fārs. This appointment was motivated by the fact that Jalāl al-Dīn Masʿūd Shāh's brother, Ghiyāth al-Dīn Kaykhusraw, who was acting as Shaykh Ḥasan Buzurg's substitute in Fārs, had failed to pay taxes to the *Dīvān*.[13] Following his arrival in Shiraz, Jalāl al-Dīn Masʿūd Shāh immediately met with hostility from his brother, who did not want to lose the material benefits associated with the region's fiscal management. He had first served as his father's representative and undoubtedly wanted to keep his position.[14] On Shaʿbān 15, 738/March 8, 1338, he had Ghiyāth al-Dīn Kaykhusraw's minister executed, thus sparking a conflict between the two brothers. Ghiyāth al-Dīn Kaykhusraw was imprisoned in Qalʿa-i Safīd,[15] where he died on Rajab 5, 739/January 17, 1339.[16] After overcoming these fratricidal struggles, Jalāl al-Dīn Masʿūd Shāh faced a series of Chupanid invasions from 740/1339 onward, further complicated by the interfamilial hostilities of the Chupanids, as was the case with the Injuids. Thus, in the space of just four years between Shaʿbān 740/February 1340 and

Rajab 744/November–December 1343, no less than five military campaigns were fought in Fārs.[17]

Five Military Campaigns: Alliances and Counter-Alliances

First Campaign: Chupanid–Injuid Alliance

Shaykh Ḥasan Kuchik had considerably weakened his Jalayrid rival, Shaykh Ḥasan Buzurg, when he installed Sulaymān Khan in power in 739/1339. In 740/1340, Shaykh Ḥasan Kuchik granted the government of Fārs, hitherto held by Jalāl al-Dīn Mas'ūd Shāh Īnjū, to his cousin Pīr Ḥusayn. To seize Shiraz, Pīr Ḥusayn allied himself with one of Jalāl al-Dīn Mas'ūd Shāh's brothers, Shams al-Dīn Muḥammad, who had been imprisoned at the same time as Ghiyāth al-Dīn Kaykhusraw because of their refusal to recognize Jalāl al-Dīn Mas'ūd Shāh's authority over Fārs. After managing to escape, Shams al-Dīn Muḥammad placed himself under the protection of the Chupanid Shaykh Ḥasan Kuchik, the Jalayirids' enemy.[18] The first clash between Jalāl al-Dīn Mas'ūd Shāh and Pīr Ḥusayn took place on Sha'bān 18, 740/February 18, 1340, at Sarvistān, where the latter inflicted a crushing defeat on the army of Jalāl al-Dīn Mas'ūd Shāh, who was forced to flee to Luristān. Pīr Ḥusayn entered Shiraz victorious in late Sha'bān 740/late February 1340,[19] but the execution of his Injuid ally Shams al-Dīn Muḥammad on Ramaḍān 18, 740/March 18, 1340, sparked an uprising among the Shirazis who were deeply attached to the Injuids. Pīr Ḥusayn was forced to flee the city, leading Jalāl al-Dīn Mas'ūd Shāh to reclaim control of his territory.[20]

Second Campaign: Chupanid–Muzaffarid Alliance

The peace was short-lived, as Pīr Ḥusayn returned about eight months later after forming an alliance with another ambitious *amīr*, the Muzaffarid Mubāriz al-Dīn Muḥammad, lord of Yazd and Kirmān.[21] Jalāl al-Dīn Mas'ūd Shāh then fled for a second time, seeking refuge in Baghdad with his protector Shaykh Ḥasan Buzurg.[22] Pīr Ḥusayn arrived at the gates of Shiraz on Rabī' II 26, 741/October 19, 1340. According to the *Shīrāz-nāma*, the population of the city put up fierce resistance for fifty days.[23] On Jumādā II 16, 741/December 7,

1340, a peace agreement was finally signed through the *qāḍī al-qudāt*, Majd al-Dīn Ismāʿīl Fālī.[24] For eighteen months, Shiraz remained under Pīr Ḥusayn's authority and was administered by his representatives: Shams al-Dīn Maḥmūd Ṣā'in Qāḍī Simnānī[25] and Ẓahīr al-Dīn Ibrāhīm Ṣavvāb.[26] The pair later participated in shaping regional policies.

Let us mention the influence of Majd al-Dīn Ismāʿīl Fālī, who belonged to a well-known family of religious scholars in Shiraz. His grandfather had been involved in the implementation of a tax reform during the time of the Salghurid atabek, Abū Bakr. The Mongol authorities respected the opinion of his family owing to their reputation among the Shirazi population. When Sughunchaq Noyan wanted to appoint Nāṣir al-Dīn Abū ʿAbd Allāh Bayḍāvī as *qāḍī al-quḍāt* of Shiraz during his second mission to Fārs in 678/1279–80, the notables of the city instead advised him to choose Rukn al-Dīn Yaḥyā, Majd al-Dīn Ismāʿīl's father.[27] The two men eventually agreed to work together but only on the condition that Rukn al-Dīn Yaḥyā's authority would take precedence over that of Nāṣir al-Dīn Bayḍāvī.[28]

Majd al-Dīn Ismāʿīl Fālī was a highly respected religious authority in the circles of the *Ordu*. He had verified Rashīd al-Dīn's religious works,[29] and he is described as one of the scholars who received presents from the minister.[30] However, it was his struggle against Öljeitü's imposition of Shiʿism as the state religion[31] that made him famous, and as such, he is mentioned in several Arab biographical dictionaries and local Persian sources.[32] A pious legend spread concerning his role in this affair: due to his stance against the Ilkhan, he was exposed to wild beasts and dogs, but none of them harmed him.[33] A hagiographic version of his conversation with Pīr Ḥusayn also appears in an edifying biography that Subkī devoted to him.[34] What emerges from this episode is that Majd al-Dīn Ismāʿīl managed to persuade the inhabitants of Shiraz to surrender to Pīr Ḥusayn, thus preventing famine and any loss of life.

Third Campaign: New Chupanid–Injuid Alliance

Rivalries within the Chupanid clan prevented Pīr Ḥusayn from holding on to power peacefully for any extended period of time. In Muḥarram 743/June 1342, he was attacked by his cousin Malik Ashraf, who had formed an alliance with the Injuid Shaykh Abū Isḥāq.[35] Shaykh Abū Isḥāq strongly resented Pīr

Ḥusayn, who had ordered the assassination of his brother, Shams al-Dīn Muḥammad, during his first attempt to seize Shiraz in 740/1340.[36] Pīr Ḥusayn gathered troops and ammunition and then marched to confront the invaders. On the way to Isfahan, his *nā'ib*, Shams al-Dīn Maḥmūd Ṣā'in Qāḍī, who was leading a contingent of armed men, as well as his ally, Amīr Jalāl al-Dīn Ṭayyib Shāh, both joined the ranks of Malik Ashraf.[37] Pīr Ḥusayn was no longer able to hold off his cousin's forces, and on Ṣafar 1, 743/July 6, 1342, he suffered a crushing defeat.[38] The sources do not explain why Shams al-Dīn Maḥmūd Ṣā'in Qāḍī and Amīr Jalāl al-Dīn Ṭayyib Shāh defected, although they probably reached an advantageous agreement with the opposing parties prior to battle. Pīr Ḥusayn returned to Tabriz to seek the assistance of his cousin, Shaykh Ḥasan Kuchik. However, the latter had him poisoned, preferring to eliminate a rival from his own clan.[39]

Shaykh Abū Isḥāq Īnjū and Malik Ashraf continued their march toward Fārs. The Injuid instructed Malik Ashraf that he had to go ahead and convince the people of Shiraz to accept their capture of the city without a fight. Shaykh Abū Isḥāq Īnjū nevertheless intended to outperform his ally, rallying the population behind him and labeling Malik Ashraf a despot. The Shirazis consequently closed the city gates to the Chupanid and set up a strong resistance.[40] After realizing that he could not take Shiraz, Malik Ashraf returned to Azerbaijan.

Fourth Campaign: New Chupanid–Injuid Alliance

Shaykh Abū Isḥāq remained the sole ruler of Shiraz and governed there until the return of his brother, Jalāl al-Dīn Masʿūd Shāh. After Pīr Ḥusayn forced him to flee Shiraz in 741/1341, he sought refuge in Baghdad with Shaykh Ḥasan Buzurg, who believed that his support for Jalāl al-Dīn Masʿūd Shāh could strengthen his position against the powerful Chupanid clan. In 743/1342–3, to help Jalāl al-Dīn Masʿūd Shāh reconquer Fārs, Shaykh Ḥasan Buzurg prepared troops commanded by a Chupanid dissident, Yāghī Bāstī, one of Shaykh Ḥasan Kuchik's uncles.[41] Shaykh Ḥasan Buzurg exploited the fratricidal divisions in the Chupanid clan to weaken his rival. To strengthen his ties with Yāghī Bāstī, Shaykh Ḥasan Buzurg asked Jalāl al-Dīn Masʿūd Shāh to appoint his Chupanid ally as governor (*ḥākim*) of Shiraz as a condition of his provision of assistance.[42] Indeed, the position of *ḥākim* was more appealing than that of *amīr*, because the governor had the responsibility of raising tax revenues, which thus gave him the opportunity to enrich himself. After arriving in Shiraz, they discovered that Shaykh Abū Isḥāq held this position of power. Immediately, Jalāl al-Dīn Mas'ūd Shāh put himself at the service of his brother.[43] He fulfilled his commitment and appointed Yāghī Bāstī as *ḥākim*. However, the Shirazis did not welcome him any more than Pīr Ḥusayn. Yāghī Bāstī's hatred drove him to assassinate Jalāl al-Dīn Mas'ūd Shāh on Sha'bān 19, 743/January 17, 1343, as he was leaving the hammam.[44] Shaykh Abū Isḥāq, whom Jalāl al-Dīn Mas'ūd Shāh had sent to Shabānkāra to collect taxes, was informed of his brother's assassination and soon returned to Shiraz to avenge this crime.[45]

According to the *Shīrāz-nāma*, on Sha'bān 20, 743/January 17, 1343, heavy fighting broke out between the followers of Yāghī Bāstī and Shaykh Abū Isḥāq.[46] Some Shirazi notables and district chiefs (*kulū*) as well as their followers (*atāba'*) sided with Shaykh Abū Isḥāq, while Kulū Ḥusayn and some notables from the neighborhoods, where Yāghī Bāstī and his troops were stationed, supported the opposition.[47] The clashes lasted for several days until Shaykh Abū Isḥāq's followers went to seek reinforcements at Kāzarūn. Shaykh Amīn al-Dīn Balyānī's biography recounts several historical events that may be corroborated by other sources. The holy man lived at the same time as Ḥāfiẓ, who designated Amīn al-Dīn as one of the five people who had a beneficial influence on the population of Fārs.[48] The shaykh had close ties with the Injuids. Sharaf al-Dīn Maḥmūd Shāh had even called his son "Shaykh Abū Isḥāq" in honor of the founder of the *kāzarūnī* order. Given Amīn al-Dīn Balyānī's spiritual authority, it is thus unsurprising that the people of Kāzarūn sympathized with the Injuid cause. Amīr Daylam Shāh, a "competent warlord," arrived from Kāzarūn with a party of followers. With the help of the city's population, he took possession of the atabek palace where Yāghī Bāstī had set up his residence. The latter was forced to flee, leaving the region in the hands of Shaykh Abū Isḥāq.[49]

Iranian culture is strongly influenced by the dualism of ancient Persia, which is symbolically expressed by the opposition of good and evil or light and darkness. This contrast is also expressed in the Qur'ān, in which light (*nūr*) stands for the true faith, right path, and knowledge, and darkness (*ẓulmāt*) represents disbelief, misguidance, and ignorance.[50] The author of the *Shīrāz-nāma* uses these concepts to juxtapose right (*ḥaqq*) and wrong (*bāṭil*):

> A group of notables and some of the population of Shiraz sided with Yāghī Bāstī. They had chosen the wrong path (*ṭarīq-i bāṭil*). A multitude of notables, the greats of the kingdom, and most of the people of Shiraz supported the cause of Shaykh Abū Isḥāq. They had chosen the right path (*ṭarīq-i ḥaqq*).[51]

These Qur'ānic notions serve as a paradigm for understanding the events taking place in the human world. Ibn Zarkūb thus makes use of these two ideas to turn the fighting and subsequent looting in Shiraz into an eschatological battle against the forces of evil, embodied by Yāghī Bāstī's supporters. The war raged in the city for a month and twenty days. Weak and tired, the people prayed to God: "Our Lord, do Thou not burden us beyond what we have the strength to bear."[52]

> Thus, while another group of horsemen and people on foot employed unconventional strategies, a troop of experienced warriors and a group of infantry joined the path of war every day … Eventually, half of the city held by Yāghī Bāstī's supporters was taken over. At the same time, a curse was cast on the Religious Law. A small group of commoners and dishonest people carried out attacks and looted. The Gog and Magog sedition breached the Iskandar dam of Islamic Law.[53]

The Injuid prince who opposed Yāghī Bāstī is thus modeled in the image of Alexander the Great, who is said to have imprisoned the impure people of the Qur'ān behind a bronze barrier. This account also alludes to the opposition between Īrān and Tūrān, which appears in Firdawsī's *Shāh-nāma*. This comparison is relevant here, because in Ibn Zarkūb's opinion, the Turko-Mongol *amīr* Yāghī Bāstī, an enemy of the Shirazi population and Shaykh Abū Isḥāq, was from Tūrān, the traditional residence of ancient Persian enemies.

Fifth Campaign: New Chupanid–Muzaffarid Alliance

At the beginning of Rajab 744/November–December 1344, the Chupanids Yāghī Bāstī and Malik Ashraf returned to Fārs, setting the region on fire and spilling blood.[54] They pillaged the region of Bavānāt and then headed for Isfahan, where Pīr Ḥusayn's former *nā'ib*, Amīr Ẓahīr al-Dīn Ibrāhīm Ṣavvāb, had joined them. As previously mentioned, after joining the ranks of Malik Ashraf in 743/1342, he then switched to the Muzaffarid side.[55] Amīr Ẓahīr al-Dīn Ibrāhīm Ṣavvāb continued his career as an administrator in Mubāriz al-Dīn's service, and it is probably through this function that he gained knowledge about the properties of notables. As Ḥāfiẓ-i Abrū claims, it was easy for him to "levy high taxes from the rich people in Ispahan."[56] From there, Yāghī Bāstī and Malik Ashraf returned to Fārs: they pillaged Abarqūh on the way and invited Mubāriz al-Dīn Muḥammad to join them to seize Shiraz. The Muzaffarid agreed on the condition that Malik Ashraf deliver to him Shams al-Dīn Maḥmūd Ṣā'in Qāḍī, whose agents were holding Qal'a-i Sīrjān,[57] a stronghold situated at the junction of the roads connecting Shiraz to Kirmān and Yazd to Hormuz.[58]

The occupation of Sīrjān was significant for Mubāriz al-Dīn Muḥammad for two reasons: first, it put him in a position to control troop movements from Fārs, and second, it allowed him to take up residence along the trade route connecting the Persian Gulf to central Iran. The presence of a minting workshop at the start of the fourteenth century attests to its economic significance.[59] In addition to the strategic importance of the site, the Muzaffarids' control of the main trade route represented an important source of wealth.

Malik Ashraf accepted Mubāriz al-Dīn Muḥammad's request to provide him with military support. He sent Shams al-Dīn Maḥmūd Sā'in Qāḍī to Yazd to seek his military assistance.[60] On Rajab 27, 744/December 15, 1343, news reached the region that Shaykh Ḥasan Kuchik had been assassinated by his wife 'Izzat Mulk.[61] Malik Ashraf preferred to return to Tabriz to take care of his own interests despite the offer from Yāghī Bāstī and Ẓahīr al-Dīn Ibrāhīm Ṣavvāb to reward him with two hundred tomans from previously collected funds if he agreed to assist them in the capture of Shiraz. Soon afterward, Yāghī Bāstī traveled to Tabriz.

By the time Malik Ashraf requested the assistance of Mubāriz al-Dīn Muḥammad, Shams al-Dīn Maḥmūd Ṣā'in Qāḍī had taken control of this strategic place coveted by the Muzaffarid. When Shams al-Dīn Maḥmūd Ṣā'in Qāḍī was delivered to Mubāriz al-Dīn Muḥammad, he was forced to cede his territory in exchange for his freedom. In addition to abandoning

Sīrjān, Shams al-Dīn Maḥmūd Ṣā'in Qāḍī was required to pay an annual tribute of ten thousand dinars to Mubāriz al-Dīn Muḥammad. He was also forbidden from forming any kind of alliance with potential Muzaffarid foes.[62] In exchange, Shams al-Dīn Maḥmūd Ṣā'in Qāḍī obtained the administration of Kirmān. However, the notables of the community had doubts about his involvement in the affairs of the province, because of his tendency to switch sides in conflicts.[63] Indeed, when Shams al-Dīn Maḥmūd Ṣā'in Qāḍī was sent to Shiraz to settle the ongoing dispute between Shaykh Abū Isḥāq and Mubāriz al-Dīn Muḥammad over the ancient Injuid possessions held in the province of Kirmān, he abandoned his mission. Probably for monetary reasons, he changed sides once again and accepted the position of vizierate offered to him by Shaykh Abū Isḥāq.[64] He acted in the same way as the officials of the local chancelleries, who were always eager to sell themselves to the highest bidder.

The return of Malik Ashraf and Yāghī Bāstī to Tabriz ended Shaykh Abū Isḥāq's political deadlock. His troops, hitherto scattered throughout Fārs, regained Shiraz.[65] Once again master of the city, Shaykh Abū Isḥāq had the *khuṭba* pronounced and coins minted in his name.[66] He dispatched emissaries to the *amīrs* of Lur and Shūlistān, the traditional allies of the Shiraz government who had sworn allegiance to him.[67] In 745/1344, Shaykh Abū Isḥāq decided to march toward Kirmān, looting along the way.[68] When he arrived in Sīrjān, Pahlavān 'Alī Dārakī, Mubāriz al-Dīn Muḥammad's *nā'ib*, delivered the city to him on the very same day. After seizing this strategic site, Shaykh Abū Isḥāq continued his advance toward Kirmān. At fifteen *farsakh* from the city, he learned that Mubāriz al-Dīn Muḥammad had gathered an army reinforced by the Mongol Awghānī and Jurmā'ī tribes. As the balance of forces was not in his favor, Shaykh Abū Isḥāq decided to negotiate a peace agreement. He requested that Amīr Ẓahīr al-Dīn Ibrāhīm Ṣavvāb be appointed as the Muzaffarid negotiator. As already mentioned, following Pīr Ḥusayn's defeat in Ṣafar 743/ July 1342, Amīr Ẓahīr al-Dīn Ibrāhīm Ṣavvāb had turned away from the cause of the Chupanids and joined the Muzaffarids. Like Ḥāfiẓ-i Abrū, Kutubī had a favorable opinion of him and viewed him as a capable and wise man.[69] However, his willingness to change alliances for his personal gain did not win him the support of Shiraz's influential figures. He was murdered within a year of his appointment.[70] This ended the political career of a man who epitomized the Iranian administrators of the time, striving to maneuver between various factions in order to protect their own interests.

Uncertain Political Line of Shaykh Abū Isḥāq Īnjū

Righteous deputies ensure
the stability of the sultan's power.[71]
It is not lawful to pray
for an oppressive *amīr*.[72]

Shaykh Abū Isḥāq's reign was fraught with conflicts with Mubāriz al-Dīn Muḥammad. He led several military campaigns in Kirmān, apparently in an attempt to recover the wealth once held by his father, Sharaf al-Dīn Maḥmūd Shāh. Pīr Ḥusayn had indeed granted the government of this province to Mubāriz al-Dīn Muḥammad as a reward for his assistance in capturing Shiraz in Jumādā II 741/November–December 1340.[73] Nevertheless, Shaykh Abū Isḥāq had great political ambitions, as he aspired to expand his authority far beyond Fārs. But his inability to assess the military strength of his rivals on the ground, his repeated betrayals of Mubāriz al-Dīn Muḥammad, and his political errors that affected his own subjects inevitably led to his failure.

The clashes between Shaykh Abū Isḥāq and Mubāriz al-Dīn Muḥammad spanned about a dozen years, from Shaykh Abū Isḥāq's first attempt to seize Kirmān in 745/1344 until his execution in 758/1357. During this period, there were constant troop movements between Fārs, Kirmān, and Yazd. Since a straightforward account of the events does not prove very useful, it seems more appropriate to examine Shaykh Abū Isḥāq's political approach and to pinpoint the factors that contributed to the Muzaffarid success. What circumstances led to the infamous failure of the military operations led by Shaykh Abū Isḥāq?

The timeline of events reveals that Shaykh Abū Isḥāq broke numerous promises and peace agreements made with Mubāriz al-Dīn Muḥammad in just four years from 745/1344 to 749/1349. Following his failed attempt to capture Kirmān in 745/1344, Shaykh Abū Isḥāq tried once again the following year, thus breaking the peace agreement. He lost many outstanding military leaders in the conflict.[74] During the first siege of Kirmān, to broker a truce with Mubāriz al-Dīn Muḥammad, Shaykh Abū Isḥāq pledged not to ally with the Mongol Awghānī and Jurmāʾī tribes.[75] In 749/1348–9, during the uprising of the Jurmāʾīs against the Muzaffarids, Shaykh Abū Isḥāq again betrayed his word and decided to take advantage of the uprising against his powerful adversary to weaken him. He pretended to send a contingent of five thousand men to bolster the Muzaffarid ranks but instead ordered them to support the Mongol tribes during the battle.[76] Shaykh Abū Isḥāq set out to attack Yazd and Maybud, which belonged to the Muzaffarids, in an effort to create a second front and reduce Mubāriz al-Dīn Muḥammad's ability to defend himself. As he failed to capture these cities, he resumed peace negotiations.[77] However, in the winter of the same year, Shaykh Abū Isḥāq broke his word once more. He sent his best military leader, Sulṭān Shāh Jāndār, to attack Kirmān again with a large contingent of men reinforced by the Awghānīs.[78] Once Shaykh Abū Isḥāq realized that his forces could not defeat Mubāriz al-Dīn Muḥammad, he dispatched Sayyid Ṣadr al-Dīn b. Mujtabā to negotiate peace. Mubāriz al-Dīn Muḥammad reminded the emissary of Shaykh Abū Isḥāq's series of betrayals, but the mediation of Sayyid Ṣadr al-Dīn b. Mujtabā eventually paid off as a new peace agreement was reached.[79] Note that a religious authority once again led the negotiation. Mubāriz al-Dīn Muḥammad, who sought to give Islamic legitimacy to his power, recognized the importance of gaining the support of the religious elites.

During four years of military campaigns, Shaykh Abū Isḥāq did not learn from his failures. In 751/1350–1, he made another attempt to capture Yazd. After the first confrontation, the city came under siege,[80] with a terrible famine wiping out a large part of the population.[81] When winter arrived, Shaykh Abū Isḥāq was forced to leave the camp. During the summer of 752/1351, he led a new campaign in Kirmān,[82] relying on Amīr Bikjakāz's military skills after he deserted the Chupanid Malik Ashraf to join him.[83] Mubāriz al-Dīn Muḥammad's army, which had formed a strong alliance with the Awghānī and Jurmāʾī tribes, won a resounding victory over their adversary on Jumādā I 14, 753/June 28, 1352,[84] and an immense booty fell into the hands of the Muzaffarids.[85]

Mubāriz al-Dīn Muḥammad, who had grown battle-weary, decided to attack Shiraz to finally oust Shaykh Abū Isḥāq.[86] It is unclear whether he initially intended to seize Fārs, because his territorial ambitions appeared to be limited to Kirmān, Yazd, and ʿIrāq-i ʿajam. However, Shaykh Abū Isḥāq's betrayals provoked the harsh response of the Muzaffarids, resulting in the capture of Shiraz and the annihilation of the Injuid family.

Capture of Shiraz

Religious scholars served as peace mediators in the conflicts between Mubāriz al-Dīn Muḥammad and Shaykh Abū Isḥāq. As already seen, in 749/1348–9, Sayyid Ṣadr al-Dīn b. Mujtabā successfully concluded tense negotiations following the second Injuid campaign in Kirmān. In 753/1352, when Shaykh Abū Isḥāq learned that Mubāriz al-Dīn Muḥammad was preparing to seize Shiraz, he sent Mawlānā ʿAḍud al-Dīn ʿAbd al-Raḥmān Ījī to negotiate peace once again.[87] Previously a prominent figure in the *Ordu* under Abū Saʿīd, he later became qadi at the Injuid court.[88] As an undisputed religious authority with political experience, his opinion was of great importance. In Sīrjān, he met with Mubāriz al-Dīn Muḥammad, who welcomed him with all the respect befitting his position as a distinguished religious scholar. To highlight his family's interest in Islam, Mubāriz al-Dīn Muḥammad asked Mawlānā ʿAḍud al-Dīn ʿAbd al-Raḥmān Ījī to recite Ibn Ḥājib's *Shaḥr-i mukhtaṣṣar* for his son Shāh Shujāʿ.[89] He then rewarded the scholar with fifty thousand dinars and gave ten thousand to the people of his retinue, but because of Shaykh Abū Isḥāq's recurrent betrayals, he refused the peace offer.[90]

Mubāriz al-Dīn Muḥammad was concerned with winning the favor of the ulemas, who held him in high esteem and saw him as a fighter for Islam. They praised his actions against the Awghānīs, who had supported Shaykh Abū Isḥāq in 749/1348, because the tribes followed Mongol law (*sunnat-i Mughūl*). Indeed, Mubāriz al-Dīn's fight against them was considered a holy war.[91] Pahlavān ʿAlī Shāh and eight hundred honorable men who had lost their lives in the battles were revered as martyrs.[92] Mubāriz al-Dīn Muḥammad always attempted to give Islamic legitimacy to his actions. In 755/1354, when he became master of Shiraz, he decided to lay siege to Isfahan and pledged allegiance to the Abbasid Caliph, ʿAbbās al-Muʿtaḍid bi-llāh Abū Bakr, in whose name he read the *khuṭba* and issued coins.[93] The ulemas of Fārs, Yazd, and Kirmān approved of his approach, because this rule had not been followed in Iran since the Mongol conquest of Baghdad.[94]

Ibn Zarkūb, who had previously been highly favorable to Shaykh Abū Isḥāq, wrote about the advance of Mubāriz al-Dīn Muḥammad's army toward Shiraz as follows: "On Rabīʿ I 1, 753/April 28, 1351, the auspicious banners [of Mubāriz al-Dīn Muḥammad] were hoisted."[95] Mubāriz al-Dīn then received a declaration: "Thou givest the Kingdom to whom Thou wilst."[96] This Qur'ānic verse was used to justify Mubāriz al-Dīn's march on Shiraz. Ibn Zarkūb portrays the city's chaotic state just before it was besieged, claiming that beggars, highway thieves, and vagrants—all of whom were needy and greedy for everything—plundered the goods of Muslims. Out of rage, they closed the doors of mosques.[97] Another Qur'ānic verse was used by Ibn Zarkūb to characterize Shaykh Abū Isḥāq as the culprit in this situation: "Truly, they are the workers of corruption."[98] This implies that Shaykh Abū Isḥāq's poor governance created this situation, making him unworthy to rule. Shaykh Abū Isḥāq's negative portrayal contrasts with that of Mubāriz al-Dīn Muḥammad, who was endowed with titles giving him legitimacy to rule in Fārs. He was the "Alexander of the time" (*Iskandar-i zamān*), he was the "Dārā of the time" (*Dārā-i dawrān*) in reference to the mythical ruler of the Kayanid dynasty, and like the Salghurids before him, he was the "heir to the kingdom of Solomon" (*varīth-i mulk-i Sulaymān*). He was also the "vivifying of the law" (*muḥyī-i sharāʿī*).[99] Mubāriz al-Dīn is also compared with the staff of Moses, capable of performing miracles (*ʿaṣā'-i Mūsā qudrat-i muʿjiza*). He put an end to the "demon of oppression" (*dīv-i ẓulm*).[100] A voice whispered a passage from the Qur'ān to the Shirazis: "He has confirmed thee with His help, and with the believers."[101] This Qur'ānic quote introduces Mubāriz al-Dīn Muḥammad as an agent of divine will. After becoming master of Shiraz, he reinstated all the clerical members to their previous positions. *Khānaqāhs*, madrasas, and mosques were decorated, while brothels (*kharābāt*) and taverns (*maykada*) were destroyed.[102] Another Qur'ānic verse unequivocally supports Ibn Zarkūb's portrayal of Shaykh Abū Isḥāq: "So God strikes both the true (*al-ḥaqq*) and the false (*al-bāṭil*). As for the scrum, it vanishes as jetsam, and what profits men abides in the earth."[103]

How can we explain Ibn Zarkūb's change of mind, when ten years earlier, he had claimed that Shaykh Abū Isḥāq's followers followed the path of truth in their fight against Yāghī Bāstī? The Injuid prince lost his main support during the siege of Shiraz. The qadi of Fārs, ʿAḍud al-Dīn Ījī, whom Shaykh Abū Isḥāq had sent to negotiate peace with Mubāriz al-Dīn Muḥammad, as well as Majd al-Dīn Sarbandī, one of his military commanders, surrendered to the Muzaffarid prince.[104]

During the siege, Shaykh Abū Isḥāq was ignorant of the danger to which he was exposed. Upon hearing the drums of Mubāriz al-Dīn Muḥammad's army, he asked his minister and companion (*nadīm*), Qavām al-Dīn Ḥasan Tamghāchī: "What will be the outcome of this affair between us and Mubāriz al-Dīn?" His minister responded in a premonitory way: "As long as I am alive, no decay will make its way into the fortress of your might."[105]

Qavām al-Dīn Ḥasan died during the siege in Rabīʿ II 754/April 1353 according to a poem of Ḥāfiẓ.[106] The minister was the protector of the poet, who dedicated several ghazals to him, including this poem in his praise:

> Of the seal-ring of His ruby lip, it is fit that a Sulaiman-like boast I should express:
>
> When mine is the *ism-i-a'zam* (the great name) of Ahriman, what fear (is it that), I have
>
> After abstinence like this, notorious for profligacy Hafiz became,
>
> What grief have I, when as patron in the world Aminu-d-Din Hasan, I have.[107]

Mubāriz al-Dīn's siege of the city lasted for more than seven months, which proved to be trying months for the Shirazis due to the unprecedented famine. As the siege prolonged, divisions emerged in the population as to whether they should resist or surrender to the enemy. Shaykh Abū Isḥāq made serious mistakes that alienated part of the population. He ordered the execution of two influential members of the Maḥalla-i Bāgh-i Naw: Amīr Sayyid Ḥājjī Ḍarrāb and a district head, a certain Ḥājjī Shams al-Dīn.[108] Shaykh Abū Isḥāq accused them of collaborating with the Muzaffarids. In fact, they supported a surrender simply to alleviate the suffering of the population. Members from one of the most prominent Shirazi families, the Bāgh-i Naw'īs, lived in this district. The notes devoted to them in *Shadd al-izār* attest to both their political influence and their piety.[109] Following these executions, the Shirazis rose up against Shaykh Abū Isḥāq, and in Ramaḍān 754/October 1353, a group of neighborhood leaders went to Mubāriz al-Dīn Muḥammad to inform him that Ra'īs 'Umar, who was the head of Maḥalla-i Murdistān, had decided to open the Bayḍā gate. Muzaffarid troops subsequently stormed the city on Shawwāl 3, 754/November 1, 1353.[110] Mubāriz al-Dīn Muḥammad entrusted the government of Shiraz to his nephew Shāh Sulṭān.

The Muzaffarids' capture of Shiraz nevertheless sparked opposition from part of the city's population.[111] In Rabī' I 755/March 26–April 24, 1354, Ay Temür,[112] one of Shaykh Abū Isḥāq's *amīrs*, and Ghiyāth al-Dīn Manṣūr, *amīr* of the Shūls, assembled their troops in Shūlistān. They arrived in Kāzarūn and discovered that Shiraz was guarded by a small garrison.[113] The inhabitants of the Bāb-i Kāzarūn neighborhood informed Ay Temür that they would let him enter the city. Shāh Sulṭān was forced to flee after Ay Temür's arrival, which led to a popular uprising. The residence of Shāh Sulṭān and Mūrdistān, a pro-Muzaffarid district, were set on fire.[114]

Mubāriz al-Dīn Muḥammad sent his son Shāh Shujā' to restore order in Shiraz. After completely plundering Shūlistān, he arrived before the city. He decided to immediately launch his attack and entered through the Bāb-i Iṣṭakhr. His opponents immediately surrendered. Shāh Shujā' then went to stay at Dār al-salṭana while fighting continued in the neighborhood of Bāb-i Kāzarūn where the population was engaged in violent combat with the help of the Shūls. Shāh Shujā' broke down the resistance after a bloody battle in which many rebels lost their lives. The remaining adversaries were captured and put to death, with their bodies being piled up in the streets.[115] This marked the end of the pro-Injuid factions in the city.

After the capture of Shiraz, Shaykh Abū Isḥāq sought refuge in Isfahan with Sayyid Jamāl al-Dīn Mīr-i Mīrān. Sayyid had declared himself as the city's governor after taking advantage of the chaos in the aftermath of Abū Sa'īd's death.[116] He was the first in a lineage that continued until the Safavid era[117] and was described as one of the "*kalāntarān* of Isfahan."[118] Shaykh Abū Isḥāq and Sayyid Jamāl al-Dīn Mīr-i Mīrān had a mutually beneficial friendship. Mubāriz al-Dīn Muḥammad wanted to permanently defeat Shaykh Abū Isḥāq. In 755/1354, he decided to besiege Isfahan. Sayyid Jamāl al-Dīn Mīr-i Mīrān set up a resistance to Mubāriz al-Dīn Muḥammad, who was forced to withdraw his troops at the start of winter.

The city surrendered in spring 758/1357 after a series of sieges. Shaykh Abū Isḥāq was apprehended and imprisoned in Ṭabarak fortress.[119]

From his prison, Shaykh Abū Isḥāq wrote a letter to Mubāriz al-Dīn Muḥammad, which was conveyed by Shihāb Munshī in the *Humāyūn-nāma*.[120] Shaykh Abū Isḥāq says to Mubāriz al-Dīn Muḥammad: "Were we not brothers? How could this have happened?" He ends his letter by wishing him felicity in both worlds and signs: "Unhappily afflicted, without sin (*bī gunāh*), Abū Isḥāq b. Maḥmūd Shah."[121] But this missive had no influence on the decision of Mubāriz al-Dīn Muḥammad.

Shaykh Abū Isḥāq was transferred to Shiraz to be held to account for the execution of Sayyid Ḥājjī Ḍarrāb. Mubāriz al-Dīn Muḥammad gave a religious justification to the trial held in the city's central square, where all of Shiraz's eminent scholars, qadis, and notables had gathered. Mubāriz al-Dīn Muḥammad asked Shaykh Abū Isḥāq why he had executed Sayyid Ḥājjī Ḍarrāb. He only answered: "We ordered it."[122] Mubāriz al-Dīn Muḥammad then condemned him to suffer the law of retaliation (*qiṣāṣ*); he was then delivered to the victim's young son, Sayyid Quṭb al-Dīn. Before his execution, which took place on Jumādā I 21, 758/May 21, 1357,[123] Shaykh Abū Isḥāq recited this quatrain:

> Alas, no eggs from the bird of life!
> There is no hope left of friend of stranger!
> Alas and alack, during this period of life!
> Nothing remains of what we have said but a tale.[124]

Thus ended the Injuid dynasty in Fārs.

Shaykh Abū Isḥāq's policy was therefore a glaring failure. Aside from his repeated betrayals, the Injuid prince lacked the intelligence to recognize that his armies were incapable of defeating his foe. We must now consider the factors that contributed to the strength of the Muzaffarid armies.

Role of Tribal Members in the Injuid and Muzaffarid Armies

At first glance, it appears that the involvement of tribal members in the two armies—particularly the powerful Awghānī and Jurmā'ī tribes, who were prompt to switch sides—had a significant impact on the outcome of the battles.[125] Mubāriz al-Dīn Muḥammad had great difficulty dealing with the unreliability of the tribes. He attempted to appease the Mongol tribes when he took control of Kirmān in 741/1340–1, as he was aware of the potential threat posed by their looting and conflicts. He requested a daughter from one of their chiefs to marry his son, Shāh Shujāʿ.[126] This matrimonial alliance, however, did not prevent the Awghānīs and the Jurmāʾīs from repeatedly rallying behind Shaykh Abū Isḥāq. The Injuid campaign in Kirmān in winter 749/1349, for example, saw some of the Mongol tribes with whom Mubāriz al-Dīn Muḥammad had made a pact defect to the opposing camp. On the orders of Mubāriz al-Dīn Muḥammad, many members of these tribes were executed in retaliation in the district of Yazd and in Kirmān.[127] In all honesty, neither Shaykh Abū Isḥāq nor Mubāriz al-Dīn Muḥammad enjoyed particularly strong support from these tribal chiefs, whose only goal was to maximize their financial gain from the alliance. Nevertheless, as we have seen in the battles between the Salghurids and the Mongol armies, the Iranian and Turkmen tribes had historically provided military support to the authority in Shiraz. Furthermore, by backing Shaykh Abū Isḥāq, the ancient Iranian tribes with roots in Persia, such as the Shūls and the Kurds, demonstrated their support for this prince of Iranian ancestry. Following the Muzaffarid conquest of Shiraz, as already mentioned, the leader of the Shūls, Amīr Ghiyāth al-Dīn Manṣūr, regained power in the city for a short time with the assistance of the Injuid commander Ay Temür. The drum was immediately sounded to announce the good news.[128] The former Injuid palace that Shāh Sulṭān had turned into his home was pillaged, and the district of Mūrdistān, which supported Mubāriz al-Dīn Muḥammad, soon found itself in the "hurricane's passage."[129] There was also ethnic solidarity between Mubāriz al-Dīn Muḥammad, who was of Arab origin, and the Arab tribes of Fārs who he rallied behind him when he helped Pīr Ḥusayn seize Shiraz in 741/1340.

The tribes played a major role in the clashes between Mubāriz al-Dīn Muḥammad and Shaykh Abū Isḥāq, although they tended to favor the latter more than his adversary. Indeed, the Injuid would have been quite powerless without the support of the Shūls, Kurds, and Turkmens. The presence of the *pahlavāns* in the Muzaffarid armies as well as the good military training of Mubāriz al-Dīn Muḥammad's sons who led his armies were critical factors in the victory of the Muzaffarids.

Muzaffarids and *Pahlavāns*

Let us first present the *pahlavāns* as a social group before examining their role in the Muzaffarid army. Primarily from large cities or rural areas, the *pahlavāns* were members of youth (*javān*) organizations. They underwent an introductory apprenticeship in archery and wrestling, the two ancient Iranian martial arts.[130] The *javān* is a young celibate man as opposed to the *katkhudā*, the head of the household. There is a Persian equivalent of the word *javān*: *barnā* or *burnā*, a term that evokes the notion of maturity. The *javānmard*, in the adjectival sense of "brave, noble, generous," denotes a mature man (*mard*) shaped by the ideals of the *javān*.[131] The *javānmard* is frequently associated with the *pahlavān*, a daring and chivalrous champion who is not afraid to put his life at risk for the oppressed. This is attested in Ibn Baṭṭūṭa's account of what happened when the Chupanid Pīr Ḥusayn tried to flee Shiraz. He arrested Tāshī Khātūn, Maḥmūd Shāh Īnjū's widow, and her son, Shaykh Abū Isḥāq, and tried to take them as captives to Tabriz. When they reached the center of the bazaar in Shiraz, Tāshī Khātūn unveiled her face and said: "It is thus, O men of Shiraz, that I am to be carried away from amongst you, I who am so-and-so, the wife of so-and-so." Thereupon, one of the woodworkers known as the Pahlavān Maḥmud rose up and said: "We shall not let you go out from our town, nor accept any such thing."[132] The people joined him, killed many of Pīr Ḥusayn's soldiers, and freed the woman and her son.[133]

It is widely assumed that the Arabic equivalent of the Persian *javān* is *fatā* (plur. *fityān*), young man. The meaning of *fityān* is contradicted in the sources. They are frequently associated with *futuwwa* in Sufism. Late Sufi treatises describe *fityān* as groups of young people who, without family ties, lived in small communities with a sense of brotherhood and mutual solidarity. In the chronicles, however, they are instead depicted as troublemakers. They are referred to by various terms such as *ʿayyār*, *awbāsh*, *shāṭir*, or even *rind*. The activities of these urban youth are well documented in Baghdad and Syria.[134] A *rind*, which originally signified a brigand or libertine, was also connected with the local vigilantes who led the urban militias. Luke Treadwell demonstrates that autonomous urban militias were common in Transoxiana in early Islam. They defended cities and engaged in guerrilla warfare against invaders.[135] We find *ʿayyārūn* in Iran, especially in the Mongol period.[136] Originally, they were often shopkeepers, blacksmiths, or weavers. They organized popular resistance against the Mongol invaders or their representatives in the cities of Khurasan. The *'ayyārūn* ousted the Mongol governor of Herat and the city's police chief, while the Mongols were unable to dislodge them when they held a fortress one hundred kilometers away.[137] The *'ayyārūn* constituted the military wing of the populace and bore names that indicated their military role such as catapult launcher (*manjinīqī*) or tower keeper (*burjī*).[138] They appeared to be similar to the *pahlavāns* at first glance, although they did not share the same goals. Indeed, the *pahlavān* concept was rooted in a traditional initiation.

The wrestler (*kushtīgīr*) became a champion, a *pahlavān*, after completing his apprenticeship with his friends and fellow pupils by his side. This training allowed him to pursue a military career.[139] The *pahlavāns* mainly lived in the Mongol milieu of Azerbaijan during the Ilkhanid period; they were mostly wrestlers from Khurasan, which had renowned martial arts schools. It is interesting to note that the exercises of the *pahlavāns* were similar to those practiced by the Mongols. The wrestling and archery practices, common to Iranian *kushtīgīr* and Mongolian *bö'e*,[140] were very much alive in Ilkhanid Iran. Amīn Bāshtīnī, the son of a wealthy landowner from Bayhaq, was Abū Sa'īd's favorite[141] and the "champion of the capital" (*pahlavān-i pāytakht*) Sulṭāniyya.[142] His brother, Jalāl al-Dīn 'Abd al-Razzāq Bāshtīnī, was the founder of the Sarbedar movement.[143] Amīn Bāshtīnī was brought from his village to the Ilkhanid court on the back of his reputation as a champion, which had been established by his brother, Jalāl al-Dīn 'Abd al-Razzāq. In an archery competition, for example, he had beaten the most famous of the *pahlavāns*, a certain Abū Muslim 'Alī Surkh Khurāsānī, whose title (*isfahsālār-i Īrān-zamīn*) indicates that he was symbolically acknowledged as the military commander of the entire Iranian nation.[144] After Abū Sa'īd's death, we find Abū Muslim 'Alī Surkh Khurāsānī among the ranks of Shaykh Ḥasan Buzurg's army at the time of his confrontation with the Chupanid forces in 738/1338.

For a *pahlavān*, two possible career paths were available. He might serve as a prince's designated champion, as Abū Muslim 'Alī Surkh Khurāsānī had done for Abū Sa'īd, thus competing against other champions in events like wrestling or archery tournaments. But the *pahlavān* could also become a military leader, governor, or guardian of a fortress.[145] In this case, the *pahlavān* emerged as a key figure, and his followers shared either his personal power (like the Sarbedars) or that of the *amīr* to whom he offered his services. The Bāshtīnīs were not the only *pahlavāns* to start vying for local power following the fall of the Ilkhanid Empire. In a sense, the Muzaffarids were also *pahlavāns* or, at the very least, close to the *pahlavān* communities.

When Amīr Muẓaffar was living in Maybud, his son, Mubāriz al-Dīn Muḥammad, was trained in armory. He drew the attention of the young people in the region, and they all went hunting together.[146] Mubāriz al-Dīn Muḥammad also resembled a great *pahlavān*, acting more like an agent tasked with maintaining order than as a leader of popular agitation. Mubāriz al-Dīn Muḥammad put an end to the raids of the Negüderis before swiftly quashing Jamāl Lūk's revolt. He thus gained respect in the *Ordu* because of these brilliant deeds. In 734/1333–4, Mubāriz al-Dīn Muḥammad went to Abū Sa'īd's court with his son, Shāh Muẓaffar, born a decade earlier. A wrestler himself, he performed arrow-based feats in public and engaged in public wrestling. He was likened to Abū Muslim 'Alī Surkh Khurāsānī.[147] In Mubāriz al-Dīn Muḥammad's entourage, a certain Akhī Shujā' al-Dīn Khurāsānī had become one of Abū Sa'īd's close confidants because of his kinship with the famous *pahlavān* Abū Muslim 'Alī Surkh Khurāsānī. As such, Akhī Shujā' al-Dīn had been appointed governor of the *vilāyat* of Bam.[148] After the Ilkhan's death, Akhī Shujā' Khurāsānī came to Kirmān and entered the service of Mubāriz al-Dīn Muḥammad, who favored him.

Being a *pahlavān* implied a certain mindset. The *pahlavāns* combined the cult of the body with excesses of all sorts, from mad generosity to the defiance of social norms, drinking, and sexual prowess. Mu'īn al-Dīn Yazdī, the author of the *Mavāhib-i ilāhī*, claims that Akhī Shujā' al-Dīn engaged in heinous acts with women, but that Mubāriz al-Dīn Muḥammad closed his eyes to them.[149] Akhī Shujā' al-Dīn did not come alone, but was accompanied by a group of fortress guards (*kutvālān*), or in other words, *pahlavāns*.[150] The man appointed by Mubāriz al-Dīn Muḥammad as *kutvāl* of Sīrjān after capturing this stronghold was also a *pahlavān*, a certain 'Alī Dārakī.

The Muzaffarid army was partly made up of Khurasanian recruits. Numerous *pahlavāns* also held high military commands. Mubāriz al-Dīn Muḥammad sent a certain Pahlavān 'Alī Shāh to fight against the Awghānīs. His son, Shāh Shujā', was also one of his best warlords. His supporters included people like Pahlavān Ṭālib[151] and Pahlavān Khurram.[152] Later on, Pahlavān Khurram was appointed governor of Isfahan as a reward for his good and loyal services in the army. In the *Jughrāfiyā-i Ḥāfiẓ-i Abrū*, the names of twelve *pahlavāns* with military responsibilities are mentioned. These bands of brave men (*bahādur*), many of whom were like the Muzaffarids from Khurasan, would have fought alongside Mubāriz al-Dīn Muḥammad and his son. Because of the strong bonds existing between the *pahlavāns* and their chief as well as between the latter and the Muzaffarids, the men who formed such an army were more loyal to the Muzaffarid cause than those in the Injuid army. Their commitment formed part of an ideology—albeit less elaborate than that of the Sarbedars, who adopted a form of messianism—associated with the ideals of the *pahlavāns*. Faced with such a disciplined and united army, the disparate forces (*lashkarī az har jins*)[153] of the opposing camp appeared weak. Shaykh Abū Isḥāq's army was occasionally led by valiant warlords such as Sulṭān Shāh Jāndār or the Jalayirid Aq Buqa. However, both soon realized that it was futile to fight the Muzaffarid troops. Sulṭān Shāh Jāndār preferred switching to the opposing camp after suffering two or three defeats, as a result of his master's inconsistent strategies. Shaykh Ḥasan Buzurg's envoy, Aq Buqa, who was sent from Baghdad to Fārs to support Shaykh Abū Isḥāq, quickly returned with his army upon learning of the situation. Although the Muzaffarid victory was based on clear military superiority coupled with Mubāriz al-Dīn Muḥammad's skillfully executed strategy, another factor worked in his favor, namely Islam.

Paradox of Muzaffarid Ideology

The Muzaffarids' victory was based on two antinomic facets: Mubāriz al-Dīn Muḥammad was able to combine the ideals of the *pahlavān* with Islam in his quest for power. The *pahlavān*'s behavior, characterized by weapon mastery, sexual prowess, and drinking, could seem shocking to any good Muslim. The aforementioned case of Akhī Shujāʿ al-Dīn Khurāsānī is not the only example mentioned in historical literature.[154] Khwāfī, the *Mujmal*'s author, who is less biased than other sources on the history of the Sarbedars, also speaks of this subversive conduct. He claims, for example, that Jalāl al-Dīn ʿAbd al-Razzāq Bāshtīnī took advantage of his rise to power to violate young boys and girls from respectable families with impunity.[155] A survey of both the literary and historical sources can no doubt confirm this outrageous behavior of the *pahlavāns*. Mubāriz al-Dīn Muḥammad, who followed a strict form of Islam but surrounded himself with *pahlavāns*, thus displayed a contradictory attitude. But why did he act in this manner? Was his goal merely to gain more power? And did these offensive recruits guarantee his success?

The *pahlavāns*, the Iranian *javānmards*, and the youth bands mentioned in the medieval sources of the Latin West have striking similarities. In 1964, Georges Duby called attention to the young members of the knighthood,[156] observing a wealth of information about young people living in the rural and urban areas of northwest France in the twelfth-century sources. Men of "good birth" were called youths in these texts using the singular or plural adjective *juvenis* or *juventus*.[157] These precise terms are used to designate a social group in the true sense of the word; as can be seen, they share similarities with the Persian terminology, which also denotes a band of youths. According to Georges Duby, in the vast majority of instances, these terms represented men of war at a particular stage of their lives. The *juvenis* was an adult who had been introduced into the world of armed men, much like the *javānmard* or *pahlavān*; in other words, he was a knight. The behavior of the *juvenis* resembles that of the *pahlavān* in every way. He traveled to the countryside in search of glory through battles and tournaments, he sought social recognition, or he chased after female prey.[158] The *juvenis*, like the *pahlavān*, placed himself and his band at the service of a lord or *condottiero* seeking to expand his power.[159]

After the central power collapsed, Mubāriẓ al-Dīn Muḥammad, the lord of Maybud who had engaged in open combat at the *Ordu* of Abū Saʿīd, benefited from the support of these brave men, the *pahlavāns*. As we have seen, he was joined by these youths in Maybud during his father's lifetime. During his many ongoing struggles with Shaykh Abū Isḥāq, what mattered most to him was the paradox between the two ideals that would determine his victory; the overriding goal was to defeat his enemy. Mubāriẓ al-Dīn Muḥammad's combination of strict Islam and *pahlavān* ideals was not the only paradoxical aspect of Iranian society at the time. For example, the sayyids who lived a pious life as recluses were also observed in the circles of the *Ordu*, embracing various administrative responsibilities that allowed them to amass an enormous wealth. Nevertheless, Mubāriz al-Dīn Muḥammad wisely decided to put an end to the protracted conflicts with Shaykh Abū Isḥāq, who had shown his complete inability to assume power. He was favored by the people of Shiraz and enjoyed military support from most of the tribes of Fārs and its surrounding principalities of Luristān and Shūlistān. However, his failure meant that the province came under the rule of a dynasty whose ancestors were Arab, not Iranian. While the *pahlavāns* were responsible for the military victory of the Muzaffarids, Islam had helped them win over the support of a sizable portion of the Shirazi population.

Following the death of the Ilkhan Abū Saʿīd when the population of Shiraz was the victim of bloody rivalries, the inhabitants of the city supported opposing parties. The lack of precise information about these factions makes it difficult to interpret the positions of the various protagonists. According to the medieval authors, Iranian cities were frequently the site of violent conflicts between two opposing factions, which should be viewed in terms of neighborhood conflicts that were just as significant as religious factionalism. For Zayn al-Dīn b. Ḥamd Allāh Mustawfī Qazvīnī, it was customary for the people of Isfahan (*ʿādat-i ahl-i Iṣfahān*) to fight each other. Every day, two-thirds of the city's population clashed with the other third.[160]

The information on the clashes between Shiraz's neighborhoods is limited. We only gain a glimpse of these conflicts when the city was under siege. In addition to religious solidarity, social organizations from Sufi orders, and paramilitary associations of the *pahlavān* type, the *kulūs* represented an important political force. The term *kulū* referred to a neighborhood leader (*ra'īs-i maḥalla*), but it could also be the head of the bazaar, who represented certain economic interests.[161] The *kulūs* played a significant role. Not only did they act on behalf of the population before the administration, but in the event of the city's surrender, they also negotiated with the invader.[162] It is worth noting that the *kulūs* always intervened during the surrender. Any divisions between the *kulūs* reflected tensions existing between the various districts of the city. At the time of the conflict between Yāghī Bāstī and Shaykh Abū Isḥāq, Kulū Ḥusayn, the spokesman for the inhabitants of the district where Yāghī Bāstī resided, had taken his side, while the other inhabitants of the city supported Shaykh Abū Isḥāq. In the case of Mubāriz al-Dīn Muḥammad's confrontation with Shaykh Abū Isḥāq, only the Bāb-i Kāzarūn district remained faithful to the Injuid cause. Kulū Fakhr al-Dīn, who had supporters in this district, made an attempt to retake the city after the Muzaffarid conquest.[163] Group alliances fluctuated in Shiraz and were only formed under external pressure. Given the description of urban clashes when a besieged city surrendered, it would appear that factionalism, which pitted districts against each other, was a key feature of medieval Iranian cities.

Amīrs' Campaigns in Fārs

First Campaign: Chupanid–Injuid Alliance

Shaʿbān 18, 740/February 18, 1340: struggle between Jalāl al-Dīn Masʿūd Shāh Īnjū and Pīr Ḥusayn
Late Shaʿbān 740/late 1340: arrival of Pīr Ḥusayn in Shiraz
Ramaḍān 28, 740/March 28, 1340: Shams al-Dīn Muḥammad Īnjū's execution and uprising of Shirazis
Pīr Ḥusayn's flight from Shiraz
Jalāl al-Dīn Masʿūd Shāh's return to Shiraz

Second Campaign: Chupanid–Muzaffarid Alliance

741/1341: return of Pīr Ḥusayn to Fārs, allied with Mubāriz al-Dīn Muẓaffar
Rabīʿ II 26, 741/October 19, 1340: Pīr Ḥusayn in front of Shiraz's gates
Jumādā II 16, 741/December 7, 1340: peace agreement
Pīr Ḥusayn governs Shiraz for a period of eighteen months

Third Campaign: New Chupanid–Injuid Alliance

Muḥarram 743/June 1342: Malik Ashraf's alliance with Shaykh Abū Isḥāq Īnjū; his fight against Pīr Ḥusayn
Ṣafar 1, 743/July 6, 1342: Pīr Ḥusayn goes back to Tabriz
Shaykh Abū Isḥāq Īnjū regains power in Shiraz

Fourth Campaign: New Chupanid–Injuid Alliance

743/1342–3: Jalāl al-Dīn Masʿūd Shāh Īnjū allied with Yāghī Bāstī
Shaʿbān 19, 743/January 17, 1343: Jalāl al-Dīn Masʿūd Shāh Īnjū murdered by Yāghī Bāstī

Shaʿbān 20, 743/January 18, 1343: struggles between supporters of Yāghī Bāstī and Jalāl al-Dīn Masʿūd Shāh Īnjū

Yāghī Bāstī's flight from Shiraz

Fifth Campaign: New Chupanid–Muzaffarid Alliance

Early Rajab 744/November–December 1344: return of Yāghī Bāstī and Malik Ashraf to Fārs; alliance with Mubāriz al-Dīn Muẓaffar to seize Shiraz

Rajab 27, 744/December 15, 1344: execution of Shaykh Ḥasan Kuchik in Tabriz

Return of Yāghī Bāstī and Malik Ashraf to Tabriz

Shaykh Abū Isḥāq Īnjū regains power in Shiraz

7

Persian *ḥukkām*: "Games of the Swords" or Corrupt Officials?

Immediately after the conquest of eastern Iran, the Mongols realized the importance of the revenues from the towns and agricultural areas that had fallen under their military control. As mentioned previously, Möngke set up a series of measures to exploit the populations of the empire. While it was relatively simple for the conquerors to militarily dominate a territory, administrative domination proved more challenging. The Mongol policy applied in Fārs is a clear example of the difficulties encountered by the Mongols when trying to establish authority over this region far from the Azerbaijani *Ordu*. Research on the Mongols often claims that while Fārs remained safe during the Mongol invasion, it was systematically exploited in the second half of the thirteenth century. So the question beckons: Was Fārs destroyed by Mongol domination or were other factors to blame for the circumstances outlined in this book?

Previous Instances of Economic Decline

When the Mongols invaded Iran, the country had been in crisis for nearly two centuries. Conflicts in urban neighborhoods, sometimes motivated by religious hostility, had wreaked havoc and impeded the development of local trade and crafts. In Isfahan in 500/1107, the Saljuq Sultan Muḥammad b. Malik Shāh inflicted a crushing defeat on the Ismāʿīlīs with the help of Sunnī networks.[1] Following this triumph, the population of Isfahan paraded through the streets, with the notable absence of the Turks. David Durand-Guédy points out that the Sunnī elites of Isfahan celebrated their victory to show that they were in charge of the local government.[2] Subsequently, tensions erupted between the Ḥanafīs and the Shāfiʿīs,[3] and this sectarian strife fueled the Mongol massacres. The invaders, inspired by the Shāfiʿīs, first subjected the Ḥanafīs to servitude before slaughtering them.[4] In Baghdad under the Buyids, Sunnīs and Shāfiʿīs had engaged in fatal clashes. More than three decades after the Saljuq takeover of the city, the severity of the religious conflicts between these two factions animated the populace of several Baghdad neighborhoods. These confessional *fitnas* had partially sacked Baghdad before the city was taken by Hülegü.[5] In the rural areas, the eleventh century witnessed the beginning of a global agricultural crisis. Vaṣṣāf describes the agricultural deterioration observed during his own lifetime in the first half of the fourteenth century. As an example, he uses Kirbāl, which was a cold fertile region to the east of Shiraz. He asserts that under the Buyid ʿAḍud al-Dawla, Kirbāl produced seven hundred thousand *kharvār* of cereals.[6] During the reign of the Salghurid atabek Saʿd b. Zangī, agricultural production had fallen to three hundred thousand *kharvār*. According to Vaṣṣāf, the production continued to decline before Ghazan's reforms. Based on 20 percent or 24 percent taxation on crops, Petrushevsky estimated that the annual grain production in Kirbāl at that time amounted to around two hundred thousand *kharvār*.[7] Based on these figures, which should be taken merely as orders of magnitude, it emerges that the agricultural crisis preceding the Ilkhanid period was indeed severe, resulting from the turbulent times that rocked the region following the decline of the Buyids and the Saljuqs.

Reasons for Recurring Administrative Dysfunctions

Rashīd al-Dīn's *Jāmiʿal-tawārīkh* describes the ravages wreaked on the rural economy with the flight of peasants and the desertification of farmlands as a double consequence of the plundering of the tribes and the brutality of both the *ilchis* and the Mongol *basqaqs*. Nevertheless, the author praises at length the reforms of Ghazan, whom he advised and inspired. Amīr Nawrūz and Ghazan's victory over Baidu in 1295 shows precisely what Michael Hope had pointed out: "a departure from the old standards of Chinggisid political authority to a new age of Islamic kingship."[8] Ghazan was a messianic king, a ruler who cared about the welfare of his Muslim subjects. Rashīd al-Dīn omits mentioning Ṣadr al-Dīn Aḥmad Khālidī Zanjānī's tax reforms in Fārs, which benefited both the *Dīvān* and the people. These reforms put an end to the incessant abuses of the *ilchis* and the *noyans*' envoys.[9] Rashīd al-Dīn thus seeks to attribute these measures to Ghazan despite his hesitant and sometimes contradictory management in Fārs.

Ghazan's famous reforms, often seen as a turning point in the Iranian administrative regime with long-lasting effects, were unlikely to change the practices in Fārs. Vaṣṣāf denounces the abuses committed in 1318 during the reign of Abū Sa'īd, when taxes were levied in the *vilāyat* of Fīrūzābād. He claims that in the span of just six months, three administrators (*ḥākim*), six agents (*nā'ib*), seven tax agents (*muqarrir*), and more than two hundred cavaliers stayed there, all at the local population's expense. The area then apparently fell into ruin.[10] Even if the author probably exaggerates about the situation, we might infer that his description partially reflects the reality. Vaṣṣaf enumerates not only the problems caused by the officials sent to the province from the *Ordu* but also the mayhem produced by the local inhabitants, even during the reign of Abū Sa'īd. He writes:

> In Shiraz, the lawless and crooks (*runūd va awbāsh*), who are like wild beasts and cattle, indulged in murder and plunder, but there was no independent and strong government to quell them; the Shūls, the Kurds, and other evildoers who are drunk without drinking wine and dance without ecstasy committed offences, night and day, cutting off the water, setting fire to houses and millstones, the *basqaqs*, however, were not strong enough to stop them.[11]

The abuses committed are no doubt undeniable. But if these testimonies that recount the misery of the population were taken from a literal perspective, the region would appear irreparably devastated. The reality is far more complicated than this. Indeed, the Mongols' destructive power was disproportionate compared with their numerical weight, which was, all things considered, rather modest.[12]

Venality of Local Officials

What were the root causes of the administrative dysfunctions that disrupted the collection of taxes in Fārs? After the death of the atabek Abū Bakr, the first wave of infamous administrative chaos erupted, leading to the gradual Mongol takeover of Fārs. The political chaos that overtook Shiraz and its surrounding area on account of the incompetence of Abū Bakr's successors favored the influence of the Ilkhans, even though they only superficially preserved the dynastic tradition through the young Salghurid princesses. Thereafter, the administration was entrusted to many prominent locals, but this strategy quickly proved ineffective, because they would use tax collection for their personal gain.[13] As indicated by the actions of Inkianu, the *Ordu* commissioned competent Turko-Mongol administrators to solve the issue. Saʿdī devoted many heartbreaking verses to Inkianu:

> Fortune has turned enough, and turns again:
> The prudent man binds not his heart to the world.[14]

Sughunchaq Noyan was appointed twice to Fārs to settle its fiscal affairs, with Ibn Zarkūb and Vaṣṣāf both praising him for his good governance. They affirm that he established justice and eliminated oppression and tyranny (*jawr va ẓulm*).[15] These Turko-Mongol officials were eager to introduce taxes to the *Dīvān*, but they were also aware that to collect the sums needed to fund the *Ordu*, it was necessary to preserve the productive apparatus of Fārs. They understood that if the levies were higher than what the population could afford, they would become so destitute that they would be unable to maintain their means of subsistence. These Turko-Mongol officials nevertheless quickly fell victim to the intrigues of their Persian collaborators at the *Ordu*. The assertions of the local population thus had a significant impact on the administrative history of Fārs. Seeing their illegal income disappear as a result of better tax administration, they thus tried to use the administrative system to their advantage. Why did they behave in this manner?

Arduous relations between the different political actors characterize the Ilkhanid period at all levels, from the divanian staff to the local subordinates. In his study, *Émirs mongols et vizirs persans*, Jean Aubin illustrated how the Persian officials and administrators were frequently subject to extraordinary setbacks that could end in bloodshed. They constantly had to satisfy the unlimited financial desires of the *Ordu*.[16] To occupy a position of authority, a Mongol or Persian protector was needed. However, to ensure the discretion of subordinates so that they would not report fraudulent activity or to obtain an advantageous position, money was an absolute necessity. This partially explains the multiple intrigues at the court of the Ilkhans, which had devastating effects on Fārs throughout this period. As already noted, these rapidly gained fortunes could vanish just as quickly in the face of embezzlement allegations by a rival who coveted this monetary influx for himself. The excessive appetite of the *Ordu* could also provoke a tax collector's downfall if he was unable to raise the demanded sums. However, despite the risks involved, the tax farm of Fārs was highly coveted, which indicates that the area was not completely destroyed economically. In the *Ordu*, the local notables fought each other to obtain the management of a simple district.

Great Traders Caught in the Turmoil

It was a total failure to maintain a fictional dynastic tradition in Shiraz through the young Salghurid princess, Abis Khātūn, supported by a local administrator. The Ilkhans thus resorted to the tax farming system, entrusting the collection of taxes to sharecroppers and appealing to great merchants to assist them in this task. The substantial financial means of the merchants attracted the attention of the Ilkhans, as they regarded them as a safe option for collecting taxes. The merchants' personal fortunes could be used to compensate for the failings of any peasants unable to pay the necessary sums. The example of the great merchants shows how quickly fortunes could be made and lost. Shams al-Dīn Muḥammad b. Malik Tāzīgū, an important international merchant, especially in the camel trade, had powerful allies in the *Ordu*. However, in a short period of time, he lost all his possessions. Not only had he failed to make the landowners pay their dues, but he also was not repaid by the *Dīvān* for the advances taken out of his own finances to cover the wages of the subordinate officials. Shams al-Dīn Muḥammad b. Malik Tāzīgū made an effort to safeguard his wealth by contributing to charitable foundations, although this did not prevent him from dying penniless in poverty. Traditionally, any assets placed in *waqf* provided the founder and his heirs with some kind of security in times of political instability.[17] However, the records indicate that during the Ilkhanid period, the wealth of these foundations was not always used for their initial purpose. The poet Pūr-i Bāha, who lived during the reign of Abaqa, was close to the Juvaynīs.[18] He is the author of a poem written on Rajab 24, 667/March 29, 1269, entitled *Kār-nāma-i awqāf-i Khwāf* ("The Book of Pious Foundations of Khwāf"), which boldly outlines the administration of mortmain property in this region of Khurasan. In his view, transferring a property to *waqf* was equivalent to throwing it in the garbage.[19] Vaṣṣāf speaks of *waqf* in terms of waste.[20] Hagiographic texts also echo these practices at this time. Amīn al-Dīn Balyānī, who was close to the Injuids, advised one of his disciples to abandon all his possessions, because:

> Of everything you turn into *waqf* ..., you have nothing left and no one benefits from what you have given. Look at what they have done with other people's *waqf*; they will do the same to your pious actions.[21]

Later, Jamāl al-Dīn Ibrāhīm Ṭībī, the famous Malik al-Islām, also experienced a reversal of fortune because of the intrigues of his powerful Persian enemy, ʿIzz al-Dīn Muẓaffar, who had received the title of "Pillar of Power" (*ʿamīd al-mulk*). In the affairs of Fārs, he was a close collaborator of the vizier Ṣadr al-Dīn Aḥmad Khālidī Zanjānī. Malik al-Islām retained his office for several years thanks to his generosity toward Mongol princesses, *noyans*, and other influential figures of the *Ordu*. During his stay at the court of Ghazan, he offered them many gifts, precious pearls, and stones. Thomas Allsen explains the value of pearls in Mongolian culture, as their usage in the portraits of the emperors and their wives shows that they had more than just ornamental value. Pearls were treasured because of their symbolic meaning, as they enhanced the social and political status of their owners. Allsen speaks of "class objects."[22] Local officials from Fārs thus sent pearls to the Mongolian authorities in order to continue enjoying their favor. Jamāl al-Dīn Ibrāhīm Ṭībī did not, however, avoid troublesome situations at the *yarghu* of Ghazan, although his unique financial status saved him from capital punishment.

The case of Malik al-Islām illustrates particularly well the role played by trade in southern Iran. He benefited both the Ilkhans and the local rulers. The rulers in Kirmān and Fārs were at odds with each other, as they both sought to control the sea and island routes of the Persian Gulf. The struggle to dominate the Sīrjān district, which lay at the crossroads of the trade routes, was primarily aimed at the control of the Yazd-Hormuz route. The Qutlughkhanids of Kirmān, particularly Terken Khātūn, had links with large traders. Bībī Terken, one of the daughters of Quṭb al-Dīn and Terken Khātūn, had married the great merchant Shams al-Dīn Muḥammad b. Tāzīgū. After Terken Khātūn's long reign, her second daughter, Pādishāh Khātūn, inherited Sīrjān. She thus dominated the economic axis linking the Persian Gulf to central Iran. And, like her mother, she frequented many great merchants and was a friend of the merchant family Ṭībī.[23]

This large network of international merchants was indeed the source of Fārs' wealth. Peter Martinez demonstrates how the Ilkhans' ministers were adept at manipulating the monetary policy to maximize trade incomes across the entire realm. Ghazan's monetary reforms, based on the advice of his ministers Rashīd al-Dīn and Tāj al-Dīn 'Alī Shāh, who were themselves involved in trade, formed part of this fiscal restructuring, which was a crucial component of the partnership between the Ilkhanid administration and the Ṭībī merchants of Qays.[24]

The Ṭībī merchants, who had prospered along the trade route between the Indian Ocean and the inland regions of Iran due to the importance of Shiraz, gradually lost their position. As we witnessed above, 'Izz al-Dīn 'Abd al-'Azīz, the son of Malik al-Islām, was executed and replaced by Maḥmūd Shāh Īnjū at the instigation of the Chupanid clan. Afterward, Qays fell into the hands of the prince of Hormuz, Quṭb al-Dīn Tahamtan II (r. 720–48/1320–47) in 720/1320. He landed on the island by surprise, appropriated the wealth that had accumulated there for decades, and killed Malik al-Islām's children and grandchildren. Only one of Malik al-Islām's sons survived, a certain Malik Shams al-Dīn, who lived at the court of Abū Sa'īd, as well as one of his grandsons, Niẓām al-Dīn Aḥmad. Both dreamed of winning back Qays.[25] In 733/1332–3, they secured a *yarligh* from the Ilkhan, which ordered the troops of Fārs and Shabānkāra to attack Hormuz to seek retribution, although Maḥmūd Shāh Īnjū, who loathed the Ṭībīs' change of fortune, sided with the prince of Hormuz. He argued that the Ṭībīs had rebelled against Abū Sa'īd's authority. Therefore, a new military coalition was formed, and the Tībī merchants, who were no longer able to control the flow of trade across the Indian Ocean, were eliminated to make way for the Injuids.[26]

The capture of Qays by the ruler of Hormuz seems to have become part of the collective memory. In the life of a Sufi shaykh of Lāristān, Sayyid Kāmal Pīr Qattālī (d. 721/1321), a lengthy and rather factual account reports the conquest of the island. The shaykh came from an important and prolific family known as the "People of the House" (*ahl al-bayt*), whose descendants still live in Bandar 'Abbās today. The factual narrative aims to emphasize Sayyid Kāmal Pīr's charisma, whose stick and sword charged with his *baraka* were the agents behind the king of Hormuz's victory over the political authorities of Qays. According to the hagiography, the Qattālīs had settled over a vast territory spanning from Shiraz to Hormuz, from the border of Iraq to the Persian Gulf islands and the Arabian Sea, from Julfar to Oman, and from Makrān to the border of Sind.[27] They earned part of their income from trade or were close to the trade network. Although it is a hagiographical narrative, this text bears witness to the importance of commercial interests connected to international trade.

Consequences of Corrupt Local Agents

The administrative situation in Shiraz echoed the volatile situation in the *Ordu*. The mere disgrace of a *noyan* implied his certain death. Shabānkāra'ī accurately describes the Mongol *amīrs* sent to the *yarghu* as the "games of swords" (*shikār-i suyūf*).[28] The *noyan* who fell from grace also dragged down his Persian associate who had placed himself under his protection, thus causing the patron to lose power both in the *Ordu* and in the province. Despite losing their backing in the capital, these local notables occasionally succeeded in keeping their position by joining forces with a new strongman of the moment. Sayyid 'Imād al-Dīn Abū Yu'lā and 'Izz al-Dīn Muẓaffar were prime examples of this attitude of Persian officials, scheming at all costs to keep themselves in power. These local notables, all corrupt, who sought a place for themselves in the Mongol court to protect their own interests, were the true perpetrators of the administrative chaos in Fārs. After losing a powerful patron, they would seek out support elsewhere and return to their administrative affairs, waiting for the day when they in turn became "judged by the *yasa*" and turned into the "games of swords."

We therefore cannot trust the medieval sources and sometimes even contemporary historiography, because they maintain the belief that Mongol domination alone was responsible for the decline of Fārs.[29] It is true, however, that the comings and goings of *basqaqs* and other *Ordu* envoys had harmful effects, not to mention the nuisance of officials living in the province. Not only were the Mongol envoys a scourge for the inhabitants of the Ilkhanate provinces, but so too were the Persian officials accompanied by large groups of troops. Fakhr al-Dīn Mustawfī Qazvīnī, governor of Anatolia, arrived in the region in 685/1286 with two of his brothers and a band of Qazvīnis.[30] Jean Aubin also mentions the case of Niẓām al-Dīn Yaḥyā Faryūmadī, who was Ghazan's minister in Anatolia in 1299–1300. He came to the province with countless Khurasanis secretaries, Azerbaijanis chamberlains, Quhistanis tax collectors, and Kirmanis stewards.[31] The Persian administrators who crisscrossed the provinces with many agents, including their compatriots, were no less troublesome than the Mongol couriers. The sources, particularly those that convey the viewpoint of the vassal principalities, complain less about the mistreatment inflicted by the Mongols than that of the divanians.[32]

In addition to the strategic disruption caused by the travel of Persian administrators and their entourage, there was the appropriation of taxes. Indeed, a large portion of the taxes levied on the population, sometimes at excessive levels, went into the pockets of the local tax farmers or their Persian associates in the *Ordu*. Nevertheless, the majority of Turko-Mongolian administrators were capable civil servants. In Anatolia in 1280, Samaghar, "righteous *amīr* and perfect *yarghuci*," stood up against the actions of Fakhr al-Dīn Mustawfī Qazvīnī.[33] In Fārs, Inkianu and Sughuncaq Noyan were capable officials, who, had they not fallen victim to the intrigues of Persian notables, could have ensured the proper management of the region.[34]

Chaotic Return to Traditional Sharing Zones

God be praised for the justice of the Sulṭān
Aḥmad, son of Shaykh Ūvais son of
Ḥasan Īlkānī, Khān son of a Khān,

emperor offspring of an emperor
he whom it is fitting to
call the Soul of the World.[35]

The death of Abū Sa'īd in 1335 marked the end of the Ilkhanid dynasty, although the roots of its decline can be traced back to his reign. Jean Aubin regards him as the first puppet Ilkhan.[36] However, the prestige of the Chinggisid lineage continued for several more years, as demonstrated by the *amīrs*' concern for a blood prince from the imperial family, as, in principle, only Chinggis Khan's descendants had the right to lead the Ilkhanate.[37] Thus, the unity of the Ilkhanid Empire was maintained in theory through various leaders, although no one dared to claim the supreme throne.[38] After Abū Sa'īd's death, the Ilkhanate was divided into several areas that corresponded globally to the traditional division of "Iran-s." In Khurasan and Māzandarān, the Ilkhan Ṭaghai Temür maintained the Chinggisid legitimacy until his death in 754/1353; Azerbaijan was practically under control of the Chupanid Shaykh Ḥasan Kuchik, even though the power laid nominally in the hands of Sulaymān Khan, a grandson of Hülegü; finally, Shaykh Ḥasan Buzurg ruled Iraq.

Despite its notorious administrative problems, Fārs remained prosperous, thus making it the object of ambition of the Injuid and Chupanid *amīrs* for nearly two decades. Troops relentlessly moved around the province, fueled by the frequent changes of alliances between the different protagonists. The Muzaffarids won the final victory over their rival *amīrs* thanks to the participation of tribes and many *pahlavāns* serving their army, notwithstanding the contradiction between their ideals and the precepts of Islam. Nevertheless, the Muzaffarids were not the only dynasty benefiting from the support of the *akhīs* and the *pahlavāns* during this period. A certain Akhī Shāh Malik served the Chupanid ruler Malik Ashrāf,[39] while Pahlavān Ḥājjī Kharbanda Sanjarī was one of the military commanders of the Jalayirid army in 777/1375.[40] In the Timurid era, there were still many *pahlavāns* holding military offices. In 790/1388, Akhī Īrān Shāh held the fortress of Sulṭāniyya for Tamerlane.[41] To remain in power, these princes inevitably relied on these groups of men, who were well trained in the art of weaponry, loyal to their allies, and capable of holding fortresses.

The new forces that made up the Ilkhanate gradually grew in strength over a period of two decades. The Chupanids prevailed in 740/1340 following their victory over Shaykh Ḥasan Buzurg. In Fārs, the duel between the Muzaffarids and the Injuids ended with the Muzaffarid capture of Shiraz in 754/1353. Although the Jalayirids were one of the strongest forces along with the Chupanids, they had to wait until 757/1356 to establish themselves under Shaykh Ūvays, Shaykh Ḥasan Buzurg's son.[42] Once established, these dynasties did not expand but were instead weakened by internal tensions.[43] The case of the Muzaffarids is a good example, as the dynasty became entangled in fratricidal struggles for twenty years, with no successor able to assert himself in Fārs. For this reason, the powers that formed on the ashes of the Persian Ilkhanate quickly disappeared from the political scene under the pressure of the Turkmen dynasties.

8

Epilogue

Other Principalities in Southern Iran

> Muẓaffar al-Dīn Muḥammad, as recounted,
> touched his white beard and said,
> "God, make it red with the blood of the martyrdom."[1]

To better understand the Ilkhanid dominance over the areas that remained relatively autonomous, it would be necessary to compare this study on Fārs with a similar one conducted on other Muslim territories or even on Christian principalities like Armenia and Georgia. This goal is evidently difficult to achieve, as it extends far beyond the scope of this research on Ilkhanid Fārs. However, it is still possible to provide some preliminary observations to make comparisons with the regional rulers who controlled several cities in southern Iran. They had mostly come to power after the collapse of the Saljuq Empire following the death of Malik Shāh in 1092. While the Salghurids in Fārs and the Qutlughkhanids in Kirmān are thoroughly chronicled, it is hard to precisely trace the history of the smaller rulers in the region who reigned independently. Indeed, the sources on the sequence of events, dates, and succession of rulers are muddled and incomplete.

Principalities on the Eve of the Mongol Invasion

A lineage of atabeks exercised power in Lur-i Buzurg, the eastern and southern part of Luristān, whose capital was Īdhaj (ancient Malāmīr). In its early days, the dynasty was known as Faḍluyya, named after a Kurdish leader from Syria who supposedly settled in the north of Luristān around 500/1106.[2] One of his descendants, Abū Ṭāhir, gained renown after a military expedition against the Shabānkāra when he was in the service of Sunqur b. Mawdūd Salghur. As a sign of gratitude, the latter bestowed on him the administration of Kūh Gīlūya, a mountainous region located northwest of Fārs on the border of Luristān.[3] Abū Ṭāhir then expanded his power over the whole of Lur-i Buzurg. He subsequently claimed the title of atabek for himself and became independent in 550/1155–6.[4] His son, Nuṣrat al-Dīn Malik Hazārasp (d. 626/1229), gave his name to the dynasty, the Hazaraspids.[5] From the region, he expelled the Shūls, who moved to Fārs, and thereafter he extended his territory toward Isfahan. Malik Hazārasp is therefore the true founder of this small principality.[6] As we will see in the local histories, the Iranian provinces had a strong Persian identity. Ibn Isfandiyār, the historian of Ṭabaristān, indicated that the scenes from Firdawsī's *Shāh-nāma* were depicted on the walls of the palace of the Bawandid sovereign Ḥusām al-Dawla Ardashīr and that its verses were recited to help people fall asleep.[7] Similar evidence exists for many other small local rulers. Shabānkāra'ī attributes to the Hazaraspids an uninterrupted royal bloodline dating back to the Kayanids:

> The Hazaraspid rulers are truly great kings, and their achievements are known to the world. Nowadays, the kings of yore cannot be found in any land, but the [Hazaraspids] still remain. They imbibe the customs and manners of the Iranian kings (*mulūk-i irān zamīn*).[8]

Historians praised Nuṣrat al-Dīn Aḥmad b. Yūsuf Shāh (r. 695–730/1296–1330),[9] the seventh atabek who spent many years at the court of the Ilkhans. Mustawfī Qazvīnī remarks that during Nuṣrat al-Dīn Aḥmad's reign, Luristān became "the envy of the multitudes," as Shabānkāra'ī reports that people from Mashriq va Maghrib flocked to Aḥmad's court and were never disappointed.[10] Ibn Baṭṭūṭa presents Nuṣrat al-Dīn Aḥmad as a king of extreme piety, who "used to wear a hair-shirt beneath his clothes next his skin."[11] Alluding to the atabek's pious reputation, Shabānkāra'ī refers to Aḥmad as "Pīr-i Aḥmad."[12] Shihāb Munshī's *Humāyūn-nāma* contains a letter addressed by "some sultans" (*baḍī-i salāṭīn*) to Nuṣrat al-Ḥaqq wa-l-Dīn Pīr Aḥmad. They call the atabek the most perfect and just king of those times (*akmāl va a'adal-i mulūk-i ayyām*).[13]

A number of works have been dedicated to Nuṣrat al-Dīn Aḥmad, regarded by his contemporaries as a just and wise ruler.[14] Shams al-Dīn 'Abd al-Laṭīf,

Rūzbihān Baqlī Shīrāzī's grandson, dedicated the *Rūḥ al-jinān* to him. In addition to an insightful hagiographical biography of his grandfather, this text includes a collection of "advice to the prince," which connected him with the ancient Persian tradition. Nuṣrat al-Dīn Aḥmad is praised as the "glorified sultan" (*sulṭān-i muʿaẓẓam*), "righteous of the world" (*ʿādil-i jahān*), and "heir to the kingdom of the Kayanids" (*varīth-i mulk-i Kayān*).[15] Another work for the prince, *Tuḥfa* ("The Gift") by Sharaf Faḍl Allāh b. ʿAbd Allāh Qazvīnī, is dedicated to the atabek as "the King of Islam (*pādishāh-i islām*), the refuge of the people of the faith," while associating him with the rulers of ancient Persia.[16]

During his long reign, Nuṣrat al-Dīn Aḥmad maintained good relations with Tabriz.[17] He probably established Mongol institutions in Luristān, specifically to fix the tax system.[18] Nuṣrat al-Dīn Aḥmad stayed away from perilous military adventures, unlike his brother Afrāsiyāb b. Yūsuf Shāh (r. c. 688–95/1290–6), whom he succeeded in 695/1296.[19] Despite Afrāsiyāb's political mistakes, the Hazaraspids managed to preserve their territory throughout the Ilkhanid period.

Another dynasty of atabeks, who descended from the Jangrū'ī tribe of the Lurs, ruled the Lur-i Kuchick in the northern and western part of Luristān, with Khurramābād as its capital.[20] It is known as Khurshīdī, after Shujāʿ ʿAlī Khurshīd, the first ruler who died at the age of one hundred in 621/1224.[21] According to Naṭanzī, until the end of 550/1106, the district had never had a governor.[22] Every year, the Caliph's officials came to fix and collect taxes until the appointment of Shujāʿ ʿAlī Khurshīd as *shiḥna* of part of Luristān on behalf of the Saljuq governor Ḥusām al-Dīn Shūhlī.[23] After the latter's death, Shujāʿ ʿAlī Khurshīd ruled independently in 580/1184–5 and took the title of atabek. From the Abbasid Caliph Nāṣir al-Dīn (r. 1180–1225), he obtained the district of Ṭarazak in Khūzistān in exchange for some of his fortresses. The dynasty survived despite numerous familial conflicts until Shāhvardī's execution for disobedience in 1006/1597 by order of Shāh ʿAbbās Safavī.

Yazd also had a ruling dynasty of atabeks, whose history is difficult to reconstruct due to the scarcity of reliable sources. The local histories of Yazd include the main relevant accounts, which, while incomplete and chronologically jumbled, primarily describe the charitable activities of the atabeks.[24] The Saljuq Sultan Arslan b. Ṭughril appointed Rukn al-Dīn Sām

b. Langar, a town garrison commander, as atabek to the two daughters of the last Kakuyid prince Farāmarz b. 'Alā' al-Dawla 'Alī.[25] Yazd historians describe Rukn-al-Dīn Sām as a gentleman and pious ruler, though incapable of governing.[26] The Saljuq Sultan Sanjar dismissed and replaced him with his brother, 'Izz al-Dīn Langar, to whom he also entrusted the government of Isfahan and Shiraz. Recognized as a brave man (*bahādur*) by historians, he reigned until 604/1207–8.[27] The atabeks of Yazd were mostly tributaries to the Saljuqs and later the Ilkhanids.[28]

On the eastern borders of Fārs, in Shabānkāra, the Ismā'īlī Kurds had established a warlike principality that was at the height of its power in the first half of the thirteenth century.[29] On the history of Shabānkāra's rulers, Muḥammad Shabānkāra'ī's chronicle, *Majma' al-ansāb*, is a useful source. Provincial in outlook, Shabānkāra'ī views the politics of the Ilkhanids through the prism of Shabānkāra, Fārs, Kirmān, or Hormuz.[30] Shabānkāra'ī provides precise information, probably because he attended the court of Shabānkāra's last sovereigns.

Like the Hazaraspids, the kings of Shabānkāra claimed that they were descended directly from the Sasanid Ardashīr I. According to the *Daftar-i Dilgushā*, the rulers of Shabānkāra are the offspring (*nazhād*) of the kings of ancient Persia, while they mint the royal coins (*sikka-i shahrīyāri*) in gold.[31] Charles Melville believes that different though comparable observations could be made about the Salghurid rulers of Fārs, but who, "as Turks, were the longterm enemies and rivals of the Shabankareh."[32] We witnessed how the rulers of Shabānkāra were able to successfully block the Salghurid atabeks' eastward thrust for a hundred years.

Nevertheless, the kings of Shabānkāra shared a dual culture, steeped in the ancient Persian tradition while adhering to strict Sunnī orthodoxy. According to the *Majma' al-ansāb*, from dawn until dusk, Muẓaffar al-Dīn Muḥammad's court (d. 659/1261) resembled a madrasa.[33] He was interested in law and Qur'ānic exegesis, and like the atabek Abū Bakr in Shiraz, he condemned scholasticism (*'ilm-i kalām*), logic (*manṭiq*), and philosophy, which he considered to be contrary to the *sharī'a*.[34] Shabānkāra's society was extremely archaic and patriarchal compared with the Salghurid court of Shiraz.[35]

Under Muẓaffar al-Dīn Muḥammad, the kingdom attained a high level of prosperity, leading to the construction of numerous religious and charitable buildings.[36] Jean Aubin, who meticulously examines the ruling class of the Shabānkāra principality, explains that it was comprised of two groups: the chamberlains (*ḥūjjāb*) in the service of the chancellery and the *amīrs*.[37] We will now observe how they helped bring the kingdom under the Ilkhanid authority.

Originally from the steppe, the Qutlughkhanids were descendants of the two Qara Khitai commanders, Baraq Ḥājib and his brother Ḥamīd Pūr, who had been captured in 1210 by the Khwārazmshāh 'Alā' al-Dīn Muḥammad in a battle against Tayangu, who was the Qara Khitai commander of Talas.[38] Impressed by their military skills, 'Alā' al-Dīn Muḥammad appointed them to important positions. Baraq Ḥājib was appointed as chamberlain and then assigned to the service of 'Alā' al-Dīn Muḥammad's son, Giyāth al-Dīn, who later appointed him as governor of Isfahan and Kirmān. In 1224, Jalāl al-Dīn, Khwārazmshāh's successor, confirmed his power and granted him the title of Qutlugh Khan ("Fortunate Khan"). After his conversion to Islam, the Abbasid Caliph recognized him and awarded him the title of Qutlugh Sulṭān ("Fortunate Sultan"). As an astute politician, Baraq Ḥājib learned to build a positive relationship with the Mongol conquerors very early in his career. He sent his son, Rukn a-Dīn Khwāja Jūq, to stay at the court of Ögödei.[39] After the death of Baraq Ḥājib in 632/1235, Rukn al-Dīn received a *yarligh* from the Great Qa'an, issued in order for him to succeed his father.[40]

While the Salghurids of Shiraz quickly lost their autonomy from the *Ordu* due to the lack of political stability among the successors of the Salghurid Abū Bakr, the princes and atabeks who ruled these small principalities of southern Iran managed to retain their independence for some time. What factors allowed these local rulers to resist a total Ilkhanid takeover of their territory?

Confirmation of Power in Exchange for Submission

Even before Hülegü's arrival in Iran, several local princes pledged their allegiance to the Great Qa'an, as seen in the case of the atabek Abū Bakr, who sent his nephew Tahamtan to Ögödei to pledge allegiance. The Great Qa'an consequently confirmed his power and territorial possessions. Every year, the atabek Abū Bakr sent a tribute to Qaraqorum, which, according to Vaṣṣāf, was only a small part of his income. According to the author of the *Tārīkh-i jadīd-i Yazd*, Aḥmad b. al-Ḥusayn, who is the only source of this information, the atabek of Yazd, Salghur Shāh, also sent gifts to Ögödei to express his allegiance. In exchange, the Great Qa'an confirmed him in his power, issuing him with a diploma of investiture (*manshūr-i pādishāhī*) and a robe of honor (*khil'a*).[41] Indeed, most of the local princes went to Qaraqorum to make an act of submission to the Great Qa'an.

We may also mention the case of Badr al-Dīn Mas'ūd (r. 640–58/1242–60), the atabek of Lur-i Kuchik, who came to power amid family rivalries between Shujā' al-Dīn Khurshīd's descendants. Since the Abbasid Caliph refused to recognize his accession, Badr al-Dīn Mas'ūd went to the court of Möngke, who kept him in his position. He participated in Hülegü's campaigns against the Ismā'īlīs and the Abbasid Caliph. He was awarded a share of the booty captured at Baghdad but died soon afterward in 658/1260.[42]

Like the Salghurids of Shiraz, the king of Shabānkāra, Muẓaffar al-Dīn Muḥammad, also sent gifts to Ögödei and told him: "This country is only mountains (*īn vilāyat kūhīst*) and the unfortunates (*bīchāragān*) who live there are poor mountain dwellers (*kūhnishīn*). They are starving and without means to survive."[43] According to Shabānkāra'ī, this speech allowed Muẓaffar al-Dīn Muḥammad to preserve his kingdom from "Mongol sedition" (*fitnat-i mughūl*).[44] The products sent from his "poor kingdom" did not, however, ensure long-term peace in his principality.

Under Ögödei, Muẓaffar al-Dīn preserved his independence by presenting an ingenious account of his kingdom's wealth. According to Shabānkāra'ī, some of the principality's inhabitants were "enemies (*dushman*) of the king," as they went to Hülegü and told him that the province was prosperous (*vilāyatī-i pur ni'mat*) and that Muẓaffar al-Dīn had many treasures. Subsequently, Hülegü sent an army to Shabānkāra.[45] Naṭanzī, who gives a slightly different version of events, says that Muẓaffar al-Dīn punished his officials if they did not perform their duties fairly. The historian then claims that the property of a certain 'Alī Ḥaydar, an official of Muẓaffar al-Dīn Muḥammad's *dīvān*, was confiscated because of his misconduct. He fled to Hülegü, who subsequently issued an order to send an army to the province.[46] Both accounts seem to allude to dysfunctions in tax collection. Although the sources are not clear, taxes were undoubtedly diverted to the benefit of certain court officials who had a vested interest in the Mongol *Ordu*. As we witnessed above, this was also a recurring issue at the Salghurid court.

In this period, Muẓaffar al-Dīn was eighty-five years old. Ṣāḥib Shabākāra'ī says that Muẓaffar al-Dīn, being endowed with royal glory (*farr-i īzadī*) for the first time since the Arab conquest,[47] decided to go into battle against the "infidels" (*kāfirān*). Before his morning prayer, he made his ablutions and informed his chamberlains: "God be praised! God gave me everything I wanted. Today, God willing, I will attain the bliss of martyrdom (*sa'ādat-i shahādat*)."[48] He chanted these lyrics while strapping on his arms:

> O chainmail of battle, you have rested a while from war,
> Now there's work to be done, be strong; be a luck ornament all round.
> Now my hero's back is bent, my Kabuli dagger no longer gleams
> I do not say this out of fear of you, or because I'm old and altered.[49]

As narrated, while touching his white beard, Muẓaffar al-Dīn said: "My God, make it red with the blood of martyrdom."[50] Like the heroes of *Shāh-nāma*, he lost his life on the battlefield on Ṣafar 6, 659/January 10, 1261.[51] The long narrative of the old king's heroic fight against the army of Hülegü's pagans resembles edifying literature. It nonetheless demonstrates the sense of Persian identity that pervaded throughout the society of Shabānkāra.

Muẓaffar al-Dīn's comrades in arms held council and removed the king's body from the battlefield before the Mongols discovered that he had been killed. The next morning, his sons, Quṭb al-Dīn Mubāriz and Ghiyāth al-Dīn Muḥammad, sent emissaries to inform the Mongol authorities that the king was ready to offer his submission.[52] Henceforth, Quṭb al-Dīn Mubāriz, who succeeded his father, was forced to pay an annual tribute of six thousand dinars in gold.[53] After the departure of the Mongols, the throne was left at the mercy of the Mongolian *noyans*, the rival members of the royal family, and the Shabānkāra'ī *amīrs* and court chamberlains who attended the *Ordu*.

Submission to the Great Qa'an entailed more than merely acknowledging his power and paying tribute; a member of the princely family was often required to stay at the Mongol *Ordu* as hostage. Such arrangements, whereby tributary rulers sent their sons or other close relatives to the Ilkhanid court, aimed to guarantee the cooperation of the subordinate dynasty. Let us cite the case of the Hazaraspid atabeks of Lur-i Buzurg, many of whom stayed at the court of the Ilkhans. Yūsuf Shāh, who had spent his youth with Abaqa, was chosen by the latter to succeed his father, Shams al-Dīn Alp Arghun, in 676/1277–8, although he still remained at the *Ordu* in line with a well-established tradition.[54] Afterward, Afrāsiyāb, Yūsuf Shāh's son, who was held hostage at the court of Arghun, was nominated by royal decree to succeed his father in 685/1286–7.[55] The strong ties between Afrāsiyāb and the Mongolian *noyan* Bolad Chingsang may have influenced this nomination.[56]

The Mongols and their vassal dynasties often forged matrimonial alliances for the sake of political rapprochement. The Ilkhans, however, chose to marry among the Turko-Mongolian elite, undoubtedly to maintain their connections with the military aristocracy.[57] There were, of course, exceptions. Although a Muslim woman was strictly forbidden from marrying a pagan, the Salghurid princess Terken Khātūn disregarded this prohibition. After Abū Bakr's death, she gave her daughter, Abish Khātūn, in marriage to Mengü Temür, Hülegü's son, in order to strengthen her position in the *Ordu*. However, this marriage had little impact on the dynasty's independence. In fact, when Abish Khātūn was sent to Shiraz to rule the province, her political mistakes led to the Ilkhans gaining complete control of Fārs.

In Kirmān, the Qutlughkhanids had kept their steppe culture even after their conversion to Islam. The famous Terken Khātūn ("Qutlugh Khātūn"), Baraq Ḥājib's daughter, declared her affinity with the Turkic world. She claimed: "I am the child of a mighty Sulṭān and the fruit of the garden that is the heart of the Turks."[58] Pādishāh Khātūn, the daughter of Quṭb al-Dīn Muḥammad and Terken Khātūn, was betrothed to the Ilkhan Abaqa in 1271–2. Initially, the mother of the young sixteen-year-old princess had expressed her reluctance about her daughter marrying an infidel. Nevertheless, this marriage had positive outcomes despite its challenges from a religious perspective. Thanks to this marriage, Terken Khātūn gained political recognition.[59]

Submission to the Great Qa'an, tribute payments, and matrimonial alliances helped the local rulers establish their power in their regions. However, it was military cooperation with Iran's new masters that truly allowed the local rulers to retain their autonomy or, in the case of insubordination, face the consequences.

Supplying the Ilkhans with Troops in Exchange for Peace

Local rulers were obliged to provide troops to the Ilkhans, either to support their territorial expansion or to restore order in the provinces in the event of a rebellion. Military contributions protected the vassal dynasties from conquest or even from complete destruction. Indeed, refusing to participate militarily in the Ilkhans' campaigns was regarded as an act of rebellion against Mongol rule. This notion is explicitly stated in Hülegü's order of submission to local Iranian dynasties, as he prepared to overcome the Ismāʿīlīs of Alamūt:

> We are on campaign to eradicate the strongholds of the Heretics by command of the Qa'an. If you come yourselves and assist us with soldiers, weapons, and provisions, your territories, troops, and homes will remain yours and your efforts will be appreciated. If you allow any negligence of this command to take place, when by God's grace we finished with them, we will head straight for you—and no excuse will be accepted—and the same thing will happen to your territories and homes that will happen to them.[60]

Emissaries were sent to all territories to announce the arrival of the conqueror's banners. According to Rashīd al-Dīn, sultans and kings bearing gifts arrived from all directions.[61] However, submission to the Mongols was viewed negatively in the Mamluk sultanate. The Damascus historian Shihāb al-Dīn al-ʿUmarī lists all the kingdoms that came under Ilkhanid control, claiming that the kings of these countries had become the "slaves" (*ʿabīd*) of the Mongol sultans.[62]

In Fārs, several sovereigns sent military support to Hülegü. The Salghurid atabek, Muḥammad Shāh, participated in the capture of Baghdad alongside the Ilkhan,[63] who temporarily spared him from execution upon hearing the news of his brother Saljūq Shāh's revolt against the Mongol authority. Muẓaffar al-Dīn Tekla, the atabek of Lur-i Buzurg, came to power in 655/1257 or 656/1258.[64] Although the Abbasid Caliph recognized his authority, Tekla joined Hülegü during the Baghdad campaign to "obey him" (*bi-sabīl-i muṭāwanat*).[65] He was included in the Kitbuqa Noyan's division. Tekla's opinions about Hülegü changed after witnessing the execution of the Abbasid Caliph and the terrible fate suffered by Muslims. He subsequently disapproved of Hülegü's actions. After discovering that his views had reached "Hülegü Khan's ears" (*gūsh-i*

Hūlāgū Khān), Tekla decided to run away to Luristān.[66] Hülegü sent his *amīrs* Kitbuqa Noyan and Sartaq Noyan to apprehend him. Tekla's brother, Shams al-Dīn Alp Arghun, who had also fought alongside the Ilkhan, advised him to find common ground with Hülegü.[67] Tekla did not confront the Mongol army but was captured and brought back to Tabriz to appear at the *yarghu*. His escape was viewed as a revolt, and he was put to death.[68] Shams al-Dīn Alp Arghun, who was appointed to replace Tekla, reigned without difficulty until his death from illness in 672/1273–4.[69]

After the first conquests, the armies of the vassal states continued to serve as reinforcements for the Ilkhans. One example is Sulṭān Ḥajjāj of Kirmān and the atabek Yūsuf Shāh of Lur-i Buzurg who participated in Abaqa's campaign against the invasion of Baraq Khan Chaghatay in Khurasan. The latter was defeated near Herat on Dhū l-Ḥijja 1, 668/July 22, 1270.[70] We can also mention the case of Shams al-Dīn Muḥammad Kart of Herat, who was ordered to pacify Sīstān in 1254–5 alongside the Mongol troops.[71]

Submission to Mongol rule, tribute payments, and military participation meant that the princes of southern Iran could preserve their independence from the Ilkhans, although their situation was tenuous, as shown by the example of Tekla, the atabek of Lur-i Buzurg. Why did these principalities eventually succumb to the Mongol yoke? The mismanagement of their fiscal affairs and revolts against the Ilkhans' power were the two main reasons why the vassal states lost their autonomy.

Consequences of Insubordination to the Ilkhans

In some cases, difficulties with tax levies were at the origin of the progressive Ilkhanid takeover of the vassal states, as clearly demonstrated in the case of the Salghurids in Shiraz. In Shabānkāra, after Muẓaffar al-Dīn Muḥammad's martyrdom in a battle against Hülegü's army, his successors maintained good relations with the Ilkhans. His grandson, Niẓām al-Dīn Ḥasan, died, just like his grandfather, chanting the verses of the *Shāh-nāma*, although he was in the ranks of the Mongol army. He fervently supported the crushing of the Salghurid atabek, Saljūq Shāh, following his dissidence in 662/1263.[72] Hülegü, as was customary, dispatched military reinforcements using local contingents, which included the *amīrs* of Shabānkāra, in order to put an end to the uprising. A royal edict invested Niẓām al-Dīn's younger brother, Nuṣrat al-Dīn Ibrāhīm, but two years later in 664/1265–6, the young prince was poisoned to death.[73] On the same day, the *amīrs* and chamberlains recommended appointing Jalāl al-Dīn Ṭayyib Shāh, who was only thirteen years old.[74] The young prince went to the *Ordu* of Abaqa, who made him a "gift (*suyughatmish*) of the Shabānkāra" and granted him the drum, the standard, and a tablet of authority.[75] In other words, the Ilkhan confirmed him in his position. According to Naṭanzī, the principality became very prosperous (*miṣr-i jāmi'*) under his governance.[76] Nevertheless, it was during Jalāl al-Dīn Ṭayyib Shāh's long reign (r. 624–81/1265–83) that the kingdom was burdened by Mongol tyranny. Shīshī Bakhshī, one of the great *amīrs* of the Ilkhans and a tax collector (*shiḥna*), came to reorganize the province's finances, that is to say, to drain the taxes toward the *Ordu*.[77] During the last years of Abaqa's reign, Jalāl al-Dīn Ṭayyib Shāh came to denounce Shīshī Bakhshī's embezzlement to the Ilkhan after he had diverted part of the taxes for his own benefit.[78] Shīshī Bakhshī was removed from office, while Jalāl al-Dīn Ṭayyib Shāh remained at the Mongol court. After Abaqa's death, Shīshī Bakhshī obtained from Ahmad Tegüder the condemnation of Jalāl al-Dīn Ṭayyib Shāh, who was executed in 681/1283 around Hamadān.[79]

Shīshī Bakhshī's hostility toward Jalāl al-Dīn Ṭayyib Shāh dated back to his time as a tax collector in Shabānkāra. Shīshī Bakhshī had asked Jalāl al-Dīn Ṭayyib Shāh to marry off his daughter to his son, but the atabek had refused. Shīshī Bakhshī saw this refusal as an offense.[80] He most likely used the political unrest triggered by Abaqa's death to become close to the new Ilkhan and exact revenge on Jalāl al-Dīn Ṭayyib Shāh. It is unclear why Ahmad Tegüder complied with Shīshī Bakhshī's request, because the Ilkhans had received military reinforcements from Shabānkāra's princes against the Salghurids of Shiraz. It should be emphasized that Shīshī Bakhshī was among the great Ilkhanid *amīrs* involved in the power struggle between Arghun and Aḥmad Tegüder. By fulfilling Shīshī Bakhshī's request, the Ilkhan may have hoped to obtain his assistance in his conflict with Arghun.[81]

The assassination of an official and the refusal to pay taxes to the *Dīvān* were usually the major causes of the Ilkhans' retaliation. Recognized as a perfect ruler by Hülegü, Abaqa, and Arghun,[82] Rukn al-Dīn Yūsuf Shāh, the atabek of Yazd, apparently lost his life for this very reason. After Ghazan's accession to the throne, Rukn al-Dīn Yūsuf Shāh neglected to pay a courtesy visit to the *Ordu*. He did not pay the taxes, even though Ghazan sent many *ilchis* to claim three years of unpaid duties from the government of Yazd.[83] According to Naṭanzī, who gives a slightly different version, the city's notables (*akābir*) came to Rashīd al-Dīn to protest about the tyranny (*jawr*) and injustice (*ẓulm*) that they had suffered at the hands of the atabek. Once Ghazan had been informed, he summoned Yūsuf Shāh to the *Ordu*, but he refused to appear.[84] Furious, Ghazan sent the *noyan* Yesüder with two hundred horsemen.[85] According to Aḥmad b. Husayn Jaʿfarī, the author of the *Tārīkh-i jadīd-i Yazd*, Yūsuf Shāh sent his mother, Khurram Turkān, to Yesüder to apologize.[86] As the latter was drinking wine with his companions, he did not respect the atabek's mother, and in his drunkenness, he tore her garment.[87] Yūsuf Shāh then openly opposed Yesüder, saying to his soldiers: "Today is the day of the great holy war (*ghazā'-i akbār*)."[88] Yūsuf Shāh attacked Yesüder at his camp, killing the Mongol *noyans* and most of his men, while taking his wife and sons captive.[89] Gazan sent another *amīr*, Muḥammad Īdājī, with thirty thousand horsemen from Isfahan. Yūsuf Shāh fled with Yesüder's wife and children to Sīstān before the arrival of the army at Yazd. Īdājī spared the population of Yazd, which came under direct Ilkhanid administration with a *darugha* appointed by Ghazan,[90] although the government remained nominally in the name of the atabeks.[91] In Naṭanzī's time, some descendants of the Yazd atabeks were still to be found "living as dervishes and farmers along with a multitude of subjects."[92]

According to Peter Jackson, the atabek sought to assert his sovereignty, because "the rapid changes of sovereign at the center which, coupled with the earlier leniency of Gaikhatu, had surely given an impression of instability and weakness."[93] However, another factor may also have played a role in Rukn al-Dīn Yūsuf Shāh's execution, specifically his ties to Amīr Nawrūz with whom he supposedly spent a year in Khurasan.[94] According to Rashīd al-Dīn, the emirate of Yazd was given by Baidu to Amīr Nawrūz's son, Sulṭān Shāh.[95] It therefore appears that besides the nonpayment of taxes and the desire for independence from the central power, other factors contributed to the execution of Rukn al-Dīn Yūsuf Shāh. The atabek probably supported a group that Ghazan intended to eliminate.

Rukn al-Dīn Yūsuf Shāh's rebellion against the Ilkhanid authority is reminiscent of the Salghurid Saljūq Shāh's revolt after his killing of one of the Mongol *basqaq* of Shiraz, or the princess Abish Khātūn, who had executed Sayyid ʿImād al-Dīn Abū Yuʿlā, the representative of the Ilkhans. However, neither Saljūq Shāh nor Abish Khātūn fostered a desire to expand their territory; they only contested Ilkhanid suzerainty. By contrast, the rebellion of Afrāsiyāb, who was the Hazaraspid atabek of Lur-i Buzurg, was certainly part of the policy of territorial expansion.

Afrāsiyāb had been held hostage at the *Ordu* of Arghun before his designation as the successor of his father Yūsuf Shāh in 1286–7. Unlike his brother Nuṣrat al-Dīn Aḥmad's rule, the historians portray Afrāsiyāb's reign in a negative light.[96] They present him as an oppressive and tyrannical figure who rebelled against the Ilkhanid power. Dissatisfied with Arghun's refusal to annex the region of Kūh Gīlūya to Hazaraspid territory, which had previously been granted to the Hazaraspids by the Salghurid atabek Sunqur b. Mawdūd, Afrāsiyāb occupied Isfahan with his cousin Qizil. They took advantage of the power vacuum left by Arghun's death in 1291 to execute Baidu, Ispahan's tax collector, and capture the city.[97] Afrāsiyāb, who had great political ambitions, dispatched relatives to take control of the regions stretching from Hamadān to the Persian Gulf, as well as Darband.[98] His revolt was finally suppressed by Mongol forces. Afrāsiyāb was taken prisoner and sent to the new Ilkhan, Gaikhatu. Two women of the Ilkhan's household, who had fond memories of the services rendered by Afrāsiyāb's father, Yūsuf Shāh, successfully interceded on his behalf. As a result, Gaikhatu pardoned him and acknowledged his authority. However, a few years later, Ghazan executed Afrāsyāb at the request of the Mongolian *amīr* Horqudaq. When he returned from collecting taxes in Fārs, Horqudaq brought back with him Afrāsiyāb, who had received the title of *sālār* "great *amīr*" and a cavalier cloth (*khilʿat-i savārī*). Horqudaq said that when he sent his agent to collect taxes in Kūh Gīlūya, the population stirred up trouble and claimed that "Afrāsiyāb took this land (*marz*) by his sword (*tīgh*) and his harm (*bāzū*) and they refused to pay *kharāj*."[99] Horqudaq added that Afrāsiyāb had assassinated the *basqaq* Baidu.[100] Ghazan flew into a rage and ordered that the atabek be executed on Dhū l-Ḥijja 28, 695/October 26, 1296.[101] Shortly after Ghazan's enthronement, as we have seen, Horqudaq was sent to Shiraz to investigate a dispute between Malik al-Islam and ʿIzz al-Dīn Muẓaffar in relation to tax collection problems in Fārs.

The Ilkhans did not always condemn the misconduct of their subordinate princes. In some circumstances, they showed pragmatism. For example, Aḥmad Tegüder had tolerated the attitude of Muẓaffar al-Dīn Maḥmūd b. Ṭayyib Shāh, who presided over the disorder raging in the Shabānkāra kingdom. The latter had surrounded himself with scoundrels (*runūd va awbāsh*), who enjoyed pranks like placing cats in women's underwear.[102] According to Shabānkāra'ī, the qadi did not apply Islamic law to marriage and divorce proceedings for three years. Muẓaffar al-Dīn Maḥmūd also indulged in drinking sessions (*majlis-i sharāb*) with his companions.[103] Aḥmad Tegüder was the first Ilkhanid ruler to convert to Islam. Vaṣṣāf has no reservation about the faith of the Ilkhan, who was "adorned with the necklace of Islam" (*qilāda-i islām-rā mutaqallid būd*) and even abstained from wine.[104] Aḥmad Tegüder turned a blind eye to Muẓaffar al-Dīn Maḥmūd b. Ṭayyib Shāh's misdemeanor, because he saw him as a potential ally against the Salghurids. These small local atabeks were usually the first to challenge the power of Shiraz. Nevertheless, Gaikhatu's leniency toward Afrāsiyāb reveals the weakness of his power.

The primary goal of the Mongol conquerors was to impose taxes and to allow trade to go unimpeded. This is why the Qa'ans, particularly Möngke, engaged in a policy of administrative centralization across the vast territory that they had conquered, relying on administrative and military collaboration with the local authorities. As the conquerors' vassals, they could either profit from their obedience or suffer the consequences.[105] The Ilkhans' dominance over all the states that were subservient to them was not expressed in the same way. They most often acted with pragmatism according to their particular interests at the time. The Ilkhanid authority experienced moments of weakness during the power struggles between the blood princes, which resulted in rapid changes of leaders at the head of the Ilkhanate. As already mentioned, several small princes and atabeks who took advantage of these circumstances tried to escape Mongolian rule and even expand their territory, but these hastily planned political ventures were largely unsuccessful and were usually suppressed in blood.

The best way for the vassal rulers to preserve the wealth and autonomy of their kingdoms was to collaborate with the Mongol *Ordu*. In Kirmān, the

Qutlughkhanids maintained good relations with the Ilkhans and enjoyed a long period of autonomy with respect to the central power. However, at the time of Ghazan, when Kirmān suffered political instability, the Qutlughkhanids lost the throne. Ascending to power in 703/1303–4, Quṭb al-Dīn Shāh Jahān refused to pay the sums owed to the *Dīvān* (*muḥaṣṣīlān-i mālhā-i dīvān*).[106] Öljeitü removed him from office and entrusted his position to Nāṣir al-Dīn Muḥammad b. Burhān, who supposedly descended from the Ghurids.[107] Nevertheless, the political stability guaranteed during the long reign of Terken Khātūn (r. 655–81/1257–82) seems to have favored the effective administrative management of Kirmān. Instead, in Fārs, the disastrous policy of the Salghurids led the Ilkhans to intervene very swiftly and directly in the tax affairs of the province. Political unrest combined with the corruption of local notables engaged in tax collection were the root causes of the province's economic downturn.

Notes

Preface

1 Charles Melville, "Concepts of Government and State Formation in Mongol Iran," in *The Coming of the Mongols*, D. Morgan and S. Stewart (eds.) (London: Tauris, 2018), 34; Charles Melville, "Concepts of Government and State Formation in Mongol Iran," in *Iran after the Mongols*, Sussan Babaie (ed.) (London: Tauris, 2019), 36.
2 Jean Aubin, "Liminaire," *Le monde iranien et l'Islam* 4/1 (1971): ix.
3 Aubin, "Liminaire," ix. See the study of Jürgen Paul on Fārs in the pre-Mongol period, "Local and Imperial Rule. Examples from Fārs (9th–10th centuries)," in *Emerging Powers in Eurasian Comparison, 200–1100. Shadows of Empire*, W. Pohl and V. Wieser (eds.) (Leiden: Brill, 2022), 329–52.
4 Charles Melville, "The Caspian Provinces: A World Apart. Three Local Histories of Mazandaran," *IrSt* 33/1–2 (2000): 45.

Introduction

1 Juvaynī/Boyle, *The History of the World Conqueror*, I, 39.
2 As a Chinese dynasty, the Kitans adopted the name Liao. Michal Biran, "The Mongols and Nomadic Identity. The Case of the Kitans in China," in *Nomads as Agents of Cultural Change. The Mongols and Their Eurasian Predecessors*, R. Amitai and M. Biran (eds.) (Honolulu: University of Hawaiʿi Press, 2015), 152–81.
3 Sergey A. Vasyutin, "The Model of the Political Transformation of the Da Liao as an Alternative to the Evolution of the Structure of Authority in the Early Medieval Pastoral Empires of Mongolia," in *Complexity of Interaction along the Eurasian Steppe Zone in the First Millennium CE*, J. Bemmann and M. Schmauder (eds.) (Bonn: Universität Bonn, 2015), 391–436.
4 Thomas T. Allsen, *Mongol Imperialism. The Policies of the Grand Qan Möngke in China, Russia and the Islamic Lands, 1251–1259* (Berkeley: University of California Press, 1987), 7.
5 One of the Mongols' aims in mobilizing the human resources of the occupied territories was to move the populations endowed with technical know-how. In

1221, Chinggis Khan transferred to Mongolia and China a hundred thousand artisans who had been taken prisoner in Transoxiana. Chinese farmers were relocated to Marv, then to Khūī in Azerbaijan, to introduce millet cultivation in those areas. Ḥamd Allāh Mustawfī Qazvīnī, who wrote around 1340, claimed that the people of Khūī were of Chinese descent; see Allsen, *Mongol Imperialism*, 9.

6 On the Kitans and the Jürchens, see Thomas J. Barfield, *Perilous Frontier. Nomadic Empires and China, 221 BC to ad 1757* (Cambridge, MA: Blackwell, 1989), 164–86; Herbert Franke, "The Forest Peoples of Manchuria: Kitans and Jurchens," in *The Cambridge History of the Early Inner Asia*, D. Sinor (ed.) (Cambridge: Cambridge University Press, 1990), 400–23.

7 David M. Farquhar, *The Government of China under Mongolian Rule* (Stuttgart: Franz Steiner, 1990), 3.

8 The Mongolian term *cherig* designates the indigenous contingents who fought in the Mongol armies; see Doerfer, III, n° 1079, 65–70.

9 His first coronation took place in 1249 in Almālīq, south of Lake Balkhash. The princes of the rival lines, the Ögödayids and the Chaghatayids, refused to recognize his enthronement on the pretext that the election of a new Qa'an was to take place in the region of Onan and Kerülen rivers, where Chinggis Khan had been proclaimed head of all the subjugated tribes; see Thomas T. Allsen, "Guard and Government in the Reign of the Grand Qan Möngke," *HJAS* 4/2 (1986): 497.

10 Jean Aubin, *Émirs mongols et vizirs dans les remous de l'acculturation* (Paris: Association pour l'avancement des études iraniennes, 1995), 17. The sources are not clear regarding Hülegü's exact mission. Was it to conquer Islamic lands and then return to Qaraqorum, or was it to found a khanate dependent on the Qa'an? On this matter, see Reuven Amitai, "Hulāgu (Hülegü) Khan," *EIr* 12: 553–4.

11 See Peter Jackson, *The Mongols and the Islamic World. From Conquest to Conversion* (New Haven, CT: Yale University Press, 2017), 125–51.

12 Thomas T. Allsen, *Culture and Conquest in Mongol Eurasia* (Cambridge: Cambridge University Press, 2001), 20–1; Reuven Amitai-Preiss, "Two Notes on the Protocol on Hülegü's Coinage," *Israel Numismatic Journal* 10 (1988–9): 117–28.

13 For a discussion of when Hülegü was awarded this title, see Allsen, *Mongol Imperialism*, 21; Thomas T. Allsen, "Changing Forms of Legitimization in Mongol Iran," in *Rulers from the Steppe. State Formation on the Eurasian Periphery* (Los Angeles: University of Southern California, 1991), 226–7; Thomas T. Allsen, "Notes on Chinese Titles in Mongol Iran," *Mongolian Studies* 14 (1991): 27. Numismatic data that are reliable in establishing the precise date show that the title was used five months after Möngke's death; see David

M. Lang, *Studies in the Numismatic History of Georgia in Transcaucasia* (New York: American Numismatic Society, 1955), 42–3; Michael Weiers, "Münzaufschriften auf Münzen mongolischer Il-Khane aus dem Iran," *The Canada-Mongolian Review* 4/1 (1978): 49. It seems that it was after the capture of Aleppo on Ṣafar 2, 658/January 18, 1260, that sources mentioned the title *īlkhān*; see Reuven Amitai-Preiss, "Evidence for the Early Use of the Title īlkhān among the Mongols," *JRAS* 3/1–3 (1991): 353–61.

14 For the term *il*, see Doerfer, II, n° 653, 194–201. In thirteenth-century Persian sources, the term *īl* accompanied by an auxiliary verb was used to denote an act of submission; see Allsen, "Changing Forms of Legitimization in Mongol Iran," 227.

15 For the term *bulgha*, see Doerfer, II, n° 768, 317–20. For the orders of submission, see Éric Voegelin, "The Mongol Orders of Submission to European Powers, 1245–1255," *Byzantion* 15 (1940–1): 378–413; Denise Aigle, "De la 'non négociation' à l'alliance inaboutie. Réflexions sur la diplomatie entre les Mongols et l'Occident latin," in *Les relations diplomatiques entre le monde musulman et l'Occident latin*, D. Aigle et P. Buresi (eds.), *Oriente moderno* 88/1, 2008, 395–436; Denise Aigle, "La paix selon l'ordre du monde des Mongols," in *Les mots de la paix*, 2017, https://www.islam-medieval.cnrs.fr/Lesmotsdelapaix/ordre-mongol/.

16 Nassima Neggaz, "The Many Deaths of the Last 'Abbāsid Caliph al-Mustaʿṣim bi-llāh (d. 1258)," *JRAS* 30/4 (2020): 585–612.

17 Neggaz, "The Many Deaths of the Last 'Abbāsid Caliph," 590–1.

18 For the religious beliefs of the Mongols, see Shīrīn Bayānī, *Dīn va dawlat dar Īrān-i 'ahd-i Mughūl* (Tihrān: Markaz-i Nashr-i Dānishgāhī, 1988), I, 1–46. The author relies mainly on Latin sources. See also Denise Aigle, *The Mongol Empire between Myth and Reality* (Leiden: Brill, 2014), 107–56.

19 Qur'ān 6: 65.

20 Juvaynī/Qazvīnī, II, 638–9.

21 For the *yasa*, see David O. Morgan, "The 'Great *Yāsā* of Chingiz Khān' and Mongol Law in the Īlkhānate," *BSOAS* 49/1 (1986): 163–76; Denise Aigle, "Le 'grand *yasa*' de Gengis-khan, l'Empire, la culture mongole et la *sharī'a*," *JESHO* 47/1 (2004): 31–79; Denise Aigle, "Mongol Law *versus* Islamic Law: Myth and Reality," in *The Mongol Empire between Myth and Reality* (Leiden: Brill, 2014), 134–56; Denise Aigle, "Yasa," in *The Mongol World*, T. May and M. Hope (eds.) (London: Routledge, 2022), 319–30. See the bibliographical article of David O. Morgan, "The 'Great *Yasa* of Chinggis Khan' Revisited," in *Mongols, Turks and Others. Eurasian Nomads and the Sedentary World*, R. Amitai and M. Biran (eds.) (Leiden: Brill, 2005), 291–308.

22 For the *yarghu*'s practices in Persian sources, see Maʿṣūme Maʿdankan, "Yāsā dar ʿahd-i Īlkhāniān," *Maʿāref* 9/1 (1992): 3–14; Maʿṣūme Maʿdankan, *Ba-yāsā rasīdagān* (Tihrān: Markaz-i Nashr-i Dānishgāhī, 1996).

23 ʿAlā' al-Dawla Simnānī, born in 659/1261, came from a wealthy family of *dīvān* officials who served the Mongol Empire. At the age of fifteen he entered the service of Arghun whom he accompanied in 683/1284 in a campaign against Aḥmad Tegüder. It was during this campaign that he had a mystical revelation and that he decided to return to Simnān to devote himself to a pious life, see Jamal J. Elias, *The Throne Carrier of God. The Life and Thought of Alā' ad-Dawla ad-Simnānī* (Albany: University of New York Press, 1995); Devin DeWeese, "ʿAlā al-Dawla Simnānī's Religious Encounters at the Mongol Court near Tabriz," in *Politics, Patronage and the Transmission of Knowledge in 13th–15th Tabriz*, J. Pfeiffer (ed.) (Leiden: Brill, 2014), 35–76.

24 The first examples are found among the Qutlughkhanids of Kirmān where undated coins were minted in the name of "The Just/the Great/Chīngīz Khān," see Allsen, "Changing Forms of Legitimization in Mongol Iran," 244.

25 Allsen, *Mongol Imperialism*, 71. The same is true of the Sa-Skya dynasty of Tibet, see *Mongol Imperialism*, 71. For the Karts of Herat (1245–1381), see Lawrence Goddard Potter, *The Kart Dynasty of Herat: Religion and Politics in Medieval Iran*, Columbia University, 1992 (unpublished Ph.D thesis); George Lane, *Early Mongol Rule in Thirteenth-Century Iran. A Persian Renaissance* (London: Routledge, 2003), 152–76.

26 On the use of these tablets, see Igor de Rachewiltz, "Two Recently Published P'ai-tzu Discovered in China," *Acta Orientalia Academiae Scientiarum Hungariae* 36/1–3 (1982): 23–7; Baohai Dang, "The Paizi of the Mongol Empire," *Zentralasiatische Studien* 31 (2001): 31–62.

27 Allsen, *Mongol Imperialism*, 70.

28 Allsen, *Mongol Imperialism*, 71.

29 In his general presentation of the regions of the Ilkhanid Empire, George Lane (*Early Mongol Rule*) only scratched the surface of the matter; Kirmān, 102–22; Shiraz, 122–52; Herat, 152–76; for Bagdad, see Hend Gilli-Elewy, *Bagdad nach dem Sturz des Kalifats. Die Geschichte einer Provinz unter ilḫanicher Herrschaft (656–735/1258–1335)* (Berlin: Klaus Schwartz Verlag, 2000); for Anatolia, see Charles Melville, "Anatolia under the Mongols," in *Cambridge History of Turkey*, I, Kate Fleet (ed.) (Cambridge: Cambridge University Press, 2009), 51–101.

30 For the term *yurt*, see Doerfer, IV, n° 1914, 212–16.

31 See John Masson Smith, "Mongol Nomadism and Middle Eastern Geography: Qīshlāqs and Tümens," in *The Mongol Empire & Its Legacy*, R. Amitai-Preiss and D. Morgan (eds.) (Leiden: Brill, 1999), 39–56. For the terms *yaylāq* and *qīshlāq*, see Doerfer, IV, n° 1941, 252–3; III, n° 1496, 479–81.

32 Ann K. S. Lambton, "Mongol Fiscal Administration in Persia (Part 1)," *StIs* 64 (1986): 79–99; Ann K. S. Lambton, "Mongol Fiscal Administration in Persia (Part 2)," *StIs* 65 (1987): 97–123.
33 Lane, *Early Mongol Rule*, 122–52.
34 'Abd al-Rasūl Khayrāndīsh, *Fārsiyān dar barādar-i Mughūlān* (Tihrān: Abādboom, 2016).

1 Notes on the Sources

1 Gabrielle M. Spiegel, "Political Utility in Medieval Historiography: A Sketch," in *The Past as Text: The Theory and Practice of Medieval Historiography* (Baltimore, MD: Johns Hopkins University Press, 1999), 85.
2 Bernard Guénée, *Histoire et culture historique dans l'Occident médiéval* (Paris: Aubier, 1991), 337.
3 Dorothea Krawulsky, *Mongolen Ilkhâne und Ideologie Geschichte* (Beirut: Verlag für islamische Studien, 1989), 29.
4 Igor de Rachewiltz, "Some Remarks on the Dating of *The Secret History of the Mongols*," *Monumenta Serica* 24 (1965): 185–205.
5 Rachewiltz, "Introduction," in *Secret History*, I, xxxvii.
6 Juvaynī/Qazvīnī, *Tārīkh-i jahāngushā*, I, 5; Juvaynī/Boyle, *The History of the World Conqueror*, I, 8.
7 Juvaynī/Qazvīnī, *Tārīkh-i jahāngushā*, I, 4–5; Juvaynī/Boyle, *The History of the World Conqueror*, I, 7.
8 For Rashīd al-Dīn's work, see Stefan Kamola, *Making Mongol History, Rashid al-Din and the Jami' al-tawarikh* (Edinburgh: Edinburgh University Press, 2019).
9 Raschid-eldin, *Histoire des Mongols de la Perse*, ed. and trans. É. Quatremère, reprint (Amsterdam: Oriental Press, 1968), 61–3; David O. Morgan, "Persian Perceptions of Mongols and Europeans," in *Implicit Understandings. Observing, Reporting and Reflecting on the Encounters between Europeans on Others Peoples in the Early Modern Era*, Stuart B. Schwartz (ed.) (Cambridge: Cambridge University Press, 1995), 209.
10 Allsen, *Culture and Conquest in Mongol Eurasia*, 88.
11 Rashīd al-Dīn/Karīmī, *Jāmi' al-tawārīkh*, 173, 178; Allsen, *Culture and Conquest in Mongol Eurasia*, 86.
12 The book was called so because gold was associated with the Chinggisid line, which was characterized as "golden," see Allsen, *Culture and Conquest in Mongol Eurasia*, 88.
13 Allsen, *Culture and Conquest in Mongol Eurasia*, 86.

14 Bar Hebraeus, *Chronicon syriacum*, ed. P. Bedjan (Paris: Maisonneuve, 1890), 521; Bar Hebraeus. *The Chronography of Gregory Abû'l-Faraj (1225–1286).* English translation by Ernest Wallis Budge (London: Oxford University Press, 1932), 444.

15 Denise Aigle, "L'œuvre historiographique de Barhebraeus. Son apport à l'histoire de la période mongole," in *Barhebraeus et la renaissance syriaque*, D. Aigle (ed.), *Parole de l'Orient* 33 (2008): 25–61.

16 Nāṣir al-Dīn Abū 'Abd Allāh Bayḍāvī, *Niẓām al-tawārīkh*, ed. B. Karīmī (Tihrān: Bunyād-i Mawqūfāt-i Duktur Maḥmūd Afshār, 1935).

17 For the cultural importance of this text, see Charles Melville, "From Adam to Abaqa," *StIr* 30 (2001): 67–86 and *StIr* 36 (2007): 7–64.

18 Charles Melville, "The Itineraries of Sultan Öljeitü, 1304–16," *Iran* 28 (1999): 55–70; Melville, "The Īlkhān Öljeitü's Conquest of Gīlān (1307): Rumour and Reality," in *The Mongol Empire & Its Legacy*, R. Amitai-Preiss and D. Morgan (eds.) (Leiden: Brill, 1990), 72–125.

19 Allsen, *Culture and Conquest in Mongol Eurasia*, 100.

20 Allsen, *Culture and Conquest in Mongol Eurasia*, 99–100.

21 Mustawfī Qazvīnī, *Tārīkh-i guzīda*, ed. Ḥusayn Navā'ī (Tihrān: Chāpkhāna-I Firdawsī, 1983).

22 Zayn al-Dīn Qazvīnī, *Dhayl-i Tārīkh-i guzīda*, ed. Īraj Afshār (Tihrān: Chāpkhāna-I Jahān, 1993).

23 Charles Melville, "Ḥamd Allāh Mustawfī's *Ẓafarnāmah* and the Historiography of the Late Ilkhanid Period," in *Iran and Iranian Studies: Essays in Honor of Iraj Afshar*, K. Eslami (ed.) (Princeton, NJ: Princeton University Press, 1998), 1–12.

24 Abū Bakr Quṭbī Aharī, *Tārīkh-i Shaykh Ūvais*, ed. J. B. Loon ('s-Gravenhague: Mouton & Co, 1954), 51.

25 See Bert Fragner, *Persophonie. Regionalität, Identität und Sprachkontakt in der Geschichte Asiens* (Berlin: Das Arabische Buch, 1999), 59–61.

26 As early as 1963, Karl Jahn drew researchers' attention to these texts, see "Study on Supplementary Persian Sources for the Mongol History of Iran," in *Proceeding of the fifth Meeting of the Permanent International Altaic Conference*, D. Sinor (ed.), Uralic and Altaic Series 23 (1963): 197–204.

27 Zekrollah Mohammadi, Amir Hossein Hatami, and Mohsen Parvish, "Persian Identity Aspects in Delgosha's System of Poems based on Shahnameh's Ferdowsi Re-creations," *Literary Text Research* 25/89 (2021): 87–114.

28 Melville, "Between Firdausī and Rashīd al-Dīn," 46. For manuscript tradition, see ibid., 48–50.

29 Charles Melville, "History and Myth: The Persianisation of Ghazan Khan," in *Irano-Turkic Cultural Contacts in the 11th-17th Centuries*, Éva M. Jeremiàs (ed.) (Piliscsaba: The Avicenna Institute of Middle Eastern Studies, [2002] 2003, 142);

Charles Melville, "Gāzān-nāma," *EIr* X:383. The *Ghāzān-nāma* is preserved in an only manuscript at the Library University of Cambridge. Now the text is edited, see Nūr al-Dīn Azhdarī, *Ghāzān-nāma*, ed. Maḥmūd Dadbbirī (Tihrān:, Mawqūfāt Ductur Maḥmūd Afshār,1381sh).

30 Melville, "Persian Local Histories: Views from the Wings," 7–14.

31 Mimi Hanaoka, *Authority and Identity in Medieval Islamic Historiography: Persian Histories from the Peripheries* (New York: Cambridge University Press, 2016).

32 The first comprehensive examination of Persian historical writing is *Persian Local Histories*, the special issue of *Iranian Studies* 33/12 (2000) edited by Charles Melville and Jürgen Paul, and more recently, Hanaoka, *Authority and Identity.*

33 Jean Aubin, "Un chroniqueur méconnu, Šabānkāra'ī," *Studia Iranica* 10/1 (1981): 213.

34 Ibn Zarkūb, *Shīrāz-nāma*, ed. Ismā'īl Vā'iẓ Javāḍī (Tihrān: Intishārāt-i Farhang-i Īrān, 1971–2). Biographical data in *Shadd al-izār*, 317–18.

35 The *faḍā'il*'s books and the geographical data are issued from the hadiths and historical texts, see R. Sellheim, "Faḍīla," *EI*[2] 2: 247–8.

36 Ibn Zarkūb organizes the biographies into several *ṭabaqāt* each devoted to a great religious figure of the region (Shaykh Kabīr, Murshid al-Dīn Abū Isḥāq Kāzarūnī, Abū Shujā' Maqārīḍī, Rūzbihān Baqlī Shīrāzī, Najīb al-Dīn Buzghush) and their contemporary shaykhs.

37 Ibn Zarkūb, *Shīrāz-nāma*, 108.

38 Mu'īn al-Dīn Abū l-Qāsim Junayd Shīrāzī, *Shadd al-izār*, ed. Muḥammad Qazvīnī (Tihrān: Chāpkhāna-i Majlis, 1948–9). Written in Arabic around 791/1389, his son 'Isā translated the work into Persian under the title *Hazār mazār* at the request of a friend in order to make the text accessible to those unfamiliar with Arabic.

39 Ja'far b. Muḥammad Ḥusaynī Ja'farī, *Tārīkh-i Yazd*, ed. Īraj Afshār (Tihrān: Bungāh-i Tarjuma wa Nashr-i Kitāb, 1959–60), "Muqaddima-i mu'allif," 6.

40 Aḥmad b. Ḥusayn b. 'Alī Kātib, *Tārīkh-i jadīd-i Yazd*, ed. Īraj Afshār (Tihrān: Intishārat-i Ibn Sīnā, 1966). On these texts, see Isabel Miller, "Local History in Ninth-Fifteenth Century Yazd: The *Tārīkh-i Jadīd-i Yazd*," *Iran* 27 (1989): 75–9.

41 Muḥammad Mufīd Mustawfī Bāfqī, *Jāmi'-i mufīdī*, ed. Īraj Afshār, 3 vols. (Tihrān: Intishārat-i Asāṭir, 2006).

42 Miller, "Local History in Ninth-Fifteenth Century Yazd," 79.

43 Maḥmūd Kutubī, *Tārīkh-i Āl-i Muẓaffar*, ed. 'Alī Navā'ī (Tihrān: Kitābfurūshī-i Ibn Sinā, 1955–6).

44 Charles Melville (ed.), *Persian Historiography* (London: Tauris, 2012), 205–6.

45 See Judith Pfeiffer, "'A Turgid History of the Mongol Empire in Persia'. Epistemological Reflections Concerning a Critical Edition of Vaṣṣāf's *Tajziyat al-amṣār wa tazjiyat al-aʿṣār*," in *Theoretical Approaches to the Transmission and Edition of Oriental Manuscripts*, J. Pfeiffer and M. Kropp (eds.) (Beirut: Orient-Institut, 2007), 107–29.

46 Vaṣṣāf, *Tajziyat al-amṣār va tazjiyat al-aʿṣār*, lithograph (Bombay, 1852).

47 There are 160 manuscripts in many libraries, Pfeiffer, "'A Turgid History of the Mongol Empire,'" 107.

48 Shabānkāraʾī, *Majmaʿ al-ansāb*, ed. Mīr Hāshim Muḥaddith (Tihrān: Amīr Kabīr, 1984).

49 Jean Aubin, "Un chroniqueur méconnu, Šabānkāraʾī," *Studia Iranica* 10/1 (1981): 213–24; Mīr Hāshim Muḥaddith, "Muqaddima," in Shabānkāraʾī, *Majmaʿ al-ansāb*, 5–6; Muḥsin Jaʿfarī Madhhab, "Dhayl-i Majmaʿ al-ansāb-i Shabānkāraʾī," *Āʾina-i mirāth* (2005): 249–552; Edmund C. Bosworth and Peter Jackson, "Shabānkāraʾī," *EI*[2] 9: 63–4; Denise Aigle, "Shabānkāraʾī," *EIr*, online edition.

50 Aubin, "Un chroniqueur méconnu, Šabānkāraʾī," 153.

51 Ḥāfiẓ-i Abrū, *Jughrāfiyā*, ed. Ṣādiq Sajjād (Tihrān: Mirāth-i Maktūb, 1977).

52 Charles Melville and Maria Subtelny, "Ḥāfeẓ-e Abru," *EIr* 11: 507–9.

53 Charles Melville, "Ḥamd-Allāh Mostawfi," *EIr* 11: 631–63; Denise Aigle, "Introduction," in Ḥamd Allāh b. Abī Bakr b. Zayn al-Dīn Ḥamd al-Mustawfī Qazvīnī, *Nuzhat al-qulūb*. Facsimile Copy of the Original Manuscript No. 4517, Fatih Library (Istanbul), copied in 855 A. H. (Tihrān: Mirath-i Maktūb, 2021), 5–12.

54 For the hagiographical genre in Iran, see the remarks of Jürgen Paul, "Hagiographic Literature in Persia and Central Asia," *EIr* 11: 536–9; Denise Aigle, *Saints hommes de Chiraz et du Fārs. Pouvoir, société et lieux de sacralité (X*[e]*-XV*[e] *s.)* (Leiden: Brill, 2023), 27–46.

55 Jean Aubin, "Introduction," in *Matériaux pour la biographie de Shah Niʿmatullah Wali Kermani*, ed. J. Aubin (Paris: Institut français de recherche en Iran, 1956), 1.

56 Aubin, "Introduction," 1.

57 Aubin, "Introduction," 1.

58 Jean Aubin, *Deux sayyids de Bam au XV*[e] *siècle. Contribution à l'histoire de l'Iran timouride* (Wiesbaden: Franz Steiner Verlag, 1956).

59 Shivan Mahendrarajah, *The Sufi Saint of Jam: History, Religion and Politics of a Sunni Shrine in Shiʿi Iran* (Cambridge: Cambridge University Press (Cambridge Studies in Islamic Civilization), 2021).

60 Aigle, *Saints hommes de Chiraz et du Fārs. Pouvoir, société et lieux de sacralité (Xe-XVe s.).*

2 Establishing and Governing an Empire

1 Ibn al-Athīr, *Chronicon*, ed. K. J. Tornberg, 12 vols (Leiden: Brill, 1851–76), XII, 233–5. Translation Bertold Spuler, *History of the Mongols*, translated from the German by Helga and Stuart Drummond (Berkeley: University of California Press, 1972), 31.

2 Thomas T. Allsen, "Population Movements in Mongol Eurasia," in *Nomads as Agents of Cultural Change*, 119.

3 Allsen, "Population Movements in Mongol Eurasia," 143.

4 David O. Morgan, *The Mongols* (Oxford: Blackwell, 1986); Thomas T. Allsen, "The Rise of the Mongolian Empire and Mongolian Rule in North China," in *The Cambridge History of China*, 6, *Alien Regimes and Border States, 907–1368*, H. Franke and D. Twitchett (eds.) (Cambridge: Cambridge University Press, 1994), 321–413.

5 David O. Morgan, "Who Ran the Mongol Empire?" *JRAS* 2 (1982): 124–36; David O. Morgan, "Mongol or Persian: The Government of Īlkhānid Iran," *Harvard Middle Eastern and Islamic Review* 3 (1996): 62–76.

6 See Thomas T. Allsen, "The Yuan Dynasty and the Uighurs in Turfan in the 13th Century," in *China Among Equals: The Middle Kingdom and its Neighbours, 10th–14th Centuries*, M. Rossabi (ed.) (Berkeley: University of California Press, 1983), 243–80; Michael R. Drompp, "Strategics of Cohesion and Control in the Türk and Uyghur Empires," in *Complexity of Interaction along the Eurasian Steppe Zone*, 437–51.

7 Michal Biran, *The Qara Khitai Empire in Eurasian History: Between China and Islam* (Cambridge: Cambridge University Press, 2005), 175–99; Michal Biran, "The Qarakhanids' Eastern Exchange: Preliminary Notes on the Silk Roads in the Eleventh and Twelfth Centuries," in *Complexity of Interaction along the Eurasian Steppe Zone*, 575–95.

8 *Secret History* § 263; Thomas T. Allsen, "Maḥmūd Yalavač," in *In the Service of the Khan. Eminent Personalities of the Early Mongol-Yüan Period (1200–1300)*, Igor de Rachewiltz, Hok Lam Chan, Ch'i-Ch'ing Hsiao, and Peter W. Geier (eds.) (Wiesbaden: Harrassowitz Verlag, 1993), 121–31.

9 The province of Bukhara designates here all of Transoxiana that fell under Mongol administration after the capture of Samarqand.

10 Yelü Ahai was one of the first supporters of the future Great Qa'an. Subsequently, he played a leading military role on the Sino-Mongolian border. He then became governor of the province of Bukhara. His son took over so that the administration of the region remained in their hands for more than twenty years.

11 Paul Buell, "Sino-Khitan Administration in Mongol Bukhara," *Journal of Asian History* 13/2 (1979): 121–51.
12 In Islamic sources, this title has become a personal name. They talk about Tūshā the *bāsqāq*, see Juvaynī/Qazvīnī, *Tārīkh-i jahāngushā,* I, 83–4. On the title *t'ai-shih* and his use by the Mongols and in Chinese sources, see Doerfer, I, n° 249, 372–4.
13 Allsen, *Mongol Imperialism*, 5–6; Michal Biran, "The Mongol Transformation: From the Steppe to Eurasian Empire," *Medieval Encounters* 10/1–3 (2004): 349.
14 Biran, "The Mongol Transformation," 346–58.
15 *Secret History* § 202–8.
16 On the Mongol terms "*yeke jarquchi*" (Persian, *yārghūchī-i buzurg*; Chinese, *ta-tuan-shih-kuan*), see Igor de Rachewiltz, "Introduction," *Secret History* 1: xxxvii; "Commentary," II, 767, 77; on the Mongol term "*jarqu*(*chi*)" (Persian, *yāghūchī*), see Doerfer, IV, n° 1785, 64–6; Igor de Rachewiltz, "Commentary," II, 771, 773; Florence Hodous, "Jarqu and Jarquchin," in *The Mongol World*, 331–40. On Shigi Qutuqu, see Paul Ratchevsky, "Sigi-Qutuqu, ein mongolische Gefolgsmann im 12.-13. Jahrhundert," *Central Asiatic Journal* 10/2 (1965): 87–120.
17 See Thomas T. Allsen, "Sharing Out the Empire: Apportioned Lands under the Mongols," in *Nomads in the Sedentary World*, A. M. Kazanov and A. Wink (eds.) (Richmond: Curzon, 2001), 172–90. The generic term in Mongolian for such "shares" was *qubi*, "Sharing Out the Empire: Apportioned Lands under the Mongols,", 176.
18 *Secret History* § 203.
19 *Secret History* § 263. This paragraph of *The Secret History of the Mongols* is important on the administrative structures set up by Chinggis Khan in the conquered provinces; see Rachewiltz, "Commentary," II, 961–4.
20 Morgan, "Mongol or Persian: The Government of Īlkhānid Iran," 68.
21 The population census was not only intended to establish the amount of taxes and raise troops but also to identify the people who could contribute their knowledge in terms of scholarship and techniques. See Allsen, *Mongol Imperialism*, 116–43.
22 Hebraeus, *Chronicon Syriacum*, 488; Budge, 416.
23 From a silver coin minted around 1244–5, see George Lane, "Arghun Aqa: Mongol Bureaucrat," *IrSt* 32/4 (1999): 461; Peter Jackson, "Arghūn Aqa," *EIr* 2: 401–2. The title "*ulugh manqul ulus bek*" is Turkic equivalent to Mongol "*yeke monggol ulus noyan*."
24 For the administrative structure of the empire, see Jackson, *The Mongols and the Islamic World*, 107–11.

25 Ann K. S. Lambton, "Kharādj," *EI*[2] 4: 1066–85. The author, however, gives too much credit to Rashīd al-Dīn's information on Ghazan's reforms.

26 Allsen, *Mongol Imperialism*, 144; see the fiscal change under the Great Qa'ans, Allsen, *Mongol Imperialism*, 144–87.

27 Juvaynī/Qazvīnī, *Tārīkh-i jahāngushā*, III, 74.

28 Allsen, *Mongol Imperialism*, 80–5.

29 On Menggeser, see Allsen, *Mongol Imperialism*, 93–4.

30 This function dates back to Han and Chin times; see Charles O. Hucker, *A Dictionary of Official Titles in Imperial China* (Standford, CA: Standford University Press, 1985), 126–7. In *Secret History*, the term *chingsang* is used in § 132, see Igor de Rachewiltz, "Commentary," II, 896. See also Doerfer, I, n° 184, 310–12. In Yüan China, *ch'en-hsiang* refer to "great advisor (of central secretariat);" David M. Farquhar, *The Government of China under Mongolian Rule* (Stuttgart: Franz Steiner, 1990), 170, 368. On Chinese titles in Ilkhanate, see Allsen, "Notes on Chinese Titles in Mongol Iran," 27–39.

31 Allsen, *Mongol Imperialism*, 93–6.

32 Allsen, "Guard and Government," 502. In Persian sources, the secretariat of Khurasan is mentioned by the term *dīvān*.

33 Buell, "Sino-Khitan Administration in Mongol Bukhara," 147.

34 On the contacts between the divanians and the Mongols at the time of Ögödei and Möngke, see Aubin, *Émirs mongols et vizirs persans*, 19–20, 25–6.

35 Allsen, *Mongol Imperialism*, 107.

36 This dual administration has its roots in the Chinese system of local government introduced by Shi Huang Ti, the first emperor who unified China (221 av. J.-C. – 210 av. J.-C.), see Donald Ostrowski, *Muscovy and the Mongols. Cross-cultural Influences on the Steppe Frontier, 1304–1589* (Cambridge: Cambridge University Press, 1998), 36.

37 *Secret History* § 274.

38 *Secret History* § 274. On use of these terms in *Secret History*, see Rachewiltz, "Commentary," II, 961–2, 1003, 1009; on *tammachin*, "Commentary," 1002, 1003, 1007.

39 On the Mongol term *darugha* (*dārūghāchī* in Persian sources), see Doerfer, I, n° 193, 319–23. On the *darughachi*, see Vladimir Barthold, *Turkestan Down to the Mongol Invasion* (London: Luzac, 1977[4]), 401; Morgan, *The Mongols*, 109, 114, 142; Francis W. Cleaves, "DaruΓa and Gerege," *HJAS* 16/1–2 (1953): 237–55; Farquhar, *The Government of China under Mongolian Rule*, 3, 7, 23, 41; Allsen, *Mongol Imperialism*, 7, 72–3; Elizabeth Endicott-West, *Mongolian Rule in China. Local Administration in the Yuan Dynasty* (Cambridge, MA: Harvard University Press, 1989), 2–3, 8, 17–8. In Islamic sources, the term *basqaq* of Turkic origin is used as the equivalent of *darughachi*. The Arabic term *shiḥna* is also used as

the equivalent of *darughachi*, but not on a regular basis; it can also designate the *yarghuchi*, the judge. On the term *basqaq*, see Doerfer, II, n° 691, 241–3. It is difficult to determine precisely the functions performed by the characters designated by these various names because the meaning of these terms varied according to periods and regions. On the terms *tamma*, *darugha*, and *basqaq* see Donald Ostrowski, "The *tamma* and the Dual-Administrative Structure of the Mongol Empire," *BSOAS* 61/2 (1998): 262–77. Donald Ostrowski (270) points out the influence in local Mongol administration of Chinese dual system which called on two governors, one for civil affairs (*t'ai-shou*) and the other for military affairs (*wei-t'ou*). According to Donald Ostrowski (ibid., 272), the *basqaq* seems to be more or less the equivalent of the military governor and the *darughachi* that of the civil governor. Discussion of terms used in Persian sources to designate tax collectors, Yazdān Farrukhī, *Barrasī-i sayr-i taḥvilāt-i dīvān-i sālārī-i mughūl-hā dar Īrān* (Tihrān: Amīr Kabīr, 2017), 43–6.

40 Cleaves, "DaruΓa and Gerege," 72.

41 On Kirmān, see Lane, *Early Mongol Rule*, 152–76.

42 Qashānī, *Tārīkh-i Ūljaytū*, 49, 198. Najīb al-Dawla died in 715/1315; his coffin was transported to Tabriz where they prayed for him according to the rite of the Muslims (*rasm-i musalmānān*). According to Bertold Spuler (*Die Mongolen in Iran. Politik, Verwaltung und Kultur der Ilchanzeit 1220–1350* (Berlin: Akademie-Verlag, 1955), 339), he died in Shiraz. He probably confuses him with another Najīb al-Dawla who was sent by Arghun to Khurasan to put down a rebellion; see Walter J. Fischel, *Jews in the Economic Political Life of Medieval Islam* (London: Royal Asiatic Society, 1968), 105.

43 Bar Hebræus explains how careers are made under the Ilkhans. He says that whoever approaches a Mongol and presents him with some money is given the coveted position, *Chronicon Syriacum*, 575.

44 See the remarks of Yazdān Farrukhī, *Barrasī-i sayr-i taḥwilāt-i dīvān*, 57, footnote 2.

45 Aubin, *Émirs mongols et vizirs persans*, 83.

46 At that time, only Khurasan was under the direct rule of the Great Qa'an. Denise Aigle, "Persia under Mongol Domination. The Effectiveness and Failings of a Dual Administrative System," *Bulletin d'études orientales* 57 (2006–7): 65–78. Table of dual administration at the administrative and judicial level in Yazdān Farrukhī, *Barrasī-i sayr-i taḥwilāt-i dīvān*, 210.

47 See Ann K. S. Lambton, *Continuity and Change in Medieval Persia* (London: Tauris, 1988), 50–61.

48 Discussion on the functions of *vizīr* and *ṣāḥib-dīvān*, Yazdān Farrukhī, *Barrasī-i sayr-i taḥwilāt-i dīvān*, 58.

49 In 1286, after Arghun's second enthronement, Qubilai conferred him the title of "Great Chancellor" (*ch'eng-hsiang*), see Aubin, *Émirs mongols et vizirs persans*, 38.
50 Hebræus, *Chronicon Syriacum*, 560; Budge, 477.
51 Lambton, *Continuity and Change*, 55.
52 See Aubin, *Émirs mongols et vizirs persans*, 29–33, 37–8, 40; Farrukhī, *Barrasī-i sayr-i taḥwilāt-i dīvān*, 123–33.
53 Aubin, *Émirs mongols et vizirs persans*, 22–4, 46–8, 58–9.
54 We also sometimes encounter the term *valī*.
55 Rashīd al-Dīn/Alizade, *Jāmiʿ al-tawārīkh*, III, 102–3; Rashīd al-Dīn/Rawshan and Mūsavī, *Jāmiʿ al-tawārīkh*, II, 939.
56 Rashīd al-Dīn/Alizade, *Jāmiʿ al-tawārīkh*, III, 103; Rashīd al-Dīn/Rawshan and Mūsavī, *Jāmiʿ al-tawārīkh*, II, 938.
57 See I. P. Petrushevsky, "The Socio-Economic Condition of Iran under the Īl-Khāns," in *Cambridge History of Iran*, V, *The Saljuq and Mongol Periods*, J. A. Boyle (ed.) (Cambridge: Cambridge University Press, 1968), 483–537; Lambton, "Mongol Fiscal Administration in Persia (Part 1)," 79–99; Lambton, "Mongol Fiscal Administration in Persia (Part 2)," 97–123; Lambton, *Continuity and Change*, 185–220. New taxes were imposed, notably the *qubchur*; on the evolution of this tax, see Lambton, "Mongol Fiscal Administration in Persia (Part 2)," 85–95; David O. Morgan, "Ḳubčūr," *EI*[2] 3: 299.
58 Vaṣṣāf, *Tajziyat al-amṣār va tazjiyat al-aʿṣār*, 161. He uses *qufchūr* for *qubchur*.
59 Vladimir Minorsky, "Pūr-i Bahā's 'Mongol' Ode," *Iranica* (1964): 299.
60 The right of residence existed before the Mongol period, but in much smaller proportions. Ghazan abolished it, but it was reinstated under Abū Saʿīd; see Petrushevsky, "The Socio-economic Condition," 535–6.
61 See Petrushevsky, "The Socio-economic Condition," 515–20; Ann K. S. Lambton, *Landlord and Peasant in Persia* (London: Tauris, 1953), 77–80; Lambton, *Continuity and Change*, 97–129; Jean Aubin, "La propriété foncière en Azerbaydjan sous les Mongols," *Le Monde iranien et l'Islam* 4 (1975–6): 79–132.
62 Lambton, *Continuity and Change*, 118.
63 Voir Kazuhiko Shiraiwa, "*Īnjū* in the *Jāmiʿ al-Tavārīkh* of Rashīd al-Dīn," *Acta Orientalia Academiae Scientiarum Hungaricae* 42/2–3 (1988): 371–6.
64 Lambton, *Continuity and Change*, 118.
65 Shabānkāraʾī, *Majmaʿ al-ansāb*, 296.
66 Among the documents discovered in the mausoleum of Ardabīl, a large number date from the Mongol period. These are most often private acts that reflect the precariousness of property titles, so much formulas guaranteeing the rights of the owner were inserted into the contracts, Monika Gronke, "Les notables iraniens à lěpoque mongole. Aspects économiques et sociaux d'après les documents du

sanctuaire d'Ardébil," in *Documents de l'Islam médiéval. Nouvelles perspectives de recherche* (Cairo: Institut français d'archéologie orientale, 1991), 121.

67 Lambton, *Landlord and Peasant in Persia*, 78. She also cites the case of the sayyids Ṭabāṭabā'ī whose property constituted in *waqf* in Fārs was transformed into *injü* of the *Dīvān*, Lambton, *Landlord and Peasant in Persia*, 78–9.

68 See Jean Aubin, "Le patronage culturel en Iran sous les Ilkhans. Une grande famille de Yazd," *Le Monde iranien et l'Islam* 3 (1975): 107–18.

69 Birgitt Hoffmann, "The Gates of Piety and Charity: Rašīd al-Dīn Faḍl Allāh as Founder of Pious Endowments," in *L'Iran face à la domination mongole*, D. Aigle (ed.) (Tihrān: Institut français de recherche en Iran, 1997), 198–201; Birgitt Hoffmann, *Waqf im mongolischen Iran. Rašiduddīns Sorge um Nachrum und Seelenheil* (Stuttgart: Franz Steiner Verlag, 2000); Birgitt Hoffmann, "In Pursuit of *Memoria* and Salvation: Rashīd al-Dīn and His Rab'i Rashīdī," in *Politics, Patronage and the Transmission of Knowledge in 13th–15th Century Tabriz*, 176.

70 Vaṣṣāf, *Tajziyat al-amṣār va tazjiyat al-a'ṣār*, 142.

71 Petrushevsky, "The Socio-economic Condition," 494–5; Lambton, *Continuity and Change*, 83–99, 210–16.

72 Aubin, "La propriété foncière," 94–5. See also Charles Melville, "Wolf or Shepherd? Amir Chupan's Attitude to Government," in *The Court of the Il-Khans, 1290–1340*, J. Raby and T. Fitzherbert (eds.) (Oxford: Oxford University Press, 1996), 82.

73 Charles Melville, "The Itineraries of Sultan Öljeitü, 1304–16," *Iran* 28 (1990): 60.

74 Melville, "The Itineraries of Sultan Öljeitü, 1304–16," 61.

75 Morgan, "Mongol or Persian: The Government of Īlkhānid Iran," 73.

76 Aubin, *Émirs mongols et vizirs persans*, 83.

3 Competent Governance under Abū Bakr Salghur

1 Stefan Kamola, "Salghurid History in the *Jāmi' al-Tawārīkh*: A Preliminary Exploration of Its Composition and Transmission," in *New Approaches to Ilkhanid History*, T. May, B. Dashdondog and Ch. P. Atwood (eds.) (Leiden: Brill, 2021), 124.

2 Edmond C. Bosworth, "Salghurides," *EI²* VIII: 1012–3; Bertold Spuler, "Atābakān-e Fārs," *EIr* 2: 895–6. The length of the reign of the first Salghurid rulers is difficult to establish. The sources are contradictory, while numismatics does not make it possible to provide dates with any degree of certainty.
On the Salghurids in Fārs see, Erdogam Merçil, *Fars atabegleri salgurlular* (Ankara: Basimevi, 1975); 'Abbās Iqbāl Āshtiyānī, *Tārīkh-i Mughūl* (Tihrān: Amīr

Kabīr, 1966–7), 379–85; Karāmat-Allāh Afsar, *Tārīkh-i bāft-i qadīmī-i Shīrāz* (Tihrān: Nashr-i Qatra, 1974), 59–88.

3 *Morals Pointed and Tales Adorned. The Bustan of Sa'di*, translated by G. M. Wickens (Toronto: University of Toronto Press, 1974), 34.

4 Faṣīḥ Khwāfī, *Mujmal*, II, 252.

5 Vaṣṣāf, *Tajziyat al-amṣār va tazjiyat al-a'ṣār*, 149. Numismatic sources attest that he ruled Fārs from 545/1150 to 1151. David Durand-Guédy, "1147: The Battle of Qara-Tegin and the Rise of Azarbayjan," *Der Islam* 92/1 (2015): 184 and footnote 79; Muḥammad 'Abd Allāh al-Sayyid Yūnis, *al-Tadāwul al-naqdī fī madīnat Shīrāz mundhu bidāyat al-dawlat al-salghūriyya wa ḥattā nihāyat al-dawlat al-muẓaffariyya*, Doctoral dissertation, University of Cairo, 2010, 25–6.

6 Sources give different dates. According to Shabānkāra'ī (*Majma' al-ansāb*, 183), he died in 570/1174–5, according to Ibn Zarkūb (*Shīrāz-nāma*, 74) and Vaṣṣāf (150) he died in 571/1175–6.

7 Shabānkāra'ī, *Majma' al-ansāb*, 183.

8 Vaṣṣāf, *Tajziyat al-amṣār va tazjiyat al-a'ṣār*, 150.

9 Ibn Zarkūb, *Shīrāz-nāma*, 73.

10 Ibn Zarkūb, *Shīrāz-nāma*, 73–4; Vaṣṣāf, *Tajziyat al-amṣār va tazjiyat al-a'ṣār*, 150; Shabānkāra'ī, *Majma' al-ansāb*, 182–3.

11 Bayḍāvī, *Niẓām al-tawārīkh*, 122.

12 Vaṣṣāf, *Tajziyat al-amṣār va tazjiyat al-a'ṣār*, 150.

13 *Shīrāz-nāma* (74) and Vaṣṣāf (150) present roughly the same version of the facts. Tughril b. Sunqur is said to have been taken prisoner by Tekla in the Fāl region. According to these two authors Tekla died in 591/1195. According to Mustawfī Qazvīnī (*Tārīkh-i guzīda*, 504) Tughril b. Sunqur succeeded his cousin Tekla, but he came into conflict with 'Izz al-Dīn Sa'd b. Zangī who took him prisoner. Tughril b. Sunqur fell in battle in 599/1202–3. *Mujmal* (II, 679) give this date for Sa'd b. Zangī's intronization.

14 Bayḍavī, *Niẓām al-tawārīkh*, 87.

15 He must therefore have reigned only a few months; it is necessary to remove the name of Tughril from the list of Salghurid rulers that appeared in many works. Edmond C. Bosworth points out this error in his article on the Salghurids, *EI*[2] 8: 10.

16 See chapter on the sources.

17 Sharaf al-Dīn Ibrāhīm b. Ṣadr al-Dīn Rūzbihān, *Tuḥfat ahl al-'irfān fī dhikr sayyid al-aqṭāb Rūzbihān*, in *Rūzbihān-nāma*, M. Dānish-Pazhūh (ed.) (Tihrān: Intishārat-i Anjuman-i Āthār-i millī, 1347sh./1969), 63.

18 b. Ṣadr al-Dīn Rūzbihān, *Tuḥfat ahl al-'irfān*, 63.

19 b. Ṣadr al-Dīn Rūzbihān, *Tuḥfat ahl al-'irfān*, 63.

20 Sources differ on the course of events between the reign of Tekla and that of Sa'd b. Zangī, Spuler, "Atābakān-e Fārs," 895.

21 Bayḍāvī, *Niẓām al-tawārīkh*, 122; Ibn Zarkūb, *Shīrāz-nāma*, 75–6; Mustawfī Qazvīnī, *Tārīkh-i guzīda*, 505.

22 Description of Sa'd b. Zangī's rule and expansive policy by Khayrāndīsh, *Fārsiyān dar barādar-i Mughūlān*, 55–62.

23 Ibn Zarkūb, *Shīrāz-nāma*, 75. On the strategic function of Sīrjān, see Jean Aubin, "La question de Sīrǧān au XIIIe siècle," *Studia Iranica* 6/2 (1977): 285–90.

24 Bayḍāvī, *Niẓām al-tawārīkh*, 122; Ibn Zarkūb, *Shīrāz-nāma*, 75; Vaṣṣāf, *Tajziyat al-amṣār va tazjiyat al-a'ṣār*, 151; Shabānkāra'ī, *Majma' al-ansāb*, 183.

25 Ibn al-Athīr, *al-Kāmil fī l-tārīkh*, XII, 316, 319.

26 Bayḍavī, *Niẓām al-tawārīkh*, 122; Mustawfī Qazvīnī, *Tārīkh-i guzīda*, 505; Vaṣṣāf, *Tajziyat al-amṣār va tazjiyat al-a'ṣār*, 153; Shabānkāra'ī, *Majma' al-ansāb*, 183–4.

27 Spuler, "Atābakān-e Fārs," 895.

28 Bayḍavī (123) gives Malik Khātūn; Vaṣṣāf, *Tajziyat al-amṣār va tazjiyat al-a'ṣār*, 154.

29 Vaṣṣāf, *Tajziyat al-amṣār va tazjiyat al-a'ṣār*, 154. *Shīrāz-nāma* (76) refers to Safīd-i Nawbanjān. Rashīd al-Dīn/Rawshan and Mūsavī, I, 433.

30 Sa'dī, *Būstān*, translation by Homa Katouzian, "Sa'dī on Love and Morals," in *The Coming of the Mongols*, 96.

31 Sa'dī dedicated his *Būstān* and *Gūlistān* to Abū Bakr b. Sa'd and Sa'd b. Abū Bakr, respectively, and his pen name derived from the names of his patrons.

32 Sources differ on the exact dates of his reign. All agree in giving as the date of his death Jumādā I or II 658, except Vaṣṣāf (180) which gives 659, the date retained by Ann K. S. Lambton ("Shīrāz," *EI*[2] 9: 492). Edmond C. Bosworth ("Salghurides," *EI*[2] 8: 1013) believes that Abū Bakr's dates are 628–58. Khayrāndīsh (*Fārsiyān dar barādar-i mughūlān*, 65) gives as dates of reign 628–59, which must now be retained.

33 Bayḍavī, *Niẓām al-tawārīkh*, 88; Ibn Zarkūb, *Shīrāz-nāma*, 80; Jean Aubin, "Les princes d'Ormuz du XIIIe au xve siècle," *Journal Asiatique* (1953): 81.

34 Jean Aubin, "La ruine de Sīrāf et les routes du golfe Persique aux XIe et XIIe siècles," *Cahiers de civilisation médiévale* 2/3 (1959): 295–301; Jean Aubin, "La survie de Shîlâu et la route du Khunj-o-Fâl," *Iran* 7 (1969): 21–37.

35 After Salghurid conquest, Qays was named *dawlat-khāna-i islām*, Aubin, "Les princes d'Ormuz," 81.

36 *Nuzhat al-qulūb*, 185–6. Ralph Kauz has dedicated a detailed article to the story of Qays, "The Maritime Trade of Kish during the Mongol Period," in *Beyond the Legacy of Genghis Khan*, L. Komaroff (ed.) (Leiden: Brill, 2006), 51–67.

37 Baḥrayn was held by the *amīr* Muḥammad b. Muḥammad b. 'Alī Mājid; he was removed by Abū Bakr, Vaṣṣāf, *Tajziyat al-amṣār va tazjiyat al-a'ṣār*, 179.

38 Qiu Yihao, "Background and Aftermath of Fakhr al-Dīn al-Ṭībī's Voyage: A Reexamination of the Interaction between the Ikhanate and the Yuan at the Beginning of the Fourteenth Century," in *New Approaches to Ilkhanid History*, 150, footnote 13.
39 Qaṭīf is a large Arabian oasis located on the southern shore of the Persian Gulf along the Bay of Tārūt, see George Rentz, "al-Qaṭīf," *EI*[2] 5: 794–6.
40 Vaṣṣāf, *Tajziyat al-amṣār va tazjiyat al-a'ṣār*, 179.
41 Vaṣṣāf, *Tajziyat al-amṣār va tazjiyat al-a'ṣār*, 179.
42 Vaṣṣāf, *Tajziyat al-amṣār va tazjiyat al-a'ṣār*, 179. Aubin, "Les princes d'Ormuz," 81; Spuler, *Die Mongolen in Iran*, 141–2.
43 Vaṣṣāf, *Tajziyat al-amṣār va tazjiyat al-a'ṣār*, 178; Aubin, "Les princes d'Ormuz," 81.
44 On the relations between the princes of Hormuz and the Salghurids after the occupation of the island, see Aubin, "Les princes d'Ormuz," 82–3.
45 Ibn Zarkūb, *Shīrāz-nāma*, 80. According to 'Abbās Iqbāl Āshtiyānī (*Tārīkh-i Mughūl*, 387), he was nicknamed *Sulṭān al-baḥr va-l-barr.*
46 Aubin, "Les princes d'Ormuz," 84.
47 Aubin, "Les princes d'Ormuz," 84.
48 Junayd Shīrāzī, *Shadd al-izār*, 218.
49 *Morals Pointed and Tales Adorned. The Bustan of Sa'di*, 10.
50 Vaṣṣāf, *Tajziyat al-amṣār va tazjiyat al-a'ṣār*, 156.
51 Vaṣṣāf, *Tajziyat al-amṣār va tazjiyat al-a'ṣār*, 157.
52 Rashīd al-Dīn/Alizade, *Jāmi' al-tawārīkh*, III, 26–7; Vaṣṣāf, *Tajziyat al-amṣār va tazjiyat al-a'ṣār*, 157.
53 See Aigle, *Le Fārs sous la domination mongole*, 71–80.
54 Sa'dī, *Būstān*, translation by Homa Katouzian, "Sa'dī on Love and Morals," 97.
55 Mohammad Younis, "The Salghurid Coinage of Fārs (Iran). Citing the Mongols: Varieties of Overlordships, Form and Content (623–685/1226–1286)," *Journal of the Oriental Society of Australia* 45 (2013): 97.
56 Vaṣṣāf, *Tajziyat al-amṣār va tazjiyat al-a'ṣār*, 163–4.
57 Vaṣṣāf, *Tajziyat al-amṣār va tazjiyat al-a'ṣār*, 164.
58 Vaṣṣāf, *Tajziyat al-amṣār va tazjiyat al-a'ṣār*, 164.
59 Vaṣṣāf, *Tajziyat al-amṣār va tazjiyat al-a'ṣār*, 156.
60 Stephen Album, "Studies in Ilkhanid History and Numismatics," *StIr* 13/1 (1984): 108.
61 Vaṣṣāf, *Tajziyat al-amṣār va tazjiyat al-a'ṣār*, 157.
62 Vaṣṣāf, *Tajziyat al-amṣār va tazjiyat al-a'ṣār*, 161.
63 Vaṣṣāf, *Tajziyat al-amṣār va tazjiyat al-a'ṣār*, 161.
64 Vaṣṣāf, *Tajziyat al-amṣār va tazjiyat al-a'ṣār*, 161.
65 Ibn Zarkūb, *Shīrāz-nāma*, 80.

66 Vaṣṣāf, *Tajziyat al-amṣār va tazjiyat al-aʿṣār,* 161.
67 Ibn Zarkūb, *Shīrāz-nāma*, 78; Vaṣṣāf, *Tajziyat al-amṣār va tazjiyat al-aʿṣār,* 161.
68 Ibn Zarkūb, *Shīrāz-nāma*, 82; Vaṣṣāf, *Tajziyat al-amṣār va tazjiyat al-aʿṣār,* 161–2.
69 The *tamgha* corresponds to the tax on trade and crafts that was introduced by the Mongols. This word of Turkic origin means: sign, mark, emblem, and by extension "seal." See Doerfer, II, n° 933, 554–65; Allsen, *Mongol Imperialism*, 159. This tax was assessed at 10 percent of the value of the transactions; Ghazan Khan would have cut it in half; Petrushevsky, "The Socio-economic Condition of Iran," 532–6.
70 Vaṣṣāf, *Tajziyat al-amṣār va tazjiyat al-aʿṣār,* 162.
71 Junayd Shīrāzī, *Shadd al-izār*, 421.
72 Vaṣṣāf, *Tajziyat al-amṣār va tazjiyat al-aʿṣār,* 163. Here, the term *amlāk* (plural of *milk*) is used as opposed to the lands of the imperial crown (*dīvānī*).
73 It seems, from reading the anecdote reported by Vaṣṣāf (162–3), that this measure was subsequently repealed because of its unpopularity.
74 Vaṣṣāf, *Tajziyat al-amṣār va tazjiyat al-aʿṣār,* 163.
75 Vaṣṣāf, *Tajziyat al-amṣār va tazjiyat al-aʿṣār,* 157; Junayd Shīrāzī, *Shadd al-izār*, 219–20; Ibn Junayd Shīrazī, *Hazār mazār*, 266–8.
76 Junayd Shīrāzī, *Shadd al-izār*, 218. Faqīh Ṣā'in al-Dīn Ḥusayn is Junayd Shīrāzī's informant. On this family see Aigle, *Saints hommes de Chiraz et du Fārs*, 324–6.
77 Junayd Shīrāzī, *Shadd al-izār*, 176–7; Ibn Junayd Shīrazī, *Hazār Mazār*, 225–6.
78 Junayd Shīrāzī, *Shadd al-izār*, 198–201; Ibn Junayd Shīrazī, *Hazār Mazār*, 243–6.
79 Ibn Zarkūb, *Shīrāz-nāma*, 82–4. Junayd Shīrāzī (Ibn Zarkūb, *Shīrāz-nāma*, 79–80) presents Abū Bakr as the best ruler of the time for his justice. Shabānkāra'ī (*Majmaʿ al-ansāb*, 184) also praises his righteousness.
80 Vaṣṣāf, *Tajziyat al-amṣār va tazjiyat al-aʿṣār,* 158.
81 Ibn Zarkūb, *Shīrāz-nāma*, 80.
82 Vaṣṣāf, *Tajziyat al-amṣār va tazjiyat al-aʿṣār,* 157. The *bazm* was a royal reception during which the king and his entourage drank wine to the sound of music, see A. S. Mélikian-Chirvani, "The Iranian *bazm* in Early Persian Sources," in *Banquets d'Orient* (Bures-sur-Yvette, 1992), 95–120.
83 Biographical record of Khwāja ʿAmīd al-Dīn Abzarī by Ibn al-Fuwaṭī, *Talkhīṣ*, II, n° 1340, 900–1. The author gives him the title of ʿAmīd al-Mulk. See also Junayd Shīrāzī, *Shadd al-izār*, 215, footnote 2, and Qazvīnī (Junayd Shīrāzī, *Shadd al-izār*, 517–27). Qazvīnī notes that, in the *Talkhīṣ*, Ibn al-Fuwaṭī gives him the *nisba* al-Fālī instead of al-Abzarī mentioned in the other sources. Qazvīnī (Junayd Shīrāzī, *Shadd al-izār*, 521, footnote 3) suggests that the *nisba* al-Fālī is attributed to him because of the proximity of the two districts or because the district of Fāl included the canton of Abzar. However, it could be that this *nisba*

was given to Khwāja 'Amīd al-Dīn Abzarī because he presumably had properties in both regions.

84 Ibn Zarkūb, *Shīrāz-nāma*, 81; Vaṣṣāf, *Tajziyat al-amṣār va tazjiyat al-a'ṣār*, 156.

85 He would have exchanged correspondence with the caliph and various religious personalities. See *Asnād va nāma-hā-i tārīkhī*, ed. Sayyid 'Alī Mu'ayyad Thābitī (Tihrān: Kitābkhāna-i Ṭahūrī, 1967), 160–91.

86 Vaṣṣāf, *Tajziyat al-amṣār va tazjiyat al-a'ṣār*, 150–1.

87 Vaṣṣāf, *Tajziyat al-amṣār va tazjiyat al-a'ṣār*, 156. He was put to death in Rabī' II 624/April 1227.

88 Vaṣṣāf, *Tajziyat al-amṣār va tazjiyat al-a'ṣār*, 157.

89 Vaṣṣāf, *Tajziyat al-amṣār va tazjiyat al-a'ṣār*, 157.

90 Ibn Zarkūb, *Shīrāz-nāma*, 84; Vaṣṣāf, *Tajziyat al-amṣār va tazjiyat al-a'ṣār*, 160. Here the title *amīr* does not refer to a military function, but it means that Amīr Fakhr al-Dīn Abū Bakr was considered as a notable.

91 Vaṣṣāf, *Tajziyat al-amṣār va tazjiyat al-a'ṣār*, 160.

92 Vaṣṣāf, *Tajziyat al-amṣār va tazjiyat al-a'ṣār*, 160.

93 Lambton, *Landlord and Peasant*, 113; Ann K. S. Lambton, "Awqāf in Persia: 6th-8th/12th-14th Centuries," *Islamic Law and Society* 4/3 (1997): 302. On the charitable foundations in Islam, see Maria E. Subtelny, *Le monde est un jardin. Aspects de l'histoire culturelle de l'Iran médiéval* (Paris: Association pour l'avancement des études iraniennes, 2000), 77–96; Maria E. Subtelny, *Timurids in Transition. Turko-Persian Politics and Acculturation in Medieval Iran* (Leiden: Brill, 2007), 154–8.

94 Vaṣṣāf, *Tajziyat al-amṣār va tazjiyat al-a'ṣār*, 163. The families of sayyids were very numerous in Shiraz where there are several important mausoleums, see Aigle, *Saints hommes de Chiraz et du Fārs*, 292–313.

95 Ibn Zarkūb, *Shīrāz-nāma*, 82.

4 Progressive Administrative Control of the Ilkhans over Fārs

1 Sa'dī, *Gulistān*, translation by Lane, *Early Mongol Rule*, 126.

2 Vaṣṣāf, *Tajziyat al-amṣār va tazjiyat al-a'ṣār*, 181; Shabānkāra'ī, *Majma' al-ansāb*, 185; Rashīd al-Dīn/Rawshan and Mūsavī, *Jāmi' al-tawārīkh*, II, 829–30. Sa'd had been commissioned by his father to wear the *kharāj* of Fārs to the Mongol court. He was probably returning from such a mission when his father died, Vaṣṣāf, *Tajziyat al-amṣār va tazjiyat al-a'ṣār*, 157. Biographical sketch of Sa'd in Junayd Shīrāzī, *Shadd al-izār*, 272–4. Account of this chaotic period in Shiraz, see Lane, *Early Mongol Rule*, 126–8.

3 According to Bayḍavī (89), he died twelve days after his name was pronounced in the *khuṭba* and struck on the coin. 'Abbās 'Iqbāl Āshtiyānī (*Tārīkh-i Mughūl*, 389) says on 17 Jumādā, that is, twelve days after the death of his father. His coffin was taken to the Madrasa-i 'Aḍudiyya in Shiraz that had been built by his mother Terken Khātūn, Vaṣṣāf, *Tajziyat al-amṣār va tazjiyat al-a'ṣār*, 181; Faṣīḥ Khwāfī, *Mujmal*, II, 328.
4 She was the atabek 'Alā' al-Dawla's sister, Vaṣṣāf, *Tajziyat al-amṣār va tazjiyat al-a'ṣār*, 181.
5 Vaṣṣāf, *Tajziyat al-amṣār va tazjiyat al-a'ṣār*, 182.
6 Vaṣṣāf, *Tajziyat al-amṣār va tazjiyat al-a'ṣār*, 182.
7 Vaṣṣāf, *Tajziyat al-amṣār va tazjiyat al-a'ṣār*, 181.
8 Vaṣṣāf, *Tajziyat al-amṣār va tazjiyat al-a'ṣār*, 181.
9 Rashīd al-Dīn/Rawshan and Mūsavī, *Jāmi' al-tawārīkh*, II, 829–30; Vaṣṣāf, *Tajziyat al-amṣār va tazjiyat al-a'ṣār*, 182; Faṣīḥ Khwāfī, *Mujmal*, II, 328. We have a coin minted in his name and those of Möngke and Hülegü, Younis, "The Salghurid Coinage of Fārs," 98.
10 Rashīd al-Dīn/Rawshan and Mūsavī, II, 830.
11 Ibn Zarkūb, *Shīrāz-nāma*, 86; Vaṣṣāf, *Tajziyat al-amṣār va tazjiyat al-a'ṣār*, 181; Faṣīḥ Khwāfī, *Mujmal* (II, 329) says 660.
12 Shabānkāra'ī, *Majma' al-ansāb*, 185.
13 *Tārīkh-i Shāhī*, 160.
14 Vaṣṣāf, *Tajziyat al-amṣār va tazjiyat al-a'ṣār*, 181.
15 Vaṣṣāf, *Tajziyat al-amṣār va tazjiyat al-a'ṣār*, 181.
16 Rashīd al-Dīn/Rawshan and Mūsavī, *Jāmi' al-tawārīkh*, II, 830; Vaṣṣāf, *Tajziyat al-amṣār va tazjiyat al-a'ṣār*, 183.
17 Vaṣṣāf, *Tajziyat al-amṣār va tazjiyat al-a'ṣār*, 183.
18 Vaṣṣāf, *Tajziyat al-amṣār va tazjiyat al-a'ṣār*, 183.
19 *Tārīkh-i Shāhī*, 160. Translation Lane, *Early Mongol Rule*, 128.
20 Vaṣṣāf, *Tajziyat al-amṣār va tazjiyat al-a'ṣār*, 181.
21 Ibn Zarkūb, *Shīrāz-nāma*, 88. Translation Lane, *Early Mongol Rule*, 128.
22 Vaṣṣāf, *Tajziyat al-amṣār va tazjiyat al-a'ṣār*, 183–4.
23 Ibn Zarkūb, *Shīrāz-nāma*, 88; Vaṣṣāf, *Tajziyat al-amṣār va tazjiyat al-a'ṣār*, 186.
24 Ibn Zarkūb, *Shīrāz-nāma*, 88; Vaṣṣāf, *Tajziyat al-amṣār va tazjiyat al-a'ṣār*, 184; *Tārīkh-i Shāhī*, 163; Faṣīḥ Khwāfī, *Mujmal*, II, 331.
25 Vaṣṣāf, *Tajziyat al-amṣār va tazjiyat al-a'ṣār*, 183–4.
26 Vaṣṣāf, *Tajziyat al-amṣār va tazjiyat al-a'ṣār*, 183. English translation by John Limbert, *Shiraz in the Age of Hafez* (Seattle, University of Washington Press, 2004), 20.
27 Vaṣṣāf, *Tajziyat al-amṣār va tazjiyat al-a'ṣār*, 165–9.

28 Rashīd al-Dīn/Rawshan and Mūsavī, II, 830; Vaṣṣāf, *Tajziyat al-amṣār va tazjiyat al-aʿṣār,* 184.
29 Vaṣṣāf, *Tajziyat al-amṣār va tazjiyat al-aʿṣār,* 185. He commands his slave to bring him the head of Terken Khātūn. No sooner, the head was brought to the atabek on a platter, Lane, *Early Mongol Rule*, 129.
30 Vaṣṣāf, *Tajziyat al-amṣār va tazjiyat al-aʿṣār,* 185–6.
31 Vaṣṣāf, *Tajziyat al-amṣār va tazjiyat al-aʿṣār,* 186.
32 Ibn ʿAbd al-Ẓāhir, *al-Rawḍ al-zāhir fī sīrat al-Malik al-Ẓāhir*, ed. ʿAbd al-ʿAzīz Ḥuwayṭir (Riyāḍ, 1976), 148; Ibn Wāṣil, *Mufarrij al-kurūb fī akhbār banī Ayyūb*, eds. Ḥasanayn Muḥammad Rabīʿ and Saʿīd ʿAbd al-Fātiḥ ʿĀshūr (Cairo, 1977), VI, 359; Maqrīzī (*Kitāb al-Sulūk li-maʿrifat duwal al-mulūk*, ed. M. ʿAbd al-Qādir, Beirut, I, 550) adds that Baybars informed them of the defeat of Hülegü's troops by the forces of Berke Khan, the ruler of the Golden Horde.
33 Baybars al-Manṣūrī al-Dawādār, *Zubdat al-fikra fī taʾrīkh al-hijra*, ed. Donald S. Richards (Beirut: Dār al-Nashr al-Kitāb al-ʿArabī, 1998), 88.
34 Vaṣṣāf, *Tajziyat al-amṣār va tazjiyat al-aʿṣār,* 186.
35 Vaṣṣāf, *Tajziyat al-amṣār va tazjiyat al-aʿṣār,* 186.
36 Vaṣṣāf, *Tajziyat al-amṣār va tazjiyat al-aʿṣār,* 186; *Tārīkh-i Shāhī*, 164–5.
37 Vaṣṣāf, *Tajziyat al-amṣār va tazjiyat al-aʿṣār,* 186.
38 Vaṣṣāf, *Tajziyat al-amṣār va tazjiyat al-aʿṣār,* 186.
39 Vaṣṣāf, *Tajziyat al-amṣār va tazjiyat al-aʿṣār,* 186. Jīrūft was famous for its pearl fisheries. This port was located a little north of the current city of Būshhir.
40 See Jean Aubin, "Références pour Lār médiévale," *Journal asiatique* (1955): 492–5.
41 Vaṣṣāf, *Tajziyat al-amṣār va tazjiyat al-aʿṣār,* 187.
42 Vaṣṣāf, *Tajziyat al-amṣār va tazjiyat al-aʿṣār,* 187.
43 Vaṣṣāf, *Tajziyat al-amṣār va tazjiyat al-aʿṣār,* 187.
44 Vaṣṣāf, *Tajziyat al-amṣār va tazjiyat al-aʿṣār,* 187. The image of Ṣiffīn is used here toward a non-Muslim.
45 Vaṣṣāf, *Tajziyat al-amṣār va tazjiyat al-aʿṣār,* 186.
46 Bayḍavī, *Niẓām al-tawārīkh*, 127.
47 Aigle, *Saints hommes de Chiraz et du Fārs*, 421–75.
48 *Tārīkh-i Shāhī*, 164; Lane, *Early Mongol Rule*, 130.
49 See Denise Aigle, "Un fondateur d'ordre en milieu rural. Le cheikh Abû Ishâq de Kâzarûn," in *Saints orientaux*, D. Aigle (ed.) (Paris: De Boccard, 1995), 181–209; Aigle, *Saints hommes de Chiraz et du Fārs*, chapter 7.
50 Vaṣṣāf, *Tajziyat al-amṣār va tazjiyat al-aʿṣār,* 189. Ḥāfiẓ-i Abrū, *Jughrafiyā*, II, 175.

51 Ibn Zarkūb, *Shīrāz-nāma*, 89; Vaṣṣāf, *Tajziyat al-amṣār va tazjiyat al-aʿṣār*, 189; *Tārīkh-i Shāhī*, 166; Shabānkāraʾī, *Majmaʿ al-ansāb*, 186–7; Faṣīḥ Khwāfī, *Mujmal*, II, 331.

52 Vaṣṣāf, *Tajziyat al-amṣār va tazjiyat al-aʿṣār*, 190–1.

53 Vaṣṣāf, *Tajziyat al-amṣār va tazjiyat al-aʿṣār*, 192.

54 Ibn Zarkūb, *Shīrāz-nāma*, 89–90; Vaṣṣāf, *Tajziyat al-amṣār va tazjiyat al-aʿṣār*, 191.

55 Vaṣṣāf, *Tajziyat al-amṣār va tazjiyat al-aʿṣār*, 191.

56 Vaṣṣāf, *Tajziyat al-amṣār va tazjiyat al-aʿṣār*, 191.

57 ʿAzīz al-Dīn Nasafī, *Kitāb al-Insān al-kāmil*, ed. Marijan Molé (Tihrān: Institut français de recherche en Iran, 1962), 321–2, and "Introduction," ibid., 18–19. On ʿAzīz al-Dīn Nasafī, see Landolt, "Nasafī, ʿAzīz," *EIr*, online edition.

58 Vaṣṣāf, *Tajziyat al-amṣār va tazjiyat al-aʿṣār*, 192.

59 *Shīrāz-nāma* (90) gives the date as 666/1267–8, but it is too late in relation to the events connected with Saljūq Shāh.

60 Vaṣṣāf, *Tajziyat al-amṣār va tazjiyat al-aʿṣār*, 192.

61 Junayd Shīrāzī, *Shadd al-izār*, 271. After his execution, he was buried in Shiraz.

62 Junayd Shīrāzī, *Shadd al-izār*, 271.

63 Vaṣṣāf, *Tajziyat al-amṣār va tazjiyat al-aʿṣār*, 192.

64 On Abish Khātūn, see Muḥammad Qazvīnī, *Yāddāsht-hā-i Qazvīnī*, ed. Īraj Afshār (Tihrān: Instishārat-i Dānishgāh-i Tihrān, 1958), I, 10–16; Bertold Spuler, "Abeš-Kātūn," *EIr* I: 210; Lambton, *Continuity and Change*, 272–5; Bruno De Nicola, *Women in Mongol Iran. The Khātūns, 1206–1335* (Edinburgh: Edinburgh University Press, 2017), 112–13.

65 Vaṣṣāf, *Tajziyat al-amṣār va tazjiyat al-aʿṣār*, 190.

66 Sources do not agree on the date of his enthronement. Vaṣṣāf (190) gives 661, but it is too early since Saljūq Shāh was killed at the end of the year 662. Bayḍavī, Rashīd al-Dīn, and the *Mujmal* give 662, a date that seems more consistent. However, it is more likely that his investiture took place after the revolt of Qāḍī Sharaf al-Dīn Ibrāhīm, therefore in 663. This is the date chosen by Bertold Spuler and Ann K. S. Lambton. On the other hand, ʿAbbās Iqbāl Āshtiyānī (*Tārīkh-i Mughūl*, 391) places the investiture of Abish Khātūn in 662.

67 Muḥammad Yūnis, *al-Tadāwul al-naqdī fī madīna Shīrāz*, 87; Muḥammad Yūnis, "The Salghurid Coinage of Fārs," 101–2. Hülegü is "the King of the World" (*pādishāh-i jahān*), but at that time, the Ilkhans were dependent on the Qaʾan of China, and his name also appears on the coins.

68 Saʿdī, *Gūlistān*, translation Lane, *Early Mongol Rule*, 134.

69 Vaṣṣāf, *Tajziyat al-amṣār va tazjiyat al-aʿṣār*, 196.

70 Vaṣṣāf, *Tajziyat al-amṣār va tazjiyat al-aʿṣār*, 193.

71 Vaṣṣāf, *Tajziyat al-amṣār va tazjiyat al-aʿṣār*, 193.

72 Ḥāfiẓ-i Abrū, *Jughrāfiyā*, II, 177–8; Rashīd al-Dīn says that at the beginning of his reign Abaqa gave the government of Fārs to the children of the atabek Abū Bakr, Rashīd al-Dīn/Alizade, *Jāmiʿ al-tawārīkh*, III, 103; Rashīd al-Dīn/Rawshan and Mūsavī, II, 939.

73 Vaṣṣāf, *Tajziyat al-amṣār va tazjiyat al-aʿṣār*, 193.

74 Vaṣṣāf, *Tajziyat al-amṣār va tazjiyat al-aʿṣār*, 193.

75 Ibn Zarkūb, *Shīrāz-nāma*, 90; Vaṣṣāf, *Tajziyat al-amṣār va tazjiyat al-aʿṣār*, 194.

76 Vaṣṣāf, *Tajziyat al-amṣār va tazjiyat al-aʿṣār*, 194; Lane, *Early Mongol Rule*, 134. A coin, minted in Shiraz in the name of Abish Khātūn, bears a Chinese character (*bao*) that Stephen Album, relying on Vaṣṣāf, wrongly attributed to Inkianu. According to a study by Russian numismatists Belyaev and Sirodovich, the *bao* script on the Mongolian coins is the symbol of legality of the ruler who issued the coin, see V. A. Belyaev and S. V. Sidorovich, "A New Interpretation of the Character *bao* on Coins of the Mongols Uluses," *Journal of the Oriental Numismatic Society* 199 (2009): 11–17; Younis, "The Salghurid Coinage of Fārs," 105; Judith Kolbas, *The Mongols in Iran. Chingiz Khan to Uljaytu 1220–1309* (London: Routledge, 2006), 169.

77 Vaṣṣāf, *Tajziyat al-amṣār va tazjiyat al-aʿṣār*, 194.

78 Vaṣṣāf, *Tajziyat al-amṣār va tazjiyat al-aʿṣār*, 195.

79 Vaṣṣāf, *Tajziyat al-amṣār va tazjiyat al-aʿṣār*, 195. The sources are silent on his fate after this case.

80 Shams al-Dīn Kāshānī, *Shahānshāh-i Tchingīzī*, 378.

81 Rashīd al-Dīn/Rawshan and Mūsavī, II, 836; Vaṣṣāf, *Tajziyat al-amṣār va tazjiyat al-aʿṣār*, 195.

82 Nāṣir al-Dīn Munshī Kirmānī, *Simṭ al-ʿulā*, ed. ʿAbbās Iqbāl Āshtiyānī (Tihrān, 1949), 35.

83 Rashīd al-Dīn/Alizade, *Jāmiʿ al-tawārīkh*, III, 52–6; Rashīd al-Dīn/Rawshan and Mūsavī, II, 881.

84 Rashīd al-Dīn/Alizade, *Jāmiʿ al-tawārīkh*, III, 77; Rashīd al-Dīn/Rawshan and Mūsavī, I, 659.

85 Rashīd al-Dīn/Alizade, *Jāmiʿ al-tawārīkh*, III, 60.

86 Bayḍavī, *Niẓām al-tawārīkh*, 132; Rashīd al-Dīn/Alizade, *Jāmiʿ al-tawārīkh*, III, 102; Rashīd al-Dīn/Rawshan and Mūsavī, II, 938; Vaṣṣāf, *Tajziyat al-amṣār va tazjiyat al-aʿṣār*, 55. Sughunchaq Noyan disappeared from the political scene in 1284. He died in Marāgha in 1290, Aubin, *Émirs mongols et vizirs persans*, 23.

87 Vaṣṣāf (195) says that Sughunchaq Noyan was *ṣāḥib-dīvān*. Ibn Zarkūb, *Shīrāz-nāma*, 92; Ḥāfiẓ-i Abrū, *Jughrāfiyā*, II, 178.

88 Vaṣṣāf, *Tajziyat al-amṣār va tazjiyat al-aʿṣār*, 195–6.

89 Vaṣṣāf, *Tajziyat al-amṣār va tazjiyat al-aʿṣār*, 195.

90 Vaṣṣāf, *Tajziyat al-amṣār va tazjiyat al-aʿṣār,* 195; Ḥāfiẓ-i Abrū, *Jughrāfiyā*, II, 178.
91 Vaṣṣāf, *Tajziyat al-amṣār va tazjiyat al-aʿṣār,* 195.
92 Ḥāfiẓ-i Abrū, *Jughrāfiyā* (II, 178) says he was appointed as *darughachi.*
93 Ibn Zarkūb, *Shīrāz-nāma*, 90; Vaṣṣāf, *Tajziyat al-amṣār va tazjiyat al-aʿṣār,* 195; Ḥāfiẓ-i Abrū, *Jughrāfiyā*, II, 178.
94 Ḥāfiẓ-i Abrū, *Jughrāfiyā*, II, 178.
95 Ibn Zarkūb, *Shīrāz-nāma*, 90; Vaṣṣāf, *Tajziyat al-amṣār va tazjiyat al-aʿṣār,* 195; Ḥāfiẓ-i Abrū, *Jughrāfiyā*, II, 178.
96 Ibn al-Suqāʿī, *Tālī Kitāb wafayāt al-aʿyān*, ed. and French trans. Jacqueline Sublet (Damascus: Institut français de Damas, 1974), 32. The author says Salanjak for Sughunchaq; see also Ṣalāḥ al-Dīn Khalīl b. Aybak Ṣafadī, *al-Wafī bi-l-wafayāt*, ed. Sven Dedering (Wiesbaden: Frantz Steiner Verlag, 1981), VI, 136–7.
97 Vaṣṣāf, *Tajziyat al-amṣār va tazjiyat al-aʿṣār,* 197.
98 Vaṣṣāf, *Tajziyat al-amṣār va tazjiyat al-aʿṣār,* 197.
99 Vaṣṣāf, *Tajziyat al-amṣār va tazjiyat al-aʿṣār,* 190.
100 The Mongols often appealed to international traders to collect taxes, see below.
101 Vaṣṣāf, *Tajziyat al-amṣār va tazjiyat al-aʿṣār,* 204; Ḥāfiẓ-i Abrū, *Jughrāfiyā*, II, 178.
102 Vaṣṣāf, *Tajziyat al-amṣār va tazjiyat al-aʿṣār,* 204; Ḥāfiẓ-i Abrū, *Jughrāfiyā*, II, 179.
103 Vaṣṣāf, *Tajziyat al-amṣār va tazjiyat al-aʿṣār,* 205.
104 Vaṣṣāf, *Tajziyat al-amṣār va tazjiyat al-aʿṣār,* 205.
105 Ibn Zarkūb, *Shīrāz-nāma*, 92.
106 Vaṣṣāf, *Tajziyat al-amṣār va tazjiyat al-aʿṣār,* 206.
107 Vaṣṣāf, *Tajziyat al-amṣār va tazjiyat al-aʿṣār,* 206.
108 Vaṣṣāf, *Tajziyat al-amṣār va tazjiyat al-aʿṣār,* 207.
109 Vaṣṣāf, *Tajziyat al-amṣār va tazjiyat al-aʿṣār,* 207.
110 Vaṣṣāf, *Tajziyat al-amṣār va tazjiyat al-aʿṣār,* 207.
111 Vaṣṣāf, *Tajziyat al-amṣār va tazjiyat al-aʿṣār,* 207.
112 Vaṣṣāf, *Tajziyat al-amṣār va tazjiyat al-aʿṣār,* 207; Ḥāfiẓ-i Abrū, *Jughrāfiyā*, II, 180–1.
113 Aubin, *Émirs mongols et vizirs persans*, 46–7.
114 Aubin, *Émirs mongols et vizirs persans*, 47.
115 Ibn Zarkūb, *Shīrāz-nāma*, 92; Ḥāfiẓ-i Abrū, *Jughrāfiyā*, II, 181.
116 Rashīd al-Dīn/Alizade, *Jāmiʿ al-tawārīkh*, III, 212.
117 A toman is the equivalent of ten thousand dinars.
118 Vaṣṣāf, *Tajziyat al-amṣār va tazjiyat al-aʿṣār,* 207.
119 Vaṣṣāf, *Tajziyat al-amṣār va tazjiyat al-aʿṣār,* 207.
120 He was enthroned on June 21, 1282, in the Alātāq.

121 Qazvīnī, *Ẓafar-nāma*, translation Hope, *Power, Politics*, 138.
122 Reuven Amitai, "The Conversion of Tegüder Ilkhan to Islam," *Jerusalem Studies in Arabic and Islam* 25 (2001): 15–43.
123 Vaṣṣāf, *Tajziyat al-amṣār va tazjiyat al-aʿṣār*, 209; Ḥāfiẓ-i Abrū, *Jughrāfiyā* II, 182.
124 Vaṣṣāf, *Tajziyat al-amṣār va tazjiyat al-aʿṣār*, 209; Ḥāfiẓ-i Abrū, *Jughrāfiyā* II, 182.
125 Vaṣṣāf, *Tajziyat al-amṣār va tazjiyat al-aʿṣār*, 209.
126 Vaṣṣāf, *Tajziyat al-amṣār va tazjiyat al-aʿṣār*, 209.
127 Lambton (*Continuity and Change*, 272–3) makes the mistake of making Ṭash Mengü and Mengü Temür, the husband of Abish Khātūn, one and the same character. This error is echoed by Lane, *Early Mongol Rule*, 143–4. Vaṣṣāf (197, 223) designates Abish Khātūn's husband by the name of Mengü, whereas in the episode in question here (210–11), it is about another character responding to the name of Ṭash Mengü.
128 Vaṣṣāf, *Tajziyat al-amṣār va tazjiyat al-aʿṣār*, 210; Ḥāfiẓ-i Abrū, *Jughrāfiyā*, II, 182.
129 Vaṣṣāf, *Tajziyat al-amṣār va tazjiyat al-aʿṣār*, 211. According to *Shīrāz-nāma* (93), he left for Qays.
130 Vaṣṣāf, *Tajziyat al-amṣār va tazjiyat al-aʿṣār*, 211.
131 Shams al-Dīn ʿAbd al-Laṭīf, *Rūḥ al-jinān fī sīrat al-shaykh Rūzbihān*, in *Rūzbihān-nāma*, ed. M. Dānishpazhūh (Tihrān: Intishārat-i Anjumān-i Āthār-i Millī, 1969), 135. Ṣadr al-Dīn Ibrāhīm was Rūzbihān's grandson; he succeeded his grandfather. Analysis of the entire anecdote concerning Bulughan in Aigle, *Saints hommes de Chiraz et du Fārs*, 558–60.
132 ʿAbd al-Laṭīf b. Ṣadr al-Dīn Rūzbihān, *Rūḥ al-jinān*, 136.
133 Vaṣṣāf (211) attributes Ṭash Mengü's bad behavior to his stupidity and dishonest nature.
134 Vaṣṣāf, *Tajziyat al-amṣār va tazjiyat al-aʿṣār*, 211; Ḥāfiẓ-i Abrū, *Jughrāfiyā*, II, 183.
135 Ḥāfiẓ-i Abrū, *Jughrāfiyā*, II, 183.
136 His full filiation is Jalāl al-Dīn Arqān b. Malik Khān b. Muḥammad b. Zangī.
137 He is also referred in the sources as Khwāja Niẓām al-Dīn Abū Bakr.
138 Ibn Zarkūb, *Shīrāz-nāma*, 94; Vaṣṣāf, *Tajziyat al-amṣār va tazjiyat al-aʿṣār*, 211.
139 Vaṣṣāf, *Tajziyat al-amṣār va tazjiyat al-aʿṣār*, 208–11; Ḥāfiẓ-i Abrū, *Jughrāfiyā*, II, 183.
140 Ibn Zarkūb, *Shīrāz-nāma*, 94; Vaṣṣāf, *Tajziyat al-amṣār va tazjiyat al-aʿṣār*, 211; Ḥāfiẓ-i Abrū, *Jughrāfiyā*, II, 183.
141 Vaṣṣāf, *Tajziyat al-amṣār va tazjiyat al-aʿṣār*, 106.
142 Vaṣṣāf, *Tajziyat al-amṣār va tazjiyat al-aʿṣār*, 211.

143 Vaṣṣāf, *Tajziyat al-amṣār va tazjiyat al-aʿṣār*, 211.

144 Subtelny, *Le monde est un jardin*, 82.

145 Vaṣṣāf, *Tajziyat al-amṣār va tazjiyat al-aʿṣār*, 217–18; *Shīrāz-nāma* (95) dates this drought three years after the death of Sayyid Abū Yuʿlā on December 30, 1284. See also Lane, *Early Mongol Rule*, 144.

146 Jackson, "Arghūn Khan," *EIr* 2: 402–4.

147 Hope, *Power, Politics*, 136.

148 On the use of seals in Ilkhanid Iran, see Gottfried Herrmann, *Persiche Urkunden der Mongolenzeit. Text- und Bildteil* (Wiesbaden: Harrassowitz Verlag, 2004), 33–42. We must distinguish the "red seal" (*altamgha*) from the "golden seal" (*altun tamgha*), which was rather used for documents relating to tax matters. See also Doerfer, II, n° 933, 554–65; Gerhard Doerfer, "Altūn Tamghā," *EIr* 1: 913–14.

149 Hebræus, *Chronicon Syriacum*, 560. He gives a detailed account of Buqa's rise, followed by its inevitable downfall, ibid., 560–3.

150 Ḥāfiẓ-i Abrū, *Jughrāfiyā*, II, 184.

151 Mustawfī Qazvīnī, *Tarīkh-i guzīda*, 595; Ḥāfiẓ-i Abrū, *Jughrāfiyā*, 2, 184.

152 Ibn Zarkūb, *Shīrāz-nāma*, 95–6; Vaṣṣāf, *Tajziyat al-amṣār va tazjiyat al-aʿṣār*, 211–12; Ḥāfiẓ-i Abrū, *Jughrāfiyā*, II, 184.

153 Vaṣṣāf, *Tajziyat al-amṣār va tazjiyat al-aʿṣār*, 212.

154 Ibn Zarkūb, *Shīrāz-nāma*, 95; Vaṣṣāf, *Tajziyat al-amṣār va tazjiyat al-aʿṣār*, 213.

155 Vaṣṣāf, *Tajziyat al-amṣār va tazjiyat al-aʿṣār*, 213.

156 Ibn Zarkūb, *Shīrāz-nāma*, 95; Vaṣṣāf, *Tajziyat al-amṣār va tazjiyat al-aʿṣār*, 213.

157 Vaṣṣāf, *Tajziyat al-amṣār va tazjiyat al-aʿṣār*, 215.

158 Ḥāfiẓ-i Abrū, *Jughrāfiyā*, 2, 185–6.

159 Vaṣṣāf, *Tajziyat al-amṣār va tazjiyat al-aʿṣār*, 215; Ḥāfiẓ-i Abrū, *Jughrāfiyā*, II, 187.

160 In Persian sources, the Negüderis are also referred to as Qaraunas, Jean Aubin, "L'ethnogenèse des Qaraunas," *Turcica* I (1969): 65–94; *Yāddāsht-hā-i Qazvīnī*, VI, 144–6.

161 Ḥāfiẓ-i Abrū, *Jughrāfiyā*, II, 186.

162 Ibn Zarkūb, *Shīrāz-nāma*, 95; Vaṣṣāf, *Tajziyat al-amṣār va tazjiyat al-aʿṣār*, 215.

163 Vaṣṣāf, *Tajziyat al-amṣār va tazjiyat al-aʿṣār*, 216, translation Lane, *Early Mongol Rule*, 147.

164 Vaṣṣāf, *Tajziyat al-amṣār va tazjiyat al-aʿṣār*, 216.

165 Vaṣṣāf, *Tajziyat al-amṣār va tazjiyat al-aʿṣār*, 217.

166 Ḥāfiẓ-i Abrū, *Jughrāfiyā*, II, 187.

167 Ḥāfiẓ-i Abrū, *Jughrāfiyā*, II, 187–8.

168 Vaṣṣāf, *Tajziyat al-amṣār va tazjiyat al-aʿṣār*, 219; Ḥāfiẓ-i Abrū, *Jughrāfiyā*, II, 188.

169 Vaṣṣāf, *Tajziyat al-amṣār va tazjiyat al-aʿṣār,* 219. He was close to Buqa, Aubin, *Émirs mongols et vizirs persans*, 38–9.

170 Ibn Zarkūb, *Shīrāz-nāma*, 96; Vaṣṣāf, *Tajziyat al-amṣār va tazjiyat al-aʿṣār,* 220; Ḥāfiẓ-i Abrū, *Jughrāfiyā*, II, 188–9.

171 Vaṣṣāf, *Tajziyat al-amṣār va tazjiyat al-aʿṣār,* 220.

172 Rashīd al-Dīn/Alizade, *Jāmiʿ al-tawārīkh,* III, 205; Vaṣṣāf, *Tajziyat al-amṣār va tazjiyat al-aʿṣār,* 221; Ḥāfiẓ-i Abrū, *Jughrāfiyā*, II, 189–90.

173 Ḥāfiẓ-i Abrū, *Jughrāfiyā*, II, 190. According to Vaṣṣāf (221), this arrangement would have lasted until the time of Gaikhatu. Every year, emissaries came to collect this sum in Shiraz.

174 Ibn Zarkūb, *Shīrāz-nāma*, 71; Vaṣṣāf, *Tajziyat al-amṣār va tazjiyat al-aʿṣār,* 222–3; Ḥāfiẓ-i Abrū, *Jughrāfiyā*, II, 190; Spuler, *Mongolen in Iran*, 210.

175 Vaṣṣāf, *Tajziyat al-amṣār va tazjiyat al-aʿṣār,* 222; Ḥāfiẓ-i Abrū, *Jughrāfiyā*, II, 190. Charāndāb-i Tabrīz is a district of Tabriz, see Dorothea Krawulsky, *Iran. Das Reich des Ilkhāne* (Wiesbaden: Ludwig Reichert, 1978), 524. Subsequently, his daughter Kürdüchin had her body transported to Shiraz, Ḥāfiẓ-i Abrū, *Jughrāfiyā*, II, 190.

176 Vaṣṣāf, *Tajziyat al-amṣār va tazjiyat al-aʿṣār,* 222.

177 Vaṣṣāf, *Tajziyat al-amṣār va tazjiyat al-aʿṣār,* 222.

178 Dominic P. Brookshaw, *Hafiz and His Contemporaries. Poetry, Performance and Patronage in Fourteenth Century Iran* (London: Tauris, 2019), 167.

179 Vaṣṣāf, *Tajziyat al-amṣār va tazjiyat al-aʿṣār,* 222; Āshtiyānī, *Tārīkh-i Mughūl*, 395, footnote 1.

5 Ilkhanid Policy in Fārs

1 Vaṣṣāf, *Tajziyat al-amṣār va tazjiyat al-aʿṣār,* 190.

2 The term *injü* designates the princely properties that had been given as appanage at the time of the extension of Mongol power in the sedentary areas of its newly conquered territory. This often took the form of pastures, revenue rights, animals, and even people, see Doerfer, II, n° 670, 220–5; Hope, *Power, Politics*, 206.

3 Vaṣṣāf, *Tajziyat al-amṣār va tazjiyat al-aʿṣār,* 230.

4 Hope, *Power, Politics*, 137.

5 Hope, *Power, Politics*, 141.

6 Rashīd al-Dīn/Alizade, *Jāmiʿ al-tawārīkh,* III, 211.

7 Arghun Aqa (d. 673/1275) was of Oirat origin, Peter Jackson, "Aghūn Āqā," *EIr* 2: 401–2.

8 Vaṣṣāf, *Tajziyat al-amṣār va tazjiyat al-aʿṣār,* 230.
9 Ibn Zarkūb, *Shīrāz-nāma*, 138–9; Vaṣṣāf, *Tajziyat al-amṣār va tazjiyat al-aʿṣār,* 230.
10 Vaṣṣāf, *Tajziyat al-amṣār va tazjiyat al-aʿṣār,* 231.
11 Aubin, *Émirs mongols et vizirs persans*, 40.
12 Vaṣṣāf, *Tajziyat al-amṣār va tazjiyat al-aʿṣār,* 223–4.
13 Vaṣṣāf, *Tajziyat al-amṣār va tazjiyat al-aʿṣār,* 224; Ḥāfiẓ-i Abrū, *Jughrāfiyā*, II, 190–1.
14 Ḥāfiẓ-i Abrū, *Jughrāfiyā*, II, 191.
15 Vaṣṣāf, *Tajziyat al-amṣār va tazjiyat al-aʿṣār,* 219–20.
16 Rashīd al-Dīn/Alizade, *Jāmiʿ al-tawārīkh,* III, 210–11.
17 Rashīd al-Dīn/Alizade, *Jāmiʿ al-tawārīkh,* III, 211–14. A more detailed list in Vaṣṣāf (232) shows that five other princes were part of the conspiracy.
18 Spuler, *Die Mongolen in Iran*, 349, 351; Hope, *Power, Politics*, 142. His brother Aruq suffers the same fate a month later in Baghdad.
19 Hope, *Power, Politics*, 143.
20 Rashīd al-Dīn/Alizade, *Jāmiʿ al-tawārīkh,* III, 210. See also Aubin, *Émirs mongols et vizirs persans*, 26.
21 On Saʿd al-Dawla and his family, see Fischel, *Jews in the Economic Political Life of Medieval Islam*, 90–117, and the more recent study by Jonathan Brack, "A Jewish Vizier and His Shīʿī Manifesto: Jews, Shīʿīs, and the Politization of Confessional Identities in Mongol-ruled Iraq and Iran (13th to 14th Centuries)," *Der Islam* 96/2 (2019): 374–403.
22 Vaṣṣāf, *Tajziyat al-amṣār va tazjiyat al-aʿṣār,* 235.
23 Aubin, *Émirs mongols et vizirs persans*, 42.
24 Vaṣṣāf, *Tajziyat al-amṣār va tazjiyat al-aʿṣār,* 235.
25 Rashīd al-Dīn/Alizade, *Jāmiʿ al-tawārīkh,* III, 219; Ibn Zarkūb, *Shīrāz-nāma*, 99.
26 Rashīd al-Dīn/Alizade, *Jāmiʿ al-tawārīkh,* III, 219; Vaṣṣāf, *Tajziyat al-amṣār va tazjiyat al-aʿṣār,* 224.
27 *Ḥāfiẓ-i Abrū, Jughrāfiyā*, II, 192.
28 Vaṣṣāf, *Tajziyat al-amṣār va tazjiyat al-aʿṣār,* 224.
29 Ḥāfiẓ-i Abrū, *Jughrāfiyā*, II, 192.
30 According to Rashīd al-Dīn (Rashīd al-Dīn/Alizade, *Jāmiʿ al-tawārīkh,* III, 220), Shams al-Dīn Ḥusayn ʿAlkānī, Niẓām al-Dīn Abū Bakr, Majd al-Dīn Abū Bakr and his son were executed at Kūshk-i Zar, a village of the Ābāda district, *Farhang-i jughrāfiyāʾī-i Īrān* (Tihrān: Intishārāt-i Dāyirah-i jugharāfiyāʾī Sitād-i Artish, 1951), VII, 193. Vaṣṣāf (228) gives Monday Rabīʿ II 19, 689/May 1, 1290, for the death of Sayf al-Dīn Yūsuf. Ibn Zarkūb (*Shīrāz-nāma*, 97) says that at the end of the year 688/1290. Fakhr al-Dīn Mubārak Shāh, Khwāja Niẓām al-Dīn

Vazīr, Khwāja Sayf al-Dīn Yūsuf, and Majd al-Dīn Rūmī were executed. It is the version of Vaṣṣāf and Rashīd al-Dīn that we must remember.

31 Vaṣṣāf, *Tajziyat al-amṣār va tazjiyat al-a'ṣār,* 225.

32 Vaṣṣāf, *Tajziyat al-amṣār va tazjiyat al-a'ṣār,* 227.

33 Vaṣṣāf, *Tajziyat al-amṣār va tazjiyat al-a'ṣār,* 228; Ḥāfiẓ-i Abrū, *Jughrāfiyā,* II, 192.

34 Vaṣṣāf, *Tajziyat al-amṣār va tazjiyat al-a'ṣār,* 247–8.

35 Aubin, *Émirs mongols et vizirs persans*, 47.

36 Aubin, *Émirs mongols et vizirs persans*, 48.

37 Vaṣṣāf, *Tajziyat al-amṣār va tazjiyat al-a'ṣār,* 332–3.

38 Thomas T. Allsen, "Mongolian Princes and Their Merchant Partners, 1200–1260," *Asia Major* 2/2 (1989): 83–4; Virgil Ciocîltan, *The Mongols and the Black Sea Trade in Thirteenth and Fourteenth Centuries* (Leiden: Brill, 2012), 1–36; Jackson, *The Mongols and the Islamic World*, 210–24.

39 On the term *ortoq*, see Doerfer, II, n° 446, 25–7.

40 In Arabic-Turkic lexicons from the eleventh to twelfth centuries, *ortoq* is always defined as a partner, by the term *sharīk* in the dictionary of Maḥmūd Kāshgharī, and by that of *socius* in the *Codex Cumanicus*, Allsen, "Mongolian Princes and Their Merchant Partners," 117.

41 Allsen, "Mongolian Princes," 94.

42 Allsen, "Mongolian Princes," 98.

43 Allsen, "Mongolian Princes," 105.

44 The wealth carried away was deposited in two fortresses in Azerbaijan where, subsequently, they were converted into gold bars that were entrusted as capital to the *ortoq*, see Allsen, "Mongolian Princes," 110. On 'Alī Bahādur at Bagdad, see Reuven Amitai-Preiss, *Mongols and Mamluks. The Mamluk-Īlkhānid War, 1260–1281* (Cambridge: Cambridge University Press, 1995), 58.

45 Allsen, "Mongolian Princes," 110.

46 Rashīd al-Dīn/Alizade, *Jāmi' al-tawārīkh,* III, 103. Rashīd al-Dīn says he administered Fārs on behalf of the atabek Abū Bakr's children.

47 According to Īraj Afshār, his name is of Arabic origin; see Afshār's commentary in *Tārīkh-i Yazd*, 210. On Khwāja Shams al-Dīn Muḥammad b. Malik Tāzīgū, see *Tārīkh-i Yazd*, 89–91, and Afshār's commentaries, *Tārīkh-i Yazd*, 210–12; *Tārīkh-i Jadīd-i Yazd*, 121–2; Rashīd al-Dīn/Alizade, *Jāmi' al-tawārīkh,* III, 103, 151–2; Ḥāfiẓ-i Abrū, *Jughrāfiyā*, II, 178–80. He had married Bībī Terken, the eldest daughter of the rulers of Kirmān, Quṭb al-Dīn Muḥammad and Qutlugh Khātūn.

48 On these charitable foundations, see Ja'farī, *Tārīkh-i Yazd*, 89–91; Kātib, *Tārīkh-i jadīd-i Yazd*, 131–3.

49 Ḥāfiẓ-i Abrū, *Jughrāfiyā*, vol. II, 178.
50 Vaṣṣāf, *Tajziyat al-amṣār va tazjiyat al-aʿṣār,* 197–8; Ḥāfiẓ-i Abrū, *Jughrāfiyā*, II, 179.
51 Rashīd al-Dīn/Alizade, *Jāmiʿ al-tawārīkh,* III, 151–2; Vaṣṣāf, *Tajziyat al-amṣār va tazjiyat al-aʿṣār,* 202; *Tārīkh-i Shāhī*, 205–8; Ḥāfiẓ-i Abrū, *Jughrāfiyā*, II, 179.
52 Rashīd al-Dīn/Alizade, *Jāmiʿ al-tawārīkh,* III, 151–2; Vaṣṣāf, *Tajziyat al-amṣār va tazjiyat al-aʿṣār,* 199.
53 Rashīd al-Dīn/Alizade, *Jāmiʿ al-tawārīkh,* III, 152. Vaṣṣāf (201) does not mention Shams al-Dīn Muḥammad b. Malik Tāzīgū, but he specifies that Bulughan fled to Isfahan with three hundred horsemen.
54 Vaṣṣāf, *Tajziyat al-amṣār va tazjiyat al-aʿṣār,* 202.
55 *Tārīkh-i Shāhī*, 207.
56 Jamāl al-Dīn Ibrāhīm has an edifying biography in the *Shadd al-izār* (342–4) from which nothing can be drawn regarding his role in Fārs. Two Arab authors penned a more informative biography about his political role. Ibn al-Suqāʿī, ed., 42–4; Ibn al-ʿImād, *Shadharāt al-dhahab*, 26. On the Ṭībī family, see Muḥammad Qazvīnī's commentaries in *Shadd al-izār*, 543–8. On the commercial activities of Jamāl al-Dīn Ibrāhīm and his sons, see Aubin, *Émirs mongols et vizirs persans*, 89–100; Eliyahu Ashtor, *A Social and Economic History of the Near East in the Middle Ages* (London: Collins, 1976), 266, under the name of Ibrāhīm Sawāmilī.
57 According to Yāqūt, Ṭīb was located midway between Wāsiṭ and the Khūzistān; the distance between these two regions was eighteen *farsakh*. Yāqūt reports the account of a merchant, Dawūd b. Aḥmad b. Saʿīd Ṭībī, which confirms the role of Ṭīb for his commercial activities; Yāqūt, III, 566.
58 Ibn al-Suqāʿī, ed., 32; Ibn Ḥajar al-ʿAsqalānī, *al-Durar al-kāmina*, I, n° 159, 59–60.
59 Ibn al-ʿImād, *Shadharāt al-dhahab*, 26.
60 Ḥāfiẓ-i Abrū, *Jughrāfiyā*, II, 194.
61 Yihao, "Background and Aftermath of Fakhr al-Dīn al-Ṭībī's Voyage," 153.
62 Vaṣṣāf, *Tajziyat al-amṣār va tazjiyat al-aʿṣār,* 505.
63 In these ports, the goods were not subject to tax levies.
64 After Taqī al-Dīn's death in 702/1302–3, Sirāj al-Dīn, a son of Jamāl al-Dīn Ibrāhīm, succeeded him, Vaṣṣāf, *Tajziyat al-amṣār va tazjiyat al-aʿṣār,* 505.
65 Aubin, "Les princes d'Ormuz," 97. In his biographical note on Malik al-Islām, the author of *Shadd al-izār* (343) recounts an edifying tale. One day, he asked God to heal a valuable horse that the doctors could not treat: his prayer was answered.
66 Vaṣṣāf, *Tajziyat al-amṣār va tazjiyat al-aʿṣār,* 267.

67 Rashīd al-Dīn, *The Successors of Genghis Khan*, trans. J. A. Boyle (New York: Columbia University Press, 1971), 307.
68 Vaṣṣāf, *Tajziyat al-amṣār va tazjiyat al-aʿṣār*, 267.
69 Rashīd al-Dīn, *The Successors of Genghis Khan*, 307.
70 Vaṣṣāf, *Tajziyat al-amṣār va tazjiyat al-aʿṣār*, 268.
71 Vaṣṣāf, *Tajziyat al-amṣār va tazjiyat al-aʿṣār*, 333.
72 Vaṣṣāf, *Tajziyat al-amṣār va tazjiyat al-aʿṣār*, 268–9.
73 Walter J. Fischel, "On the Iranian Paper Currency *al-chāw* of the Mongol Period," *JRAS* (1939): 601–4; Karl Jahn, "Paper Currency in Iran: A Contribution to the Cultural and Economic History of Iran in the Mongol Period," *Journal of Asian History* 4 (1970): 101–35; Peter Jackson, "Čāv," *EIr* 5: 96–7; Jackson, *The Mongols and the Islamic World*, 276. See Rashīd al-Dīn's report on the confusion in the Ilkhanate after the introduction of paper money, Rashīd al-Dīn/Thackson, 413–14.
74 Vaṣṣāf, *Tajziyat al-amṣār va tazjiyat al-aʿṣār*, 271.
75 Vaṣṣāf, *Tajziyat al-amṣār va tazjiyat al-aʿṣār*, 279.
76 Vaṣṣāf, *Tajziyat al-amṣār va tazjiyat al-aʿṣār*, 277.
77 Abatay Noyan had been commander of Hülegü's army center.
78 Vaṣṣāf, *Tajziyat al-amṣār va tazjiyat al-aʿṣār*, 284.
79 Vaṣṣāf, *Tajziyat al-amṣār va tazjiyat al-aʿṣār*, 284.
80 Vaṣṣāf, *Tajziyat al-amṣār va tazjiyat al-aʿṣār*, 284.
81 Bertold Spuler, "Baydū," *EIr* 3: 887–8.
82 Rashīd al-Dīn/Karīmī, *Jāmiʿ al-tawārīkh*, 850.
83 Allsen, "Changing Forms of Legitimization in Mongol Iran," 230.
84 Charles Melville, "Pādishāh-i islām: The Conversion of Sultan Maḥmūd Ghāzān Khān," *Pembroke Papers* 1 (1990): 159–77. However, after his conversion to Islam, Ghazan built his authority on both Islam and Chinggisid ideology, see Aigle, *The Mongol Empire*, 255–305.
85 Rashīd al-Dīn/Alizade, *Jāmiʿ al-tawārīkh*, III, 611; Aubin, *Émirs mongols et vizirs persans*, 61.
86 Rashīd al-Dīn/Alizade, *Jāmiʿ al-tawārīkh*, III, 613.
87 Rashīd al-Dīn/Alizade, *Jāmiʿ al-tawārīkh*, III, 615.
88 This new legitimacy is visible in the currency. According to Ibn Faḍl Allāh al-ʿUmarī (*Das mongolische Weltreich: al-ʿUmarī's Darstellung der mongolischen Reiche in seinem Werk Masālik al-abṣār fī mamālik al-amṣār*, ed. Klaus Lech, Wiesbaden, 1968, ed., 15), Ghazan inscribed only his own name on coins (*al-qān ṣāḥib al-takht*), omitting that of the Great Qa'an. This testimony is confirmed by coins minted in Iran. There are, however, a few coins minted in Transcaucasia that bear the Mongolian formula: "In the might of Heaven (*Tngri*), struck by

Ghazan." See Allsen, "Changing Forms of Legitimization in Mongol Iran," 230–1; Allsen, *Culture and Conquest*, 31–2. Aigle, *The Mongol Empire*, 189–98.

89 Aubin, *Émirs mongols et vizirs persans*, 61–4.

90 Rashīd al-Dīn/Alizade, *Jāmi' al-tawārīkh,* III, 618; Vaṣṣāf, *Tajziyat al-amṣār va tazjiyat al-a'ṣār,* 325.

91 Vaṣṣāf, *Tajziyat al-amṣār va tazjiyat al-a'ṣār,* 327.

92 Bertold Spuler (*Die Mongolen in Iran*, 95) refers him under the name Ḥājjī Beg.

93 Vaṣṣāf, *Tajziyat al-amṣār va tazjiyat al-a'ṣār,* 327.

94 Vaṣṣāf, *Tajziyat al-amṣār va tazjiyat al-a'ṣār,* 327.

95 Rashīd al-Dīn/Alizade, *Jāmi' al-tawārīkh,* III, 618.

96 Aubin, *Émirs mongols et vizirs persans*, 62.

97 Ḥāfiẓ-i Abrū, *Jughrāfiyā* (II, 193) says he was *ḥākim*.

98 Horqudaq appears in Ghazan's circle in 690/1291. He was one of his great *amīrs* in Khurasan, Rashīd al-Dīn/Thackson, 426, 428; Vaṣṣāf, *Tajziyat al-amṣār va tazjiyat al-a'ṣār,* 327; Aubin, *Émirs mongols et vizirs persans*, 54.

99 Vaṣṣāf, *Tajziyat al-amṣār va tazjiyat al-a'ṣār,* 330.

100 Vaṣṣāf, *Tajziyat al-amṣār va tazjiyat al-a'ṣār,* 331.

101 Rashīd al-Dīn/Alizade, *Jāmi' al-tawārīkh,* III, 324; Jean Aubin, *Émirs mongols et vizirs persans*, 66–7.

102 Vaṣṣāf, *Tajziyat al-amṣār va tazjiyat al-a'ṣār,* 330.

103 Vaṣṣāf, *Tajziyat al-amṣār va tazjiyat al-a'ṣār,* 335–6. On the tortures inflicted on 'Izz al-Dīn Muẓaffar, see Ma'ṣūma Ma̱'dankan, *Ba-yāsā rasīdagān*, 50–1.

104 Vaṣṣāf, *Tajziyat al-amṣār va tazjiyat al-a'ṣār,* 339–40.

105 Vaṣṣāf, *Tajziyat al-amṣār va tazjiyat al-a'ṣār,* 339–40; Ḥāfiẓ-i Abrū, *Jughrāfiyā*, II, 194.

106 In the pre-Mongol period, the term *mulūk-i aṭrāf* designed collectively the local and regional rulers, see Jürgen Paul, "Who Were the *mulūk Fārs*?" in *Transregional and Regional Elites. Connecting the Early Islamic Empire*, H.-L. Hagemann and S. Heidemann (eds.) (Berlin: De Gruyter, 2020), I, 117–46.

107 Rashīd al-Dīn/Alizade, *Jāmi' al-tawārīkh,* III, 325–7; Vaṣṣāf, *Tajziyat al-amṣār va tazjiyat al-a'ṣār,* 354–6; Ma'dankan, *Ba-yāsā rasīdagān*, 29–30.

108 Vaṣṣāf, *Tajziyat al-amṣār va tazjiyat al-a'ṣār,* 348–9.

109 According to Ḥāfiẓ-i Abrū (*Jughrāfiyā*, II, 194), he retained this office until the end of Ghazan's reign.

110 Vaṣṣāf, *Tajziyat al-amṣār va tazjiyat al-a'ṣār,* 350.

111 Vaṣṣāf, *Tajziyat al-amṣār va tazjiyat al-a'ṣār,* 348–9.

112 Vaṣṣāf, *Tajziyat al-amṣār va tazjiyat al-a'ṣār,* 347.

113 In 692/1293, Taichu was removed by Ṣadr al-Dīn Aḥmad Khālidī Zanjānī.

114 Lambton, "Mongol Fiscal Administration in Persia," 115, footnote 2.

115 Vaṣṣāf, *Tajziyat al-amṣār va tazjiyat al-a'ṣār,* 404.

116 Vaṣṣāf, *Tajziyat al-amṣār va tazjiyat al-aʿṣār,* 404.

117 Ghazan's reign had also an impact on the administration in Anatolia, which passed under the direct control of the Ilkhans. All appointments were decided in the *Ordu*, and there was a complete lack of administrative stability, see Melville, "Anatolia under the Mongols," 51–100.

118 Vaṣṣāf, *Tajziyat al-amṣār va tazjiyat al-aʿṣār,* 436–7.

119 Vaṣṣāf, *Tajziyat al-amṣār va tazjiyat al-aʿṣār,* 505. Ḥāfiẓ-i Abrū, *Jughrāfiyā* (II, 194) gives another version of the events according to which Öljeitü appointed a new *basqaq* in Fārs at the start of his reign, although he left the management of affairs to Malik al-Islām. Vaṣṣāf's version is more credible.

120 Qāshānī (154) refers him as Khwāja ʿIzz al-Dīn Qūhakī. Moreover, he would have been the assistant (*nā'ib*) of the minister Tāj al-Dīn ʿAlī Shāh, see Qāshānī, 116.

121 Vaṣṣāf, *Tajziyat al-amṣār va tazjiyat al-aʿṣār,* 438.

122 Vaṣṣāf, *Tajziyat al-amṣār va tazjiyat al-aʿṣār,* 437.

123 Vaṣṣāf, *Tajziyat al-amṣār va tazjiyat al-aʿṣār,* 439.

124 Vaṣṣāf, *Tajziyat al-amṣār va tazjiyat al-aʿṣār,* 439.

125 Vaṣṣāf, *Tajziyat al-amṣār va tazjiyat al-aʿṣār,* 507.

126 Vaṣṣāf, *Tajziyat al-amṣār va tazjiyat al-aʿṣār,* 507. Fakhr al-Dīn Aḥmad had accompanied his father to Tabriz in 697/1297–8. He was then sent as an envoy to Temür Qa'an in China by Ghazan. He had previously been appointed by his father to administer the maritime districts of Fārs, see Aubin, "Les princes d'Ormuz," 98–9. Fakhr al-Dīn Aḥmad, who received ten tomans of gold from the royal treasury, was to carry out commercial transactions in which 70 percent of the profit was for the Ilkhan and 30 percent for the merchant, see Yihao, "Background and Aftermath of Fakhr al-Dīn al-Ṭībī's Voyage," 155–6.

127 Vaṣṣāf, *Tajziyat al-amṣār va tazjiyat al-aʿṣār,* 506–7. Qāshānī (117) says that his death occurred on Tuesday Jumādā II 12, 710/November 6, 1310; according to *Shīrāz-nāma* (99) his death occurred in Rabīʿ I 706/September 10–October 9, 1306.

128 Ḥāfiẓ-i Abrū, *Jughrāfiyā*, II, 194.

129 Ḥāfiẓ-i Abrū, *Jughrāfiyā*, II, 194.

130 Ḥāfiẓ-i Abrū, *Jughrāfiyā*, II, 195.

131 Ḥāfiẓ-i Abrū, *Jughrāfiyā*, II, 195. When the situation of ʿIzz al-Dīn ʿAbd al-ʿAzīz was compromised on the continent, while he subsequently controlled Qays, Qaṭīf, Baḥrayn, and Baṣra, he sought to strengthen his position in the Persian Gulf while trying to seize Hormuz; see Aubin, "Les princes d'Ormuz," 100–1.

132 Ḥāfiẓ-i Abrū, *Jughrāfiyā*, II, 194. Qāshānī (154) erroneously refers to him as Jamāl al-Dīn b. Naʿīm b. ʿAbd al-Salām.

133 Ḥāfiẓ-i Abrū, *Jughrāfiyā*, II, 194.
134 Qāshānī, *Tārīkh-i Ūljaytū,* 163; Ibn Zarkūb, *Shīrāz-nāma,* 99–101; Ḥāfiẓ-i Abrū, *Jughrāfiyā*, II, 195. See also Aubin, "Les princes d'Ormuz," 100.
135 Qāshānī, *Tārīkh-i Ūljaytū,* 103.
136 Ḥāfiẓ-i Abrū, *Jughrāfiyā*, II, 201.
137 Jean Aubin, "Le patronage culturel en Iran sous les Ilkhans. Une grande famille de Yazd," *Le Monde iranien et l'Islam* 3 (1975): 110. Members of this family financed pious constructions in towns farther from Yazd such as Kāzarūn, Aigle, *Saints hommes de Chiraz et du Fārs*, 600.
138 Ibn al-Fuwaṭī, *Talkhīṣ*, I, 455–6; Ibn Ḥajar al-ʿAsqalānī, *Durar al-kāmina,* II, 454–5.
139 Aubin, "Le patronage culturel," 110; Josef Van Ess, *Der Wesir und seine Gelehrten: Zu Inhalt und Entstehungs-geschịchte der theologischen Schriften des Rašīduddīn Faḍlullāh (gest. 718/1318)* (Wiesbaden: Franz Steiner Verlag, 1981), 27.
140 Jaʿfarī, *Tārīkh-i Yazd*, 32. The author of *Tārīkh-i jadīd-i Yazd* (83) errs in saying that he obtained this office from Abū Saʿīd in 737/1336–7.
141 Shabānkāraʾī, *Majmaʿ al-ansāb*, 288.
142 Ḥāfiẓ-i Abrū, *Jughrāfiyā*, II, 199.
143 Ḥāfiẓ-i Abrū, *Jughrāfiyā*, II, 197. On Muzaffarids' origin, Maḥmūd Kutubī, *Tārīkh-i Āl-i Muẓaffar*, 3; Faṣīḥ Khwāfī, *Mujmal*, II, 293; Peter Jackson, "Muẓaffarides," *EI*[2] 8: 821–3; Hans Robert Römer, "The Jalayirids, Muzaffarids and Sarbadārs," in *Cambridge History of Iran*, V, *The Saljuq and Mongol Periods*, J. A. Boyle (ed.) (Cambridge: Cambridge University Press, 1975), 11–15.
144 Ḥāfiẓ-i Abrū, *Jughrāfiyā*, II, 198. On the early career of Amīr Muẓaffar, see Qāsim Ghanī, *Tārīkh-i ʿaṣr-i Ḥāfiẓ*, 68–9.
145 Ḥāfiẓ-i Abrū, *Jughrāfiyā*, II, 198.
146 Ḥāfiẓ-i Abrū, *Jughrāfiyā*, II, 198.
147 Ḥāfiẓ-i Abrū, *Jughrāfiyā*, II, 198.
148 Ḥāfiẓ-i Abrū, *Jughrāfiyā*, II, 199.
149 Mustawfī Qazvīnī, *Tārīkh-i guzīda*, 601. Shabānkāraʾī (272) gives the Jumādā I 5, 717/August 16, 1317.
150 Ḥāfiẓ-i Abrū, *Jughrāfiyā*, II, 200; Naṭanzī, *Muntakhab al-tawārīkh-i Muʿīnī*, 180.
151 Jamāl Lūk belonged to the Arab tribe of Khafāja, see Jean Aubin, "Références pour Lār médiévale," *Journal asiatique* (1955): 500. In Turkic, *lūk* means "one-humped camel," see Abel Pavet de Courteille, *Dictionnaire turk-oriental* (Amsterdam: Philo Press, 1972), 494.
152 Naṭanzī, *Muntakhab al-tawārīkh-i Muʿīnī*, 180–1.
153 Ḥāfiẓ-i Abrū, *Jughrāfiyā*, II, 202.

154 Faṣīḥ Khwāfī, *Mujmal*, III, 39–40. The sayyid refused all the riches offered by the sultan to settle for a simple Qur'ān.

155 Shabānkāra'ī, *Majma' al-ansāb*, 288–9.

156 *Mujmal* (III, 53) is, it seems, the only source to give the date of Kürdüchin's death, which would have occurred in Sulṭāniyya. She was then buried in Shiraz.

157 Ibn Zarkūb, *Shīrāz-nāma*, 103; Vaṣṣāf, *Tajziyat al-amṣār va tazjiyat al-a'ṣār*, 624. Kürdüchin was first married to the Qutlughkhanid Soyurghatmish. She played an important role in the politics of Kirmān. She then married Amīr Saltilmish and finally Amīr Ṭaghai, who would have been summoned to Shiraz as *basqaq* in 720/1320, Āshtiyānī, *Tārīkh-i Mughūl*, 410. On Kürdüchin, see Muḥammad Qazvīnī's remarks in *Shadd al-izār*, 282–3, see also Lambton, *Continuity and Change*, 273, 275–6, 286–7, and Shirīn Bayānī, *Zan dar Īrān dar 'aṣr-i Mughūl* (Tihrān: Kawīr, 1973–4), 10. She was appointed as *ḥākim* of Kirmān by Baidu, Vaṣṣāf, *Tajziyat al-amṣār va tazjiyat al-a'ṣār*, 284. On Kürdüchin in Kirmān, see Qāsim Ghanī, *Tārīkh-i 'aṣr-i Ḥāfiẓ*, 3–6; Lane, *Early Mongol Rule*, 144, 149.

158 Vaṣṣāf, *Tajziyat al-amṣār va tazjiyat al-a'ṣār*, 624–5. According to *Shīrāz-nāma* (103), which is the only source to mention this event, after the death of Kürdüchin, her niece Sulṭān Khātūn succeeded her in Shiraz, although this information is probably incorrect.

159 Charles Melville, "Čobān," *EIr* 5: 875–8; Charles Melville and 'Abbās Zaryab, "Chobanids," *EIr* 5: 496–502.

160 Charles Melville, *The Fall of Amir Chupan and the Decline of the Ilkhanate, 1327–37: A Decade of Discord in Mongol Iran* (Bloomington: Indiana University, 1999).

161 Shabānkāra'ī, *Majma' al-ansāb*, 296–7. Naṭanzī (170) erroneously writes that Sharaf al-Dīn Maḥmūd Shāh had married Ghiyāth al-Dīn Muḥammad Rashīdī's daughter, but in another place (172) he does mention Jalāl al-Dīn Mas'ūd Shāh.

162 Shabānkāra'ī, *Majma' al-ansāb*, 297; Melville, *The Fall of Amir Chupan*, 36.

163 Ibn Zarkūb, *Shīrāz-nāma*, 101. Ibn Zarkūb adds that he removed the tyranny (*ẓulm*) from the region, *Shīrāz-nāma*, 102.

164 Naṭanzī, *Muntakhab al-tawārīkh-i Mu'īnī*, 170.

165 Shabānkāra'ī, *Majma' al-ansāb*, 296. It is the only source to mention the name of Mubārak Shāh.

166 Shabānkāra'ī, *Majma' al-ansāb*, 296.

167 It was possible that 'Izz al-Dīn 'Abd al-'Azīz's actions against Hormuz were carried out with support from the Ilkhanid government, Aubin, "Les princes d'Ormuz," 101. Ḥāfiẓ-i Abrū (*Jughrāfiyā*, II, 195) says that he ruled, for some years, the coastal areas and the islands (*sāḥil-i daryā va jazā'ir*). According to *Shīrāz-nāma* (100), 'Izz al-Dīn 'Abd al-'Azīz is said to have taken over the government of Fārs at the start of Abū Sa'īd's reign.

168 Charles Melville, "Wolf or Shepherd? Amir Chupan's Attitude to Government," in *The Court of the Il-Khans, 1290–1340*, J. Raby and T. Fitzherbert (eds.) (Oxford: Oxford University Press, 1996), 85.

169 'Izz al-Dīn 'Abd al-'Azīz was accused of conspiring with the wife of Dimashq Khwāja; she would have liked to assassinate him using magic and poison, Melville, "Wolf or Shepherd?" 85.

170 As Melville ("Wolf or Shepherd?" 85) suggests, in this case Amīr Chūpān failed to thwart the plots and gave credence to the charges against 'Izz al-Dīn 'Abd al-'Azīz. *Majma' al-ansāb* (296) incorrectly says that 'Izz al-Dīn 'Abd al-'Azīz was executed by Amīr Chūpān. The other sources say that he was killed at the instigation of Dimashq Khwāja.

171 Naṭanzī (172) gives 726/1326. Here again the terminology is not exact in the sources. The *Shīrāz-nāma* (101) says that Sharaf al-Dīn Maḥmūd Shāh made himself independent. According to Ḥāfiẓ-i Abrū, *Jughrāfiyā* (II, 202), it was thanks to Amīr Chūpān that he was appointed governor of the province, but the event is placed at the time of the affair between Sayyid 'Aḍud al-Dīn and Mubāriz al-Dīn Muḥammad, in 716/1317.

172 Ibn Zarkūb, *Shīrāz-nāma*, 102; Stephen Album, "Studies in Ilkhanid History and Numismatics," *Studia Iranica* 13/1 (1984): 63–4.

173 Ibn Zarkūb, *Shīrāz-nāma*, 103.

174 Melville, *The Fall of Amir Chupan*, 40, footnote 114.

175 Shabānkāra'ī, *Majma' al-ansāb*, 297–8. Melville (*The Fall of Amir Chupan*, 36, footnote 103) points out that the date given by Shabānkāra'ī, 35 khānī, that is, the beginning of March 1336, is too late. The editor of the text has rectified as (7)35, other sources give 734.

176 Muḥammad b. Mas'ūd Sūzanī, *Dīvān-i Ḥakīm Sūzanī Samarqandī*, ed. Nāṣir al-Dīn Shāh Ḥusaynī (Tihrān: Amīr Kabīr, 1959), 129.

177 Ibn Zarkūb, *Shīrāz-nāma*, 103; Ḥāfiẓ-i Abrū, *Jughrāfiyā*, II, 202.

178 Details of this revolt in Ibn Zarkūb, *Shīrāz-nāma*, 103–4; Shabānkāra'ī, *Majma' al-ansāb*, 297–8; Aharī, *Tārīkh-i Shaykh Ūvais*, 58. The *amīrs* cited are Muḥammad Beg, Maḥmūd b. Īsan Qutlugh, Muḥammad Pīltan, and Sulṭān Shāh b. Nīkrūz, who were hostile to Musāfir Īnāq.

179 Maḥmūd b. 'Uthmān, *Miftāḥ al-hidāya va miṣbāḥ al-'ināya*, ed. 'Imād al-Dīn Shaykh al-Ḥukamā'ī (Tihrān: Kitābkhāna-i Millī, 1995), 56.

180 Maḥmūd b. 'Uthmān, *Miftāḥ al-hidāya*, 55.

181 Maḥmūd b. 'Uthmān, *Miftāḥ al-hidāya*, 55.

6 Fārs amid the Rivalries of Chupanids, Injuids, and Muzaffarids

1 Ḥāfiẓ-i Abrū, *Dhayl-i Jāmi' al-tawārīkh*, 144.

2 Charles Melville, "The End of the Ilkhanate and after: Observations on the Collapse of the Mongol World Empire," in *The Mongols' Middle East: Continuity and Transformation in Ilkhanid Iran*, B. De Nicola and Ch. Melville (eds.) (Leiden: Brill, 2016), 309–35; Patrick Wing, *The Jalayirids. Dynastic State Formation in the Mongol Middle East* (Edinburg: Edinburg University Press, 2016), 74–94.

3 See Melville and Zaryab, "Chobanids," 496–502.

4 The origin of the dynasty begins at Ilka Noyan, hence the name Ilkanids by which it is also known. Their official chronicler, Aharī, gives them the name of Jalā'īr. See Römer, "The Jalayirids, Muzaffarids and Sarbadārs," 11–16; John Masson Smith, "Djalāyir, Djalāyirides," *EI*[2] 2: 411–12; *Yāddāsht-hā-i Qazvīnī*, I, 160; Wing, *The Jalayirids*, 2016.

5 On this period, see Melville, *The Fall of Amir Chupan*; Aigle, *Le Fārs face à la domination mongole*, 165–71.

6 Wing, *The Jalayirids*, 85–94.

7 Four years older than Jamāl al-Dīn Shaykh Abū Isḥāq, Shams al-Dīn Muḥammad was born in 717/1317–18 in the same year as the Chupanid Shaykh Ḥasan Kuchik, *Mujmal*, III, 26.

8 Jamāl al-Dīn Shaykh Abū Isḥāq was born on Jumādā 4, 721/July 1, 1321, *Mujmal*, III, 32.

9 Naṭanzī, *Muntakhab al-tawārīkh-i Mu'īnī*, 170.

10 Arpa Ke'ün, a descendant of Ariq Böke, a brother of Hülegü, had been enthroned by Ghiyāth al-Dīn Muḥammad Rashīdī, on Rabī' II 18, /December 5, just five days after the death of Abū Sa'īd, Aigle, *Le Fārs face à la domination mongole*, 165. Sharaf al-Dīn Maḥmūd Shāh was accused of wanting to put a descendant of Hülegü on the throne, *Le Fārs face à la domination mongole* , 166.

11 'Alī Pādishāh was the chief of the Oirat tribe, see Charles Melville, " 'Ali-Padshah and the Oirat moment," in *The Fall of Amir Chupan*, 46–53.

12 According to Naṭanzī (173), Jalāl al-Dīn Mas'ūd Shāh would have gone to Shaykh Ḥasan Buzurg as a representative. See also Aharī, *Tārīkh-i Shaykh Ūvais*, 60. Stephen Album ("Studies in Ilkhanid History and Numismatics," 75, footnote 74) errs in saying that Arpa Ke'ün sent him to Anatolia to be his deputy.

13 Aharī (64–5) is the only one to mention this important detail.

14 Ibn Zarkūb, *Shīrāz-nāma*, 103–4.

15 Ibn Zarkūb, *Shīrāz-nāma*, 104; Naṭanzī, *Muntakhab al-tawārīkh-i Muʿīnī*, 173.
16 Ibn Zarkūb, *Shīrāz-nāma*, 105; Faṣīḥ Khwāfī, *Mujmal*, III, 55.
17 Chronology of the campaigns at the end of the chapter.
18 Ibn Zarkūb, *Shīrāz-nāma*, 104; Naṭanzī, *Muntakhab al-tawārīkh-i Muʿīnī*, 173.
19 Ibn Zarkūb, *Shīrāz-nāma*, 105.
20 Ibn Zarkūb, *Shīrāz-nāma*, 105; Naṭanzī, *Muntakhab al-tawārīkh-i Muʿīnī*, 173; Samarqandī, *Maṭlaʿ-i saʿdayn*, I, 184; Faṣīḥ Khwāfī, *Mujmal*, III, 57.
21 Ḥāfiẓ-i Abrū, *Jughrāfiyā*, II, 205; Samarqandī, *Maṭlaʿ-i saʿdayn* (I, 186) says that Pīr Ḥusayn sent an envoy to Amīr Ghāzī in Yazd to make an alliance.
22 Samarqandī, *Maṭlaʿ-i saʿdayn*, I, 197.
23 Ibn Zarkūb, *Shīrāz-nāma*, 105–6.
24 Ibn Zarkūb, *Shīrāz-nāma*, 106; Samarqandī, *Maṭlaʿ-i saʿdayn*, I, 197–8.
25 Khwandmīr, *Dastūr al-vuzarāʾ*, 240–1.
26 Ibn Zarkūb, *Shīrāz-nāma*, 106; Naṭanzī, *Muntakhab al-tawārīkh-i Muʿīnī*, 173–4; Khwandmīr, *Dastūr al-vuzarāʾ*, 242–3.
27 Vaṣṣāf, *Tajziyat al-amṣār va tazjiyat al-aʿṣār,* 205. Bayḍāvī began writing his *Niẓām al-tawārīkh* between Sughunchaq Noyan's two stays in Fārs. At the end of the chronicle, Bayḍāvī praises the Mongol *amīr,* which could be a reflection of the success of his appointment as *qāḍī al-quḍāt* of Shiraz, Charles Melville, "From Adam to Abaqa," *Studia Iranica* 30/1 (2001): 82.
28 Vaṣṣāf, *Tajziyat al-amṣār va tazjiyat al-aʿṣār,* 205–6.
29 On Majd al-Dīn Ismāʿīl Fālī's certificates, see Ess, *Der Wesir und seine Gelehrten*, 20, 26.
30 Rashīd al-Dīn, *Mukātibat*, 58.
31 Jean Calmard, "Le chiisme imamite sous les Ilkhans," in *L'Iran face à la domination mongole*, 261–92; Judith Pfeiffer, "Öljeytü's Conversion to Shiʿism (709/1309) in Muslim Narrative Sources," *Mongolian Studies* 22 (1999): 35–67.
32 Ibn Zarkūb, *Shīrāz-nāma*, 127–9; Junayd Shīrāzī, *Shadd al-izār*, 423–6; according to *Hazār Mazār* (144–6) his name was Mawlānā Majd al-Dīn Abū Ibrāhīm Ismāʿīl; Faṣīḥ Khwāfī, *Mujmal*, III, 82–3; Subkī, IX, n° 1344, 400–3; Ibn al-ʿImād, *Shadharāt al-dhahab*, VIII, 308.
33 Junayd Shīrāzī, *Shadd al-izār*, 424; Subkī, *Ṭabaqāt al-shāfiʿiyya*, 401; Ibn Baṭṭūṭa, *The Travels of Ibn Baṭṭūṭa, A.D. 1325–1354*, II, 303–4.
34 The name of Pīr Ḥusayn is not mentioned, although there is talk of a dispute between the people of Shiraz and a ruler who laid siege to the city. Majd al-Dīn Ismāʿīl b. Yaḥyā Fālī and some notables left Shiraz to negotiate peace with the attackers. They threw stones at him, but none of them hit him, Subkī, *Ṭabaqāt al-shāfiʿiyya*, IX, 401.
35 Ibn Zarkūb, *Shīrāz-nāma*, 106.

36 Kutubī, *Tārīkh-i Āl-i Muẓaffar,* 22; Ḥāfiẓ-i Abrū, *Jughrāfiyā*, II, 206; Naṭanzī, *Muntakhab al-tawārīkh-i Muʿīnī*, 175.
37 Kutubī, *Tārīkh-i Āl-i Muẓaffar,* 21–2; Ḥāfiẓ-i Abrū, *Jughrāfiyā*, II, 206; Samarqandī, *Maṭlaʿ-i saʿdayn*, I, 206.
38 Ibn Zarkūb, *Shīrāz-nāma*, 106–7; Kutubī, *Tārīkh-i Āl-i Muẓaffar,* 22; Naṭanzī, *Muntakhab al-tawārīkh-i Muʿīnī*, 175–6.
39 Shaykh Ḥasan Kuchik gave him the choice between sword and poison, Kutubī, *Tārīkh-i Āl-i Muẓaffar,* 22; Faṣīḥ Khwāfī, *Mujmal*, III, 62; Samarqandī, *Maṭlaʿ-i saʿdayn*, I, 207.
40 Kutubī, *Tārīkh-i Āl-i Muẓaffar,* 22; Ḥāfiẓ-i Abrū, *Jughrāfiyā*, II, 206.
41 Aharī, *Tārīkh-i Shaykh Ūvais,* 69; Ḥāfiẓ-i Abrū, *Jughrāfiyā*, II, 206.
42 Ibn Zarkūb, *Shīrāz-nāma*, 112; Aharī, *Tārīkh-i Shaykh Ūvais,* 69; Ḥāfiẓ-i Abrū, *Jughrāfiyā*, II, 206.
43 Ibn Zarkūb, *Shīrāz-nāma*, 113.
44 Ibn Zarkūb, *Shīrāz-nāma*, 112; Naṭanzī, *Muntakhab al-tawārīkh-i Muʿīnī*, 174.
45 Ibn Zarkūb, *Shīrāz-nāma*, 112; Naṭanzī, *Muntakhab al-tawārīkh-i Muʿīnī*, 174.
46 If the date given by the *Shīrāz-nāma* is correct, the revolt of the Shirazis began as soon as the news of Jalāl al-Dīn Masʿūd Shāh's assassination was known, before the return of Shaykh Abū Isḥāq to Shiraz, which seems quite plausible.
47 Ibn Zarkūb, *Shīrāz-nāma*, 114–15; Ḥāfiẓ-i Abrū, *Jughrāfiyā*, II, 206–7.
48 Ḥāfiẓ, *Dīvān*, II, 1065.
49 Ibn Zarkūb, *Shīrāz-nāma*, 114–15; Ḥāfiẓ-i Abrū, *Jughrāfiyā*, II, 207; Naṭanzī, *Muntakhab al-tawārīkh-i Muʿīnī*, 174–5. According to the *Majmaʿ al-ansāb* (315), the *julūs* of Shaykh Abū Isḥāq in Shiraz took place on the date of these events. He says that his authority was exercised over Fārs, the *garmsīrāt*, Isfahan, Luristān, and Shūlistān. In addition to Fārs where he sought to impose himself, he even mentions the allies who later gave him their support when he opposed the Muzaffarid Mubāriz al-Dīn Muḥammad.
50 See Mohammad Mokri, *La lumière et le feu dans l'Iran ancien et leur démythification en Islam* (Leuven: Peeters, 1982[2]), 90, 99–100.
51 Ibn Zarkūb, *Shīrāz-nāma*, 114–15.
52 Qur'ān 2: 286.
53 Ibn Zarkūb, *Shīrāz-nāma*, 115.
54 Ibn Zarkūb, *Shīrāz-nāma*, 118. The *Dhayl-i Tārīkh-i guzīda* (27–30) places these events in 742/1341–2.
55 Kutubī, *Tārīkh-i Āl-i Muẓaffar,* 25; Ḥāfiẓ-i Abrū, *Jughrāfiyā*, II, 208.
56 Ḥāfiẓ-i Abrū, *Jughrāfiyā*, II, 207.
57 Kutubī, *Tārīkh-i Āl-i Muẓaffar,* 23–4; Ḥāfiẓ-i Abrū, *Jughrāfiyā*, III, 105. His son, Mawlānā Khwāja ʿImād al-Mulk, was his deputy.

58 Jean Aubin, "La question de Sīrjān au XIIIe siècle," *Studia Iranica* 6/2 (1977): 285–90. See the history of Sīrjān by 'Alī Akbar Bakhtiyārī, *Sīrjān dar ā'yīna-i zamān* (Kirmān, 1999. On these events see, *Sīrjān dar ā'yīna-i zamān*, 86–9.
59 Aubin, "La question de Sīrjān," 289.
60 Kutubī, *Tārīkh-i Āl-i Muẓaffar*, 23; Ḥāfiẓ-i Abrū, *Jughrāfiyā*, II, 208.
61 Faṣīḥ Khwāfī, *Mujmal*, III, 27; Ḥāfiẓ-i Abrū, *Jughrāfiyā* (III, 105) and *Dhayl-i Tārīkh-i guzīda* (29) give 742/1341–2. 'Izzat Mulk and the women around her were killed, dismembered, and eaten by followers of Shaykh Ḥasan Kuchik, Samarqandī, *Maṭla' al-sa'dayn*, I, 188–90. See also Ma'ṣūma Ma'dankan, *Ba-yāsā rasīdagān*, 150–1.
62 Kutubī, *Tārīkh-i Āl-i Muẓaffar*, 24; Khwandmīr, *Dastūr al-vuzārā'*, 241–2.
63 Kutubī, *Tārīkh-i Āl-i Muẓaffar*, 24.
64 Shams al-Dīn Maḥmūd Ṣā'in Qāḍī's son, born in 708/1308–9, will also become Shaykh Abū Isḥāq's vizier in 747/1346; Faṣīḥ Khwāfī, *Mujmal*, III, 17; Jean Aubin, "La question de Sīrjān," 29.
65 Kutubī, *Tārīkh-i Āl-i Muẓaffar*, 24; Ḥāfiẓ-i Abrū, *Jughrāfiyā*, II, 209.
66 Kutubī, *Tārīkh-i Āl-i Muẓaffar*, 24. On the coins struck by Shaykh Abū Isḥāq, see Ernst von Bergmann, "Münzen der Indschuiden," *Numismatische Zeitschrift* 3 (1871): 143–65; Muḥammad Yūnis, *al-Tadāwul al-naqdī fī madīna Shīrāz*, 233.
67 Ḥāfiẓ-i Abrū, *Jughrāfiyā*, II, 209.
68 Kutubī, *Tārīkh-i Āl-i Muẓaffar*, 24.
69 Kutubī, *Tārīkh-i Āl-i Muẓaffar*, 25; Ḥāfiẓ-i Abrū, *Jughrāfiyā*, II, 209.
70 Kutubī, *Tārīkh-i Āl-i Muẓaffar*, 25.
71 Maḥmūd b. 'Uthmān, *Miftāḥ al-hidāya*, 99–100.
72 Maḥmūd b. 'Uthmān, *Miftāḥ al-hidāya*, 102.
73 Ḥāfiẓ-i Abrū, *Jughrāfiyā*, II, 205; Naṭanzī, *Muntakhab al-tawārīkh-i Mu'īnī*, 176.
74 Kutubī, *Tārīkh-i Āl-i Muẓaffar*, 25–6; Naṭanzī, *Muntakhab al-tawārīkh-i Mu'īnī*, 177; Faṣīḥ Khwāfī, *Mujmal* (III, 54–5) gives the date of 749, but it is too late. This date probably corresponds to the failed attempt to attack Kirmān with the help of the Awghānīs during the winter of 749/1349. Shaykh Abū Isḥāq's military commander, tired of his master's incoherent policy, had decided to side with Mubāriz al-Dīn Muḥammad. According to Vaṣṣāf (201), the Jurmā'īs had contracted marriages with the inhabitants of the villages of this region.
75 Kutubī, *Tārīkh-i Āl-i Muẓaffar*, 28; Ḥāfiẓ-i Abrū, *Jughrāfiyā*, III, 117. These tribes are given as Mongols and in the process of settlement in the Kirbāl from 676/1278, Vaṣṣāf, *Tajziyat al-amṣār va tazjiyat al-a'ṣār*, 202.
76 Kutubī, *Tārīkh-i Āl-i Muẓaffar*, 27–8; Ḥāfiẓ-i Abrū, *Jughrāfiyā*, III, 117.
77 Kutubī, *Tārīkh-i Āl-i Muẓaffar*, 30; Ḥāfiẓ-i Abrū, *Jughrāfiyā*, III, 118.
78 Kutubī, *Tārīkh-i Āl-i Muẓaffar*, 30; Ḥāfiẓ-i Abrū, *Jughrāfiyā*, III, 118.

79 Kutubī, *Tārīkh-i Āl-i Muẓaffar,* 30; Ḥāfiẓ-i Abrū, *Jughrāfiyā*, III, 118. Sayyid Ṣadr al-Dīn b. Mujtabā probably belonged to the family of Sayyid ʿAḍud al-Dīn Muḥammad b. Yuʿlā b. Mujtabā who was responsible for the tax in Fārs under Öljeitü.

80 Detailed description of the engines of war used for the siege is in Naṭanzī, *Muntakhab al-tawārīkh-i Muʿīnī*, 178.

81 According to the *Mujmal* (III, 77), the dead were no longer buried because, starving, people ate them. See also Qāsim Ghanī, *Tārīkh-i ʿaṣr-i Ḥāfiẓ*, 92.

82 Kutubī, *Tārīkh-i Āl-i Muẓaffar,* 34–5; Ḥāfiẓ-i Abrū, *Jughrāfiyā*, III, 124.

83 The sources give different spellings for the name of this *amīr*: Bīkjakāz (Kutubī, *Tārīkh-i Āl-i Muẓaffar,* 34), Nīkchuvāz (Naṭanzī, *Muntakhab al-tawārīkh-i Muʿīnī*, 178), and Bīkchīkār (Ḥāfiẓ-i Abrū, *Jughrāfiyā*, III, 124).

84 Ḥāfiẓ-i Abrū, *Jughrāfiyā*, III, 124.

85 Kutubī, *Tārīkh-i Āl-i Muẓaffar,* 35; Ḥāfiẓ-i Abrū, *Jughrāfiyā*, III, 124. He used part of this booty to make embellishments to the tomb of the great Sufi of Shiraz, Abū ʿAbd Allāh b. Khafīf Shīrāzī, known as Shaykh Kabīr.

86 Kutubī, *Tārīkh-i Āl-i Muẓaffar,* 37; Ḥāfiẓ-i Abrū, *Jughrāfiyā*, III, 124.

87 Kutubī, *Tārīkh-i Āl-i Muẓaffar,* 36; Ḥāfiẓ-i Abrū, *Jughrāfiyā*, II, 208.

88 Josef Van Ess, "al-Idjī," *EI*[2] 3: 1047–8; Josef Van Ess, *Erkenntnislehre des ʿAḍuddadin al-Ījī*, Wiesbaden, 1996; Carl Brockelman, *Geschichte der arabischen Literatur* (Leiden: Brill, 1949), II, 208–9.

89 Kutubī, *Tārīkh-i Āl-i Muẓaffar,* 37.

90 Kutubī, *Tārīkh-i Āl-i Muẓaffar,* 37.

91 Kutubī, *Tārīkh-i Āl-i Muẓaffar,* 28.

92 Kutubī, *Tārīkh-i Āl-i Muẓaffar,* 28.

93 His son Shāh Shujāʿ (r. 759–65/1359–84) continued to mention the name of the Caliph of Cairo on his currency.

94 Kutubī, *Tārīkh-i Āl-i Muẓaffar,* 45.

95 Ibn Zarkūb, *Shīrāz-nāma*, 120.

96 Qur'ān 3: 26.

97 Ibn Zarkūb, *Shīrāz-nāma*, 121.

98 Qur'ān 2: 12.

99 Ibn Zarkūb, *Shīrāz-nāma*, 120–1.

100 Ibn Zarkūb, *Shīrāz-nāma*, 122.

101 Qur'ān 8: 62.

102 Ibn Zarkūb, *Shīrāz-nāma*, 122.

103 Qur'ān 13: 17.

104 Khwāndmīr, *Ḥabīb al-siyar*, III, 287–8; Khwāndmīr/Thackston, *Habibu's-Siyar. The History of the Mongols and Genghis Khan (tome 3)*, 160.

105 Khwāndmīr, *Ḥabīb al-siyar*, III, 288; Khwāndmīr/Thackston, *Habibu's-Siyar. The History of the Mongols and Genghis Khan (tome 3)*, 160.
106 Qavām al-Dīn Ḥasan Tamghāchī, as his name suggests, held the "seal" (*tamghā*).
107 Ḥafiẓ, *The Dīvān*. Translated by Henry Wilberforce Clarke, Government of India Office Printing, 1891, 726.
108 Kutubī, *Tārīkh-i Āl-i Muẓaffar*, 40; Ḥāfiẓ-i Abrū, *Jughrāfiyā*, II, 211.
109 Aigle, *Saints hommes de Chiraz et du Fārs*, chapter 2.
110 Kutubī, *Tārīkh-i Āl-i Muẓaffar*, 40; Ḥāfiẓ-i Abrū, *Jughrāfiyā*, II, 211.
111 Account of all these events in Kutubī, *Tārīkh-i Āl-i Muẓaffar*, 40–3; Ḥāfiẓ-i Abrū, *Jughrāfiyā*, II, 211–13; Faṣīḥ Khwāfī, *Mujmal*, III, 83.
112 Ay Temür is possibly identical to "Amīr Tīmūr Ghulām" who was *amīr al-umarā'* of Shaykh Abū Isḥāq. He is quoted in the unpublished charts of Naṭanzī, see Denise Aigle, "Les tableaux dynastiques du *Muntaḫab al-tawārīḫh-i Mu'īnī*," *StIr* 21/1 (1993): 67–83.
113 Kutubī, *Tārīkh-i Āl-i Muẓaffar*, 42; Ḥāfiẓ-i Abrū, *Jughrāfiyā*, II, 210–11.
114 Kutubī, *Tārīkh-i Āl-i Muẓaffar*, 43; Ḥāfiẓ-i Abrū, *Jughrāfiyā*, II, 113.
115 Ḥāfiẓ-i Abrū, *Jughrāfiyā*, II, 113.
116 Kutubī, *Tārīkh-i Āl-i Muẓaffar*, 46.
117 Jamāl al-Dīn Mīr-i Mīrān was the *ra'īs* of Isfahan in the years 1349–56, Kutubī, *Tārīkh-i Āl-i Muẓaffar*, 45–6, 53, see also Jean Aubin, "Šāh Ismā'īl et les notables de l'Iraq persan. Études safavides I," 40; Rosemarie Quiring-Zoche, *Isfahan im 15. und 16. Jahrhundert* (Freiburg: Klaus Schwarz Verlag, 1980), 228–9.
118 Khwāndmīr, *Ḥabīb al-siyar*, III, 290. The term *kalāntar* refers to the one who manages the affairs of the inhabitants of a city, or even to a district chief (*ra'īs-i maḥalla*). In the *Lughat-nāma* (XII, 18502), the term *kalāntar* is the synonym of *kulū*.
119 The guardian of the fortress had delivered this stronghold to the Muzaffarids, Ḥāfiẓ-i Abrū, *Jughrāfiyā*, II, 215.
120 Shihāb Munshī was secretary at the court of the Muzaffarids, like his father. He collected in the *Humāyūn-nāma* letters written between the mid-eighth century and the mid-ninth century, see Rukn al-Dīn Humāyūn Farrakh, "Muqaddima," in *Humāyūn-nāma*, Tihrān, 4–7; this letter is reproduced in *Asnād va nāma-hā-i tārīkhī*, 304–5.
121 Shihāb Munshī, *Humāyūn-nāma*, 151–2.
122 Khwāndmīr, *Ḥabīb al-siyar*, III, 291; Khwāndmīr/Thackston, *Habibu's-Siyar. The History of the Mongols and Genghis Khan (tome 3)*, 162.
123 Faṣīḥ Khwāfī, *Mujmal*, III, 87–8; Kutubī, *Tārīkh-i Āl-i Muẓaffar*, 53–4; *Dhayl-i Tārīkh-i guzīda* (57) gives the end of 757/1356; Ḥāfiẓ-i Abrū (*Jughrāfiyā*, II, 215–17) gives Jumādā I 30, 757/May 31, 1356; Naṭanzī, *Muntakhab al-tawārīkh-i Mu'īnī*, 184–5; Shabānkāra'ī, *Majma' al-ansāb*, 317–18. Ḥāfiẓ

gave this date for the assassination of Shaykh Abū Isḥāq in a fragment of poetry, Ghanī, *Tārīkh-i ʿaṣr-i Ḥāfiẓ*, 119–21; Ḥāfiẓ, *Dīvān*, ed. Khanlarī, II, n° 24, 1576.

124 Ḥāfiẓ-i Abrū, *Jughrāfiyā*, II, 217; Khwāndmīr, *Ḥabīb al-siyar*, III, 291; Khwāndmīr/Thackston, *Habibu's-Siyar. The History of the Mongols and Genghis Khan (tome 3)*, 162.

125 During the Ilkhanid period, these Mongol tribes settled in Fārs. According to Vaṣṣāf three hundred families of Jurmāʾīs were sent to the Dārābjird region during Arghun's reign, where their settlement is attested around 740/1340 by Shabānkāraʾī, Jean Aubin, *Émirs mongols et vizirs persans*, 79.

126 Ḥāfiẓ-i Abrū, *Jughrāfiyā*, III, 129. From this marriage were born three sons, Sulṭān Ūvays, Shiblī, and Jahāngīr, and a daughter, Sulṭān Pādishāh.

127 Kutubī, *Tārīkh-i Āl-i Muẓaffar*, 35.

128 Kutubī, *Tārīkh-i Āl-i Muẓaffar*, 42–3; Ḥāfiẓ-i Abrū, *Jughrāfiyā*, II, 212. The *Shīrāz-nāma* does not mention this event.

129 Ḥāfiẓ-i Abrū, *Jughrāfiyā*, II, 212.

130 The terms *javān* and *pahlavān* are often associated, see, for example, Khwāndmīr, *Ḥabīb al-siyar*, III, 451.

131 The quality of *javānmardī* has the Arabic equivalent of *futuwwa*, created around the eighth century as opposed to *muruwwa*, the virtue of the mature man. The *Lughat-nāma* (V, 7892–3) gives as equivalent to the *javānmard*, the *fatā* and the *ṣāḥib-futuwwa*. See also Llyod Ridgeon (ed.), *Javanmardi: The Ethics and Practice of Persianate Perfection* (London: Gingko, 2018). The characters whose name is composed of the term *akhī* attached to a name, for example, Akhī Shujāʿ, are also considered as *pahlavān*. In Anatolia in the thirteenth and fourteenth centuries, the *akhīs* were the heads of associations of young people organized into corporations. This word of Turkic origin is already attested in Iran in the pre-Mongolian period; it means generous, Franz Taeschner, "Akhī," *EI*[2] 1: 983.

132 Ibn Baṭṭūṭa, *The Travels of Ibn Baṭṭūṭa, A.D. 1325–1354*, II, 307–8.

133 Ibn Baṭṭūṭa, *The Travels of Ibn Baṭṭūṭa, A.D. 1325–1354*, II, 308.

134 For the activities of the *ʿayyārūn*, see Deborah Tor, *Violent Order: Religious Warfare, Chivalry, and the* ʿayyār *Phenomenon in the Medieval Islamic World* (Würzburg: Orient-Institut Istanbul, 2007). She studies in Chapter 7 the relationship between *ʿayyār* and *futuwwa*. See also L. Hanaway, "ʿAyyār in Persian sources," *EIr* 3: 161–3.

135 Luke Treadwell, "Urban Militias in the Eastern Islamic World (Third-Fourth Centuries AH/Ninth-Tenth Centuries CE)," in *Late Antiquity: Eastern Perspectives*, T. Bernheimer and A. Silverstein (eds.) (Cambridge: Cambridge University Press, 2012), 128–44.

136 Mohsen Zakeri, "The 'Ayyārān of Khurassan and the Mongol Invasion," in *Proceedings of the Third European Conference of Iranian Studies* (Cambridge, 11th to 15th September 1995), Part 2 *Mediaeval and Modern Persian Studies*, Ch. Melville (ed.) (Wiesbaden: Franz Steiner Verlag, 1999), 269–76.
137 Zakeri, "The 'Ayyārān," 271.
138 Zakeri, "The 'Ayyārān," 275.
139 Lexicographers give *amīr* as an equivalent of the term *pahlavān*.
140 In the Mongolian languages, the term *bö'e* designates the shaman, but it also means the wrestler, the athlete. It is impossible, in the Mongolian language, to distinguish the shaman from the wrestler; on the use of this word, see Roberte Hamayon, *La chasse à l'âme. Esquisse d'une théorie du chamanisme sibérien* (Nanterre: Société d'ethnologie, 1990), 142, 506.
141 Khwāfī, *Mujmal*, III, 50–1; Mīrkhwānd, *Rawḍat al-ṣafā'*, V, 600; Khwāndmīr, *Ḥabīb al-siyar*, III, 356; Khwāndmīr/Thackston, *Habibu's-Siyar. The History of the Mongols and Genghis Khan (tome 3)*, 201.
142 Mīrkhwānd, *Rawḍat al-ṣafā'*, V, 600.
143 Aigle, "Sarbedārs," *EIr* online edition.
144 Shabānkāra'ī, *Majma' al-ansāb*, 315, 343; Mīrkhwānd, *Rawḍat al-ṣafā'*, V, 600.
145 The term *kutvāl* is sometimes found as a synonym of *pahlavān*, Shabānkāra'ī, *Majma' al-ansāb*, 343.
146 Naṭanzī, *Muntakhab al-tawārīkh-i Mu'īnī*, 180.
147 Ḥāfiẓ-i Abrū, *Jughrāfiyā*, II, 200–1; Samarqandī, *Maṭla'-i sa'dayn*, I, 194.
148 Kutubī, *Tārīkh-i Āl-i Muẓaffar*, 19; Shabānkāra'ī, *Majma' al-ansāb*, 343.
149 Mu'īn al-Dīn Yazdī, *Mavāhib-i ilāhī dar tārīkh-i Āl-i Muẓaffar*, ed. Sa'īd Nafīsī (Tihrān: Chāpkhāna-i Iqbāl, 1947–8), 132.
150 Shabānkāra'ī, *Majma' al-ansāb*, 343.
151 On this character, see Ḥāfiẓ-i Abrū, *Jughrāfiyā*, II, 260, 268.
152 He derives his *nisba*, Jalālī, from the *laqab* of his master Jalāl al-Dīn Shāh Shujā'. On Pahlavān Khurram, see Ḥāfiẓ-i Abrū, *Jughrāfiyā*, II, 225, 237, 239–40.
153 Ḥāfiẓ-i Abrū, *Jughrāfiyā*, II, 214.
154 Many examples in Dihkhudā, *Lughat-nāma*, IV: 5830.
155 Faṣīḥ Khwāfī, *Mujmal*, III, 54–5.
156 Georges Duby, "Dans la France du Nord-Ouest. Au XIIe siècle: les 'Jeunes' dans la société aristocratique," *Annales. Économie, Sciences sociales* 5 (1964): 835–46. Reprint in *Féodalité*, Paris, 1996.
157 Duby, "Dans la France du Nord-Ouest," 835.
158 Duby, "Dans la France du Nord-Ouest," 835.
159 Martin Aurell, who studies the conflicts between the *juvenes* and their fathers in Western chivalry, explains that while waiting for their inheritance, sons were often doomed to vagrancy, leading them to put themselves at the service

of the highest bidder among the lords, see "La parenté déchirée: les luttes intrafamiliales au Moyen Âge," in *Rompre la concorde familiale typologie, imaginaire, questionnements*, M. Aurell (ed.) (Turnhout: Brepols, 2010), 12.

160 Qazvīnī, *Dhayl-i Tārīkh-i guzīda*, 50.

161 Dihkhudā, *Lughat-nāma*, XII, 18502.

162 For the *kulūs*' involvement in conflicts in Muzaffarid Fārs, see Aigle, *Saints homme de Chiraz et du Fārs*, 142–3.

163 Kutubī, *Tārīkh-i Āl-i Muẓaffar*, 40–1; Ḥāfiẓ-i Abrū, *Jughrāfiyā*, II, 210; Khwāfī, *Mujmal*, 83.

7 Persian *ḥukkām*: "Games of the Swords" or Corrupt Officials?

1 David Durand-Guédy, *Iranian Elites and Turkish Rulers. A History of Iṣfahān in the Saljuq Period* (London: Routledge, 2010), 174–81.

2 Durand-Guédy, *Iranian Elites and Turkish Rulers*, 181.

3 Durand-Guédy, *Iranian Elites and Turkish Rulers*, 200–4.

4 Hossein Mirjafari, "The Ḥaydarī-Niʿmatī Conflicts in Iran," *IrSt* 12/3–4 (1979): 136.

5 Vanessa Van Renterghem, *Les élites bagdadiennes au temps des Seldjoukides*, I (Beirut: Institut français du Proche-Orient, 2015), 448.

6 The *kharvār* corresponded to one hundred *mann*, but the weight of the *mann* varied from city to city. In Shiraz, it was worth 3.3 kg; on the value of the *mann* in Iran, see Walter Hinz, *Islamische Masse und Gewichte* (Leiden: Brill, 1955), 17–21.

7 Vaṣṣāf, *Tajziyat al-amṣār va tazjiyat al-aʿṣār*, 445; Petrushevsky, "The Socio-economic Condition," 491.

8 Hope, *Power, Politics*, 159.

9 Qāshānī, *Tārīkh-i Ūljaytū*, 603–4; Aubin, *Émirs mongols et vizirs persans*, 48.

10 Vaṣṣāf, *Tajziyat al-amṣār va tazjiyat al-aʿṣār*, 690.

11 Vaṣṣāf, *Tajziyat al-amṣār va tazjiyat al-aʿṣār*, 633.

12 The population of Mongolia was estimated at seven hundred thousand people at the time of Chinggis Khan, which is the reason why he had to incorporate the conquered populations to enlarge the territory, see Thomas T. Allsen, "Ever Closer Encounters: The Appropriation of Culture and the Apportionment of Peoples in the Mongol Empire," *Journal of Early Modern History* 1 (1997): 4; Biran, "The Mongol Transformation: From the Steppe to Eurasian Empire," 348.

13 David Durand-Guédy (*Iranian Elites and Turkish Rulers*, 220–5) studied the tyranny exercised by local personnel on populations, especially villagers.

14 Saʿdī, *Kulliyāt*. Translation Lane, *Early Mongol Rule*, 134.

15 Ibn Zarkūb, *Shīrāz-nāma*, 92; Vaṣṣaf, *Tajziyat al-amṣār va tazjiyat al-aʿṣār,* 205.

16 Aubin, *Émirs mongols et vizirs persans*, 83.

17 Subtelny, *Le monde est un jardin*, 79; Lambton, *Landlord and Peasant*, 113; Lambton, "Economy IV.-V. From the Arab Conquest to the End of the Il-Khanids," *EIr* 8: 126.

18 Lane, *Early Mongol Rule*, 236–9. After the restoration of Nishapur, following the earthquake of 666/1267, Pūr-i Bāha dedicated a long poem to Abaqa in which he refers to the Ilkhan as "Nūshīrvān of our Time, the Lord of the World, the Sovereign of the Earth," Vladimir Minorsky, "Pūr-i Bāha's 'Mongol Ode,'" *Iranica* (1964): 294; on Pūr-i Bāha's poems ibid., 292–302.

19 Subtelny, *Le monde est un jardin*, 84.

20 Vaṣṣāf, *Tajziyat al-amṣār va tazjiyat al-aʿṣār,* 204.

21 Maḥmūd b. ʿUthmān, *Miftāḥ al-hidāya*, 157.

22 Thomas T. Allsen, *The Steppe and the Sea. Pearls in the Mongol Empire* (Philadelphia: University of Pennsylvania Press, 2019), 13.

23 Aubin, "La question de Sīrjān," 287.

24 A. P. Martinez, "Regional Mint Outputs and the Dynamic of Bullion Flows through the Īl-Xānate," *Journal of the Turkish Studies* 8 (1984): 173.

25 Aubin, "Le royaume d'Ormuz," 105.

26 Aubin, "Le royaume d'Ormuz," 105.

27 Aigle, *Saints hommes de Chiraz et du Fārs*, 772–8.

28 Shabānkāraʾī, *Majmaʿ al-ansāb*, 266.

29 For example, we can cite the book on the Ilkhanid Fārs by ʿAbd al-Rasūl Khayāndish whose title (*Fārs People Against Mongols*) is significant from the perspective of its author.

30 Aubin, *Émirs mongols et vizirs persans*, 83; Jackson, *The Mongols and the Islamic World*, 275.

31 Aubin, *Émirs mongols et vizirs persans*, 83; Jackson, *The Mongols and the Islamic World*, 274.

32 Aubin, *Émirs mongols et vizirs persans*, 83–4.

33 Aubin, *Émirs mongols et vizirs persans*, 83.

34 The harmful role of certain local notables is not specific to the Ilkhanid period, Jürgen Paul cites similar cases in the pre-Mongol period, but it seems on a lesser scale, see "Armies, Lords and Subjects in Medieval Iran," 73–5.

35 Ḥāfiẓ, *Dīvān*, ed. Khanlarī, n° 463. Translation in Hafez. *Translations and Interpretations of the Ghazals* by Geoffrey Squires (Ohio: Miami University Press, 2014), 167.

36 Aubin, *Émirs mongols et vizirs persans*, 85.
37 Peter Jackson (*The Mongols and the Islamic World*, 382–9) studied the importance of Chinggisid legitimacy down to the Timurids.
38 Aigle, *Le Fārs face à la domination mongole*, 165–71.
39 Samarqandī, *Maṭla'-i sa'dayn*, 1/1, 232; Faṣīḥ Khwāfī, *Mujmal*, III, 72.
40 Samarqandī, *Maṭla'-i sa'dayn*, 1/2, 484. He died at Sulṭāniyya in 798, Faṣīḥ Khwāfī, *Mujmal*, III, 139.
41 Samarqandī, *Maṭla'-i sa'dayn*, I/2, 608.
42 Shaykh Ūvays claimed a number of royal titles for himself, including sultan, khan, and *ṣāḥib-qirān* (Lord of auspicious conjunction), as heir to the Ilkhanate and the ideal Muslim ruler, see Wing, *The Jalayirids*, 129–43.
43 But to this factor the spread of the plague in the decades of 740s/1340s and 750s/1350s, and the subsequent economic tension would have also played a part, see Michael W. Dols, *The Black Death in the Middle East* (Princeton, NJ: Princeton University Press, 1977).

8 Epilogue: Other Principalities in Southern Iran

1 Shabānkāra'ī, *Majma' al-ansāb*, 165. The king of Shabānkāra pronounced this sentence before going into battle against the troops of Hülegü. I would like to thank Mohsen Ashtiyani and Michael Hope for reading and commenting on the draft of this epilogue.
2 Vladimir Minorsky, "Lur-i Buzurg," *EI*[2] 5: 832–4; Bertold Spuler, "Atābakān-e Lorestān," *EIr* II: 896–7; Bertold Spuler, "Hazāraspides," *EI*[2] 3: 347–8; Āshtiyānī, *Tārīkh-i mughūl*, 442–8.
3 Mustawfī Qazvīnī, *Nuzhat al-qulūb*, ed., 127; trans., 127.
4 The Hazaraspids were not in fact tutors to princes, as the term *atabek* would imply, they adopt the title in a nominal fashion. The rulers of the dynasty sometimes used the title *malik*, Louise Marlow, "Teaching Wisdom. A Persian Work of Advice for Atabeg Ahmad of Luristan," in *Mirror for the Muslim Prince: Islam and the Theory of Statecraft*, M. Boroujerdi (ed.) (Syracuse: Syracuse University Press, 2013), 122, footnote 2.
5 Date given by Āshtiyānī, *Tārīkh-i mughūl*, 448.
6 Bertold Spuler, "Hazāraspides," *EI*[2] III: 347; Āshtiyānī, *Tārīkh-i Mughūl*, 448.
7 Melville, "Concepts of Government and State Formation in Mongol Iran," 36.
8 Shabānkāra'ī, *Majma' al-ansāb*, 206. Translation O. Otsuka, "The Hazaraspid Dynasty's Legendary Kayanid Ancestry: The Flowering of Persian Literature

under the Patronage of Local Rulers in the Il-khanid Period," *Journal of Persian Studies* 12 (2019): 182.

9 The uncertainty of Aḥmad's regnal dates reflects a lack of unanimity in the sources, see Marlow, "Teaching Wisdom," 122, footnote 1.

10 Mustawfī Qazvīnī, *Tārīkh-i guzīda*, 548; Shabānkāra'ī, *Majma' al-ansāb*, 208–9.

11 Ibn Baṭṭūṭa, *The Travels of Ibn Baṭṭūṭa, A.D. 1325–1354*, II, 289.

12 Shabānkāra'ī, *Majma' al-ansāb*, 209.

13 Shihāb Mushī, *Humāyūn-nāma*, 62.

14 Marlow, "Teaching Wisdom," 132–7; Otsuka, "The Hazaraspid Dynasty's Legendary Kayanid Ancestry," 187–92.

15 Shams al-Dīn 'Abd al-Laṭīf b. Ṣadr al-Dīn Rūzbihān, *Rūḥ al-jinān fī sīrat al-shaykh Rūzbihān*, in *Rūzbihān-nāma* M. Dānish-Pazhūh (ed.) (Tihrān: Intishārat-i Anjumān-i Āthār-i Millī, 1347sh./1969), 369.

16 Marlow, "Teaching Wisdom," 139. The name of the author of the *Tuḥfa* does not appear in the only manuscript of the text, but it has been attributed by scholars to Sharaf Faḍl Allāh b. 'Abd Allāh Qazvīnī, "Teaching Wisdom," 137–8.

17 Mustawfī Qazvīnī, *Tārīkh-i guzīda*, 548–9; Shabānkāra'ī, *Majma' al-ansāb*, 208–9.

18 This information does not appear in the printed edition, but it derives from the manuscript preserved in the Royal Asiatic Society, see Marlow, "Teaching Wisdom," 125, footnote 6.

19 Afrāsiyāb had tried to extend his power outside the Lur-i Buzurg, see *infra*.

20 Vladimir Minorsky, "Lur-i Kuchick," *EI*[2] 5: 834–5; Bertold Spuler, "Atābakān-e Lorestān," *EIr* 2: 897–8. Āshtiyānī, *Tārīkh-i Mughūl*, 449–52. They are also known as Jangardī.

21 Early history of the dynasty, Mustawfī Qazvīnī, *Tārīkh-i guzīda*, 552–3; Naṭanzī, *Muntakhab al-tawārīkh-i Mu'īnī*, 53–4.

22 Naṭanzī, *Muntakhab al-tawārīkh-i Mu'īnī*, 53–4.

23 Mustawfī Qazvīnī, *Tārīkh-i guzīda*, 551.

24 Ja'far, *Tārīkh-i Yazd*, 38–46; Kātib, *Tārīkh-i jadīd-i Yazd*, 64–79; Bāfqī, *Jāmi'-i mufīdī*, 83–92; Āshtiyānī, *Tārīkh-i Mughūl*, 401–3.

25 He had been killed at the battle of Qaṭvān in 536/1141 in which the Qara Khitai inflicted a crushing defeat on the Saljuqs. He had no son likely to succeed him, Ja'farī, *Tārīkh-i Yazd*, 21; Kātib, *Tārīkh-i jadīd-i Yazd*, 65. The Kakuyides were from Daylam, Edmund C. Bosworth, "Kākūyides," *EI*[2] 4: 485–7.

26 Ja'farī, *Tārīkh-i Yazd*, 23; Kātib, *Tārīkh-i jadīd-i Yazd*, 67; Bāfqī, *Jāmi'-i mufīdī*, 84.

27 Ja'farī, *Tārīkh-i Yazd*, 23; Kātib, *Tārīkh-i jadīd-i Yazd*, 67; Bāfqī, *Jāmi'-i mufīdī*, 84.

28 Ann K. S. Lambton, "Yazd," *EI*[2] 11: 327–35; S. C. Fairbanks, "Atābakān-e Yazd," *EIr* 2: 900–2; Āshtiyānī, *Tārīkh-i Mughūl*, 401–3.

29 On the Shabānkāra's kings, see Aubin, *Émirs mongols et vizirs persans*, 69–80. Ibn Balkhī distinguishes the Kurds from the Shabānkāra ethnic group, which consisted of five clans. Historiography of the Mongol period knows only the Ismā'īlīs, Aubin, *Émirs mongols et vizirs persans*, 71–2.

30 Aigle, "Šabānkāra'ī," *EIr* online edition.

31 Zekrollah Mohammadi, Amir Hossein Hatami, and Mohsen Parvish, "Persian Identity Aspects in Delgosha's System of Poems Based on Shahnameh's Ferdowsi Re-creations," *Literary Text Research* 25/89 (2021): 99.

32 Charles Melville, "Concepts of Government and State Formation in Mongol Iran," in *Iran after the Mongols*, 37.

33 Shabānkāra'ī, *Majma' al-ansāb*, 160.

34 Shabānkāra'ī, *Majma' al-ansāb*, 160.

35 Aubin, *Émirs mongols et vizirs persans*, 72.

36 Shabānkāra'ī, *Majma' al-ansāb*, 160. Muẓaffar al-Dīn Muḥammad had a mosque built in Īj and another built in the rock in 652/1254, 'Imād al-Dīn Shaykh al-Ḥukamā'ī, "Naqsh-i katība-hā-i khwānda-i nashda-i masjid-i sangī-i dārāb," 88–91.

37 Aubin, *Émirs mongols et vizirs persans*, 73.

38 Ḥamīd Pūr was integrated into the Khwārazmshāh army. Details of the establishment of Baraq Ḥājib in Kirmān in Michal Biran, *The Empire of the Qara Khitai*, 87–8; Lane, *Early Mongol Rule*, 102–3; Jackson, *The Mongols and the Islamic World*, 246–7.

39 His name sometimes appears as Rukn al-Dīn Khwāja Mubārak, Lane, *Early Mongol State*, 283, footnote 563.

40 Jackson, *The Mongols and the Islamic World*, 256.

41 Kātib, *Tārīkh-i jadīd-i Yazd*, 72.

42 Mustawfī Qazvīnī, *Tārīkh-i guzīda*, 557; Naṭanzī, *Muntakhab al-tawārīkh-i Mu'īnī*, 59–60.

43 Shabānkāra'ī, *Majma' al-ansāb*, 164.

44 Shabānkāra'ī, *Majma' al-ansāb*, 164.

45 Shabānkāra'ī, *Majma' al-ansāb*, 164–5.

46 Naṭanzī, *Muntakhab al-tawārīkh-i Mu'īnī*, 4–5.

47 Mohammadi, Hossein Hatami, and Parvish, "Persian Identity Aspects in Delgosha's System of Poems," 100.

48 Shabānkāra'ī, *Majma' al-ansāb*, 165.

49 Shabānkāra'ī, *Majma' al-ansāb*, 165. Translation Melville, "Concepts of Government and State Formation in Mongol Iran," 36.

50 Shabānkāra'ī, *Majma' al-ansāb*, 165.

51 Shabānkāra'ī, *Majma' al-ansāb*, 166.

52 Shabānkāra'ī, *Majma' al-ansāb*, 165.

53 Naṭanzī, *Muntakhab al-tawārīkh-i Mu'īnī*, 5. He uses the term *ṭā'at* to express submission to Hülegü.

54 This date is given by 'Abbās Iqbāl Āshtiyānī (*Tārīkh-i Mughūl*, 448), but all the dates of the reigns are questionable due to the imprecision of the sources.

55 Naṭanzī, *Muntakhab al-tawārīkh-i Mu'īnī*, 45–6. Aḥmad, brother of Afrāsiyāb, replaced him as hostage at Tabriz.

56 Allsen, *Culture and Conquest*, 73–4; Jackson, *The Mongols and the Islamic World*, 256.

57 Jackson, *The Mongols and the Islamic World*, 258.

58 Munshī Kirmānī, *Simṭ al-'ulā*, 70; Shabānkāra'ī, *Majma' al-ansāb*, 201. Translation Lane, *The Early Mongol Rule*, 98.

59 Biography by Bruno De Nicola, "Pādshāh Khatun. An Example of Architectural, Religious, and Literary Patronage in Ilkhanid Iran," in *The Mongols' Middle East: Continuity and Transformation in Ilkhanid Iran*, 273–4.

60 Rashīd al-Dīn/Karīmī, *Jāmi' al-tawārīkh*, 688; Rashīd al-Dīn/Thackson, *Jami'ut-Tawarikh*, 341.

61 Rashīd al-Dīn/Karīmī, 688.

62 Shihāb al-Dīn al-'Umarī, *Maṣālik al-mamālik*, ed., 86.

63 According to Shams al-Dīn Kāshānī, he remained for some time in Hülegü's entourage since he accompanied him to Samarqand, *Shāhnāma-i Tchingīzī*, 310.

64 On Tekla's career before Hülegü's arrival in Iran, see Mustawfī Qazvīnī, *Tārīkh-i guzīda*, 542–4; Naṭanzī, *Muntakhab al-tawārīkh-i Mu'īnī*, 41–3; 'Abbās Iqbāl Āshtiyānī, *Tārīkh-i Mughūl*, 444–5.

65 Mustawfī Qazvīnī, *Tārīkh-i guzīda*, 543.

66 Mustawfī Qazvīnī, *Tārīkh-i guzīda*, 543; Naṭanzī, *Muntakhab al-tawārīkh-i Mu'īnī*, 43.

67 Mustawfī Qazvīnī, *Tārīkh-i guzīda*, 544; Naṭanzī, *Muntakhab al-tawārīkh-i Mu'īnī*, 43.

68 Mustawfī Qazvīnī, *Tārīkh-i guzīda*, 543–4; Naṭanzī, *Muntakhab al-tawārīkh-i Mu'īnī*, 43; Ma'ṣūma Ma'dakān, *Ba-yāsā rasīdagān*, 40.

69 Date given by Āshtiyānī, *Tārīkh-i Mughūl*, 445.

70 Faṣīḥ Khwāfī, *Mujmal*, 2, 338.

71 Allsen, *Mongol Imperialism*, 75; Jackson, *The Mongols and the Islamic World*, 253–4.

72 Shabānkāra'ī, *Majma' al-ansāb*, 169. Nizām al-Dīn Ḥasan's role in this battle is akin to epic literature.

73 Shabānkāra'ī, *Majma' al-ansāb*, 169; Vassaf, 424. Hülegü also gave him the daughter of Saljūq Shāh in marriage. The sources do not specify the reason for his

removal, but there were many power struggles between the *amīrs* and the court chamberlains of the Shabānkāra.

74 Shabānkāra'ī, *Majma' al-ansāb*, 169–70; Naṭanzī, *Muntakhab al-tawārīkh-i Mu'īnī*, 6.

75 Shabānkāra'ī, *Majma' al-ansāb*, 169–70; Naṭanzī, *Muntakhab al-tawārīkh-i Mu'īnī*, 6.

76 Shabānkāra'ī, *Majma' al-ansāb*, 170; Naṭanzī, *Muntakhab al-tawārīkh-i Mu'īnī*, 6.

77 *Majma' al-ansāb* (170–1) calls him Shīshī Ba'shī, for Bakhshī. He was probably a Buddhist. Naṭanzī (6) calls him Amīr Īghūr Sīsī.

78 Shabānkāra'ī, *Majma' al-ansāb*, 171; Naṭanzī, *Muntakhab al-tawārīkh-i Mu'īnī*, 6–7.

79 Shabānkāra'ī, *Majma' al-ansāb*, 171; Naṭanzī, *Muntakhab al-tawārīkh-i Mu'īnī*, 7.

80 Shabānkāra'ī, *Majma' al-ansāb*, 171.

81 Rashīd al-Dīn/Thackson, *Jami'ut-Tawarikh*, 389, 392, 393.

82 Shabānkāra'ī, *Majma' al-ansāb*, 212.

83 Shabānkāra'ī, *Majma' al-ansāb*, 212; Naṭanzī, *Muntakhab al-tawārīkh-i Mu'īnī*, 32-3; Ja'farī, *Tārikh-i Yazd*, 26; Kātib, *Tārīkh-i jadīd-i Yazd*, 74–5.

84 Naṭanzī, *Muntakhab al-tawārīkh-i Mu'īnī*, 32–3.

85 Shabānkāra'ī, *Majma' al-ansāb*, 212; Naṭanzī, *Muntakhab al-tawārīkh-i Mu'īnī*, 33; Kātib, *Tārīkh-i jadīd-i Yazd*, 75; Vaṣṣāf, *Tajziyat al-amṣār va tazjiyat al-a'ṣār*, 253.

86 Kātib, *Tārīkh-i jadīd*-i Yazd's author is the only one to give the name of Rukn al-Dīn Yūsuf Shāh's mother.

87 Kātib, *Tārīkh-i jadīd-i Yazd*, 75.

88 Naṭanzī, *Muntakhab al-tawārīkh-i Mu'īnī*, 33.

89 Shabānkāra'ī, *Majma' al-ansāb*, 213; Naṭanzī, *Muntakhab al-tawārīkh-i Mu'īnī*, 34; Ja'farī, *Tārikh-i Yazd*, 27; Kātib, *Tārīkh-i jadīd-i Yazd*, 75.

90 Naṭanzī, *Muntakhab al-tawārīkh-i Mu'īnī*, 34; Ja'farī, *Tārikh-i Yazd*, 27; Kātib, *Tārīkh-i jadīd-i Yazd*, 75. The sources give different reports on the events. According to the *Majma' al-ansāb* (213–14), sent to the *yarghu* after his rebellion, Yūsuf Shāh was initially pardoned by Ghazan. But later he would have been executed because Yūsuf Shāh had refused to participate in the Syrian campaign, see Naṭanzī, *Muntakhab al-tawārīkh-i Mu'īnī*, 34; Kātib, *Tārīkh-i jadīd-i Yazd*, 77. Like Hülegü before his conquest of Alamūt, according to Nūr al-Dīn Muḥammad Azhdārī (*Ghāzān-nāma*, 270–1), Ghazan sent orders to many Muslim and Christian princes asking them to join his armies before his first campaign in Syria. The princes of Shabānkāra and Fārs apparently refused, although the author does not speak of their fate.

91 Āshtiyānī, *Tārīkh-i Mughūl*, 402–3.

92 Naṭanzī, *Muntakhab al-tawārīkh-i Mu'īnī*, 34.

93 Jackson, *The Mongols and the Islamic World*, 264–5.
94 Āshtiyānī, *Tārīkh-i Mughūl*, 402.
95 Rashīd al-Dīn/Thackson, *Jami'ut-Tawarikh*, 436.
96 Mustawfī Qazvīnī, *Tārīkh-i guzīda*, 546–7.
97 Mustawfī Qazvīnī, *Tārīkh-i guzīda*, 546.
98 Mustawfī Qazvīnī, *Tārīkh-i guzīda*, 547.
99 Nūr al-Dīn Muḥammad Azhdārī, *Ghāzān-nāma*, 176; Rashīd al-Dīn/Thackson, 443.
100 Mustawfī Qazvīnī, *Tārīkh-i guzīda*, 548; Naṭanzī, *Muntakhab al-tawārīkh-i Mu'īnī*, 45–7.
101 Mustawfī Qazvīnī, *Tārīkh-i guzīda*, 548; Naṭanzī, *Muntakhab al-tawārīkh-i Mu'īnī*, 45–7.
102 Shabānkāra'ī, *Majma' al-ansāb*, 172.
103 Shabānkāra'ī, *Majma' al-ansāb*, 172.
104 Vaṣṣāf, *Tajziyat al-amṣār va tazjiyat al-a'ṣār*, 104. Translation Peter Jackson, *The Mongols and the Islamic World*, 278.
105 On the burdens and benefits of vassalage in the Mongol Empire, see Charles Melville, "Anatolia under the Mongols," in *Cambridge History of Turkey*, I, Kate Fleet (ed.) (Cambridge: Cambridge University Press, 2009), 51–101; B. Dashdondog, *The Mongols and the Armenians (1220-1335)* (Leiden: Brill, 2011), particularly on military cooperation; J. Martin, *Treasure of the Land of Darkness. The Fur Trade and Its significance for Medieval Russia* (Cambridge: Cambridge University Press, 1986), 163–7.
106 Qashānī, *Tārīkh-i Ūljaytū*, 43; Faṣīḥ Khwāfī, *Mujmal*, III, 12.
107 Jackson, *The Mongols and the Islamic World*, 267.

Bibliography

Primary Literature

Aharī, Abū Bakr Quṭbī. *Tārīkh-i Shaykh Ūvais*. Edited by J. B. Loon. 's-Gravenhague: Mouton, 1954.

Asnād va nāma-hā-i tārīkhī. Edited by Sayyid 'Alī Mu'ayyad Thābitī. Tihrān: Kitābkhāna-i Ṭahūrī, 1346sh./1963.

Azhdarī, Nūr al-Dīn, *Ghāzan-nāma*. Edited by Maḥmūd Dadbbirī. Tīhrān: Bunyād-i Mawqūfāt-i Ductur Maḥmūd Afshār, 1381sh./2003.

Bāfqī, Muḥammad Mufīd Mustawfī. *Jāmi'-i mufīdī*. Edited by. Īraj Afshār. 3 vols. Tihrān: Intishārat-i Asāṭir, 1385sh./2006.

Bar Hebraeus. *Chronicon Syriacum*. Edited by Paul Bedjan. Paris: Maisonneuve, 1890.

Bar Hebraeus. *The Chronography of Gregory Abû'l-Faraj (1225–1286)*. English translation by Ernest Wallis Budge. London: Oxford University Press, 1932.

Baybars al-Manṣūrī al-Dawādār, Rukn al-Dīn. *Zubdat al-fikra fī ta'rīkh al-hijra*. Edited by Donald S. Richards. Beirut: Dār al-Nashr al-Kitāb al-'Arabī, 1998.

Bayḍāvī, Nāṣir al-Dīn Abū 'Abd Allāh. *Niẓām al-tawārīkh*. Edited by Mīr Hāshim Muḥaddith. Tihrān: Bunyād-i Mawqūfāt-i Duktur Maḥmūd Afshār, 1382sh./2003.

Dawlatshāh Samarqandī. *Tadhkirat al-shu'arā'*. Edited by Muḥammad 'Abbāsī. Tihrān: Kitābfurūshī-i Bārānī, s.d.

Faṣīḥ Khwāfī, Aḥmad b. Jalāl al-Dīn. *Mujmal-i Faṣīḥī*. Edited by Muḥammad. Farrukhī. 3 vols. Mashhad: Bāstān, 1339sh./1960–1.

Hafez. *Translations and Interpretations of the Ghazals*. Geoffrey Squires. Ohio: Miami University Press, 2014.

Ḥāfiẓ, Shams al-Dīn. *Dīvān*. Edited by Parvīz Khanlarī. 2 vols. Tihrān: Chāpkhāna-i Nayl, 1359sh./1979[1].

Ḥafiẓ. *The Dīvān*. Translated by Henry Wilberforce Clarke. Government of India Office Printing, 1891.

Ḥāfiẓ-i Abrū. *Jughrāfiyā-i Ḥāfiẓ-i Abrū*. Edited by Ṣādiq Sajjādī. 3 vols. Tihrān: Mirāth-i Maktūb, 1375–8sh./1997–9.

Ḥāfiẓ-i Abrū. *Zubdat al-tawārīkh*. Edited by Sayyid Kamāl al-Dīn Javādī. 2 vols. Tihrān: Nashr-i Nay, 1372sh./1993.

Ḥāfiẓ-i Abrū. *Dhayl-i Jāmiʿ al-tawārīkh*. Edited by Khānbābā Bayānī. Tihrān: Intishārāt-i Anjumān-i Āthār-i Millī, 1350sh./1971.

Ḥamd Allāh Mustawfī Qazvīnī. *Nuzhat al-qulūb*. Edited by and English translation by Guy Le Strange. 2 vols. Leiden: Brill, 1915, 1919.

Ḥamd Allāh Mustawfī Qazvīnī. *Tārīkh-i guzīda*. Edited by Ḥusayn Navāʾī. Tihrān: Chāpkhāna-i Firdawsī, 1362sh./1983.

Ibn ʿAbd al-Ẓāhir, Muḥyī al-Dīn. *al-Rawḍ al-zāhir fī sīrat al-Malik al-Ẓāhir*. Edited by ʿAbd al-ʿAzīz Ḥuwayṭir. Riyāḍ: n.p., 1396/1976.

Ibn al-Athīr. *al-Kāmil fī l-tārīkh*. Edited by C. J. Tornberg. 14 vols. Leiden: Brill, 1851–76.

Ibn al-ʿImād. *Shadharāt al-dhahab fī akhbār man dhahab*. Edited by ʿAbd al-Qādir Arnaʾūṭ and Maḥmūd Arnaʾūṭ. 11 vols. Beirut: Dār al-Kutub al-ʿilmiyya, 1406–16/1986–95.

Ibn al-Fuwaṭī, *Talkhīṣ majmaʿ al-adāb fī muʿjam al-alqāb*. Edited by Muṣṭafā Jawād, 4 vols. Damascus: Wizārat al-Thaqafat wa-l-Irshād al-Qawmī, 1962–7.

Ibn aṣ-Ṣuqāʿī, Faḍl Allāh. *Tālī kitāb wafayāt al-aʿyān (Un fonctionnaire chrétien dans l'administration mamelouke)*. Edited by and French translation by Jacqueline Sublet. Damascus: Institut français de Damas, 1974.

Ibn Balkhī. *Fārs-nāma*. Edited by Guy Le Strange and Reynold A. Nicholson. London: The Cambridge University Press, 1921 (Partial translation by Guy Le Strange, *Description of the Province of Fars in Persia at the Beginning of the Twelfth Century A.D. From the MS. Of Ibn al-Balkhi in the British Museum*, London, 1912).

Ibn Baṭṭūṭa. *The Travels of Ibn Baṭṭūṭa, A.D. 1325–1354*. English translation by Hamilton Alexander Gibb. 4 vols. Cambridge: Hakluyt Society, 1958–94.

Ibn Ḥajar ʿAsqalānī. *al-Durar al-kāmina fī aʿyān al-miʾa al-thāmina*. 4 vols. Heydarabad, 1929–32.

Ibn Junayd Shīrazī, ʿIsā. *Hazār mazār*. Edited by Nūrānī Viṣāl. Shīrāz: Intishārāt-i Kitābkhāna-i Aḥmadī Shīrāzī, 1364sh./1975–6.

Ibn Khallikān, *Wafayāt al-aʿyān*. Edited by Iḥsān ʿAbbās. 8 vols. Beirut: Dār Ṣādir, 1968–72.

Ibn Wāṣil, Jamāl al-Dīn Muḥammad, *Mufarrij al-kurūb fī akhbār banī Ayyūb*. 6 vols. Edited by Ḥasanayn Muḥammad Rabīʿ and Saʿīd ʿAbd al-Fātiḥ ʿĀshūr. Cairo, 1977.

Ibn Zarkūb. *Shīrāz-nāma*. Edited by Ismāʿīl Vāʿiẓ Javādī. Tihrān: Intishārāt-i Farhang-i Īrān, 1350sh./1971–2.

Jaʿfarī, Jaʿfar b. Muḥammad Ḥusaynī. *Tārīkh-i Yazd*. Edited by Īraj Afshār. Tihrān: Bungāh-i Tarjuma wa Nashr-i Kitāb, 1338sh./1959–60.

Junayd Shīrāzī, Mu'īn al-Dīn Abū l-Qāsim. *Shadd al-izār*. Edited by Muḥammad Qazvīnī. Tihrān: Chāpkhāna-i Majlis, 1328sh./1948–9.

Juvaynī, 'Aṭā' Malik. *Tārīkh-i jahāngushā*. Edited by Muḥammad Qazvīnī. 3 vols. Leiden: Luzac, 1912–37.

[Juvaynī, 'Aṭā' Malik]. *The History of the World Conqueror*. Translation by J. Andrew Boyle. 2 vols. Manchester: Manchester University Press, 1958.

Kāshānī, Shams al-Dīn. *Shahnāma-i Chingīzī*. Edited by Vaḥīd Qanbarī Nanīz. Tihrān: Intishārāt-i Ductur Maḥmūd Afshār, 1399sh./2020.

Kātib, Aḥmad b. Ḥusayn b. 'Alī. *Tārīkh-i jadīd-i Yazd*. Edited by Īraj Afshār. Tihrān: Intishārāt-i Ibn Sīnā, 1345sh./1966.

Khwāndmīr, Ghiyāth al-Dīn. *Dastūr al-vuzarā'*. Edited by Sa'īd Nafisī. Tihrān: Iqbāl, 1317sh./1938–9.

Khwāndmīr, Ghiyāth al-Dīn. *Ḥabīb al-siyar fī akhbār afrād bashar*. Edited by M. Dabīr Siyāqī. 4 vols. Tihrān: Khayyām, 1333sh./1955–6.

[Khwāndmīr, Ghiyāth al-Dīn]. *Habibu's-Siyar. The History of the Mongols and Genghis Khan (tome 3)*. Translated and annotated by Wheeler M. Thackston, London: I.B. Tauris, 2012.

Kutubī, Maḥmūd. *Tārīkh-i Āl-i Muẓaffar*. Edited by 'Alī Navā'ī. Tihrān: Kitābfurūshī-i Ibn Sinā, 1334sh./1955–6.

Maḥmūd b. 'Uthmān. *Miftāḥ al-hidāya va miṣbāḥ al-'ināya*. Edited by 'Imād al-Dīn Shaykh al-Ḥukamā'ī. Tihrān: Kitābkhāna-i Millī, 1376sh./1995.

Maqrīzī, Taqī al-Dīn Aḥmad. *Kitāb al-Sulūk li-ma'rifat duwal al-mulūk*. Edited by M. 'Abd al-Qādir. 8 vols. Beirut: Dār al-Kutub al-'ilmiyya, 1997.

Mīrkhwānd, Muḥammad. *Tārīkh-i Rawḍat al-ṣafā'*. Edited by 'Abbās Parvīz. Tihrān: Intishārāt-i Aṣāṭir 1338–9sh./1960.

Morals Pointed and Tales Adorned. The Bustan of Sa'di. Translated by G. M. Wickens. Toronto: University of Toronto Press, 1974.

Munshī Kirmānī, Nāṣir al-Dīn. *Simṭ al-'ulā*. Edited by 'Abbās Iqbāl Āshtiyānī. Tihrān: Intishārāt-i Majjala-i Yādgār, 1328sh./1949.

Nasafī, 'Azīz al-Dīn. *Kitāb al-Insān al-kāmil*. Edited by Marijan Molé. Tihrān: Institut français de recherche en Iran, 1341sh./1962.

Naṭanzī, Mu'īn al-Dīn. *Muntakhab al-tawārīkh-i Mu'īnī*. Edited by Jean Aubin. Tihrān: Kitābfurūshī-i Khayyām, 1336sh./1957.

Qashānī, Abū l-Qāsim Muḥammad. *Tārīkh-i Ūljaytū*. Edited by M. Hambly. Tihrān: Bungāh-i Tarjuma va Nashr-i Kitāb, 1348sh./1969.

Qazvīnī, Zayn al-Dīn. *Dhayl-i Tārīkh-i guzīda*. Edited by Īraj Afshār. Tihrān: Chāpkhāna-i Jahān, 1372sh./1993.

Raschid-eldin. *Histoire des Mongols de la Perse*. Edited by and French translation É. Quatremère. Paris: Imprimerie Nationale, 1836 (Reprint, Amsterdam, Oriental Press, 1968).

Rashīd al-Dīn Faḍl Allāh Hamadānī. *Mukātibat-i Rashīdī*. Edited by Muḥammad Shafī'. Lahore: Dānishgāh-i Pānjab, 1974.

Rashīd al-Dīn Faḍl Allāh Hamadānī. *Jāmi' al-tawārīkh*. vol. III. Edited by A. A. Alizade, A. A. Romaskevich, and A. A. Khetagurov. Baku, 1957.

Rashīd al-Dīn Faḍl Allāh Hamadānī. *Jāmi' al-tawārīkh*. Edited by Bahman Karīmī. Tihrān, 1959–60.

Rashīd al-Dīn Faḍl Allāh Hamadānī. *Tārīkh-i mubārak-i Ghāzānī*. Edited by Karl Jahn. s'Gravenhague: Mouton, 1957.

[Rashīd al-Dīn Faḍl Allāh Hamadānī] *Jami'u't-Tawarikh (tome 1). Compedium of Chronicles by Rashiduddin Fazlullah*, III. Translated and annotated by Wheeler M. Thackson. London: I.B. Tauris, 2012.

Rashīd al-Dīn, *The Successors of Genghis Khan*. English translation J. A. Boyle. New York: Columbia University Press, 1971.

Ṣafadī, Ṣalāḥ al-Dīn Khalīl b. Aybak. *al-Wafī bi-l-wafayāt*. Edited by Sven Dedering. Vol. VI. Wiesbaden: Frantz Steiner Verlag, 1981.

Sakhāwī, Shams al-Dīn Abū l-Khayr Muḥammad. *Ḍaw' al-lāmi' fī a'yān al-qarn al-tāsi'*. 12 vols. Cairo, 1934–6.

Samarqandī, 'Abd al-Razzāq. *Maṭla'-i sa'dayn*. Edited by 'Abd al-Ḥusayn Navā'ī. Tihrān: Mu'assa-i Muṭāla'āt va Taḥqīqāt-i Farhangī, 1353sh./1975.

Shabānkāra'ī, Muḥammad b. 'Alī. *Majma' al-ansāb*. Edited by M. Hāshim Muḥaddith. Tihrān: Amīr Kabīr, 1363sh./1984.

Shams al-Dīn 'Abd al-Laṭīf b. Ṣadr al-Dīn Rūzbihān. *Rūḥ al-jinān fī sīrat al-shaykh Rūzbihān*, in *Rūzbihān-nāma*. Edited by M. Dānishpazhūh. Tihrān: Intishārāt-i Anjumān-i Āthār-i Millī, 1347sh./1969.

Sharaf al-Dīn Ibrāhīm b. Ṣadr al-Dīn Rūzbihān, *Tuḥfat ahl al-'irfān fī dhikr sayyid al-aqṭāb Rūzbihān*, in *Rūzbihān-nāma*. Edited by M. Dānishpazhūh. Tihrān: Intishārāt-i Anjuman-i Āthār-i millī, 1347sh./1969.

Shihāb Munshī. *Humāyūn-nāma*. Edited by Rukn al-Dīn Humāyūn Farrakh. Tihrān: Intishārāt-i Dānisgāh-i Millī-i Īrān.

Subkī, 'Abd al-Wahhāb. *Ṭabaqāt al-shāfi'iyya*. Edited by Nūr al-Dīn Sharība. 10 vols. Cairo, 1323–4/1906.

Sūzanī, Muḥammad b. Mas'ūd. *Dīvān-i Ḥakīm Sūzanī Samarqandī*. Edited by Nāṣir al-Dīn Shāh Ḥusaynī. Tihrān: Amīr Kabīr, 1338sh./1959.

Tārīkh-i Shāhī Qarākhitāyān. Edited by Muḥammad Ibrāhīm Bāstānī Pārīzī. Tihrān, 2535shsh./1976.

The Secret History of the Mongols. A Mongolian Epic Chronicle of the Thirteenth Century. Translation by Igor de Rachewiltz. 2 vols. Leiden: Brill, 2004.

al-ʻUmarī, Aḥmad b. Faḍl Allāh. *Das mongolische Weltreich. Al-ʻUmarī's Darstellung der mongolischen Reiche in seinem Werk Masālik al-abṣār wa mamālik al-amṣār*. Edited by and translated by K. Lech. Wiesbaden: Harrassowitz, 1968.

Vaṣṣāf. *Tajziyat al-amṣār va tazjiyat al-aʻṣār*. Lithograph. Bombay, 1259/1852.

Yāqūt. *Muʻjam al-buldān*. 5 vols. Beirut: Dār al-Ṣādir, 1986.

Yazdī, Muʻīn al-Dīn. *Mavāhib-i ilāhī dar tārīkh-i Āl-i Muẓaffar*. Edited by Saʻīd Nafīsī. Tihrān: Chāpkhāna-i Iqbāl, 1326sh./1947–8.

Yūnis, Muḥammad ʻAbd Allāh al-Sayyid. *al-Tadāwul al-naqdī fī madīnat Shīrāz mundhu bidāyat al-dawlat al-salghūriyya wa ḥattā nihāyat al-dawlat al-muẓaffariyya*. Doctoral dissertation, Cairo, 2010.

Secondary Literature

Afsar, Karāmat-Allāh. *Tārīkh-i bāft-i qadīmī-i Shīrāz*. Tihrān: Nashr-i Qatra, 1974.

Aigle, Denise. "Introduction." In Ḥamd Allāh b. Abī Bakr b. Zayn al-Dīn Ḥamd al-Mustawfī Qazvīnī, *Nuzhat al-qulūb*. Facsimile Copy of the Original Manuscript No 4517, Fatih Library (Istanbul), copied in 855 A. H. Tihrān: Mirath-i Maktūb, 2021, 5–12.

Aigle, Denise. "L'œuvre historiographique de Barhebraeus. Son apport à l'histoire de la période mongole." In *Barhebraeus et la renaissance syriaque*. Edited by Denise Aigle. In *Parole de l'Orient* 33 (2008): 25–61.

Aigle, Denise. *Le Fārs sous la domination mongole (XIIIe-XIVe s.). Politique et fiscalité*. Paris: Association pour l'avancement des études iraniennes, 2005.

Aigle, Denise. "Le 'grand *yasa*' de Gengis-khan, l'empire, la culture mongole et la *sharīʻa*." *Journal of the Economic and Social History of the Orient* 47/1 (2004): 31–79.

Aigle, Denise. "Les tableaux dynastiques du *Muntaḫab al-tavāriḫ-i Muʻinī*: une originalité dans la tradition historiographique persane." *Studia Iranica* 21/1 (1992): 67–83.

Aigle, Denise. "Loi mongole *vs* loi islamique. Entre mythe et réalité." *Annales. Histoire, Sciences Sociales* 5/6 (2005): 971–96.

Aigle, Denise. *The Mongol Empire between Myth and Reality*. Leiden: Brill, 2014.

Aigle, Denise. "Persia under Mongol domination. The effectiveness and failings of a dual administrative system." In *Le pouvoir à l'Âge des sultanats dans le Bilād al-Šām/Power in the Age of the Sultanates in the Bilād al-Šām* (Seminar

ACOR-IFPO, Amman 15–16 May 2005). Edited by Bethany Walker and Jean-François Salles. In *Bulletin d'Études Orientales* 57 (2006–7): 65–78.

Aigle, Denise. "Šabānkāra'ī." *Encyclopædia Iranica*. Online edition.

Aigle, Denise. *Saints hommes de Chiraz et du Fārs. Pouvoir, société et lieux de sacralité (Xe-XVe s.)*. Leiden: Brill, 2023.

Aigle, Denise. "Sarbedārs." *Encyclopædia Iranica*. Online edition.

Aigle, Denise. "Un fondateur d'ordre en milieu rural. Le cheikh Abû Ishâq de Kâzarûn." In *Saints orientaux*. Edited by Denise Aigle. Paris: De Boccard, 1995, 181–209.

Aigle, Denise. "Yasa." In *The Mongol World*. Edited by Timothy May and Michael Hope. London: Routledge, 2022, 319–30.

Album, Stephen. "Studies in Ilkhanid History and Numismatics." *Studia Iranica* 13/1 (1984): 49–116.

Allsen, Thomas T. "Changing Forms of Legitimization in Mongol Iran." In *Rulers from the Steppe. State Formation on the Eurasian Periphery*. Los Angeles: University of Southern California, 1991, 223–41.

Allsen, Thomas T. *Culture and Conquest in Mongol Eurasia*. Cambridge: Cambridge University Press, 2001.

Allsen, Thomas T. "Ever Closer Encounters: The Appropriation of Culture and the Apportionment of Peoples in the Mongol Empire." *Journal of Early Modern History* 1/1 (1997): 2–23.

Allsen, Thomas T. "Guard and Government in the Reign of the Grand Qan Möngke." *Harvard Journal of Asian Studies* 4/2 (1986): 495–521.

Allsen, Thomas T. "Maḥmūd Yalavač." In *In the Service of the Khan. Eminent Personalities of the Early Mongol-Yüan Period (1200–1300)*. Edited by Igor de Rachewiltz, Hok Lam Chan, Ch'i-Ch'ing Hsiao, and Peter W. Geier. Wiesbaden: Harrassowitz Verlag, 1993, 1210–31.

Allsen, Thomas T. *Mongol Imperialism. The Policies of the Grand Qan Möngke in China, Russia, and the Islamic Lands, 1251–1259*. Berkeley: University of California Press, 1987.

Allsen, Thomas T. "Mongolian Princes and Their Merchant Partners, 1200–1260." *Asia Major* 2/2 (1989): 83–126.

Allsen, Thomas T. "Notes on Chinese Titles in Mongol Iran." *Mongolian Studies* 14 (1991): 27–39.

Allsen, Thomas T. "Population Movements in Mongol Eurasia." In *Nomads as Agents of Cultural Change. The Mongols and Their Eurasian Predecessors*. Edited by Reuven Amitai and Michal Biran. Honolulu: University of Hawai'i Press, 2015, 119–51.

Allsen, Thomas T. "The Rise of the Mongolian Empire and Mongolian Rule in North China." In *The Cambridge History of China. 6 Alien regimes and border states, 907–1368*. Edited by Herbert Franke and Denis C. Twitchett. Cambridge: Cambridge University Press, 1994, 321–413.

Allsen, Thomas T. "Sharing Out the Empire: Apportioned Lands under the Mongols." In *Nomads in the Sedentary World*. Edited by Anatoly M. Kazanov and André Wink. Richmond: Curzon, 2001, 172–90.

Allsen, Thomas T. *The Steppe and the Sea. Pearls in the Mongol Empire*. Philadelphia: University of Pennsylvania Press, 2019.

Allsen, Thomas T. "The Yuan Dynasty and the Uighurs in Turfan in the 13th Century." In *China Among Equals: The Middle Kingdom and Its Neighbours, 10th–14th Centuries*. Edited by Morris Rossabi. Berkeley: University of California Press, 1983, 243–80.

Amitai-Preiss, Reuven. "Evidence for the Early Use of the Title Ilkhan Among the Mongols." *Journal of the Royal Asiatic Society* 3/1–3 (1991): 353–61.

Amitai-Preiss, Reuven. *Mongols and Mamluks. The Mamluk-Īlkhānid War, 1260–1281*. Cambridge: Cambridge University Press, 1995.

Amitai-Preiss, Reuven. "Two Notes on the Protocol on Hülegü's Coinage." *Israel Numismatic Journal* 10 (1988–9): 117–28.

Amitai, Reuven. "Hulāgu (Hülegü) Khan." *Encyclopædia Iranica* 12: 553–4.

Amitai, Reuven. "The Conversion of Tegüder Ilkhan to Islam." *Jerusalem Studies in Arabic and Islam* 25 (2001): 15–43.

Āshtiyānī, ʿAbbās Iqbāl. *Tārīkh-i Mughūl*. Tihrān: Amīr Kabīr, 1345sh./1966.

Ashtor, Eliyahu. *A Social and Economic History of the Near East in the Middle Ages*. London: Collins, 1976.

Aubin, Jean. *Deux sayyids de Bam au xve siècle. Contribution à l'histoire de l'Iran timouride*. Wiesbaden: Franz Steiner Verlag, 1956.

Aubin, Jean. *Émirs mongols et vizirs dans les remous de l'acculturation*. Paris: Association pour l'avancement des études iraniennes, 1995.

Aubin, Jean. "Introduction." In *Matériaux pour la biographie de Shah Niʿmatullah Wali Kermani*. Edited by Jean Aubin. Paris: Institut français de recherche en Iran, 1956, 1–19.

Aubin, Jean. "La question de Sīrjān au XIIIe siècle." *Studia Iranica* 6/2 (1977): 285–90 (Reprint in *Études sur l'Iran médiéval. Géographie historique et société*. Edited by and introduction by Denise Aigle. Paris: Association pour l'avancement des études iraniennes, 2018, 47–52).

Aubin, Jean. "L'ethnogenèse des Qaraunas." *Turcica* 1 (1969): 65–94. (Reprint in *Études sur l'Iran médiéval. Géographie historique et société*. Edited by and introduction by Denise Aigle. Paris: Association pour l'avancement des études iraniennes, 2018, 251–77).

Aubin, Jean. "La propriété foncière en Azerbaydjan sous les Mongols." *Le Monde iranien et l'Islam* 4 (1975–6): 79–132. (Reprint in *Études sur l'Iran médiéval. Géographie historique et société*. Edited by and introduction by Denise Aigle. Paris: Association pour l'avancement des études iraniennes, 2018, 171–219).

Aubin, Jean. "La ruine de Sīrāf et les routes du golfe Persique aux XIe et XIIe siècles." *Cahiers de civilisation médiévale* 2/3 (1959): 295–301. (Reprint in *Études sur l'Iran médiéval. Géographie historique et société*. Edited by and introduction by Denise Aigle. Paris: Association pour l'avancement des études iraniennes, 2018, 53–62).

Aubin, Jean. "La survie de Shîlâu et la route du Khunj-o-Fâl." *Iran* 7 (1969): 21–37. (Reprint in *Études sur l'Iran médiéval. Géographie historique et société*. Edited by and Introduction by Denise Aigle. Paris: Association pour l'avancement des études iraniennes, 2018, 63–90).

Aubin, Jean. "Le patronage culturel en Iran sous les Ilkhans. Une grande famille de Yazd." *Le Monde iranien et l'Islam* 3 (1975): 107–118. (Reprint in *Études sur l'Iran médiéval. Géographie historique et société*. Edited by and introduction by Denise Aigle. Paris: Association pour l'avancement des études iraniennes, 2018, 131–42).

Aubin, Jean. "Les princes d'Ormuz du XIIIe au XVe siècle." *Journal Asiatique* 241/1 (1953): 77–138.

Aubin, Jean. "Liminaire." *Le monde iranien et l'Islam* 1 (1971): i–ix.

Aubin, Jean. "Références pour Lār médiévale." *Journal asiatique* (1955): 491–505.

Aubin, Jean. "Šāh Ismā'īl et les notables de l'Iraq persan. Études safavides I." *Journal of the Economic and Social History of the Orient* 2 (1959): 37–81.

Aubin, Jean. "Un chroniqueur méconnu, Šabānkāra'ī." *Studia Iranica* 10/1 (1981): 213–24. (Reprint in *Études sur l'Iran médiéval. Géographie historique et société*. Edited by and introduction by Denise Aigle. Paris: Association pour l'avancement des études iraniennes, 2018, 143–54).

Aurell, Martin. "La parenté déchirée: les luttes intra-familiales au Moyen-Age." In *Rompre la concorde familiale typologie, imaginaire, questionnements*. Edited by Martin Aurell. Turnhout: Brepols, 2010, 7–60.

Bakhtiyārī, 'Alī Akbar. *Sīrjān dar ā'yīna-i zamān*. Kirmān: Kirmānshināsī, 1378sh./1999.

Barfield, Thomas J. *Perilous Frontier. Nomadic Empires and China, 221 BC to ad 1757*. Cambridge: Blackwell, 1989.

Barthold, Vladimir. *Turkestan Down to the Mongol Invasion*. London: Luzac, 1977[4].

Bayānī, Shīrīn. *Dīn va dawlat dar Īrān-i 'ahd-i Mughūl*. Tihrān: Markaz-i Nashr-i Dānishgāhī, 1367sh./1988.

Bayānī, Shirīn. *Zan dar Īrān dar 'aṣr-i Mughūl*. Tihrān: Kawīr, 1352sh./1973–4.

Bell, Paul. "Sino-Khitan Administration in Mongol Bukhara." *Journal of Asian History* 13/2 (1979): 121–51.

Bergmann, Ernst von. "Münzen der Indschuiden." *Numismatische Zeitschrift* 3 (1871): 143–65.

Biran, Michal. "The Mongol Transformation: From the Steppe to Eurasian Empire." *Medieval Encounters* 10/1–3 (2004): 339–61.

Biran, Michal. "The Mongols and Nomadic Identity. The Case of the Kitans in China." In *Nomads as Agents of Cultural Change. The Mongols and Their Eurasian Predecessors*. Edited by Reuven Amitai and Michal Biran. Honolulu: University of Hawai'i Press, 2015, 152–81.

Biran, Michal. "The Qarakhanids' Eastern Exchange: Preliminary Notes on the Silk Roads in the Eleventh and Twelfth Centuries." In *Complexity of Interaction along the Eurasian Steppe Zone in the first Millennium CE*. Edited by Jan Bemmann and Michael Schmauder. Bonn: Universität Bonn, 2015, 575–95.

Biran, Michal. *The Qara Khitai Empire in Eurasian History: Between China and Islam*. Cambridge: Cambridge University Press, 2005.

Bosworth, Edmund C. "Kākūyides." *Encyclopédie de l'Islam*² 4: 485–7.

Bosworth, Edmond C. "Salghurides." *Encyclopédie de l'Islam*² 8: 1012–3.

Bosworth, Edmund C. and Peter Jackson. "Shabānkāra'ī." *Encyclopédie de l'Islam*² 9: 63–4.

Brockelman, Carl. *Geschichte der arabischen Literatur*. 5 vols. Leiden: Brill, 1949.

Brookshaw, Dominic P. *Hafiz and His Contemporaries. Poetry, Performance and Patronage in Fourteenth Century Iran*. London: Tauris, 2019.

Calmard, Jean. "Le chiisme imamite sous les Ilkhans." In *L'Iran face à la domination mongole*. Edited by Denise Aigle. Tihrān: Institut français de recherche en Iran, 1997, 261–92.

Ciocîltan, Virgil. *The Mongols and the Black Sea Trade in Thirteenth and Fourteenth Centuries*. Leiden: Brill, 2012.

Cleaves, Francis W. "DaruΓa and Gerege." *Harvard Journal of Asiatic Studies* 16/1–2 (1953): 237–55.

Dang, Baohai. "The Paizi of the Mongol Empire." *Zentralasiatische Studien* 31 (2001): 31–62.

Dashdondog, Bayarsaikhan. *The Mongols and The Armenians (1220–1335)*. Leiden: Brill, 2011.

De Nicola, Bruno. "Pādshāh Khatun. An Example of Architectural, Religious, and Literary Patronage in Ilkhanid Iran." In *Along the Silk Roads in Mongol Eurasia*.

Generals, Merchants, and Intellectuals. Edited by Michal Biran, Jonathan Brack, and Francesca Fiaschetti. Oakland: University of California, 2020, 270–89.

De Nicola, Bruno. *Women in Mongol Iran. The Khātūns, 1206–1335*. Edinburgh: Edinburgh University Press, 2017.

DeWeese, Devin. "'Alā al-Dawla Simnānī's Religious Encounters at the Mongol Court near Tabriz." In *Politics, Patronage and the Transmission of Knowledge in 13th–15th Tabriz*. Edited by Judith Pfeiffer. Leiden: Brill, 2014, 35–76.

Dihkhudā, *Lughat-nāma*. Tihrān: Chāp-i Dānishgāh-i Tihrān, 1372–3sh./1993–5.

Doerfer, Gerhard. "Altūn Tamghā." *Encyclopædia Iranica* I: 913–4.

Doerfer, Gerhard. *Türkische und mongolische Elemente in Neupersischen*. 4 vols. Wiesbaden: Franz Steiner Verlag, 1963–75.

Dols, Michael W. *The Black Death in the Middle East*. Princeton, NJ: Princeton University Press, 1977.

Drompp, Michael R. "Strategis of Cohesion and Control in the Türk and Uyghur Empires." In *Complexity of Interaction along the Eurasian Steppe Zone in the First Millennium CE*. Edited by Jan Bemmann and Michael Schmauder. Bonn: Universität Bonn, 2015, 437–51.

Duby, Georges. "Dans la France du Nord-Ouest. Au XIIe siècle: les 'Jeunes' dans la société aristocratique." *Annales. Économie, Sciences sociales* 5 (1964): 835–46. (Reprint in *Féodalité*. Paris: Gallimard, 1996).

Durand Guédy, David. *Iranian Elites and Turkish Rulers. A History of Iṣfahān in the Saljuq Period*. London: Routledge, 2010.

Durand-Guédy, David. "1147: The Battle of Qara-Tegin and the Rise of Azarbayjan." *Der Islam* 92/1 (2015): 161–96.

Elias, Jamal J. *The Throne Carrier of God. The Life and Thought of Alā' ad-Dawla ad-Simnānī*. Albany: University of New York Press, 1995.

Endicott-West, Elizabeth. "Merchant Associations in Yüan China: The Ortoγ." *Asia Major* 2/2 (1989): 127–54.

Endicott-West, Elizabeth, *Mongolian Rule in China. Local Administration in the Yuan Dynasty*. Cambridge, MA: Harvard University Press, 1989.

Fairbanks, S. C. "Atābakān-e Yazd." *Encyclopædia Iranica* 2: 900–2.

Farhang-i jughrāfiyā'ī-i Īrān. 7 vols. Tihrān, 1330sh./1951.

Farquhar, David M. *The Government of China under Mongolian Rule*. Stuttgart: Franz Steiner, 1990.

Farrukhī, Yazdān. *Barrasī-i sayr-i taḥvilāt-i dīvān-sālārī-i mughūl-hā dar Īrān*. Tihrān: Amīr Kabīr, 1396sh./2017.

Fischel, Walter J. *Jews in the Economic Political Life of Medieval Islam*. London: Royal Asiatic Society, 1968.

Fragner, Bert. *Persophonie. Regionalität, Identität und Sprachkontakt in der Geschichte Asiens*. Berlin: Das Arabische Buch, 1999.

Franke, Herbert. "The Forest Peoples of Manchuria: Kitans and Jurchens." In *The Cambridge History of the Early Inner Asia*. Edited by Denis Sinor. Cambridge: Cambridge University Press, 1990, 400–23.

Ghanī, Qāsim. *Tārīkh-i ʿaṣr-i Ḥāfiẓ*. Tihrān, 1321sh./1941.

Gilli-Elewy, Hend. *Bagdad nach dem Sturz des Kalifats. Die Geschichte einer Provinz unter ilḫanicher Herrschaft (656–735/1258–1335)*. Berlin: Klaus Schwartz Verlag, 2000.

Gronke, Monika. "Les notables iraniens à lĕpoque mongole. Aspects économiques et sociaux d'après les documents du sanctuaire d'Ardébil." In *Documents de l'Islam médiéval. Nouvelles perspectives de recherche*. Edited by Yūsuf Rāghib. Cairo: Institut français d'archéologie orientale, 1991, 117–22.

Guénée, Bernard. *Histoire et culture historique dans l'Occident médiéval*. Paris: Aubier, 1991.

Hamayon, Roberte. *La chasse à l'âme. Esquisse d'une théorie du chamanisme sibérien*. Nanterre: Société d'ethnologie, 1990.

Hanaoka, Mimi, *Authority and Identity in Medieval Islamic Historiography: Persian Histories from the Peripheries*. New York: Cambridge University Presse, 2016.

Hanaway, L. "ʿAyyār in Persian sources." *Encyclopædia Iranica* 3: 161–3.

Herrmann, Gottfried. *Persiche Urkunden der Mongolenzeit. Text-und Bildteil*. Wiesbaden: Harrassowitz Verlag, 2004.

Hinz, Walter, *Islamische Masse und Gewichte*. Leiden: Brill, 1955.

Hoffmann, Birgitt. "The Gates of Piety and Charity: Rašīd al-dīn Faḍl Allāh as Founder of Pious Endowments." In *L'Iran face à la domination mongole*. Edited by Denise Aigle. Tihrān: Institut français de recherche en Iran, 1997, 198–201.

Hoffmann, Birgitt. "In Pursuit of *Memoria* and Salvation: Rashīd al-Dīn and His Rabʿ- i Rashīdī." In *Politics, Patronage and the Transmission of Knowledge in 13th–15th Century Tabriz*. Edited by Judith Pfeiffer. Leiden: Brill, 2014, 171–85.

Hoffmann, Birgitt. *Waqf im mongolischen Iran. Rašīduddīns Sorge um Nachrum und Seelenheil*. Stuttgart: Franz Steiner Verlag, 2000.

Hope, Michael. *Power, Politics and Tradition in the Mongol Empire and the Īlkhānate of Iran*. Oxford: Oxford University Press, 2016.

Hucker, Charles O. *A Dictionnary of Official Titles in Imperial China*. Standford, CA: Standford University Press, 1985.

Jackson, Peter. "Arġūn Aqa." *Encyclopædia Iranica* 2: 401–2.

Jackson, Peter. "Čāv." *Encyclopædia Iranica* 5: 96–7.

Jackson, Peter. *The Mongols and the Islamic World: From Conquest to Conversion*. New Haven, CT: Yale University Press, 2017.

Jackson, Peter. "Muẓaffarides." *Encyclopédie de l'Islam*[2] 8: 821–23.

Ja'farī Madhhab, Muḥsin. "Dhayl-i Majma' al-ansāb-i Šabānkāra'ī." *Ā'ina-yi mirāth* 30 (1384sh./2005): 249–55.

Jahn, Karl. "Paper Currency in Iran: A Contribution to the Cultural and Economic History of Iran in the Mongol Period." *Journal of Asian History* 4 (1970): 101–35.

Jahn, Karl, "Study on Supplementary Persian Sources for the Mongol History of Iran." In *Proceding of the Fifth Meeting of the Permanent International Altaic Conference*. Edited by D. Sinor. Uralic and Altaic Series 23 (1963): 197–204.

Javanmardi. The Ethics and Practice of Persianate Perfection. Edited by Llyod Ridgeon. London: Ginko, 2018.

Kamola, Stefan. *Making Mongol History, Rashid al-Din and the Jami' al-tawarikh*. Edinburgh: Edinburgh University Press, 2019.

Kamola, Stefan. "Salghurid History in the *Jāmi' al-Tawārīkh*: A Preliminary Exploration of Its Composition and Transmission." In *New Approaches to Ilkhanid History*. Edited by Timothy May, Bayarsaikhan Dashdondog, and Christopher P. Atwood. Leiden: Brill, 2021, 122–44.

Katouzian, Homa. "Sa'dī on Love and Morals." In *The Coming of the Mongols*. Edited by David Morgan and Sarah Stewart. London: Tauris, 2018, 95–127.

Kauz, Ralph. "The Maritime Trade of Kish during the Mongol Period." In *Beyond the Legacy of Genghis Khan*. Edited by Linda Komaroff. Leiden: Brill, 2006, 51–67.

Khayrāndīsh, 'Abd al-Rasūl. *Fārsiyān dar barādar-i mughūlān*. Tihrān: Abādboom, 1394sh./2016.

Kolbas, Judith. *The Mongols in Iran. Chingiz Khan to Uljaytu 1220–1309*. London: Routledge, 2006.

Krawulsky, Dorothea. *Iran. Das Reich des Ilkhāne: eine topographische-historiche Studie*. Wiesbaden: Ludwig Reichert, 1978.

Krawulsky, Dorothea. *Mongolen Ilkhâne und Ideologie Geschichte*. Beirut: Verlag für islamische Studien, 1989.

Lambton, Ann K. S. "Awqāf in Persia: 6th–8th/12th–14th Centuries." *Islamic Law and Society* 4/3 (1997): 298–318.

Lambton, Ann K. S. *Continuity and Change in Medieval Persia*. London: Tauris, 1988.

Lambton, Ann K. S. "Kharādj." *Encyclopédie de l'Islam*[2] 4: 1066–85.

Lambton, Ann K. S. "Economy IV.-V. From the Arab Conquest to the End of the Il-Khanids." *Encyclopædia Iranica* 8: 107–32.

Lambton, Ann K. S. “Mongol Fiscal Administration in Persia (part 1).” *Studia Islamica* 64 (1986): 79–99.

Lambton, Ann K. S. “Mongol Fiscal Administration in Persia (part 2).” *Studia Islamica* 65 (1987): 97–123.

Lambton, Ann K. S. *Landlord and Peasant in Persia*. London: Tauris, 1953.

Lambton, Ann K. S. “Shīrāz.” *Encyclopédie de l’Islam*² 9: 491–7.

Lambton, Ann K. S. “Yazd.” *Encyclopédie de l’Islam*² 11: 327–35.

Landolt, Hermann. “Nasafi, ‘Aziz.” *Encyclopædia Iranica*. Online edition.

Lane, George. “Arghun Aqa: Mongol Bureaucrat.” *Studia Iranica* 32/4 (1999): 459–82.

Lane, George. *Early Mongol Rule in Thirteenth-Century Iran. A Persian Renaissance*. London: Routledge, 2003.

Lang, David M. *Studies in the Numismatic History of Georgia in Transcaucasia*. New York: American Numismatic Society, 1955.

Limbert, John. *Shiraz in the Age of Hafez*. Seattle: University of Washington Press, 2004.

Ma‘dankan, Ma‘ṣūme. *Ba-yāsā rasīdagān*. Tihrān: Markaz-i Nashr-i Dānishgāhī, 1375sh./1996.

Ma‘dankan, Ma‘ṣūme. “Yāsā dar ‘ahd-i Īlkhāniān.” *Ma‘āref* 9/1 (1371sh./1992): 3–14.

Mahendrarajah, Shivan, *The Sufi Saint of Jam: History, Religion and Politics of a Sunni Shrine in Shi‘i Iran*. Cambridge: Cambridge University Press (Cambridge Studies in Islamic Civilization), 2021.

Marlow, Louise. “Teaching Wisdom. A Persian Work of Advice for Atabeg Ahmad of Luristan.” In *Mirror for the Muslim Prince: Islam and the Theory of Statecraft*. Edited by M. Boroujerdi. Syracuse: Syracuse University Press, 2013, 122–59.

Martin, Janet. *Treasure of the Land of Darkness. The Fur Trade and Its Significance for Medieval Russia*. Cambridge: Cambridge University Press,1986.

Martinez, A. P. “Regional Mint Outputs and the Dynamics of Bullion Flows through the Īl-Xānate.” *Journal of the Turkish Studies* 8 (1984): 147–73.

Mélikian-Chirvani, A. S. “The Iranian *bazm* in Early Persian Sources.” In *Banquets d’Orient*. Res Orientales. IV. Bures-sur-Yvette, 1992, 95–120.

Melville, Charles. “Anatolia under the Mongols.” In *Cambridge History of Turkey*. I. Edited by Kate Fleet. Cambridge: Cambridge University Press, 2009, 51–101.

Melville, Charles. “Between Firdausī and Rashīd al-Dīn: Persian Verse Chronicles of the Mongol Period.” *Studia Islamica* 104/105 (2007): 45–65.

Melville, Charles. “The Caspian Provinces: A World Apart. Three Local Histories of Mazandaran.” *Iranian Studies* 33/1–2 (2000): 45–91.

Melville, Charles. “Čobān.” *Encyclopædia Iranica* 5: 875–8.

Melville, Charles. "Concepts of Government and State Formation in Mongol Iran." In *The Coming of the Mongols*. Edited by David Morgan and Sarah Stewart. London: Tauris, 2018, 33–54.

Melville, Charles. "Concepts of Government and State Formation in Mongol Iran." In *Iran after the Mongols*. Edited by Sussan Babaie. London: Tauris, 2019, 33–54.

Melville, Charles. *The Fall of Amir Chupan and the Decline of the Ilkhanate, 1327–37: A Decade of Discord in Mongol Iran*. Bloomington: Indiana University, 1999.

Melville, Charles. "From Adam to Abaqa." *Studia Iranica* 30 (2001): 67–86.

Melville, Charles. "From Adam to Abaqa." *Studia Iranica* 36 (2007): 7–64.

Melville, Charles. "Ḥamd Allāh Mustawfī's *Ẓafarnāmah* and the Historiography of the Late Ilkhanid Period." In *Iran and Iranian Studies: Essays in Honor of Iraj Afshar*. Edited by Kambiz Eslami. Princeton, NJ: Princeton University Press, 1998, 1–12.

Melville, Charles. "Ḥamd-Allāh Mostawfī." *Encyclopædia Iranica* 11: 631–63.

Melville, Charles. "History and Myth: The Persianization of Ghazan Khan." In *Irano-Turkic Cultural Contacts in the 11th–17th Centuries*. Edited by Éva M. Jeremiàs. Piliscsaba: The Avicenna Institute of Middle Eastern Studies, 2002 [2003], 133–60.

Melville, Charles. "The Īlkhān Öljeitü's Conquest of Gīlān (1307): Rumor and Reality." In *The Mongol Empire & Its Legacy*. Edited by Reuven Amitai-Preiss and David Morgan. Leiden: Brill, 1990, 72–125.

Melville, Charles. "The Itineraries of Sultan Öljeitü, 1304–16." *Iran* 28 (1999): 55–70.

Melville, Charles. "Pādishāh-i Islām: The Conversion of Sultan Maḥmūd Ghāzān Khān." *Pembroke Papers* 1 (1990): 159–77.

Melville, Charles. "Persian Local Histories: Views from the Wings." *Iranian Studies* 33/1–2: 7–14.

Melville, Charles. "Wolf or Shepherd? Amir Chupan's Attitude to Government." In *The Court of the Il-Khans, 1290–1340*. Edited by Julian Raby and Teresa Fitzherbert. Oxford: Oxford University Press, 1996, 79–93.

Melville, Charles and 'Abbās Zaryab. "Chobanids." *Encyclopædia Iranica* 5: 496–502.

Melville, Charles and Maria Subtelny. "Ḥāfeẓ-e Abru." *Encyclopædia Iranica* 11: 507–9.

Merçil, Erdogam. *Fars atabegleri salgurlular*. Ankara: Türk Tarih Kurumu Basimevi, 1975.

Miller, Isabel. "Local History in ninth-fifteenth Century Yazd: The *Tārīkh-i Jadīd-i Yazd*." *Iran* 27 (1989): 75–9.

Minorsky, Vladimir. "Lur-i Buzurg." *Encyclopédie de l'Islam*[2] 5: 832–34.

Minorsky, Vladimir. "Lur-i Kuchick." *Encyclopédie de l'Islam*[2] 5: 834–35.

Minorsky, Vladimir. "Pūr-i Bahā's 'Mongol' Ode." *Iranica* (1964): 274–305.

Mirjafari, Hossein. "The Ḥaydarī-Ni'matī Conflicts in Iran." *Iranian Studies* 12/3–4 (1979): 135–61.

Mohammadi, Zekrollah, Amir Hossein Hatami, and Mohsen Parvish. "Persian Identity Aspects in Delgosha's System of Poems Based on Shahnameh's Ferdowsi Re-creations." *Literary Text Research* 25/89 (2021): 87–114.

Mokri, Mohammad. *La lumière et le feu dans l'Iran ancien et leur démythification en Islam*. Leuven: Peeters, 1982[2].

Morgan, David O. "The 'Great *Yasa* of Chinggis Khan' Revisited." In *Mongols, Turks and Others. Eurasian Nomads and the Sedentary World*. Edited by Reuven Amitai and Michal Biran. Leiden: Brill, 2005, 291–308.

Morgan, David O., "The 'Great *Yāsā* of Chingiz Khān' and Mongol Law in the Īlkhānate." *Bulletin of the School of Oriental and African Studies* 49/1 (1986): 163–76.

Morgan, David O. "Ḳubčūr." *Encyclopédie de l'Islam*[2] 3: 299.

Morgan, David O. "Mongol or Persian: The Government of Īlkhānid Iran." *Harvard Middle Eastern and Islamic Review* 3 (1996): 62–76.

Morgan, David O., *The Mongols*. Oxford: Blackwall, 1986.

Morgan, David O. "Persian Perceptions of Mongols and Europeans." In *Implicit Understandings. Observing, Reporting and Reflecting on the Encounters between Europeans on Others Peoples in the Early Modern Era*. Edited by Stuart B. Schwartz. Cambridge: Cambridge University Press, 1995, 201–17.

Morgan, David O. "Who Ran the Mongol Empire?" *Journal of the Royal Asiatic Society* 2 (1982): 124–36.

Muḥaddith, Mīr Hāshim. "Muqaddima." In Muḥammad b. 'Alī Shabānkāra'ī. *Majma' al-ansāb*. Edited by M. Hāshim Muḥaddith. Tihrān, 1363sh./1984, 5–15.

Neggaz, Nassima. "The Many Deaths of the Last 'Abbāsid Caliph al-Musta'ṣim bi-llāh (d. 1258)." *Journal of the Royal Asiatic Society* 30/4 (2020): 585–612.

Ostrowski, Donald. *Muscovy and the Mongols. Cross-cultural Influences on the Steppe Frontier, 1304–1589*. Cambridge: Cambridge University Press, 1998.

Ostrowski, Donald. "The *tamma* and the Dual-administrative Structure of the Mongol Empire." *Bulletin of the School of Oriental and African Studies* 61/2 (1998): 262–77.

Otsuka, Osamu. "The Hazaraspid Dynasty's Legendary Kayanid Ancestry: The Flowering of Persian Literature under the Patronage of Local Rulers in the Il-khanid Period." *Journal of Persian Studies* 12 (2019): 181–205.

Paul, Jürg*en*. "Armies, Lords and Subjects in Medieval Iran." In *The Cambridge World History of Violence*. Edited by Matthiew Gordon, Richard Kaeuper, and Harriett Zurndorfer. II. Cambridge: Cambridge University Press, 2020, 58–78.

Paul, Jürgen. "Local and Imperial Rule. Examples from Fārs (9th–10th centuries)." In *Emerging Powers in Eurasian Comparison, 200–1100. Shadows of Empire*. Edited by Walter Pohl and Veronika Wieser. Leiden: Brill, 2022, 329–52.

Paul, Jürgen. "Who Were the *mulūk Fārs*?" In *Transregional and Regional Elites. Connecting the Early Islamic Empire*. Edited by Hannah-Lena Hagemann and Stefan Heidemann. Berlin: De Gruyter, 2020, 117–46.

Pavet de Courteille, Abel. *Dictionnaire turk-oriental*. Amsterdam: Philo Press, 1972.

Perry, John R. "Toward a Theory of Iranian Urban Moieties: The Ḥaydariyyah and Niʿmatiyyah Revisited." *Iranian Studies* 32/1 (1999): 51–70.

Persian Historiography. Edited by Charles Melville. London: Tauris, 2012.

Petrushevsky, Igor P. "The Socio-economic Condition of Iran under the Īl-Khāns." In *Cambridge History of Iran*. V. *The Saljuq and Mongol Periods*. Edited by John A. Boyle. Cambridge: Cambridge University Press, 1968, 483–537.

Pfeiffer, Judith. " 'A Turgid History of the Mongol Empire in Persia'. Epistemological Reflections Concerning a Critical Edition of Vaṣṣāf's *Tajziyat al-amṣār wa tazjiyat al-aʿṣār*." In *Theoretical Approaches to the Transmission and Edition of Oriental Manuscripts*. Edited by Judith Pfeiffer and Manfred Kropp. Beirut: Orient-Institut, 2007, 107–29.

Pfeiffer, Judith. "Öljeytü's Conversion to Shiʿism (709/1309) in Muslim Narrative Sources." *Mongolian Studies* 22 (1999): 35–67.

Potter, Lawrence Goddard. *The Kart Dynasty of Herat: Religion and Politics in Medieval Iran*. Columbia University, 1992 (unpublished Ph.D thesis).

Quiring-Zoche, Rosemarie. *Isfahan im 15. und 16. Jahrhundert*. Freiburg: Klaus Schwarz Verlag, 1980.

Rachewiltz, Igor de. "Some Remarks on the Dating of *The Secret History of the Mongols*." *Monumenta Serica* 24 (1965): 185–205.

Rachewiltz, Igor de. "Two Recently Published P'ai-tzu Discovered in China." *Acta Orientalia Academiae Scientiarum Hungariae* 36/1–3 (1982): 23–7.

Ratchevsky, Paul. "Sigi-Qutuqu, ein mongolische Gefolgsmann im 12.-13. Jahrhundert." *Central Asiatic Journal* 10/2 (1965): 87–120.

Rentz, George. "al-Qaṭīf." *Encyclopédie de l'Islam*^{2} 5: 794–6.

Römer, Hans Robert. "The Jalayirids, Muzaffarids and Sarbadārs." In *Cambridge History of Iran*. V. *The Saljuq and Mongol Periods*. Edited by John A. Boyle. Cambridge: Cambridge University Press, 1975, 1–39.

Ṣafā', Ḏabīḥ Allāh. *Tārīkh-i adabiyāt dar Īrān*, 5 vols. Tihrān: Amīr Kabīr, 1342–6sh./1963–77.

Schwartz, Paul. *Iran im Mittelalter*. Hidesheim: Georg Olms Verlag, 1969 (1st ed. Leipzig: Otto Harrassowitz, 1896).

Sellheim, R. "Faḍīla." *Encyclopédie de l'Islam*² 2: 247–48.

Shaykh al-Ḥukamā'ī, 'Imād. "Naqsh-i katība-hā-i khwānda-i nashda-i masjid-i sangī-i dārāb dar shināsā'ī kār-kardan va tārīkh-i sākht-banā." *Pazhūhish-hā-i 'ulūm-i tārīkhī* 8/2 (1395sh./2016): 81–94.

Shiraiwa, Kazuhiko. "*Īnjū* in the *Jāmi' al-Tavārīkh* of Rashīd al-Dīn." *Acta Orientalia Academiae Scientiarum Hungaricae* 42/2–3 (1988): 371–6.

Smith, John Masson. "Djalāyir, Djalāyirides." *Encyclopédie de l'Islam*² 2: 411–2.

Smith, John Masson. "Mongol Nomadism and Middle Eastern Geography: Qīshlāqs and Tümens." In *The Mongol Empire & Its Legacy*. Edited by Reuven Amitai-Preiss and David Morgan. Leiden: Brill, 1999, 39–56.

Spiegel, Gabrielle M. *The Past as Text. The Theory and Practice of Medieval Historiography*. Baltimore, MD: Johns Hopkins University Press, 1999.

Spuler, Bertold. "Abeš-Kātūn." *Encyclopædia Iranica* 1: 210.

Spuler, Bertold. "Atābakān-e Fārs." *Encyclopædia Iranica* 2: 895–6.

Spuler, Bertold. "Atābakān-e Lorestān." *Encyclopædia Iranica* 2: 896–7.

Spuler, Bertold. *Die Mongolen in Iran. Politik, Verwaltung und Kultur der Ilchanzeit 1220–1350*. Berlin: Akademie-Verlag, 1995.

Spuler, Bertold. "Hazāraspides." *Encyclopédie de l'Islam*² 3: 347–8.

Spuler, Bertold. *History of the Mongols*. Translated from the German by Helga and Stuart Drummond. Berkeley: University of California Press, 1972.

Subtelny, Maria E. *Le monde est un jardin. Aspects de l'histoire culturelle de l'Iran médieval*. Paris: Association pour l'avancement des études iraniennes, 2000.

Subtelny, Maria E. *Timurids in Transition. Turko-Persian Politics and Acculturation in Medieval Iran*. Leiden: Brill, 2007.

Taeschner, Franz. "Akhī." *Encyclopédie de l'Islam*² 1: 331–3.

Tor, Deborah. *Violent Order: Religious Warfare, Chivalry, and the* 'ayyār *Phenomenon in the Medieval Islamic World*. Würzburg: Orient-Institut Istanbul, 2007.

Treadwell, Luke. "Urban Militias in the Eastern Islamic World (Third-Fourth Centuries AH/Ninth-Tenth Centuries CE)." In *Late Antiquity: Eastern Perspectives*. Edited by Teresa Bernheimer and Adam Silverstein. Cambridge: Cambridge University Press, 2012, 128–44.

Van Ess, Josef. "al-Idjī." *Encyclopédie de l'Islam*² 3: 1047–8.

Van Ess, Josef. *Erkenntnislehre des 'Aḍuddadin al-Īcī: Übersetzung and Kommentar der ersten Buches seiner Mawāqif*. Wiesbaden: Franz Steiner Verlag, 1996.

Van Ess, Josef. *Gelehrten: Zu Inhalt und Entstehungs-geschichte der theologischen Schriften des Rašīduddīn Faḍlullāh (gest. 718/1318)*. Wiesbaden: Franz Steiner Verlag, 1981.

Van Renterghem, Vanessa. *Les élites bagdadiennes au temps des Seldjoukides*, 2 vols. Damascus: Institut français du Proche-Orient, 2015.

Vasyutin, Sergey A. "The Model of the Political Transformation of the Da Liao as an Alternative to the Evolution of the Structure of Authority in the Early Medieval Pastoral Empires of Mongolia." In *Complexity of Interaction along the Eurasian Steppe Zone in the first Millennium CE*. Edited by Jan Bemmann and Michael Schmauder. Bonn: Universität Bonn, 2015, 391–436.

Voegelin, Éric. "The Mongol Orders of Submission to European Powers, 1245–1255." *Byzantion* 15 (1940–1): 378–413.

Watabe, Ryoko. "The Local Administration of the Ilkhānid Dynastie: A Case of Fārs." *Annals of the Japan Association for Middle East Studies* 12 (1997): 185–216 (in Japanese).

Weiers, Michael. "Münzaufschriften auf Münzen mongolischer Il-Khane aus dem Iran." *The Canada-Mongolian Review* 4/1 (1978): 41–62.

Wing, Patrick. *The Jalayirids. Dynastic State Formation in the Mongol Middle East*. Edinburgh: Edinburgh University Press, 2016.

Woods, John E. "A Note on the Mongol Capture of Iṣfahān." *Journal of Near Eastern Studies* 36/1 (1977): 49–52.

Yāddāsht-hā-i Qazvīnī. Edited by Īraj Afshār. 7 vols. Tihrān: Instishārat-i Dānishgāh-i Tihrān, 1337–42sh./1958–63.

Yihao, Qiu. "Background and Aftermath of Fakhr al-Dīn al-Ṭībī's Voyage: A Reexamination of the Interaction between the Ikhanate and the Yuan at the Beginning of the Fourteenth Century." In *New Approchs to Ilkhanid History*. Edited by Timothy May, Bayarsaikhan Dashdondog, and Christopher Atwood. Leiden: Brill, 2021, 147–75.

Younis, Mohammad. "The Salghurid Coinage of Fārs (Iran). Citing the Mongols: Varieties of Overlordships, Form and Content (623–685/1226–1286)." *Journal of the Oriental Society of Australia* 45 (2013): 93–115.

Zakeri, Mohsen. "The 'Ayyārān of Khurassan and the Mongol Invasion." In *Proceedings of the Third European Conference of Iranian Studies, held in Cambridge, 11th to 15th September 1995*, Part 2 *Mediaeval and Modern Persian Studies*. Edited by Charles Melville. Wiesbaden: Franz Steiner Verlag, 1999, 269–76.

Index

Abaqa, Ilkhan 4, 31, 58, 59, 60, 61, 62, 63, 73, 74, 79, 80, 128, 142, 144, 145, 196 n.19
Abarqūh 104
Abatay Noyan 83
'Abbās al-Mu'taḍid bi-llāh Abū Bakr, Abbasid Caliph 108
Abbasid Caliph 1, 3, 4, 44, 52, 108, 137, 139, 140, 143
'Abd al-Rasūl Khayrāndīsh 7
'Abd al-Salām 89
Abish Khātūn, Salghurid atabek 52, 57–8, 61, 63, 65–71, 73, 75, 77, 82, 92, 142, 147
Abū 'Ali Daqqāq, sufi shaykh 92
Abū Bakr b. Sa'd, Salghurid atabek 41–9, 51–3, 55, 60, 71, 73–4, 100, 108, 126, 138–9, 142, 166 n.37
Abū Muslim 'Alī Surkh Khurāsānī 115–16
Abū Sa'īd, Ilkhan 7, 14–16, 20, 36, 91–5, 97–8, 108, 111, 115–16, 118–19, 125, 129, 132, 185 n.167
Abū Ṭāhir, Lur-i Buzurg atabek 136
'Aḍud al-Dawla Fanā Khusraw, Buyid prince 74
'Aḍud al-Dīn 'Abd al-Raḥmān Ījī 108, 110
'Aḍud al-Dīn Amīr Ḥājjī 54
'Aḍud al-Dīn Muḥammad b. Abī Yu'lā b. Mujtabā (Sayyid) 90, 92
Afrāsiyāb b. Yūsuf Shāh, Lur-i Buzurg atabek 137, 142, 147–8, 198 n.19, 200 n.55
Afrāsiyāb, legendary Turanian hero 94
Aharī, Abū Bakr Quṭbī 15, 187 n.4, 13
Aḥmad Shīrāzī, Mu'īn al-Dīn Abū l-'Abbās 17, *see* Ibn Zarkūb
Aḥmad Tegüder, Ilkhan 31, 36, 61, 63–7, 73, 87, 92, 145, 148, 154 n.23
Akhī Īrān Shāh 132
Akhī Shāh Malik 132
Akhī Shujā' al-Dīn Khurāsānī 116
'Alā' al-Dawla Simnānī 4, 154 n.23
'Alā' al-Dawla, Yazd atabek 54–5
'Alā' al-Dīn Muḥammad Khwārazmshāh 41, 139
Alamūt 2, 3, 143, 201 n.90
Alghanchi, Salghurid princess 66, 70, 73
'Alī Bahādūr, Ilkhanid governor of Baghdad 79
'Alī Ḥaydar 140
'Alī Kātib, Aḥmad b. Ḥusayn 18
'Alī Pādishāh, Ilkhan 98, 187 n.11
Allsen, Thomas 1, 6, 15, 25, 128
Alp Arslan, Saljuq Sultan 39
Altaju Noyan 54–5, 58
'Amīd al-Dīn Abū Naṣr Abzarī (Khwāja) 45, 76
Amīn Bāshtīnī 115
Amīr Bikjakāz 107
Amīr Chūpān 36, 92–3, 186 n.170, 171
'Amr b. al-Hudhayl al-'Abdī 12
Anatolia 2, 6–7, 33, 36–7, 95, 98, 131
Aq Buqa, Jalayirid *amīr* 117
Arabian Sea 43
Ardashīr, Sasanid ruler 138
Arghun Aqa, Mongol governor of Iran 27–9, 74
Arghun, Ilkhan 31, 46, 63–4, 67–9, 73–8, 83–5, 142, 144–5, 147, 154 n.23, 162 n.42, 193 n.125
Arigh Böke, son of Tolui 28
Armenia 135
Armenians 2
Arpa Ke'ün, Ilkhan 98, 187 n.10, 12
Arrajān 44
Arslan b. Ṭughril, Saljuq Sultan 137
Ashtu 89
'Aṭā' Malik Juvaynī 3, 11, 12, 29, 33
Aubin, Jean 22–3, 30, 36, 62, 85, 90, 126, 131–2, 139
Awdamish 68–9

Awghānīs, Mongol tribes 105, 107–8, 112–13, 116, 190 n.74
Ay Temür 111, 113, 192 n.112
ʻAyn Jālūt 2
Azerbaijan 2, 4, 5, 7, 13, 35, 40, 101, 115, 123, 132, 152 n.5, 179 n.44
Azhdarī, Nūr al-Dīn Muḥammad 16, 201 n.90
ʻAzīz al-Dīn Nasafī 56

Badr al-Dīn Masʻūd, Lur-i Kuchik atabek 140
Baghdad 1, 2, 4, 11, 15, 22, 30, 33, 36, 47, 52, 59, 60, 76, 79, 83, 86, 88, 99, 101, 109, 114, 117, 124, 140, 143, 178 n.18
Bahāʼ al-Dīn Ayāz, prince of Hormuz 85
Bahāʼ al-Dīn Juvaynī 11
Baḥrābād 56
Baḥrayn 42, 60, 82, 86
Baidu, Ilkhan 78, 83–4, 125, 146
Baidu, Isfahan tax collector 147
Baiju, Mongol commander 2
Balyānī, Amīn al-Dīn, sufi shaykh 92, 95, 102, 128
Bam 23, 116
Bandar ʻAbbās 130
Bar Hebraeus 13–14, 27, 31, 162 n.43
Baraq Ḥājib, Qutlughkhanid Sultan of Kirmān 139
Baraq, Chaghatayid Khan 144
Baṣra 86
Batu, Golden Horde Khan 27–8
Baybars, Mamluk Sultan 54
Berke Khan, Golden Horde Khan 59, 172 n.66
Bībī Salgham, Salghurid princess 52, 57, 73
Bilād al-Rūm 39
Bilād al-Shām 2
Bolad Chingsang, Mongol Noyan 13, 142
Buell, Paul 28
Bukhra 26, 159 n.9, 10
bulgha, rebel, rebellion 3, 43
Bulghai, Mongol secretary 28
Bulughan, Ilkhanid governor of Shiraz 60, 63–5, 68, 80, 175 n.131, 180 n.53
Buqa, Ilkhanid noyan and viceroy 31, 62, 67, 74–6, 78, 117
Buyids 4, 17, 124

Caspian Sea 5
Caucasus 1
Central Asia 1, 9, 25, 26
Ceylon 42
Chaghatayid 2, 152 n.9
Charāndāb-i Tabrīz 70
Cherik 68–9
China 1, 2, 13, 15, 25, 26, 28, 59, 67, 79, 80, 81, 85, 89, 152 n.5, 161 n.30, 36, 172 n.67, 183 n.126
Chinese 1, 2, 13, 15, 25, 26, 28, 79, 83, 152 n.5
Chinggis Khan 2, 4, 7, 11, 12, 14, 25, 26, 27, 28, 43, 91, 132, 152 n.5, 9, 160 n.19, 195 n.13
Chormaqan Qorchi, Mongol noyan 29
Chupanids 15, 97–8, 103, 105, 132–3

D'Ohsson 12
Damür Temür 56, 58
Darband 147
darugha, *darughachi*, governor, khan's representative in conquered regions 2, 29, 32
Daylam Shāh (Amīr) 102
Dimashq Khwāja, Ilkhanid noyan 93, 186 n.169, 170
Diyāʼ al-Dīn Masʻūd 18
Diyar Bakr 33, 76, 83, 98
Duby, Georges 118
Durand Guédy, David 124
Durbai 33

Egypt 9
Eldegüzids 5
Euphrates 14

Faḍluyya, Shabānkāra atabek 39
Fakhr al-Dīn 29
Fakhr al-Dīn Abū Bakr, Abū Bakr minister 48, 51–2
Fakhr al-Dīn Ḥasan Shīrāzī (Sayyid) 74–5
Fakhr al-Dīn Mubārak Shāh 75, 77, 178 n.30
Fāl 46
Faqīh Sāʼin al-Dīn Ḥusayn 47
Farāmaz b. ʻAlāʼ al-Dawla ʻAlī, Kakuyid prince 138
Firdawsī 9, 15–16, 103, 136

Fīrūzābād 125
Fragner, Bert 16

Gaikhatu, Ilkhan 36, 78, 80–4, 87, 147–8
Georgia 135
Georgians 2
Ghazan Khan, Ilkhan 13, 16, 30, 35–6, 84–8, 93, 124–5, 128–9, 131, 146–7, 149, 163 n.60, 168 n.69, 181 n.84, 182 n.98, 183 n.117, 126
Ghiyāth al-Dīn Kaykhusraw Īnjū 94, 98–9
Ghiyāth al-Dīn Manṣūr 111, 113
Ghiyāth al-Dīn Muḥammad b. Muẓaffar al-Dīn Muḥammad, king of Shabānkāra 141
Ghiyāth al-Dīn Muḥammad Rashīdī, Ilkhanid minister 15, 19–20, 93, 95, 185 n.161, 187 n.10
Ghuzz 4, 5
Gīlān 5
Gog and Magog 103
Golden Horde 9, 171 n.32
Guénée, Bernard 10, 12
Gurgīn-Milādīs, princes of Lār dynasty 55

Ḥāfiẓ-i Abrū 20, 61, 80–1, 94, 104–5
Ḥāfiẓ 110
Ḥājjī Ḍarrāb (Sayyid) 110, 112
Ḥājjī Narīn, brother of Nawrūz 31, 85
Ḥājjī Shams al-Dīn 110
Hamadān 41, 63, 83, 145, 147
Ḥamīd Pūr, Qara Khitai commander of Kirmān 139
Ḥanafīs 124
Hanaoka, Mimi 16
Hazaraspids 136–8, 147, 197 n.4
Herat 5, 20, 115, 144
Hope, Michal 125
Hormuz 20, 41–3, 60, 82, 85, 104, 129–30, 138, 183 n.131, 185 n.167
Horqudaq, Ilkhanid governor 85, 147, 182 n.98
Hülegü, Ilkhan 1, 2, 11, 13, 16, 28–30, 32, 36, 44–5, 49, 51–59, 61, 70, 76, 78–9, 124, 132, 139–45, 152 n.10, 171 n.32, 187 n.10, 171 n.32, 181 n.77, 187 n.10, 197 n.1, 199 n.53, 200 n.63, 64, 73, 201 n.90
Ḥusām al-Dīn Ardashīr, Bawandid ruler 136
Ḥusām al-Dīn b. Fakhr al-Dīn 29
Ḥusām al-Dīn Muḥammad 64–5
Ḥusām al-Dīn Shūhlī, Saljuq governor 137
Ḥusām al-Dīn 'Umar Shīrzādī Qazvīnī 69, 75

Ibn al-'Imād 81
Ibn al-Fuwaṭī, 'Abd al-Razzāq 22, 90
Ibn al-Suqā'ī 60
Ibn Balkhī 21, 198 n.29
Ibn Baṭṭūṭa 21, 36, 91, 114, 136
Ibn Ḥajar al-'Asqalānī 90
Ibn Ḥājib 108
Ibn Isfandiyār 136
Ibn Khurdādhbih 20
Ibn Ya'qūb Sayfī 6
Ibn Zarkūb 17–18, 45, 53, 93, 103, 109–10, 126, *see* Mu'īn al-Dīn Abū l-'Abbās Aḥmad Shīrāzī
Īdhaj (Malāmir) 135
Īj 54
il, peace, submission 3, 43
Imād al-Dīn Abū Yu'lā (Sayyid) 60, 62–4, 67–70, 75, 130, 147 n.145
Imād al-Dīn Mīrāthī 45
India 42, 80–2, 85
Injuids 15, 92–5, 98–9, 202, 128–9, 133
Inkianu, Mongol governor 58–9, 126, 131, 173 n.76
Īrān 94, 103
Isan Qutlugh 19, 186 n.178
Isfahan 41, 54, 95, 101, 104, 108, 111, 117, 119, 123–4, 136, 138, 139, 146, 180 n.53, 189 n.49
Ismā'īlī, Kurds tribes 138, 198 n.29
Ismā'īlīs 2, 14, 123, 140, 143
Iṣṭakhr, fortress 41, 53, 69
Istifchiaq Sukurchi 88
'Izz al-Dīn 'Alavī (Sayyid) 46, 48
'Izz al-Dīn Langar, Yazd atabek 138
'Izz al-Dīn Muẓaffar b. Muḥammad 76, 78, 82–3, 85, 128, 130, 148
'Izz al-Dīn Qūhadī 88
'Izz al-Dīn Sa'd b. Zangī, Salghurid atabek 7, 41, 47, 70, 76, 124, 165 n.13
'Izzat Mulk, wife of Shaykh Ḥasan Kuchik Chūpān 104

Ja'farī, Muḥammad b. Ḥasan 18, 146
Jackson, Peter 146
Jalāl al-Dīn 'Abd al-Razzāq Bāshtīnī 115, 117
Jalāl al-Dīn Arqan, Abish Khātūn's minister 66, 70, 175 n.136
Jalāl al-Dīn Mas'ūd Shāh Īnjū 93–5, 98–9, 101–2, 189 n.146
Jalāl al-Dīn Ṭayyib Shāh (Amīr) 101
Jalāl al-Dīn Ṭayyib Shāh, king of Shabānkāra 145
Jalāl al-Dīn Ṭūra'ī 33
Jalayirids 97, 99, 133
Jamāl al-Dīn Dastajirdānī, Ilkhanid minister 85
Jamāl al-Dīn Mīr-i Mīrān (Sayyid) 111, 192 n.117
Jamāl al-Dīn Miṣrī 47
Jamāl al-Dīn Muḥammad (Sayyid) 69
Jamāl al-Dīn Shaykh Abū Isḥāq Īnjū 7, 17, 19, 97–8, 100–3, 105–14, 117–19, 187 n.7, 8, 189 n.46, 49, 190 n.64, 74, 192 n.112, 123
Jamāl Lūk 91, 116, 184 n.151
Jangrū'ī 137
Jibāl 41
Jīrūft 54–5
Jochi Noyan 67
Jochid 2, 27
Joshi Noyan 75–7
Junayd Shīrāzī, Mu'īn al-Dīn Abū l-Qāsim 17–18, 43
Jürchens 1, 2, 152 n.6
Jurmā'īs, Mongol tribes 105, 107, 112–13, 190 n.74, 193 n.125
Jushkab Oghul, Ilkhanid prince 76
Juvaynīs 4, 15, 35, 63, 128

Kāmal Pīr Qattālī (Sayyid) 130
Kamola, Stefen 39
Karts 5–6
Kāshānī, Shams al-Dīn 16, 59, 200 n.63
Kāshgharī, Maḥmūd 39
Kayāl 81
Kayanids 136–7
Kaykhusraw II 2
Kāzarūn 55, 92, 102
Kelja 56–8
Kerülen river 2, 152 n.9
Khafāja, Arab tribes 54
Khālidīs 85
Khurasan 2, 4, 5, 7, 20, 27, 28, 29, 33, 56, 64, 83, 84, 91, 92, 115, 117, 128, 132, 144, 146, 161 n.32, 162 n.42, 46, 182 n.98
Khurram Turkān, mother of Yūsuf Shāh, Yazd atabek 146
Khurramābād 137
Khūzistān 12, 137, 180 n.57
Khwāf 91
Khwāfī, Faṣīḥ Aḥmad 22, 117
Khwāndmīr, Ghiyāth l-Dīn 22
Khwārazmshāhs 11, 15, 29
Kirbāl 124, 190 n.74
Kirmān, province 4, 5, 6, 7, 18, 19, 20, 29, 31, 32, 41, 52, 54, 56, 64, 69, 80, 91, 99, 104, 105, 106, 107, 108, 109, 113, 128, 135
Kirmān, ville 106, 107, 108, 116, 128, 129, 139, 148
Kitans 1, 2, 151 n.2, 152 n.6, *see* Liao dynasty
Kitbuqa Noyan 143–4
Köse Dagh 2
Krawulsky, Dorothea 11
Kūh Gīlūya 136, 147
Kulū Fakhr al-Dīn 119
Kulū Ḥusayn 102, 119
Kürdüchin, Salghurid princess 66, 70, 73, 82, 92, 177 n.175, 185 n.156, 157, 158
Kutubī, Maḥmūd 19, 116

Laḥsa 82
Lambton, Ann 7
Lane, George 7
Lār 54–5
Lāristān 130
Liao dynasty 1, *see* Kitans
Lur-i Buzurg 64, 135–6, 142–4, 147
Lur-i Kuchik 64, 140
Luristān 99, 119, 135–7, 144, 189 n.49
Lurs, tribes 42, 54, 137

Ma'bar 42, 81
Madrasa-i 'Aḍudiyya 87, 92, 170 n.3
Maghrib 136
Mahdi 56
Mahendrarajah, Shivan 23

Maḥmūd Qalhātī, prince of Hormuz 42, 60
Maḥmūd Shāh, Muzaffarid 19
Maḥmūd Yalavach 26
Majd al-Dīn Ismā'īl Fālī 46, 48, 100
Majd al-Dīn Rūmī 77, 179 n.30
Majd al-Mulk Yazdī 31–2
Makrān 130
Malik al-Islām 81–3, 85–6, 88–9, 93, 128–9, 148, *see* Jamāl al-Dīn Ibrāhīm Ṭībī
Malik Ashraf, Chupanid *amīr* 100–1, 103–5, 107, 132
Malik Shāh, Saljuq Sultan 123, 135
Malika Khātūn, daughter of 'Izz al-Dīn Sa'd b. Zangī 41
Malipatān 81
Mamluks 9
Manchuria 1, 152 n.6
Manchus 1
Marāgha 13, 22, 30, 173 n.86
Martinez, Peter 129
Mashriq 136
Maybud 91, 107, 116, 118
Māzandarān 5, 84, 132
Melville, Charles 15, 138
Menggeser 28
Mengü Temür, son of Hülegü 52, 61, 66, 69–70, 73, 82, 92, 142, 175 n.127
Mesopotamia 2, 12
Ming Qutlugh 88
Möngke, Great Qa'an 2, 6, 27, 28, 29, 32, 44, 79, 123, 140, 148, 152 n.13, 161 n.34, 170 n.9
Mongolia 1, 3, 5–6, 12, 25, 28–9, 79, 152 n.5, 195 n.13
Morgan, David 25, 36
Mosoul 83
Mu'īn al-Dīn Yazdī 19, 116
Mubārak Shāh Īnjū 93
Mubariz al-Dīn Muḥammad 19, 35, 91, 99, 104–13, 116–19, 186 n.171, 189 n.49, 190 n.74
Mūghān 7, 85
Muḥammad b. Malik Shāh, Saljuq Sultan 123
Muḥammad b. Yahyā 20
Muḥammad Beg 60, 186 n.145
Muḥammad Īdājī 146
Muḥammad Pahlavān, Azerbaijan atabek 40
Muḥammad Qushchi 87
Muḥammad Shāh b. Salghur Shāh, Salghurid atabek 52–3, 143
Muḥammad Tughlugh Shāh, Sultan of Delhi 91, 92
Munshī Kirmānī, Nāṣir al-Dīn 18–19
Muqarrab al-Dīn Abū l-Mafākhir Mas'ūd, Abū Bakr's minister 55
Musāfir Īnāq 94–5, 186 n.178
Musta'ṣim bi-llāh (al-), Abbasid Caliph 3, 44
Mustawfī Bāfqī, Muḥammad Mufīd 18
Mustawfī Qazvīnī, Fakhr al-Dīn 37, 131
Mustawfī Qazvīnī, Ḥamd Allāh 15, 20–1, 119, 136, 152 n.5
Muẓaffar al-Dīn Maḥmūd b. Ṭayyib Shāh, king of Shabānkāra 148
Muẓaffar al-Dīn Muḥammad, king of Shabānkāra 135, 138, 140, 144, 199 n.36
Muẓaffar al-Dīn Sunqur b. Mawdūd, Salghurid atabek 39, 136, 147
Muẓaffar al-Dīn Tekla, Lur-i Buzurg atabek 143, 144
Muzaffarids 7, 18–19, 97, 104–5, 107–8, 110–11, 113, 116–17, 119, 133, 192 n.120

Najīb al-Dawla, governor of Nawbanjān 30, 162 n.42
Nāṣir al-Dīn Bayḍāvī 14–15, 40, 100
Nāṣir al-Dīn Muḥammad b. Burhān Ghurid 149
Nāṣir al-Dīn Saltimish 85
Naṣīr al-Dīn Ṭūsī 3
Nāṣir al-Dīn, Abbasid Caliph 137
Naṭanzī, Mu'īn al-Dīn 20, 91, 93, 137, 140, 145–6, 185 n.161, 186 n.171, 187 n.12
Nawbanjān 30, 44
Nawrūz, Amīr, Ilkhanid noyan and viceroy 31, 83–5, 124, 146
Nāz Khātūn 36
Negüderis 69, 77, 80–1, 91, 116
Nishapur 92
Niẓām al-Dīn Abū Bakr, Terken Khātūn's minister 52, 175 n.137, 178 n.30
Niẓām al-Dīn Vazīr (Khwāja) 61–4, 66, 68–9, 77

Niẓām al-Dīn Faryūmadī 131
Niẓām al-Dīn Ḥasan, king of Shabānkāra 54–5, 144
Niẓām al-Mulk, Saljuq minister 30
Nuṣrat al-Dīn Aḥmad, Lur-i Buzurg atabek 136–7, 147
Nuṣrat al-Dīn Ibrāhīm, king of Shabānkāra 145
Nuṣrat al-Dīn Malik Hazārasp, Lur-i Buzurg atabek 136

Oghul Beg 54
Oghuz 39
Ögödei, Great Qa'an 2, 27, 29, 43, 49, 52, 79, 139, 140, 161 n.34
Oirat, tribe 27, 62
Öljei Khātūn, wife of Hülegü 61, 69–70
Öljeitü, Ilkhan 15–16, 30, 36, 88–93, 100, 149, 183 n.119, 190 n.79
Oman 130
Ordo Qiya 76–7
Ordu 5, 6, 8, 10, 14, 20, 30, 33, 34, 35, 36, 45, 52, 53, 54, 58, 59, 61, 62, 63, 64, 65, 66, 67, 68, 69, 73, 74, 75, 76, 78, 80, 82, 83, 85, 86, 87, 88, 89, 90, 91, 92, 93, 94, 95, 100, 108, 116, 118, 123, 125, 126, 127, 128, 130, 131, 139, 141, 142, 145, 146, 148, 149, 183 n.117
Oxus 14

Pādishāh Khātūn, Ṣafvat al-Dīn, Qutlughkhanid princess 18, 129, 142
Pahlavān 'Alī Dārakī 105, 116
Pahlavān 'Alī Shāh 116
Pahlavān Ḥājjī Kharbanda Sanjarī 132
Pahlavān Khurram 116
Pahlavān Maḥmūd 114
Pahlavān Ṭālib 116
pahlavāns 113–19, 132
paiza, tablet of authority 6, 62
Pandays princes 81
Patān 81
Persian Gulf 42–3, 55, 60, 82, 104, 129–30, 147
Petrushevsky, I. P. 124
Pīr Ḥusayn, Chupanid *amīr* 99–102, 104–6, 113–14, 188 n.21, 34
Pontic-Caspian steppe 9
Prophet Muḥammad 33, 48–9, 91
Pūl-i Kuvār 56
Pūr-i Bāha 128

Qāḍī Sharaf al-Dīn Ibrāhīm 56–7, 91, 172 n.66
Qal'a-i Safīd 44, 55, 98
Qal'a-i Sīrjān 104
Qal'a-i Ṭabarak 95, 117
Qal'a-i Ushkūnvān 47
Qara Bagh 97–8
Qara Khitai 25, 94, 139, 198 n.25
Qaraqorum 5, 6, 11, 79, 139, 140, 152 n.10
Qāshānī, Abū l-Qāsim 15, 30, 183 n.120, 126, 132
Qaṭīf 42, 82
Qattālīs, 130 Julfar 130
Qavām al-Dīn Bukharī 62, 64–5, 70
Qavām al-Dīn Ḥasan Tamghāchī, Shaykh Abū Isḥāq Īnjū minister 110
Qāvurd, Saljuq prince of Kirmān 5
Qays 42, 60–1, 81–2, 85–6, 88–9, 129–30
Qazvīn 67
Qazvīnīs 131
qīshlāq, winter pastures 7
Qizil, cousin of atabek Afrāsiyāb 147
Qubilai, Great Qa'an 13, 59, 67, 76, 163 n.43
Quchan 76
Qūhistān 2, 75
Qunchuqbal, Ilkhanid noyan 83
Qurumishi 83
Quṭb al-Dīn b. Ḥājjī Ḍarrāb (Sayyid) 112
Quṭb al-Dīn Mubāriz b. Muẓaffar al-Dīn Muḥammad, king of Shabānkāra 141
Quṭb al-Dīn Muḥammad, Qutlughkhanid Sultan of Kirmān 6, 29, 142, 179 n.47, 187 n.12, 193 n.131
Quṭb al-Dīn Shāh Jahān, Qutlughkhanid Sultan of Kirmān 149
Quṭb al-Dīn Tahamtan II, prince of Hormuz 129
Qutlugh Bitikchi 54
Qutlugh Terken Khātūn, regent of Kirmān 18
Qutlughkhanids 5, 18, 54, 129, 135, 139, 142, 149, 154 n.24
Quṭuz, Mamluk Sultan 2

Ra'īs 'Umar 111

Rachewiltz, Igor de 11
Raḍī al-Dīn Bābā Iftikhārī, Ilkhanid malik of Mosul 33
Rashīd al-Dīn 11–16, 19, 30, 35, 39, 82, 84, 87–8, 90, 100, 124–5, 129, 143, 146, 161 n.25
Ray 84
Rukn al-Dīn Abū Muḥammad Manṣūr (Rāstgūy) 47
Rukn al-Dīn b. Langar, Yazd atabek 137
Rukn al-Dīn Khwāja Jūq, Qutlughkhanid Sultan of Kirmān 139
Rukn al-Dīn Yaḥyā b. Majd al-Dīn Ismā'īl 100
Rukn al-Dīn Yūsuf Shāh, Yazd atabek 146–7
Russia 1
Rūzbihān Baqlī, sufi shaykh 40, 65, 137

Sa'd al-Dawla, Ilkhanid minister 76–8
Sa'd al-Dīn Ḥamū'ī, soufi shaykh 56
Sa'd al-Dīn Sāvajī, Ilkhanid minister 87
Sa'dī 42, 59, 71, 126
Sādaq Tarkhān 87
Ṣadr al-Dīn Aḥmad Khālidī Zanjānī, Ilkhanid minister 32, 36, 62, 78, 82–86, 125, 128, 182 n.113
Ṣadr al-Dīn b. Mujtabā (Sayyid) 107–8, 190 n.79
Ṣadr al-Dīn Ibrāhīm b. Rūzbihān, sufi shaykh 65
Ṣāḥib Shabānkāra'ī 16, 141
Salghur Shāh, Yazd atabek 140
Salghur 39
Salghurids 5, 7, 14, 39, 41–2, 44, 52, 54–5, 61, 66, 92, 109, 113, 135, 139–40, 144–5, 148–9
Saljuqs 4, 5, 29, 30, 31, 39, 46, 124, 138, 198 n.25
Samaghar Noyan 37, 131
Sarban 75
Sarbedars 115–17
Sartaq Noyan 144
Sayf al-Dīn Yūsuf 62, 64–5, 68, 70, 77, 179 n.30
Sayf al-Dīn, prince of Hormuz 43
Shabānkāra, district 32, 64, 83, 86, 91, 94, 102, 129, 136, 138, 139, 140, 141, 144, 145
Shabānkāra, kings 39, 41, 46
Shabānkāra, tribe 39, 41, 46
Shabānkāra'ī, Muḥammad 16, 20, 35, 52, 90, 93–4, 130, 136, 138, 140, 148
Shādī Bitikchi 58
Shāfi'īs 124
Shāh 'Abbās, Safavid ruler 137
Shāh Rukh, Timurid Sultan 20
Shāh Shujā', Jalāl al-Dīn, Muzaffarid prince 19, 108, 111, 113, 116
Shāh Sulaymān, Safavid ruler 18
Shāh Sulṭān, Muzaffarid prince 111, 113
Shāhvardī 137
Shams al-Dawla, Ilkhanid governor of Fārs 76–8
Shams al-Dīn 'Abd al-Laṭīf Rūzbihānī, sufi shaykh 137
Shams al-Dīn Alp Arghun, Lur-i Buzurg atabek 142, 144
Shams al-Dīn Ḥusayn 'Alkānī 60, 70, 76–7, 178 n.30
Shams al-Dīn Maḥmūd Sā'in Qāḍī 100–1, 104–5, 190 n.64
Shams al-Dīn Malik 62–3
Shams al-Dīn Miyāq 52, 54
Shams al-Dīn Muḥammad b. Malik Tazīgū 80–1, 127, 129
Shams al-Dīn Muḥammad Īnjū 98–9, 101, 187 n.7
Shams al-Dīn Muḥammad Juvaynī 14, 29–32, 60, 64, 80, 87
Shams al-Dīn Muḥammad Kart 6, 144
Shams al-Dīn 'Umar Mashhadī 56
Sharaf al-Dīn Maḥmūd Shāh Īnjū 92–5, 97–8, 102, 106, 112, 114, 129, 185 n.161, 186 n.171, 187 n.1
Sharaf al-Dīn Muẓaffar, founder of the Muzafarid dynasty 35
Sharaf al-Dīn Simnānī 76, 85, 87
Sharaf Faḍl Allāh b. 'Abd Allāh Qazvīnī 137
sharī'a 3, 36, 47, 138
Shaykh Ḥasan Buzurg, founder of the Jalayirid dynasty 95, 97–9, 101, 115, 117, 132–3
Shaykh Ḥasan Kuchik, founder of the Chupanid dynasty 99–102, 104–6, 113–14, 187 n.39

Shaykh Murshid al-Dīn Abū Isḥāq, sufi shaykh 55
Shaykh Ūvays, Jalayarid Sultan 16, 133, 193 n.126, 197 n.43
Shigi Qutugu, Mongol noyan 27–8
Shihab al-Dīn al-'Umarī 143
Shihab Munshī 112, 136
Shiraz 5, 7, 17–21, 33, 40–9, 51–61, 63–70, 73–7, 80, 82–3, 85–114, 119–20, 124–7, 129–30, 133, 138–40, 142, 144–5, 147–8, 162 n.42, 170 n.3, 185 n.157, 158, 195 n.7
Shīshī Bakhshī, Ilkhanid governor of Fārs 145
Shujā' 'Alī Khurshīd, Lur-i Kuchik atabek 137
Shūlistān 105, 111, 119, 189 n.49
Shūls 53, 55, 57, 80, 111, 113, 125, 136
Sikpur, Ilkhanid noyan 31
Sind 130
Sīrāf 42, 46, 60
Sīrjān 41, 104–5, 108, 116, 129
Sīstān 69
Spuler, Berthold 31
Subkī 100
Sughunchaq Noyan, Ilkhanid viceroy 31–3, 59–62, 66, 68, 100, 126, 173 n.86, 87, 188 n.27
Sulaymān Khan, Ilkhan 99
Sulṭān Ḥajjaj, Qutlughkhanid Sultan of Kirmān 144
Sulṭān Shāh Jandār 107, 117
Sulṭān Shāh, son of Amīr Nawrūz 146
Sulṭāniyya 7, 95, 115, 132, 185 n.156
Sunnī 123–4, 138
Sūzanī Samarqandī 94
Syria 9, 59, 114, 135, 201 n.90

Ṭabartū 51
Tabriz 54, 61–2, 67–70, 75–6, 78, 83–5, 89, 91, 93, 101, 104–5, 114, 137, 144
Ṭaghachar, Ilkhanid noyan 32, 62–3, 67, 74, 77–8, 83–4
Ṭaghai Temür, Ilkhan 132
Tahamtan 43, 52, 139
Taichu, Ilkhanid governor of Fārs 78, 87
Taichu, son of Mengü Temür 70
Tāj al-Dīn 'Alī Shāh, Ilkhanid minister 30, 36, 90, 129
Tāj al-Dīn Muḥammad Abzarī 47
Talas 139
Tamerlane 44, 132
Ṭamghach Khan, Qara Khitai ruler 94
Tang-i Shikam 80
Ṭarazak 137
Tārūt 42
Tāshī Khātūn, widow of Maḥmūd Shāh Īnjū's widow 114
Tayangu 139
Tekla b. Zangī b. Mawdūd, Salghurid atabek 40–1, 165 n.13
Tekla, Lur-i Buzurg atabek 143–4
Terken Khātūn, Qutlughkhanid princess 18, 129, 142, 149
Terken Khātūn, Salghurid princess 51–4, 57, 61, 71, 73, 87, 142, 170 n.3, 171 n.29
Terken Khātūn, Yazd atabek 54
Ṭībī, Fakhr al-Dīn Aḥmad b. Jamāl al-Dīn Ibrāhīm 89, 183 n.126
Ṭībī, 'Izz al-Dīn 'Abd al-'Azīz b. Jamāl al-Dīn Ibrāhīm 89, 93–4, 129, 185 n.167, 186 n.169
Ṭībī, Jamāl al-Dīn Ibrāhīm 30, 60–1, 80–1, 128, *see* Malik al-Islām
Ṭībī, Malik Shams al-Dīn b. Jamāl al-Dīn Ibrāhīm 129
Ṭībī, merchant family 129
Ṭībī, Niẓām al-Dīn, grandson of Jamāl al-Dīn Ibrāhīm 129
Ṭībī, Taqī al-Dīn, brother of Jamāl al-Dīn Ibrāhīm 81
Tolui, Great Qa'an 2, 28
Transcaucasia 2, 181 n.88
Transoxiana 4, 114, 152 n.5
Treadwell, Luke 114
Ṭughan Qūhistānī, Ilkhanid noyan 75, 77, voir Ṭughan Taraqay
Ṭughan Taraqay 75, voir Ṭughan Qūhistānī
Tughril b. Sunqur, Salghurid atabek 40–1, 165 n.13
Tughril, Saljuq Sultan 5
Tuladay 69
Tumaq 90
Tungus 1
Tūrān 94, 103
Turmens, tribes 53, 56–7, 80, 113

Ṭūs 28
Tutiyaq 60

Umar, Caliph 43, 93

Vaṣṣāf (Shiḥāb al-Dīn ʿAbd Allāh Shīrāzī) 19–20, 34–5, 37, 40, 44–5, 47–49, 52–53, 56–8, 60–1, 66, 71, 73–7, 81, 87, 92, 124–6, 128, 230, 148

Wāsiṭ 86

Yāghī Bāstī, Chupanid *amīr* 101–5, 110, 119
Yāqūt 21, 180 n.57
yarghu, trial, interrogation, court of inquiry 4, 59, 69, 70, 75, 86, 128, 130, 144, 154 n.22, 201 n.90
yarghuchi, magistrate, judge 4, 28, 32, 37, 69
yasa (Persian *yāsā*), normative Mongol law 4, 36, 67, 69, 70, 130
yaylāq, summer pastures 7
Yazd 18, 35, 41, 51, 54–5, 64, 69, 80, 90–1, 99, 104, 106–9, 113, 129, 137–8, 140, 146
Yelü Ahai 26
Yelü Mensü-kü 26
Yesüder, Mongol noyan 146
Yüan dynasty 26
Yul Qutlugh 74
yurt, encampment, pasturelands 7
Yūsuf Shāh, Lur-i Buzurg atabek 142

Ẓahīr al-Dīn Ibrāhīm Ṣavvāb 100, 104–5
Zangī b. Mawdūd, Salghurid atabek 39–40
Zayn al-Dīn b. ʿAbd al-Salām 89–90
Zayn al-Dīn Qazvīnī 15, 20, 119

www.ingramcontent.com/pod-product-compliance
Lightning Source LLC
Chambersburg PA
CBHW071824300426
44116CB00009B/1429
9780755645770